SPIN DICTATORS

SPIN DICTATORS

THE CHANGING FACE OF TYRANNY
IN THE 21ST CENTURY

SERGEI GURIEV AND DANIEL TREISMAN

PRINCETON UNIVERSITY PRESS

PRINCETON AND OXFORD

Published by Princeton University Press
41 William Street, Princeton, New Jersey 08540
99 Banbury Road, Oxford OX2 6JX

press.princeton.edu

All Rights Reserved
ISBN 978-0-691-21141-1
ISBN (e-book) 978-0-691-22446-6

British Library Cataloging-in-Publication Data is available

Editorial: Bridget Flannery-McCoy and Alena Chekanov
Production Editorial: Jenny Wolkowicki
Jacket design: Karl Spurzem
Production: Erin Suydam
Publicity: Kate Hensley and Kathryn Stevens

Jacket images: Shutterstock

This book has been composed in Arno Pro

Printed on acid-free paper. ∞

Printed in the United States of America

10 9 8 7 6 5 4 3 2 1

To Katia, Sasha, and Andrei

— S G

To Susi, Alex, and Lara

— D T

CONTENTS

PREFACE

Early in the twenty-first century, global politics hit a major milestone. For the first time, the number of democracies in the world surged past the tally of authoritarian states. As this seismic "third wave" crested, experts identified 98 countries with free government, compared to 80 still controlled by dictators.[1] The optimism was infectious. New information technologies, globalization, and economic development seemed to be calling "time's up" on strongman rule. As countries modernized, tyranny was becoming obsolete.

The celebrations did not last long. In fact, they hardly got started. Within a few years, the advance of freedom had petered out, yielding what some quickly termed a "democratic recession." A dramatic financial crisis, born in the United States, sent the global economy crashing, undercutting faith in Western governance. By 2019, the number of democracies had fallen to 87 while that of dictatorships was back up to 92. In the West, liberalism was proving little match for populism, while in the East, all eyes were turned to China's meteoric rise. The millennial exuberance gave way to a sense of gloom.

Today's political pessimism is a bit overdone. By most measures, global democracy remains not far below its all-time high. But the dark mood points to a genuine puzzle. Even if dictatorships are not taking over, the question is how they can survive at all—and even prosper—in an ultramodern world. Why, after all the brutal manias of the twentieth century—from fascism to communism—have been discredited, do we still see new autocracies rising from the ashes? And what to make of the strongmen who are embracing tools of modernity, using Western technologies to challenge Western ways of life?

With its unmatched population and explosive growth, China has been pegged as the counterargument to liberal democracy. Its economic success—hardly dented by the 2008–9 slump or even the 2020 Covid crisis—seems to contradict the equation of development with popular rule. And yet, outside the metropolises of Beijing and Shanghai and the glittering entrepôts of Hong Kong and Macau, most of the country remains quite poor, its population still manageable by industrial-era and even preindustrial methods. The bigger puzzle is the survival of unfree government in affluent societies such as Singapore and Russia, where university degrees are more common than in most Western democracies. Do such cases offer a glimpse into an authoritarian future?

This book is an attempt to explain the nature of current dictatorships. It grew out of a mixture of research and personal experience. We both spent years tracking the rise of Putin's system in Russia, through academic analysis and firsthand observation. His regime came to seem to us not unique but rather an exemplar of trends that were reshaping authoritarian states worldwide—from Hugo Chávez's Venezuela and Viktor Orbán's Hungary to Mahathir Mohamad's Malaysia and Nursultan Nazarbayev's Kazakhstan. Observers struggle with what to call these leaders. Some fall for their pantomime of democracy; others offer awkward analogies to historical strongmen, labeling Putin a "tsar" or Erdoğan a "sultan." We see all these rulers as converging on a novel—though not unprecedented—approach that can preserve autocracy for a while in even modern, globalized settings. The key to this is deception: most dictators today conceal their true nature. So the first step is to understand how they operate. In the chapters that follow, we explore why these regimes emerged, how they work, what threats they pose, and how the West can best resist them.

The book is based on theoretical and empirical research that we have published in economics and political science journals. Our hope here is to make the key ideas more accessible. Wherever possible, we back up our claims with references to published studies (including our own) and data. A variety of tables and graphs appear in an online supplement, accessible via https://press.princeton.edu/books/spin-dictators. We refer to this material in the respective chapters' closing sections titled "Checking the Evidence."

Over the years, many colleagues and friends have shared thoughts on the ideas we present here. We are grateful to Alberto Alesina, Maxim Ananyev, Marina Azzimonti, Timothy Besley, Bruce Bueno de Mesquita, Brett Carter, Chao-yo Cheng, George Derpanopoulos, Tiberiu Dragu, Georgy Egorov, Cherian George, Lisa George, Francesco Giavazzi, Gilat Levy, Andrew Little, Elias Papaioannou, Torsten Persson, Richard Portes, Andrea Prat, Eugenio Proto, Gerard Roland, Arturas Rozenas, Miklos Sarvary, Paul Seabright, Daniel Seidmann, David Skarbek, Konstantin Sonin, Francesco Squintani, Eoghan Stafford, David Stromberg, Guido Tabellini, Gergely Ujhelyi, Qian Wang, Feng Yang, and Fabrizio Zilibotti. Cevat Aksoy, Anders Aslund, Jonathan Aves, Danny Bahar, Carles Boix, Maxim Boycko, Javier Corrales, Tim Frye, Barbara Geddes, Scott Gehlbach, Susan Landesmann, Lee Morgenbesser, Peter Pomerantsev, Molly Roberts, Dani Rodrik, Michael Ross, Andrei Shleifer, Andrei Soldatov, Art Stein, Milan Svolik, Adam Szeidl, Ferenc Szucs, Michel Treisman, Josh Tucker, David Yang, and Ekaterina Zhuravskaya read all or parts of the manuscript and offered invaluable comments, as did two anonymous readers. We thank Andrei Shleifer in particular for encouraging us to develop our arguments into a book. Of course, we are solely responsible for any remaining mistakes. Kevin Gatter, Nikita Melnikov, and Ekaterina Nemova provided excellent research assistance. At Princeton University Press, we benefited from the expert guidance and encouragement of Bridget Flannery-McCoy, Sarah Caro (now at Basic Books), Eric Crahan, and Alena Chekanov.

INTRODUCTION

CHAPTER 1

FEAR AND SPIN

Dictators have been changing. The classic tyrants of the twentieth century—Adolf Hitler, Josef Stalin, Mao Zedong—were larger-than-life figures responsible for the deaths of millions. They set out to build new civilizations within their tightly guarded—and sometimes expanding—borders. That meant controlling not just people's public behavior but also their private lives. To do that, each created a disciplined party and a brutal secret police. Not every old-school dictator was a genocidal killer or the prophet of some utopian creed. But even the less bloodthirsty ones were expert at projecting fear. Terror was their all-purpose tool.

However, toward the end of the century something changed. Strongmen around the world started turning up to meetings in conservative suits instead of military uniforms. Most stopped executing their opponents in front of packed football stadiums. Many flew to the annual business conference in the Swiss resort of Davos to schmooze with the global elite. These new dictators hired pollsters and political consultants, staged citizen call-in shows, and sent their children to study at universities in the West. They did not loosen their grip over the population—far from it, they worked to design more effective instruments of control. But they did so while acting the part of democrats.

Not all autocrats have made this leap. North Korea's Kim Jong-Un and Syria's Bashar al-Assad would fit well into a scrapbook of twentieth-century despots. In China and Saudi Arabia, rulers have digitized the old fear-based model instead of replacing it. But the global balance has shifted. Among leaders of nondemocracies today, the representative figure is no longer a totalitarian tyrant like Josef Stalin, a sadistic butcher like Idi Amin, or even a reactionary general like Augusto Pinochet. He is a suave manipulator like Hungary's Viktor Orbán or Singapore's Lee Hsien Loong—a ruler who pretends to be a humble servant of the people.[1]

This new model is based on a brilliant insight. The central goal remains the same: to monopolize political power. But today's strongmen realize that in current conditions violence is not always necessary or even helpful. Instead of terrorizing citizens, a skillful ruler can control them by reshaping their beliefs about the world. He can fool people into compliance and even enthusiastic approval. In place of harsh repression, the new dictators manipulate information. Like spin doctors in a democracy, they spin the news to engineer support. They are *spin dictators*.[2]

THE PUTIN PUZZLE

We came to this subject through a particular case. In March 2000, Russians elected a former KGB lieutenant colonel with little political experience as their president. Vladimir Putin claimed to accept the principles of democracy, although his instincts clearly pulled in a different direction. For some time, it was not obvious—perhaps even to him—where he would take his country. As the economy boomed, his ratings soared.

Putin preserved democratic appearances while emphasizing the need to build a cohesive, modern state. At first, centralizing control seemed reasonable after the turbulent 1990s. But he did not stop, and after a while the measures he was taking to strengthen executive power—his power—were visibly undermining checks and balances. The scope for political contestation narrowed.

The battering ram that broke through democratic constraints was Putin's own popularity. He used it to get supporters elected to the parliament and to bully the country's unruly regional governors. With a mix of law enforcement and business leverage, he tamed the previously tycoon-dominated but competitive media. Even as he kept the form of national elections, he and his aides left less and less to chance. Putin and his United Russia Party could almost always have won a free and fair vote. But they still used pressure and tricks to inflate their landslides.

Democracies are never perfect. For a time, the flaws in Russia's politics looked much like those in other middle-income, semi-free countries such as Argentina, Mexico, and Romania. Almost all such states suffer from corruption, tainted elections, and insecure press freedom. Political leaders often abuse their authority over police and judges. Still, these flaws typically coexist with some popular accountability.

But by the time Putin returned to the presidency in 2012, after four years as prime minister, he was clearly operating from a different playbook. In late 2011, a wave of demonstrations had swept Moscow and other cities over fraud in that year's parliamentary election. The sight of up to one hundred thousand people in the streets alarmed Putin and his advisors. They struck back, arresting peaceful protesters, squeezing disloyal politicians out of parliament, and harassing the remaining independent media.

We both watched closely as this process unfolded. Sergei headed a Moscow university specializing in economics and advised the Russian government. Daniel was a professor in the West studying Russia's postcommunist politics. In the spring of 2013, Sergei received a visit from some of Putin's security agents, who confiscated his emails and copied his computer hard drive. He had helped write a critical analysis of the latest court verdict against Mikhail Khodorkovsky, a billionaire who had been jailed on a dubious charge. Apparently, the Kremlin did not like this analysis. Soon after, Sergei moved to France.[3]

The system Putin forged in Russia is distinctively authoritarian. But it is an authoritarianism of an unfamiliar type. Unlike Stalin, Putin has not murdered millions and imprisoned millions more. Even Leonid Brezhnev, who led the Soviet Union in its later, softer phase, from 1964 to 1982, locked thousands of dissidents in labor camps and psychiatric hospitals, banned all opposition parties, and held no elections that were even slightly competitive. Opposition rallies were out of the question. All media broadcast a mind-numbing ideological discourse. Foreign radio stations were jammed and most citizens were kept from international travel by a rusting iron curtain.

Putin's regime—now more than twenty years old—is different. It does not run on Soviet-style censorship. One can publish newspapers or books that call the man in the Kremlin a dictator.[4] The catch is that most people do not want to read them. Nor has the system run on fear, although that may now be changing. Occasional acts of political violence occurred, usually in murky circumstances. But the Kremlin always denied responsibility.[5] And, although Putin's political opponents are increasingly anxious, most Russians have not seemed scared.[6] Many have quite readily accepted a skewed vision of reality that Putin's media helped to shape. The authorities under communism, with their May Day parades and ritual elections, tried to create the illusion of consent. Under Putin, many Russians consented to illusions.[7]

As we examined the system that was emerging, we realized Putin's style of rule was not unique. From Hugo Chávez in Venezuela to Viktor Orbán in Hungary, nondemocratic leaders were using a common set of techniques.[8] Quite a few drew inspiration from the pioneer of this new brand, Lee Kuan Yew. Starting in the 1960s, the long-serving leader of Singapore had shaped his country into a formidable model of political control. That might sound surprising. Singapore claims to be a democracy and is often taken for one. It holds regular elections. But a key innovation of the new autocrats is precisely to claim to be democratic. "You are entitled to call me whatever you like," Lee once retorted to a critical journalist, "but . . . do I need to be a dictator when I can win, hands down?"[9] He failed to add that always winning, hands down, was the calling card of a modern dictator.

TWENTIETH-CENTURY TYRANTS

What exactly is a dictatorship? In the Roman Republic, where the term originated, it meant a temporary grant of absolute power to a leader to handle some emergency. These days, the word is used to refer to any nondemocratic government. It has become synonymous with authoritarianism and autocracy. We follow that usage in this book. A democracy, in turn, is a state whose political leaders are chosen in free and fair elections in which all—or almost all—adult citizens have the right to vote. A *liberal* democracy combines free elections with the rule of law, constitutionally protected civil liberties, and institutional checks and balances.

Before the twentieth century, no states were fully democratic. Even those that held free and fair elections denied most women the vote.[10] Only five countries had universal *male* suffrage in 1900—and not the United States, where African Americans were disenfranchised in the Jim Crow South.[11] Besides a handful of restricted suffrage republics like the United States, most political systems fell into three baskets: *monarchies*, in which a king or queen ruled, sometimes constrained by a constitution and a partly representative parliament; *oligarchies*, in which factions of the rich governed; and *colonies*, administered by a foreign power.

That changed in the twentieth century as democracy spread in three great waves.[12] The first peaked around 1920 as new states splintered from the European empires destroyed by World War I and Western governments liberalized their voting rules. The second occurred between the late 1940s and early 1960s as the winners of World War II imposed democracy on the losers and former colonies in Asia and Africa held elections. The third wave—a true tsunami—started with Portugal's "Carnation Revolution" in 1974, picked up speed as communism collapsed around 1990, and reached its apex in the mid-2000s. By 2015, more than half of all countries—containing 53 percent of the world's population—were electoral democracies, and about one in four was a liberal democracy.[13]

Yet, even as democracy expanded, dictatorship did not disappear; the first two democratic waves were followed by reversals. In two demoralizing periods, free government seemed to crumble. First came the 1930s—a "low, dishonest decade," in W. H. Auden's phrase—when authoritarians swept the European continent. Dictatorship did not just rebound: it mutated. A few monarchies hung on in countries such as Yugoslavia and Romania. Yet, alongside them, new forms of tyranny emerged that were better adapted to the mass politics that democracy itself had ushered in. During and after World War I, millions of politically inexperienced workers and veterans cast ballots for the first time. They did so in the wake of a global bloodletting that had discredited the liberal belief in ever-continuing progress.

Two new types of regime—communist and fascist—set out to mobilize the lower classes. Each promised a complete transformation of society. Vladimir Lenin's Bolsheviks aimed to build communism in the remnants of the Russian Empire. The Nazis, under Adolf Hitler, planned an Aryan empire. On taking power, both forced the public to adopt an ideology distilled from the leader's scribblings. Raymond Aron called these "secular religions." Like traditional faiths, they stated truths not to be questioned, redirected attention from current hardship to a utopian future, and defined rituals that could sort true believers from heretics.[14] Both Lenin and Hitler inspired imitators in Europe and beyond.

A third new model—corporatism—aimed not to mobilize the masses into politics but to demobilize them into private life. Conservatives such as Portugal's António Salazar and Spain's Francisco Franco wanted to restore social deference and Catholic hierarchy.[15] In place of noisy parliaments, they created consultative chambers where selected spokesmen of social groups could advise the leader. Like the other two forms, corporatism was born out of disgust with the present. But while fascists and communists sought to escape into an imagined future, corporatists hoped to return to an imagined past.

Fascism died in the flames of World War II, while communism survived and spread. Corporatism hung on in Spain and Portugal, with distant echoes in regimes such as Juan Perón's in Argentina.[16] The second authoritarian surge began in the 1960s as postwar democratization ran out of steam. Fragile postcolonial republics fell to ruthless strongmen, while military juntas seized power in economically volatile Latin America. In this crop of dictators, some aimed, like the communists and fascists, to mobilize people into active support. Others sought, like the corporatists, to quiet them down. Socialist revolutionaries like Nasser in Egypt (mobilizational) shared the world stage with free-market reactionaries like Pinochet in Chile (demobilizational) and kleptocrats like Mobutu in Zaire (demobilizational). Aging communist regimes often progressed from mobilization to demobilization, still clinging to the same revolutionary doctrines, which just grew ever more ritualized.

As this brief review suggests, twentieth-century dictatorships were diverse. Still, most shared certain features. To begin with, the vast majority used *violent repression*. They used it to reshape society, to extract resources from the population, and to defeat and deter opposition. The scale of slaughter varied. Stalin and Mao are blamed for tens of millions of deaths. Some others got by with "only" thousands (e.g., Ferdinand Marcos of the Philippines) or hundreds (e.g., Algeria's Chadli Bendjedid).[17] During any leader's time in office, the intensity of violence might fluctuate. Some, like General Franco, came in with a bang; others, like Bashar al-Assad, ramped up the killing later. Either way, most left a bloody trail.[18]

And most were deliberately public about their violence. They turned killing into a form of gruesome theater. Some executed political opponents in front of mass audiences. Zaire's Mobutu, for instance, hanged four former cabinet ministers before a crowd of fifty thousand.[19] Or they displayed the bodies of rivals to terrorize their followers. The Haitian strongman François "Papa Doc" Duvalier propped a headless corpse at a street corner in Port-au-Prince for three days with a sign reading "renegade."[20] Almost all adopted a menacing rhetoric to spread anxiety and discourage challenges. Iraq's Saddam Hussein spoke of "cutting off necks" and "evildoers . . . who have thrust their poisoned dagger into our back."[21] Spain's Franco warned of "internal subversion" by an enemy who "lies in wait for opportunities to penetrate."[22]

At the same time, most twentieth-century dictators sought *comprehensive control over public communications*. Some banned or nationalized all private media. Others censored the press and intimidated journalists. For citizens, observing the rules governing public speech and writing became a test of loyalty, part of the mechanism by which leaders kept order. Criticizing the regime was generally taboo.

As with violence, dictators were open about their censorship. Some, like Hitler and Mao, burned books in huge bonfires. Others, like Pinochet, sent soldiers to sanitize the bookstores. The Soviet Union created an explicit censorship agency, Glavlit, to purge all broadcasts and publications of forbidden topics. Penalties could be brutal. Critical writers often disappeared into the prison camps. State propaganda was also overt and often heavy-handed. It was produced in propaganda departments and— in its ubiquity and authoritative style—communicated the regime's strength and determination as much as any particular message.

Many dictators sought to *isolate their countries*. Quarantine was usually incomplete; most authoritarian states traded with their neighbors. Some, when they thought they could get away with it, invaded them. But virtually all viewed the outside world with suspicion. Unreliable visitors, inconvenient information, and other contaminants were blocked at the frontier. Those admitted were monitored. When technology permitted, dictators jammed foreign broadcasts, and they often censored or banned foreign newspapers. Many kept citizens *in*, hoping to limit knowledge of the world and conserve manpower.[23] In most communist countries, travel abroad required government approval; in some, such as Albania and Romania, attempting to emigrate without permission was a capital crime.

Finally, although totalitarians claimed a mystical identification with their people, the leading twentieth-century dictators *derided parliamentary democracy* as practiced in the West. Many claimed to be building new, superior political orders. The most brazen stole the word itself—as in "the German Democratic Republic" or "the Democratic People's Republic of Korea"—but subverted its meaning, eliminating any hint of pluralism or liberal constraint. Postcolonial leaders like Ghana's Kwame Nkrumah saw multiparty elections as a legacy of imperialists. Parliamentary institutions, he said, offered only "chaos, confusion, corruption, nepotism, and misery."[24] Zaire's Mobutu declared simply: "Democracy is not for Africa."[25] Elections, when held, were celebrations of the rulers rather than moments of choice.

In short, most dictators maintained power by repressing any opposition, controlling all communications, punishing critics, (often) imposing an ideology, attacking the ideal of pluralist democracy, and blocking most cross-border flows of people and information. The key principle behind all these practices was simple: intimidation. The typical twentieth-century autocrat was a dictator of fear.

NEW AND IMPROVED

And yet, as we looked around in the 2000s, we saw something different. The men calling the shots in most nondemocracies seemed to come from another mold. There was Hugo Chávez, a charismatic former paratrooper, who commandeered Venezuela's airwaves to romance his country's poor. Chávez marginalized the opposition but jailed few of its members—and most of those only after a failed coup almost ousted him.[26] In Singapore, there was Lee Hsien Loong, a brilliant, Cambridge-educated technocrat, who posted photographs of sunrises on Facebook and served as patron of an NGO promoting kindness.[27] Lee's People's Action Party had won more than 89 percent of seats in all thirteen parliamentary elections since the country's independence, almost rivaling the Soviet Communist Party.[28] Yet, as of 2015 Singapore had only one "prisoner of conscience," according to Amnesty International—a sixteen-year-old blogger arrested for posting an obscene cartoon.[29] In Russia, Vladimir Putin denied there was anything undemocratic about his regime. His goons specialized in low-visibility harassment, pursuing their targets with fabricated court cases. All three of these leaders favored international openness, held frequent elections, and boasted high approval ratings. On the surface, they had little in common—a Latin American caudillo, a cerebral overachiever, a sphinx-like former spy. But that just made the parallels more intriguing.

Were these disciplinarians in well-pressed suits as different from their predecessors as they seemed? And, if so, what explained the change?

We spent several years puzzling over these questions. To begin, we plunged into literature about autocracies, past and present, immersing ourselves in histories, works of political science, journalists' accounts, and a range of other sources. Starting inductively, we looked for patterns in how rulers dominated their societies. This reading convinced us that Chávez, Lee, Putin, and various others did, indeed, share a distinctive modus operandi—one focused more on shaping public opinion than on violent repression. Each was unique in some ways. Yet, the common elements defined a school of authoritarian rule unlike the main twentieth-century approach.

But how to be sure? We first checked the logic, formulating our understanding of the strategy as a mathematical model. Next, we sought to measure just how widespread the new approach had become. Scouring existing databases, we gathered information on authoritarian governments and collected new data of our own. These confirmed that there had, indeed, been a striking shift from the dictatorship of fear to that of spin. We refer to these statistics in later chapters (in sections titled "Checking the Evidence"). For those who are interested, our journal articles spell out the details, and additional graphs and tables can be found in an online supplement.[30] We will focus here on characteristic cases, illustrative examples, and stories. This book builds on research and data but it is not an academic monograph. Our goal is to sketch the history of authoritarian evolution and suggest an interpretation. We document the spread of spin dictators and describe the methods they use to stay in power.

Along the way, we have been influenced by a range of recent work in political science and economics.[31] Some of this is already well-known; other items deserve a broader audience.

Many scholars, for instance, have sought to explain the stability of classic, violent autocracies—the regimes that we call dictatorships of fear. How do such rulers avoid being overthrown in revolutions? One way, as our colleagues have shown, is to intimidate citizens with propaganda that conveys the dictator's power and resolve.[32] Another is to keep potential rebels from coordinating on a plan to storm the barricades.[33] Acting together, citizens can achieve safety in numbers. So dictators must keep them divided—and terrified.[34]

These arguments clarify how some twentieth-century fear dictators survived for so long—and why, in the end, their regimes often crumbled without warning. They have less to say about the new-style cases. Most assume that citizens hate the dictator: only fear keeps them from revolting. But what if citizens actually like their ruler and do not want to storm the barricades? In Putin's Russia, Lee's Singapore, and Orbán's Hungary, revolutionaries have certainly existed. But they have always constituted a minority. In each case, the leader has been—as best one can tell—genuinely popular.[35] Spin dictators survive not by disrupting rebellion but by removing the desire to rebel.

Other recent works have described some features of spin dictatorship. Almost all autocracies these days hold elections, and not all are empty rituals. As Andreas Schedler has noted, we live in an age of electoral authoritarianism. In an influential book, Steven Levitsky and Lucan Way pointed out that many elections held by dictators are—although unfair—not completely unfree. Opposition parties run and even have some chance of winning.[36] Political scientists have explored the ploys, con games, and bureaucratic abuses that autocrats around the world have used to secure victories.[37] Some study how dictators control the media. Others consider how new surveillance and information technologies are being used to turbocharge repression.[38]

We build on these ideas. Our aim is to synthesize and integrate them, suggesting an overarching logic. (In a few places, we will also disagree with our colleagues' interpretations.) The bottom line is that spin dictators are not just old-school violent tyrants who have learned a few new tricks. They have forged a distinct, internally consistent approach. The key elements—manipulating the media, engineering popularity, faking democracy, limiting public violence, and opening up to the world—complement each other to produce a model of unfree governance that is spreading. Understanding this is not just an intellectual challenge: it is crucial for the West to craft effective responses.

THE RULES OF SPIN

Although spin dictatorship has become salient recently, it is not entirely new. Indeed, some insights into it are hundreds of years old. Since the ancient Greeks, most writers on tyranny have focused on the dictatorship of fear. Rulers kill, torture, imprison, and threaten their subjects to secure obedience. They spy on citizens and spread distrust among them. Aristotle called these techniques "the Persian and barbaric arts."[39] Montesquieu alluded to the "prince's ever-raised arm," always poised to strike.[40] Fear, he wrote, "must beat down everyone's courage and extinguish even the slightest feeling of ambition."[41] More recent theorists such as Franz Neumann and Hannah Arendt placed terror—along with ideology—at the heart of modern dictatorship.[42]

Yet, from the start, some thinkers also saw another possibility. Besides the "old traditional method," Aristotle described a second approach. This second type of ruler claimed to be not a violent usurper but "a steward and a king," governing for the benefit of all. He spent money to "adorn and improve his city" and cultivated an image of moderation and piety. Although still a tyrant, ruling in his own interest, he tried to seem "not harsh, but dignified."[43] He inspired reverence rather than fear. Although enslaved, his subjects did not realize it.

Later, in a similar vein, Machiavelli advised princes to use "simulation and dissimulation."[44] Since most people are influenced by appearances rather than reality, an ambitious ruler should create illusions. He "need not have all the good qualities . . . but he must seem to have them."[45] How to fool the public depends on context: "The prince can gain popular favor in many ways." But obtaining public support is crucial. "I will only say in conclusion that a prince must have the people on his side."[46]

Spin dictators heed Machiavelli's advice and copy Aristotle's second type of tyrant. Rather than intimidating citizens into submission, they use deception to win the people over. To govern in this way entails following a few rules.

The first is to *be popular*. Unlike classic despots, spin dictators must care about their approval ratings. As Machiavelli noted, they can win popular favor in various ways. Good economic performance helps. In any regime, prosperity tends to boost the incumbent's appeal.[47] This is hugely important and should not be forgotten even as we focus on other, complementary paths to popularity. Citizens infer from economic growth that the ruler must be a skilled manager. Leaders of all kinds—democrats and authoritarians—take credit for booming markets when they can.

But no economy booms all the time. So each brand of autocrat invests in a backup. Dictators of fear use repression to contain discontent as the economy tanks. They make sure citizens are too scared to protest.

Spin dictators may end up repressing as a last resort, reverting to the old-school approach in extremis. But that means giving up on broad popularity. Instead, their first line of defense, when the truth is against them, is to distort it. They manipulate information.

To do this effectively requires foresight. In good times, they prepare for bad. Claiming responsibility for successes—even those caused by luck—they build a reputation for professionalism. And, like Aristotle's second tyrant, they pretend to govern for the benefit of all. At the same time, they consolidate control over the media, often discreetly in order to preserve its credibility, quietly buying off owners and encouraging self-censorship. This enables them, at tougher moments, to divert attention from disappointing outcomes and retarget blame to others. Despite failures, spin dictators can remain popular for a while.

Of course, they are not the first to manipulate information. Some twentieth-century totalitarians were innovative propagandists. What is different is *how* spin dictators skew the news. The classic fear dictators imposed elaborate ideologies and loyalty rituals. Their control was comprehensive, their propaganda intimidating. Some were accused of brainwashing their citizens. Spin dictators use subtler methods—less Maoist agitprop, more Madison Avenue. And the content differs. Where twentieth-century strongmen relished violent imagery—recall Saddam's "poisoned dagger"—spin dictators adopt a cooler rhetoric of competence and expertise, sometimes with a light socialist or nationalist veneer.

When the facts are good, they take credit for them; when bad, they have the media obscure them when possible and provide excuses when not. Poor performance is the fault of external conditions or enemies. And disappointing outcomes are cast as still better than others could achieve. Dictators contrast their own leadership with a deeply unattractive pseudo-alternative, specially chosen to make them look better. Loyal journalists slander any genuine rival. Throughout, the dictator frames issues and shapes the public agenda to his advantage.

When this works, spin dictators are loved rather than feared. For twenty years, Putin's approval never dipped below 60 percent. Even Chávez's opponents acknowledged his popularity. But they are not loved by all. In any modern society, authoritarian or democratic, people can be divided into two groups. To begin with, there are *the informed*—the stratum of college-educated, media-savvy, and internationally connected citizens. Its members are skilled at getting and communicating political information. They may be co-opted by those in power, but they are generally hard to fool. In dictatorships, the informed see through the leader's lies, recognizing him as out for himself and far less competent than state broadcasts pretend. They would like to replace him with a better alternative. But they are too few and therefore too weak to do so alone. They need the help of the rest of society—the *general public*.[48]

The spin dictator's key challenge is to prevent the informed from puncturing his popularity and mobilizing the public against him. But how? When state coffers are full, he can co-opt his critics. He can buy their silence or even hire them to produce his propaganda. In Putin's Russia and Nazarbayev's Kazakhstan, pro-regime TV networks recruited the country's talented college graduates. Other leaders—from Peru's Alberto Fujimori to Hungary's Viktor Orbán—have bribed private media barons with payoffs, scoops, and government advertising. When short of money, dictators censor the informed and their media. As growth rates and state revenue fell in Russia and Kazakhstan recently, press restrictions tightened. In fact, most dictators do a bit of both: some critics are cheaper to censor, others to bribe.

A key insight is that one need not censor everything. Indeed, in a spin dictatorship, press restrictions that are too blatant can backfire. Rulers want citizens to think the media are relatively free. So when they censor, they also censor the fact that they are censoring. Where fear dictators burn books and ban private newspapers, spin dictators mostly just push criticism to the fringes, keeping national TV for themselves.[49] They do not care what the chattering classes say about them in private—or even in public before a small audience. Dissident intellectuals are allowed their edgy journals, cable shows, and foreign newspapers, so long as demand is low. What matters is *mass* support. To divide the public from the informed, rulers insult the latter, question their motives, label them unpatriotic or elitist, and inflame cultural resentments.

Having won mass appeal, the leader *uses his popularity to consolidate power*. This is the second rule of spin dictatorship. Popularity is a fluid asset that can fall as well as rise. So it makes sense to invest some of it into other levers of control. To cash in his high ratings, a spin dictator calls elections and referenda and, winning huge victories, claims a mandate to adjust political and legal institutions. He enacts constitutional changes, packs courts and regulatory bodies with loyalists, and gerrymanders voting districts to build a cushion of institutional support.

The third rule is to *pretend to be democratic*. Today, large majorities in almost all countries—whatever their histories and political systems—favor democracy.[50] A worldwide network of liberal states and international organizations promotes popular government. Those autocrats who continue to rule by fear defy this global opinion. Spin dictators, by contrast, pretend to embrace the vogue for freedom. Of course, many abroad see through their hypocrisy. But at home—and even abroad—many others do not.

Twentieth-century fear dictators often locked their borders, limiting travel and information transmission. Spin dictators *open up to the world*—the fourth rule. Occasionally, they restrict foreign media. But mostly they welcome flows of people, capital, and data and find ways to profit from them. They join international institutions and disrupt any missions that might be turned against them. They target potentially friendly groups in the West with Internet propaganda and hack or harass vocal opponents. And they employ the subterranean infrastructure of offshore companies and banks to safeguard their cash and co-opt Western elites.

The final—and most important—rule is to *avoid violent repression*, or at least conceal or camouflage it when used. In modern societies, brutal acts tend to discredit the leader. For a spin dictator, visible violence against the public is a mark of failure. When the model works and the ruler is popular, terrorizing ordinary citizens is not just unnecessary but counterproductive. It undercuts the desired image of enlightened, responsive leadership.

That does not mean spin dictators are pacifists. Fighting civil wars or ethnic insurgencies, they can be brutal. (In fact, democracies too are often ruthless when facing armed challenges—consider India in Kashmir.)[51] In Peru, Fujimori viciously suppressed the Sendero Luminoso Maoist guerrillas. Russia's second Chechen war, which Putin began in 1999, caused tens of thousands of deaths.[52] Where history has predisposed the public against small ethnic minorities—especially those that can be blamed for terrorism—spin dictators can profit by targeting them. They also sometimes repress journalists to censor their reporting. Still, when they do, they try to hide their involvement or disguise the purpose. Instead of arresting critics for their writing, they fabricate charges of tax evasion, fraud, or—even better—embarrassing offenses likely to alienate the writer's followers. Kazakhstan, for instance, prosecuted a well-known journalist for allegedly raping a minor, in a case Human Rights Watch suggested was "politically motivated."[53]

To recap, spin dictators manipulate information to boost their popularity with the general public and use that popularity to consolidate political control, all while pretending to be democratic, avoiding or at least camouflaging violent repression, and integrating their countries with the outside world.

Two caveats are important. We sometimes refer to spin dictatorship as a "new" model, contrasting it with the "old" practices of fear dictators. But, as noted, it is not completely new. In almost every era, at least a few autocrats have chosen deception over violence. As we saw, Aristotle first described the approach, probably with the Athenian tyrant Peisistratus in mind.[54] In nineteenth-century France, Napoleon III anticipated some techniques of later spin dictators.[55] What was new in the late twentieth century was a dramatic shift in the balance between types. Spin dictatorship grew from a marginal variety into the most common form.

The second caveat concerns our division of dictatorships into two neat groups. Again, this makes discussion simpler. But most real-world phenomena vary along a spectrum. That is certainly true of political regimes. Perfect democracy is an "ideal type" that exists only in textbooks, not life. Actual governments are more or less democratic. The same is true of nondemocratic leaders. They may be closer to the dictatorship of fear or the dictatorship of spin, but few will be entirely one or the other. Most rulers depart from the blueprint in some respect. But they come close.

So who are some recent spin dictators? In Singapore, Lee Kuan Yew helped develop the model between about 1970 and 1990. His successors, Goh Chok Tong (1990–2004) and Lee Hsien Loong (2004–), embraced Lee's style of rule. Other cases include Mahathir Mohamad in Malaysia (1981–2003) and his successors, Abdullah Ahmad Badawi (2003–9) and Najib Razak (2009–18); Nursultan Nazarbayev in Kazakhstan (1992–2019); Hugo Chávez in Venezuela (1999–2013); Vladimir Putin in Russia (2000–present); Recep Tayyip Erdoğan in Turkey (2003 until at least 2016, when massive arrests following a failed coup suggest possible backsliding to fear dictatorship); Rafael Correa in Ecuador (2007–17); and Viktor Orbán in Hungary (2010–present).[56] We also include Peru's Alberto Fujimori as an early borderline case, especially in the late 1990s, although state killings were relatively frequent in the early 1990s as the army fought Sendero Luminoso.[57] Some of these leaders inherited more or less democratic systems and converted them into spin dictatorships. Others did not need to. We will return to these cases repeatedly in the chapters that follow.

As this list suggests, the model comes in various flavors. Some practitioners, like Chávez, are on the left; others, like Orbán, are on the right. Some seek to mobilize their populations, others to calm them down. Some, like Chávez and Correa, are "populists," attacking "entrenched elites" or "the deep state" on behalf of "the people." Others, such as Lee Kuan Yew and Putin, are enthusiastic backers of the state, "deep" or otherwise. (Erdoğan attacks the "deep state" while packing the regular state with his allies.) Some, like Orbán, embrace cultural conservatism and ethnically charged anti-immigrant sentiment. Others, like Nazarbayev, emphasize ethnic and religious harmony.[58] Spin dictatorships also vary in their institutional form. Many are personalist, focused on a single individual, but they can also be dominant-party regimes (Malaysia, Singapore), military ones (Algeria under Bouteflika), or even monarchies (Kuwait under Sheikh Sabah al-Ahmad Al Sabah). Still, spin dictators share certain common features that distinguish them from fear dictators. We summarize the differences in table 1.1.[59]

TABLE 1.1. Two Models of Dictatorship

Dictatorships of fear	Dictatorships of spin
Rule through fear	*Rule through deception*
Much violent repression—many political killings and political prisoners	Little violent repression—few political killings or political prisoners
Violence publicized to deter others	Violence concealed to preserve image of enlightened leadership
Comprehensive censorship	Some opposition media allowed
Censorship public—book burnings, official bans	Censorship covert—private media co-opted when possible
Official ideology sometimes imposed	No official ideology
Heavy-handed propaganda combined with loyalty rituals	More subtle propaganda to foster image of leader competence
Liberal democracy derided	Pretense of democracy
International flows of people and information often restricted	Generally open to international flows of people and information

How has the balance between fear and spin changed? The chapters to come will spell out the details, but for now here's a quick overview. To distinguish the types empirically, we use two simple rules of thumb. Like any such rules, these miss nuances and may get the odd case wrong, but they help identify the broad trends. As noted, spin dictators hold elections, avoid overt violence against political opponents, and permit at least some critical media. Our rule of thumb focuses on these aspects. We classify a leader as a spin dictator if under his rule all the following are true:

(a) the country is a nondemocracy, *and*
(b) national elections are held in which at least one opposition party is allowed to run, *and*
(c) at least a few media outlets criticize the government each year, *and*
(d) fewer than 10 state political killings occur each year on average, *and*
(e) fewer than 1,000 political prisoners are held in any year.[60]

Dictators of fear employ violent repression and aim for complete control over public communications. We classify a leader as a fear dictator if under his tenure:

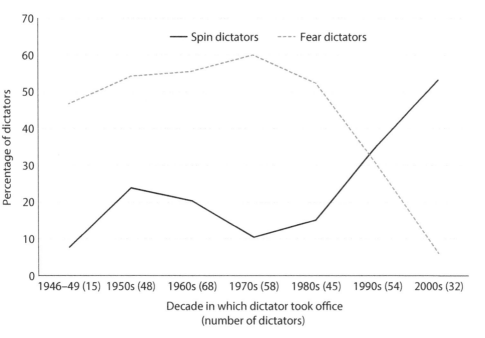

FIGURE 1.1. Shares of Fear Dictators and Spin Dictators in Successive Cohorts of Leaders

Source: Guriev and Treisman, Authoritarian Control Techniques Database;
V-DEM, V.10; Polity IV.

Note: Number of dictators in the given period in parentheses.
"Dictators": leaders who were in power for at least 5 years and whose state had a Polity2
rating of less than 6 in all 5 years. "Fear" and "spin" dictators defined as in the text.

(a) the country is a nondemocracy, *and*

(b) in at least one year few or no media outlets criticize the government, *and*

(c) 10 or more state political killings occur each year on average,
and/or

(d) 1,000 or more political prisoners are held in at least one year.[61]

The remaining dictators—29 percent of the total in 1946–2015—are
hybrids.

Figure 1.1 shows the change over time. We compare the proportions
of spin and fear dictators in successive cohorts of leaders.[62] Violent repression often varies during a leader's tenure. Some shock the population into submission early on with a brutal purge or massacre and then

do not need to kill as much for a while.[63] Others start softly but later escalate. To take this into account, we average the number of state political killings over each dictator's total years in power and compare the number of political prisoners held under each dictator at its peak. Since estimates will be noisy if taken over too short a period, we focus on just those leaders who lasted in office for at least five years.[64] As can be seen, fear dictatorships plunge from 60 percent of the total in the 1970s cohort to less than one-tenth in the 2000s cohort. The proportion of spin dictatorships soars from 13 to 53 percent.[65]

OTHER EXPLANATIONS

We argue that dictators are substituting spin for fear. But another possibility is that they have just become more efficient at repression. Perhaps they have found ways to keep people terrified using less actual violence. New information technology makes it easier to monitor and target dissidents. To take advantage of this, dictators of all types have been deploying everything from street cameras and facial recognition technology to GPS trackers. Is that all that is going on?

We do not think so. It is true that better surveillance could, in principle, reduce the need for violence. Deterrence works by threatening offenders with punishment. The force of such threats depends on both the penalty and the odds of getting caught. If the odds of detection rise, a dictator can soften the punishment without weakening the deterrent. As monitoring capacity grows, rulers can replace "high-intensity" with "low-intensity coercion."[66] Even better, they can detain troublemakers in advance rather than penalize them after the fact.[67]

Still, that something *could* happen does not mean it will. Orwell did not think that high-tech surveillance would reduce terror. Far from it, comprehensive monitoring and brutal punishment merged in his "Big Brother." Recent research suggests that today's remaining fear dictators are using new digital tools together with—not instead of—more violent techniques.[68] And that makes sense. If repression has become more cost-effective, economic logic suggests we should see more of it, not less.

Besides, even if new surveillance technology explained the fall in violence, that would still leave the puzzle of other recent changes in dictators' tactics. If low-intensity repression is so effective, why conceal its use, weakening its deterrent force? Why pretend to embrace democracy and respect freedom of opinion instead of doubling down on fear-based methods? Why work so hard to be popular if one can control citizens through their smartphones? We agree that some fear dictators have merely digitized their coercive techniques—Saudi Crown Prince Mohammed bin Salman ("MBS") comes to mind. But those leaders have not given up on violence. Meanwhile, others have adopted a whole new model.

That model has, itself, benefited from new information tools. In fact, technological advances enhance the efficiency of both fear and spin.[69] The Internet allows for low-cost, selective censorship that filters information flows to different groups. Social networks can be hijacked to disseminate sophisticated propaganda, with pitches tailored to specific audiences and the source concealed to increase credibility. Spin dictators can mobilize trolls and hackers to manipulate elections. So even if new information technology facilitates fear dictatorship, it could facilitate spin dictatorship even more.

Other skeptics suggest it is not dictators that are growing less violent but societies that are becoming less rebellious. As people get richer, they become more risk averse. With more to lose, citizens lose their taste for revolution. A dictator may need less graphic brutality and fewer explicit threats to keep such a population in line.

That sounds plausible. But, while it may be true in some cases, it does not seem to hold in general. In fact, the well-off often appear *more* of a threat to dictators than the poor. The affluent may, indeed, have more to lose. But they also have greater capacity to resist—greater organizational skill, resources, and networks—and a stronger demand for political freedom. They are harder than the poor to buy off with material payoffs.

Some evidence supports this. In 2017–20, the World Values Survey (WVS) polled citizens of 19 authoritarian states. The pollsters divided respondents into three income categories—"high," "medium," and "low"—based on their own assessments of their relative income. One question asked whether political violence was ever justifiable. Although most said no, in 9 of the 19 countries the "rich" respondents were readier to justify political violence than the "poor" ones.[70] In Hong Kong, for instance, 27 percent of high-income respondents answered 6 or higher on a 10-point scale that ranged from "never justifiable" (1) to "always justifiable" (10), compared to just 8 percent of low-income respondents. Even in mainland China, more rich than poor respondents chose high numbers. Tolerance for political violence was also greater among the rich than the poor in Azerbaijan, Belarus, Ethiopia, Jordan, Macau, Russia, and Ukraine.

Of course, the well-off might talk like revolutionaries but balk at actually revolting. But their survey answers, at least, suggest otherwise. The WVS did not ask about revolutions, but it did about less extreme opposition actions. In 20 nondemocracies, it asked whether respondents had attended peaceful demonstrations. In 14 of these, more rich than poor respondents said they had done so.[71] In Hong Kong, again, 31 percent of high-income respondents—but just 12 percent of low-income ones—said yes. And in 15 of the 20 countries more rich than poor respondents said they had participated in an unofficial strike.

Affluence may reduce the impulse to rebel in a few cases such as Singapore. But in other relatively rich autocracies—from the Gulf states to Russia, Malaysia, Turkey, and Kazakhstan—leaders seem anything but nonchalant about political unrest. And they often seem more worried about protest by the well-off than about unrest among the poor, who, in Russia and Turkey, for instance, constitute the dictator's support base. If these rulers use less violence than their predecessors, that is not because the enrichment of society has left them feeling more secure.

DIVIDING LINES

Most autocrats since 1945 are easy to peg as fear or spin dictators. But about a quarter are hybrid cases. In some countries—Qatar, the UAE, and Laos, for instance—leaders have barred opposition parties and public criticism of the government but without much violent repression. In others—for example, Sri Lanka, Bangladesh, and Algeria—rulers have used considerable violence and yet tolerated—or perhaps failed to suppress—opposition media.

China seems, at first, difficult to classify. When we talk to experts on the country, many are struck by how many features of spin dictatorship fit the regime in Beijing. Compared to Mao's savagery, violence has definitely declined. In most places these days, dissidents are less likely to be hustled off to a labor camp than invited by a secret policeman to "tea," the euphemism for a warning chat. Although scathing about Western systems—democracy "would not fit us and it might even lead to catastrophic consequences," Xi said in 2014—Chinese leaders do often describe their government as a different kind of democracy.[72] Certain private media are tolerated, and online censors sometimes just slow traffic down rather than ban sites outright.[73]

Yet, non-China specialists see the country as a blatant case of rule by fear. In restive regions, repression has been merciless. More than a million Uighurs, Kazakhs, and others have been herded into reeducation camps in Xinjiang, and those still outside live in terror.[74] Their every move is tracked by intrusive surveillance equipment. Xi clearly hopes his toughness there will intimidate pro-democracy campaigners in Hong Kong. Separatists anywhere in China, he said in 2019, "will be smashed into pieces."[75] Attempts to divide China would "end in crushed bodies and shattered bones."[76] Between June 2019 and January 2021, more than 10,200 Hong Kong protesters were arrested.[77] And much of this repression is quite open. Although at first Beijing tried to block reports about Xinjiang, leaders quickly switched to defending the camps.[78] Even in non-minority regions, dissidents are forced to make chilling televised confessions, the goal of which can only be to spread fear.[79]

For a while, China seemed to be heading toward spin dictatorship. Party chiefs Jiang Zemin (1989–2002) and Hu Jintao (2002–12) each allowed some public discussion of liberal ideas.[80] Amid the partial commercialization of China's media, some investigative reporting appeared.[81] China's main nightly news show, *Xinwen Lianbo*, remained so stilted and propagandistic that anyone watching it for news, quipped one commentator, must "be lying or . . . mentally impaired."[82] Yet, other channels introduced slick animated "explainer" videos, infographics, and patriotic documentaries.[83] However, Xi, who took over in 2012, reversed course. Besides stepping up repression in Xinjiang, Tibet, and Hong Kong, he cracked down on the press, firing investigative teams and jailing more journalists.[84] The pro-regime tone in the state-controlled *People's Daily* is today more effusive than at any time since the Cultural Revolution.[85] Even the commercialized newspapers—although devoting fewer inches to high-level politics—have become just as positive about the regime.[86]

Like Saudi Arabia under MBS, China under Xi is a strange mix of ruthless repression, outdated ideology, modern stagecraft, and cutting-edge information technology. Both states use hackers and trolls to dominate social networks, while tracking dissidents online.[87] Both leaders are more media savvy and comfortable with international openness than the classic twentieth-century tyrants. Yet, both remain wedded to rule by fear. Abroad, the Saudis deny responsibility for violent acts such as the 2018 assassination of the journalist Jamal Khashoggi.[88] But at home repression is publicized in order to intimidate. The authorities held some thirty thousand political prisoners in 2018, according to the Islamic Human Rights Commission, and public floggings, beheadings, and the display of corpses continue.[89] As journalist Ben Hubbard reports: "fear is so widespread that . . . many Saudis avoid talking on the phone or put their devices in the fridge when they meet."[90] Although updating the dictatorship of fear, Beijing and Riyadh remain committed to its central principle.

Some, hearing our argument, have suggested parallels between spin dictators and certain politicians in ostensibly democratic countries. In Italy, Silvio Berlusconi's dominance of the country's media shaped his governing style. Populist leaders like Néstor and Cristina Kirchner in Argentina and Andrés Manuel López Obrador in Mexico have used the tricks of spin dictators to co-opt mainstream media and marginalize critics.[91] In the United States, Donald Trump tried to use his Twitter account to mobilize support behind his undemocratic projects.

That spin dictators resemble politicians in low-quality democracies—and even some higher-quality ones—is not surprising. After all, spin dictators are *trying* to look like democratic politicians. And spin dictatorships often emerge when weak democracies are hijacked by unscrupulous leaders. In their early days, Orbán's Hungary, Erdoğan's Turkey, and Putin's Russia seemed to many—us included—to be not autocracies but flawed democracies. Today, we definitely place them on the authoritarian side. Since regimes vary along a spectrum, we should expect the boundary between the most threadbare democracy and the mildest dictatorship to be a fuzzy one.

It is also easy to mistake spin dictatorships for illiberal democracies— that is, democracies in which freely elected governments fail to protect civil rights and discriminate against minorities.[92] Orbán, for one, boasts openly of his illiberalism. But, in fact, spin dictators are not democrats at all. They do not just attack the civil rights of minorities—they manipulate the elections by which majorities might otherwise remove them from power.

Why do more democracies not slide into spin dictatorship? It is not for lack of effort by unscrupulous politicians. Yet, in stable democracies, something holds them back. The tradition in political science is to say that this something is democratic *institutions*. Multiparty elections, constitutional checks and balances, legal procedures, and independent judiciaries stop budding dictators in their tracks. Such rules and procedures are obviously important. And yet, as we show throughout this book, formal institutions do not act by themselves. Often, they fail to constrain leaders.[93] The essence of spin dictatorship is to conceal autocracy within formally democratic institutions. Modern authoritarians manipulate elections, disable checks and balances, rewrite constitutions, and pack courts with loyalists.[94]

The real question is not whether a state has the right formal institutions but what prevents leaders from subverting them. We argue that protection lies in the active resistance of the informed.[95] Just as in dictatorships, this subset of the population—those with higher education, communication skills, and international connections—plays a crucial role. In modern democracies, the highly educated tend to work in information-rich jobs that develop organizational talent and detailed knowledge of how the system operates. When they are numerous and well resourced, the informed can document abuses by incumbents, communicate them to the public, organize social and political movements, field effective electoral campaigns and protests, take abusers to court, and coordinate with international agencies and foreign governments. They can oppose attempts to usurp power—just as, in the United States in 2016–21, millions of lawyers, judges, officials, activists, journalists, and others pushed back against the initiatives of a nihilist in the White House. Without the actions of such people, a well-written constitution cannot help much.[96] The robust resistance of informed citizens is what secures the institutions of free government and makes them work.[97]

WHAT'S NEXT?

In the chapters to come, we will break down the elements of spin dictatorship. We will see how its practitioners avoid and disguise political violence (chapter 2), win over citizens with sophisticated propaganda (chapter 3), manage the media without crude censorship (chapter 4), fake democracy (chapter 5), and engage with the outside world (chapter 6). In each case, we will highlight striking cases, focusing on individual leaders whose early experiments helped to develop the model. We will contrast practices of recent spin dictators with those of their more overt twentieth-century predecessors. Wherever possible, we will back up our illustrations with references to more systematic data (in the "Checking the Evidence" sections and the book's online supplement).[98]

Having described the two models, we suggest an interpretation of the historical shift from fear to spin in chapter 7. What triggered this, we argue, was a cocktail of forces associated with modernization and globalization. In fact, these are the same forces that fueled the explosive "third wave" of democracy after 1974. Modernization and globalization create pressures for political openness. Spin dictatorship is the way rulers resist. They avoid real democracy by faking it. And yet, if modernization and globalization persist, the pressures intensify. In the absence of major oil wealth, these forces eventually nudge countries all the way into democracy.

Spin dictators put this off as long as possible. To do so, they must silence the informed by co-opting or censoring them. Yet, economic development swells the size of this group, rendering it more expensive to neutralize. So, in modern settings, spin offers only a temporary respite, albeit one that can last for years under a skilled operator. The effectiveness of this strategy is one reason why—although modernization generally creates conditions for democracy—the transition may come with a delay. We close, in chapter 8, with our best guess about what comes next for spin dictatorships, along with some thoughts about how the West should respond. But let's turn now to the experience of the model's pioneer as he first came to grips with the political costs of open repression.

PART I

HOW IT'S DONE

CHAPTER 2

DISCIPLINE, BUT DON'T PUNISH

In September 1956, Singapore's Chinese-speaking students took over their middle schools. The colonial authorities had dissolved the students' union and arrested its leaders, saying the organization had been infiltrated by communists.[1] In protest, thousands of teenagers flooded onto their school grounds, barricading themselves inside and pitching tents as sympathetic parents smuggled in food.

The colony's new chief minister, Lim Yew Hock, struck back with force, sending police with tear gas to evict the students. As if on cue, riots broke out across the city. Mobs rampaged, tipping over vehicles and setting fire to buildings. In the mayhem, thirteen people were killed and more than one hundred injured.[2] With the help of British troops, helicopters, armored cars, and roadblocks, Lim crushed the revolt. But by then he had discredited himself with the Chinese community that made up three-quarters of Singapore's population.[3]

To an ambitious young lawyer and political organizer named Lee Kuan Yew, Lim's clumsy reaction offered a lasting lesson. Lee had grown up in Singapore during the wartime Japanese occupation. To make ends meet, he had found a job translating news dispatches in the Japanese administration's propaganda department.[4] After the war, he studied law at Cambridge University before heading back to plunge into Singapore politics as the colony edged toward independence from Britain.

Lee did not disagree with the thrust of Lim's approach. He, too, when he became prime minister, would use the threat of revolutionary conspiracies to crack down on dissent. In the early 1960s, he sent police to arrest his more radical rivals.[5] Even after the British left, Lee kept the Internal Security Act—legislation permitting the indefinite detention of suspects—on the books for decades, long after any serious communist threat had disappeared.

Nor was Lee queasy about the use of force. Asked about the political opposition, he liked to adopt the tone of a gangster. He would put on his knuckle-dusters, he snarled, or fetch a hatchet and meet his adversaries in a dark alley.[6] During the war, the young Lee had been impressed by the ruthless effectiveness of the Japanese invaders. "I had not yet read Mao's dictum that 'power grows out of the barrel of a gun,'" he wrote later, "but I knew that Japanese brutality, Japanese guns, Japanese bayonets and swords, and Japanese terror and torture settled the argument as to who was in charge."[7]

The 1950s were a tense time. In 1949, Mao's insurgents had seized power in Beijing, sending a jolt of pride and radicalism through Singapore's Chinese diaspora. Soon after, war erupted in Korea. Britain, overstretched around the globe, was leaving its Asian colonies, one by one. In 1950, communist agents had attempted unsuccessfully to assassinate Singapore's British governor, Franklin Gimson.[8] There was plenty of reason to take the student rebellion seriously.

What struck Lee about Lim's response was not its violence but its ineptness. It taught him, he wrote, how "not to be tough and flat-footed."[9] Rather than persuade or trick the teenagers into going home, Lim had ordered in riot troops amid a shower of tear-gas canisters. Lee believed the real battle was for hearts and minds. And Lim had lost them. He was out of office by 1959, defeated in the election that brought Lee and his party to power—for life.

"I resolved," wrote Lee, "that . . . I would never make the same mistakes. I would think of a way of obliging the parents themselves to grab their children from the schools and take them home. Special Branch could pick up the leaders after the students had dispersed."[10]

Decades later, Lee—by then Singapore's long-serving leader—watched in horror as Chinese tanks mowed down that country's protesting students in Tiananmen Square. Although he felt sympathy for the victims, Lee's main reaction was—as it had been with Lim in

1956—despair at the leaders' ham-fisted response. "Why such force, I asked myself," he recalled. "These are not stupid people. They know what the world will think."[11]

Lee had forged a bond of mutual respect with Deng Xiaoping, the Chinese leader. Visiting Singapore in 1978, Deng had been amazed at what Lee had made of the once impoverished colonial outpost. In the eleven years since then, Lee had set out to mentor Deng and his team, advising them on economic policy.[12] It was painful, now, to see his friends blundering. The next year, Li Peng, who, as China's premier, had ordered the troops into Tiananmen Square, visited Singapore. Lee berated him for staging such a "grand show" before the world media. Li Peng, according to Lee, replied with humility: "We are completely inexperienced in these matters."[13]

By that point, Lee had built a new model of tight political control in Singapore, based on minimizing visible repression. Political scientist Cherian George called his approach "calibrated coercion."[14] It enabled Lee to dominate public life as completely as most overt dictators. In election after election, his People's Action Party won almost all the seats in parliament. A timid domestic media carefully avoided angering the government.[15] Political protests were extremely rare.[16]

Yet, Lee achieved this in a way that—as best one could tell—left him genuinely popular with many ordinary Singaporeans.[17] By the 1980s, there were very few political prisoners in the country's jails, and—although anti-crime measures were strict, with caning used to punish vandalism and drug abuse—there was little overt political repression.

BLOOD LANDS

Today this approach has become familiar. But in 1959, as Lee first took office, authoritarian rule was identified with violence. This chapter explores the remarkable evolution that followed. We trace how Lee and other innovators gradually devised more sophisticated and covert methods of coercion. And, with new data on state killings and political prisoners as well as other sources, we document the trend from harsh deterrence to low-intensity repression.

To appreciate this change, it is important to recall the starting point. In the 1950s, the world was still struggling to digest the horrors of Stalin's purges and Hitler's Holocaust. Around the globe, brutal regimes continued to kill their citizens by the thousands.

In communist states, the body counts were staggering. Backed by Moscow, Stalinist regimes had seized power across Eastern Europe, crushing resistance and purging the population. In just their first four years, Romania's leaders executed some 75,000 "enemies of the people." Another 100,000 perished in the Râmnicu Sărat prison.[18] In China, around 35 million starved in Mao's Great Leap Forward famine of 1958–60.[19] Their deaths resulted from the dictator's stubbornness and the zeal of local officials rather than deliberate political murder.[20] But Mao's Cultural Revolution and other political campaigns would end another 2.5 million lives. As revolution spread, the corpses continued to accumulate. Tens of thousands—maybe many more—were executed in North Korea and North Vietnam. Mengistu Haile Mariam, the Marxist dictator of Ethiopia, slaughtered 60,000 in his country's "red terror" in the 1970s. Millions of Cambodians—almost a quarter of the population, by widely accepted estimates—died in Pol Pot's "killing fields."[21]

But it was not just totalitarian ideologues who were shedding blood. Anticommunists also murdered on an industrial scale. Syngman Rhee's men in South Korea killed about 100,000 civilians before the Korean War and hundreds of thousands more during and after it.[22] As General Suharto seized power in Indonesia in 1965, massacres caused 500,000 to one million deaths.[23] In Latin America as well, anticommunism served as a pretext for butchery. Argentina's generals killed or "disappeared" 15,000–30,000 people in 1976–83, while next door General Pinochet's soldiers murdered 3,000–5,000 Chileans.[24] Other dictators required little ideological or geopolitical rationale. Postcolonial Africa threw up a rogues' gallery of bloodthirsty strongmen. Macias Nguema of Equatorial Guinea slaughtered about 50,000, Hissène Habré of Chad around 40,000.[25]

Those dissidents not murdered were often locked up. Across the unfree world, dictators packed real or alleged foes into prisons, labor colonies, concentration camps, and mental hospitals. The global persecution network stretched from the Soviet Union's "Gulag Archipelago" to Latin America's "penal islands." Almost everywhere, political prisoners were tortured.

Not all dictators were equally ruthless. As we will see in the data later, at least a few in every period got by with little killing. Yet, even those who spared the hangman still often imprisoned dissidents by the thousands. Egypt's Nasser executed only a limited number of Muslim Brothers. But his secret police could round up 20,000 political prisoners at a time.[26] In Argentina, the populist Juan Perón killed few but jailed more than 14,000 opponents.[27] Some prewar European dictators are considered relatively mild. Poland's Marshal Józef Piłsudski and Hungary's Admiral Miklós Horthy retained pieces of the democratic facade and—at least compared to what came later—showed restraint. Still, Piłsudski arrested 5,000 of his critics in 1930 and created "one of the first modern concentration camps for political prisoners."[28] The White Terror of 1919, amid which Horthy took power, featured "several thousand executions and tens of thousands of arrests." Horthy's former head bodyguard collected the ears of murdered communists.[29]

Violent repression was the key tool of twentieth-century dictators. But it was not the *only* tool. Some won popularity with anticolonial or military victories. Others, such as the leaders of Mexico's Partido Revolucionario Institucional (PRI), engineered support with economic development and patronage. In Africa, "big men" co-opted pyramids of followers, often within their ethnic group, by selectively disbursing benefits.[30] Still, even in these cases, fear and violence often lurked in the background. Mexico's regime massacred students, peasants, and unionists on many occasions.[31] The bosses might hand out bread, but they also had bayonets.

Almost as striking as the violence was the way rulers went about it. Most of the time, the killing, torture, and imprisonment were deliberately publicized. Twentieth-century dictators took pride in their gory exploits and made sure citizens knew about them. In this, they seemed to be reverting to a model of punishment that had become obsolete in the West by 1900. Medieval and early modern Europe were known for the gruesome punishments imposed for everything from minor crimes to regicide. Suspects might be broken on the wheel or the rack; burned at the stake; hung, drawn, and quartered; or all of the above. Executions and torture were public spectacles, with citizens encouraged to attend and applaud. The pillory, by its design, invited popular participation. Those who survived punishment were deliberately scarred to advertise their crimes: some were branded on the forehead; others had their nose or ears cut off.

Yet, as Michel Foucault described, the West underwent a revolution in penal philosophy and practices between 1760 and 1840. The deliberate infliction of pain gave way to more "humane" and invisible punishments, sometimes combined with attempts at rehabilitation.[32] Public executions disappeared, torture became unfashionable, and imprisonment was reconceived as a program for reform as much as retribution. Why things changed is not entirely clear, although many suppose that Enlightenment values played a key part.[33] Foucault also argued, more controversially, that the replacement of corporal punishment with less visible forms of discipline facilitated the spread of such power mechanisms into a broad range of social settings.

Twentieth-century dictators reversed this trend. They rejected the squeamishness of modern liberals, unapologetically embracing violence. They combined new technologies of mass production, transport, weapons, and communications with the traditional goals of inflicting pain and spreading fear. And they restored the very public face of political repression, along with the expectation that loyal citizens would participate.

Many autocrats made killing into a public event. Kim Jong-Il had a firing squad execute one factory director before a stadium packed with 150,000 onlookers.[34] Equatorial Guinea's Macias Nguema reportedly finished off 150 of his enemies in the capital's soccer arena as speakers played the pop song "Those Were the Days." Sudan's President Gaafar Nimeiry hanged a leading political opponent in front of 1,000 observers.[35]

Far from avoiding publicity, some clearly relished it. General Franco of Spain invented a special sentence for those whose death he wanted to advertise broadly: *garotte y prensa* ("strangulation by garotte with press coverage").[36] To refresh spectators, he set up coffee and churro stalls around one of his killing fields.[37] Many boasted of their brutality. "They regard me as an uneducated barbarian," Hitler stormed after the Reichstag fire. "Yes, we are barbarians! We want to be barbarians!"[38] President Hastings Banda of Malawi publicly recalled how his enemies had served as "food for crocodiles."[39] He bragged to parliament of the new prison he had built at Dzeleka to house his opponents: "I will keep them there and they will rot."[40] General Muammar Gaddafi of Libya ridiculed rulers who sought to conceal their responsibility by having enemies run over by cars or quietly poisoned. When he executed someone, Gaddafi insisted, he did it "on television."[41]

When the public was not around to watch a killing, dictators used the corpses to communicate. Rafael Trujillo, of the Dominican Republic, had the body of one dead rebel hoisted in a chair and driven around his home province. Peasants were forced to dance around the cadaver.[42] King Ahmad bin Yahya of Yemen ordered the heads of executed "traitors" to be "hung on the branches of trees as a warning."[43] Many other autocrats—from Papa Doc Duvalier to Ferdinand Marcos— prominently displayed the mutilated bodies of regime opponents. Mengistu broadcast pictures of his torture victims.

Among Latin American strongmen, exhibiting corpses became a macabre tradition. Under Batista in Cuba, "hundreds of mangled bodies were left hanging from lamp posts or dumped in the streets."[44] In Guatemala, the newspaper *Prensa Libre* published regular "cadaver reports" in the early 1980s for those who might have missed the originals, detailing the scars. Readers learned to associate distinctive mutilations with the police, army, and presidential guard.[45] Some dictators turned torture, itself, into a show. Under Pakistan's General Zia, political prisoners were "publicly flogged . . . by bare-chested wrestlers" and loudspeakers were set up to transmit the victims' screams.[46]

Arrests, themselves, sometimes doubled as performances. Although Argentina's military junta often replaced deaths by "disappearances," the detentions could be very public. Up to fifty soldiers or paramilitaries might burst into a victim's house at night, brandishing revolvers and grenades, yelling into loudspeakers, and flashing searchlights as helicopters circled overhead. They often halted traffic and sometimes cut electricity to an entire city block.[47] In the Dominican Republic, Trujillo's thugs patrolled the streets in characteristic black Volkswagen Beetles.

To emphasize their toughness, dictators adopted military titles such as Generalissimo (Franco, Trujillo, Stalin) and Marshal (Josip Broz Tito).[48] Former soldiers continued to wear uniforms. But many with no military background also dressed up in martial costumes. Stalin had a special outfit made in the austere Imperial style, with striped pants, gray tunic, and epaulettes.[49] Mussolini donned the garb of the fascist Militia, adding an insignia.[50] Fidel Castro rarely took off his khakis.[51] As we detail in the next chapter, dictators of all ideologies adopted a vocabulary of the battlefield. Mussolini called his fascist party "a real army."[52] Under him, Italians fought a "Battle for Grain," a "Battle for Land," and even a "War on Flies."[53] Communists engaged in "'struggle' and 'combat' on 'fronts' to achieve 'breakthroughs' in production and cultural 'victories.'"[54]

Some went a step further, militarizing society. By the late 1930s, all Italian children from age six were expected to put on fascist uniforms and march with toy rifles.[55] Even toddlers posed for photographs in black shirts.[56] In Chinese primary schools under Mao, pupils learned to fire air rifles by shooting at posters of Chiang Kai-shek and "American imperialists."[57] The college curriculum included drills in throwing grenades and shooting with live ammunition. Soviet high schools taught "basic military training" to both boys and girls.[58] Iraqi teenagers practiced military skills as members of Ashbal Saddam (Saddam's Cubs).[59]

In short, these societies were steeped in violence and martial imagery to an extent hard to conceive from within modern democracies—or the kind of disciplined stronghold that Lee Kuan Yew crafted in Singapore.

CALCULUS OF KILLING

What did twentieth-century dictators hope to achieve with all this bloodshed? And why were they so public about their violence?

To some, the only possible explanation was mental illness. Indeed, it is hard to see those ordering mass killings as completely normal. Psychologists who reviewed biographies of Hitler, Saddam Hussein, and

Kim Jong-Il found signs of paranoia, narcissism, sadism, and schizo-phrenic tendencies.[60] Still, psychopathology seems inadequate as a general account. Many dictators showed advanced cognitive skills and strategic thinking. Saddam Hussein, Pol Pot, and Macias Nguema struck some who met them as insane, but others did not.[61] Rather than driven by inner voices, many autocrats found violence useful.

But to what end? One use of force was to crush bureaucratic resistance. That clearly motivated Lenin early on and Mao during the Cultural Revolution. Lenin threatened to jail subordinates for red tape and wrote to one: "You deserve a beating!"[62] Still, this does not explain violence against the general public. Repression was often imposed by a loyal bureaucracy rather than on a disloyal one.

Some dictators used violence to reshape society in revolutionary ways. Communists sought to liquidate entire classes or social groups.[63] Even before Stalin collectivized agriculture, Lenin declared "ruthless war on the kulaks," rich peasants whom he characterized as "bloodsuckers," "spiders," "leeches," and "vampires." He also favored the execution of prostitutes and syphilitics.[64] Franco's fascists aimed to eliminate the left; Hitler targeted Jews, gypsies, homosexuals, and the handicapped. In these and many other autocracies, mass killing was supposed to "purify" the population.

Besides restructuring society, some aimed to remake individuals. To Mussolini, violence was a creative force. It would turn effete Italians into heroic Romans. His countrymen were "a bunch of . . . chattering 'mandolin players'" unprepared for the "Darwinian struggle between nations." "The Italian race is a race of sheep," he told his foreign minister. "You need to keep them lined up and in uniform from morning until night. And they need the club, the club, the club."[65] Tens of thousands who resisted disappeared into "concentration camps, political prisons, work houses, confinement colonies, and sites of internment."[66]

Another use of violence was to discipline workers and squeeze resources from the population. Stalin and Mao may not have consciously wished to starve millions of peasants, but their determination to extract surplus to fund rapid industrialization had that effect. They both led crusades against "grain profiteers," "parasites," "disorganizers," and "saboteurs." Since many peasants did resist collectivization, the policy is hard to imagine without force. Stalin's Gulag furnished free labor for construction projects like the Moscow Metro. Of the roughly 170,000 prisoners who dug the Belomor Canal, carting away dirt and rock with wooden spades and handmade wheelbarrows, more than 25,000 died.[67] On a smaller scale, Latin America's "bureaucratic authoritarian" juntas in the 1960s and 1970s set out to repress labor unions and lower wages in order to stimulate growth.

Yet, by far the most common motive for violence was to defend the regime. Harsh repression protected dictators in several ways. Most obviously, it eliminated or weakened political enemies. The list of targets was long. Besides kulaks, Lenin took aim at counterrevolutionaries, White Guards, and Cossacks. Stalin added provocateurs, Trotskyites, agents of fascism and American imperialism, wreckers, and traitors.[68] Besides using violence to purify the German stock, Hitler ordered followers to destroy anti-Nazi forces such as the communists, social democrats, and opponents of Nazism in the German churches. Latin American strongmen sent death squads to murder anyone believed to be hostile to their rule—from peasants and labor leaders to students and university professors.[69]

Of course, many of the victims were innocent scapegoats. But, from the dictator's perspective, so much the better. Even poorly targeted violence could deter potential opponents and reinforce the public's docility. The key was to demonstrate ruthlessness. As Pakistan's General Zia put it: "Martial Law should be based on fear."[70] "Why should we fear a bit of shock?" Chairman Mao asked. "We want to be shocking."[71] Stalin, in 1939, drew a direct connection between state violence and public loyalty:

> In 1937 Tukhachevsky, Yakir, Uborevich, and other fiends were sentenced to be shot. After that, the elections to the Supreme Soviet of the USSR were held. In these elections, 98.6 percent of the total vote was cast for the Soviet government. At the beginning of 1938 Rosengolts, Rykov, Bukharin, and other monsters were sentenced to be shot. After that, the elections to the supreme soviets of the union

republics were held. In these elections, 99.4 percent of the total vote was cast for the Soviet Government.[72]

Of course, Stalin's vote tallies are not to be trusted. But executing a few "fiends" and "monsters" certainly did remind citizens to vote the "right" way.

Violence also helped with propaganda. Stalin insisted on extracting confessions from his political rivals before having them shot. They had to admit to what the writer Arthur Koestler called "absurd and hair-raising lies."[73] Stalin personally oversaw some interrogations, inserting or deleting phrases in the "confessions."[74] After a stay in the notorious "Torture Dacha" near Vidnoe, south of Moscow, the great theater director Vsevolod Meyerhold confessed to spying for Britain and Japan and fingered other leading artists.[75] The top Bolshevik Nikolai Bukharin admitted to "organizing kulak uprisings" and "preparing terrorist acts" but balked at adding the murders of Leningrad party boss Sergei Kirov and writer Maxim Gorky.[76]

Why the emphasis on obtaining ridiculous "confessions" that both torturer and victim knew were untrue? In Orwell's *1984*, the party leader, O'Brien, sees forcing dissidents to recant as an end in itself, part of the exercise of power: "Power is in tearing human minds to pieces and putting them together again in new shapes of your own choosing."[77] But Orwell's contemporary Koestler, who had known the Bolsheviks Stalin purged, saw it as a matter of public messaging. In his masterpiece *Darkness at Noon*, Koestler's cold-blooded interrogator, Gletkin, tells the imprisoned Bolshevik, Rubashov, "The only way in which you can still serve the Party is as a warning example—by demonstrating to the masses, in your own person, the consequences to which opposition to the Party policy inevitably leads."[78] Scapegoats helped to convince citizens of the need for obedience, vigilance, and continual effort.

And, absurd as the confessions were, many inside and outside the Soviet Union believed them. Sometimes, the truth seemed just too grotesque to accept. After watching the trial of Radek and his "co-conspirators," the U.S. ambassador in Moscow, Joseph Davies, reported that any court would have found the defendants guilty. To stage such a show, Davies wrote, would have required "the genius of Shakespeare."[79] KGB agents compiled secret reports on how the public was responding. Among workers, some found it fishy that all of Lenin's comrades had been fascist spies. But others disagreed. Quite a few wished only that more Bolshevik leaders had been shot.[80] For those who saw through Stalin's gory pantomime, the trials showed the danger of falling under suspicion. For those who did not, they conjured up a terrifying world of treachery and blood.

Public confessions also played a role in Iran under the Shah. Radio broadcast "interviews" with leftists who, after a spell in Evin Prison, renounced their former views and praised the regime.[81] Similar recantations continued under Khomeini—the Ayatollah himself sometimes previewed the videos.[82] Prisoners would admit to treason, espionage, foreign subversion, terrorism, or religious offenses such as eclecticism, religious deviation, and ideological contamination.[83] Again, the goal seems to have been propaganda. To ordinary citizens, the confessions presented a world of hidden evils and lurking traitors against which the authorities were the only protection. At the same time, they demoralized regime opponents. Even those who saw the forced nature of the recantations were depressed to see their heroes groveling.[84]

Repression deters opposition by threatening punishment. But less conscious mechanisms may also help. Psychological research suggests perceived dangers—even those unrelated to politics—can make people more pessimistic, risk averse, and supportive of authoritarian policies and leaders.[85] Political scientist Lauren Young found that in Zimbabwe under Robert Mugabe, prompting people to think about snakes, witchcraft, or even just walking in the dark sharply reduced their readiness to attend opposition meetings or joke about the president.[86]

Finally, violent repression can bind citizens to the regime by making them complicit. Those who participate in brutal acts—or cause them by informing on peers—feel a need to justify this to themselves. The easiest way to banish guilt is to believe the victim guilty. Understanding this, dictators sought to involve citizens in their violence. Stalin's collectivization allowed poor peasants to rape, murder, and expropriate their richer neighbors. Bukharin was shocked by "the profound psychological change" in communists who participated: "Instead of going mad, they accepted terror as a normal administrative method."[87] Mao's Cultural Revolution was an orgy of decentralized carnage. The Argentine military in the 1970s rotated officers through the death squads and detention centers to ensure that no one's hands remained clean. As one officer put it: "The idea was to compromise everyone."[88] The same logic lay behind the practice of forcing citizens to attend executions. Such killings were less distressing if one could convince oneself of their necessity.

Almost all these motives require repression to be open and visible. To deter, threats must be communicated. To instill anxiety, dangers should loom all around. Enlisting citizens in terror or invigorating effete Italians is hard to do in secret. One exception is the extraction of confessions by torture: such confessions are more convincing if they seem uncoerced, so Stalin's jailers used sleep deprivation rather than beatings on show trial defendants. That might seem inconsistent with the practice of publicizing the use of force. But the death sentences that followed the trials were published prominently in the newspapers.

Of course, to say violent repression was public does not mean that most citizens knew—or discussed—the true dimensions of the terror in their midst. Even many in the dictator's circle would have lacked comprehensive information. A partial picture is enough to generate fear. And, in all autocracies, citizens protect themselves by clinging to denial, averting their eyes, and constructing justifications. Life is easier when you "know what not to know." The state's crimes become, in the phrase of anthropologist Michael Taussig, a "public secret"—generally recognized but never articulated.[89]

LEE'S SOFTER TOUCH

Against this backdrop, Lee Kuan Yew's less ferocious approach stood out. By the late 1970s, he had released most of his political prisoners. He was finding ever less visible ways to neutralize opposition. Rather than crush student protests, he simply closed down the main Chinese-language university, Nanyang, on the pretext of falling enrollments, folding it into the University of Singapore. His officials tightly regulated student organizations and vetted new faculty for soundness. "Up to 1975," writes Cherian George, "the government won its battles with students through the use of force; after that, it won without a fight."[90]

To constrain critics, Lee used restrictions rather than outright bans, allowing him to claim that politics were free. Newspapers that offended were permitted to publish, but with their circulation capped. Many faced defamation suits. Protests were allowed, but only with a license and few participants. In 2000, Lee's successors set up a "Speakers' Corner" in Hong Lim Park to show the regime's respect for freedom of expression.[91] Within its confines, orators could hold forth without being arrested. Still, they had to register first with local police and await permission. A sign warned that their speech would be recorded and kept for possible use in trials against them. They were not allowed to use loudspeakers, arouse "racial or religious enmity," insult those in authority, or make "wild gesticulations."[92]

Opposition leaders were not banned from parliament. But legal judgments and fines could keep them out. When politicians criticized him, Lee pounced on the undocumented claim and sued for defamation or libel. Repeated heavy penalties drove opponents into bankruptcy, disqualifying them from running for office.[93] Between 1971 and 1993, eleven opposition politicians went bankrupt after losing suits to government officials, according to the country's attorney general.[94] The law also required bankrupts to get permission to travel abroad, which gave the government a way to avoid embarrassment overseas.[95] Lee himself admitted the political use of bankruptcy. In 2003, discussing certain opposition activists, he told the Straits Times: "If we had considered them serious political figures, we would not have kept them politically alive for so long. We could have made them bankrupt earlier."[96]

Throughout, Lee's goal was to sustain public support and marginalize the opposition. He might deride politicians who cared only about opinion polls. But he knew his authority, in this new system, depended on keeping his ratings high. Leaders who lost the public's respect, he said, could "stumble along from day to day and pretend that it's business as usual. But nobody really takes the Government seriously."[97] A leader who stayed popular did not need violent repression—indeed, violence would backfire. And popularity, in turn, made it easier to monopolize power.

Singapore's system of stealthy control inspired others. Across Eurasia, authoritarians hailed Lee as a trailblazer. President Putin awarded him Russia's prestigious Order of Honor. Kazakhstan's President Nazarbayev added his country's Order of Friendship.[98] "We met often," the Kazakh leader said. "I considered him a good friend, I adopted his experience."[99] Kazakh officials made frequent study trips to Singapore.[100] Thailand's Thaksin Shinawatra discussed with Lee "what modern-day leaders and governments need to do to be effective."[101] Lee's admirers imitated his innovations. From Cambodia, Indonesia, Malaysia, and Myanmar to Russia, Turkey, and even Rafael Correa's Ecuador, rulers took to harassing journalists and opposition politicians with defamation and libel suits.[102] After Singapore created its "Speakers' Corner" in 2000, similar "Speakers' Corners" appeared in two Moscow parks.[103]

Chinese leaders repeatedly flirted with Singapore and its model. Deng Xiaoping sent hundreds of delegations to probe the island's successes. Under Jiang in the 1990s and Hu in the 2000s, Beijing's potentates often seemed to be steering toward some version of Lee's system. But, although they improved their public relations, China's leaders never seemed ready to renounce violent repression. Their regime remained a mix of old and new.

MOSCOW METHODS

Lee was the great pioneer. But elsewhere others were also glimpsing the logic of spin dictatorship. In the Soviet bloc, tactics were evolving. When Stalin died in 1953, his successors, thankful to have survived, freed millions from the prison camps. But Khrushchev, the champion of de-Stalinization, was out by the mid-1960s, replaced by cadres eager to restore discipline. They started with a few show trials of literary dissidents.[104]

This backfired spectacularly. The targets turned out to be not cringing victims but articulate thinkers who ran rings around the poorly prepared judges. Their courageous statements circulated through new *samizdat* (self-publication) networks, sometimes reaching the West. The BBC, Radio Liberty, and Deutsche Welle quickly broadcast them back into Russia to the millions of short-wave radio listeners. The show trials of regime opponents ended up show trials of the regime.

First, a twenty-four-year-old poet from Leningrad, Joseph Brodsky, was tried and sentenced to exile with labor. "Who appointed you a poet?" the judge demanded. "Who appointed me to the human race?" Brodsky replied. The Western poets John Berryman, W. H. Auden, and Stephen Spender took up his cause.[105] Two writers who had published satirical works in France, Yuli Daniel and Andrei Sinyavsky, were arrested in 1965. This triggered the first public protest since the war, along with appeals by leading cultural figures and scientists. Stalin's daughter, Svetlana Alliluyeva, defected to the United States soon after, saying the writers' persecution had convinced her the system would never reform.[106] When a journalist circulated a samizdat report on the trial, he too was arrested, sparking another demonstration and further arrests. By late 1968, more than 1,500 people had signed letters denouncing the prosecutions.[107] The Kremlin seemed to be losing control.

How to respond? Some Politburo members wanted to co-opt the cultural elite. The unlikely advocate of a soft line was Brezhnev's chief policeman, Interior Minister Nikolai Shchelokov. The best option, he told Brezhnev, was "not to execute our enemies publicly but smother them with embraces."[108] Shchelokov had become acquainted with the famous cellist Mstislav Rostropovich and his wife, the opera singer Galina Vishnevskaya. Through them, he had met their house guest, the writer Alexander Solzhenitsyn. Crude repression seemed to him counterproductive in the more educated society the USSR was becoming. Shchelokov sought to civilize the police. He insisted that agents treat the public politely.[109] He opened a new academy, under the composer Aram Khachaturian, to polish his officers' rough edges. He pressed for lighter sentences for women and children. He even looked into designing a new, low-caliber pistol to make police shootings less lethal.[110]

In the Politburo infighting, Shchelokov lost out to a steelier rival, the KGB chief Yuri Andropov. (After Andropov became general secretary in 1982, a relentless corruption probe drove Shchelokov to suicide.) Andropov agreed that something had to change. But rather than humanizing the regime, he sought just to target and hide repression better. He closed political trials to the public, holding them in remote spots few foreign correspondents could reach. He also stepped up confinement of dissidents in psychiatric hospitals, which allowed Soviet leaders to claim they were not political prisoners but mentally ill. This also backfired; gruesome reports of writers injected with psychotropic drugs sparked outrage abroad. But, again, the impulse was to conceal the political nature of persecution.

To reduce visibility, Andropov also softened the punishments for minor transgressions. The number of anti-Soviet leaflets, letters, and graffiti doubled between 1967 and 1981, according to KGB reports.[111] Yet, despite this troubling trend, Andropov's men charged fewer of the captured authors with crimes—10 percent in 1967 but only 3 percent in 1981.[112] Instead, most minor offenders were treated with "prophylaxis." They were summoned to the KGB's office, questioned, warned, and sent home.

The communist bloc's greatest innovation was the refinement of low-visibility harassment. Dissidents who ignored KGB warnings were demoted at work or fired and evicted from their apartments. Their telephones were disconnected, driver's licenses suspended, typewriters confiscated.[113] Their children were denied college admission. Those who still had telephones received menacing anonymous calls. Others were insulted or physically threatened by "indignant citizens" or plainclothes agents.[114] Although some were still sentenced to labor camps, Andropov's men preferred frequent searches and interrogations, short-term preventive detentions, and house arrest.[115] Dissident physicist Andrei Sakharov, exiled to the provincial capital Gorky (now Nizhny Novgorod), received envelopes in the mail full of dead cockroaches or photographs of mutilated faces. Saplings he and his wife planted in their garden were cut down. If they left their short-wave radio at home, KGB agents would vandalize it while they were out.[116]

Sakharov's treatment was still quite crude. It was the East Germans, under Erich Honecker, who perfected such harassment. Known as

Zersetzung—literally "corrosion"—the method aimed to disrupt the target's personal life and career, isolate him from friends and family, and make him question his own sanity. One Lutheran pastor active in the peace movement was first stopped—wrongly—for speeding. Police then engineered a car accident and prosecuted him for drunk driving, although he had been sober. Abusive notes appeared on trees near his home. Rumors reached the pastor's wife that he was sleeping with one of his parishioners. Eventually, threatened with a trumped-up criminal prosecution, the pastor fled to West Germany. He had been effectively neutralized—all without realizing the Stasi's role in his ordeal.[117]

The mind games could be subtle. In one case, Stasi agents snuck into a woman's apartment and rearranged the furniture. The first time, they rehung the pictures. The next, they mixed up spice jars in the kitchen. On another occasion, they replaced the woman's favorite tea with a different brand. They moved towels in the bathroom and repositioned flower pots on the windowsills. When the victim complained to friends, nobody believed her. Confused and disoriented, victims of such interventions lost the energy to continue political activities.[118]

The search for less obvious methods of repression did not turn the communist countries into spin dictatorships. Although less glaring than under Stalin, ideology and fear remained in the background. Elections still did not pretend to offer any real choice. The late Soviet bloc remained far from Lee's Singapore. But even behind the Iron Curtain methods were changing.

THE NEW PLAYBOOK

By the late 1990s, many dictators had gotten the memo. Of course, not all of them did: old-school thugs like Saddam Hussein and Kim Jong-Il still terrorized their citizens. Even relatively modern strongmen turned brutal amid civil wars or ethnic insurgencies. But many were converging on a repertoire of softer techniques. Some of these refined tricks of pioneering fear dictators. But others originated with the new masters of spin.

Arresting dissidents for nonpolitical crimes. Nicolae Ceaușescu's eureka moment came in the fall of 1967. "With inventiveness and creativity," the Romanian leader told his security chief, "we can find countless ways to get rid of political criminals, without giving the Western media any reason to squawk about us. We can arrest them as embezzlers or speculators, accuse them of dereliction of their professional duties, or whatever else best fits each case. Once a fellow's in prison, he's yours."[119] In jail as elsewhere, Ceauşescu noted, "accidents can happen."

Since then, other dictators have shown great "inventiveness and creativity." Kazakhstan's President Nazarbayev prosecuted journalists for money laundering and raping minors. He charged a political rival with corruption and weapons possession.[120] In Russia, opposition leader Aleksei Navalny's supposed crimes include defrauding lumber and cosmetics companies and illegal elk hunting.[121] Another oppositionist was arrested for swearing in public.[122] In Turkey, Erdoğan jailed a leading Kurdish politician for "using a fake health report to avoid military service."[123]

The most "inventive and creative" rulers find crimes that are not just nonpolitical but disreputable. Sex offenses work well, especially when primed by rumors. Accusing an opponent of evading military service, as Erdoğan did, paints the victim as a coward. To those reputed to be honest, corruption allegations give the appearance of hypocrisy.

Malaysia's Prime Minister Mahathir Mohamad seemed to follow the script in 1998. His former deputy, Anwar Ibrahim, had defected to the opposition. Police arrested Anwar for corruption. But they also accused him of sodomy, then illegal in Malaysia and culturally taboo. However, as Lee Kuan Yew pointed out to his colleague from across the Strait, Mahathir had made two key mistakes.[124] First, he used the Draconian Internal Security Act rather than an ordinary statute, thus exposing the case's political underpinnings. Second, Anwar appeared in court days later with a dramatic black eye. The image, published widely, set off opposition protests. After first claiming Anwar had deliberately injured himself, the police chief had to admit he had personally beaten the politician in his cell. The effect—accentuating the regime's brutality rather than obscuring it—was the opposite of that intended. Anwar emerged the political victor.[125]

Revolving door detentions. Rather than sentencing dissidents to long prison terms, dictators can neutralize them—with less negative publicity—using repeated, short detentions. In Cuba, Fidel Castro jailed some political prisoners for more than ten years. His brother Raúl, in charge from 2008 to 2021, preferred to detain activists for just a few days—long enough to intimidate and disrupt but usually not to generate international campaigns for their release.[126] By 2019, Russia's Navalny had been sentenced to thirteen short jail spells, most lasting from ten to thirty days.[127] At one point, the authorities seemed to change tack: a judge sentenced him to five years for embezzlement. Yet, in a bizarre reversal, the prosecutor general intervened to appeal, and the sentence was suspended.

Imprisoning popular activists for long terms risks creating martyrs. Russia's authorities have jailed a number of obscure protest participants and even imprisoned Navalny's less political brother, Oleg. Eventually, in 2021, the authorities did send Navalny himself to a labor colony for two and a half years, after an apparent attempt by the security services to secretly poison him failed. But his incarceration came across as an act of desperation. And the authorities continued to present him as an ordinary criminal—a commercial fraudster who had to be locked up for violating parole. When previously unknown victims have managed to attract media and public attention, their sentences have been cut. In 2019, a student and blogger, Yegor Zhukov, was accused of violating the law on protests and threatened with a labor camp term. But after he delivered a courageous and articulate courtroom speech, a translation of which made it onto the *New Yorker*'s website, his sentence was suspended.

Bankrupting the opposition. In Singapore, as mentioned, bankruptcy renders candidates ineligible for parliament, and financial penalties for defamation can be large. As the opposition politician Joshua Jeyaretnam campaigned for office in the 1970s and 1980s, he faced repeated lawsuits. The penalties eventually added up to more than $900,000.[128] Not only did these keep him out of parliament, they forced him to spend much of the next decade seeking funds to avoid prison. Another opposition candidate was sued for $5.65 million after he called government leaders' characterization of him as a "dangerous Chinese chauvinist" a lie.[129]

As so often, Singapore blazed the trail. But others followed. When Putin faced a wave of protests in 2011–12, he drastically increased financial penalties: the average fine for violating the protest law increased fivefold between 2012 and 2018.[130] In 2019, the Russian government went further: organizers of protest rallies (including Navalny and a few colleagues) were sued for millions of dollars supposedly to pay for the repair of trampled lawns, obstructed public transportation, and even overtime police work.[131] Dozens of Russian activists found their personal bank accounts frozen as the government launched a $15 million money laundering investigation into Navalny's foundation.[132] In Ecuador, an opposition newspaper faced bankruptcy after a court found it and its journalists guilty of libel and ordered them to pay $40 million to the country's president, Rafael Correa.[133] In the end, Correa relented. The beauty of such techniques is that to uninformed observers the opposition activist or journalist can genuinely seem the guilty party.

Regulations and restrictions. Rather than banning some activity completely, dictators can permit inferior alternatives. To opposition groups that want to rally in the city center, they can offer a muddy field on its outskirts, far from public transportation. They can direct those who want to speak freely to a designated location—recall Singapore's and Russia's "Speakers' Corners."[134] While permitting opposition organizations, they can require them to register, declare themselves "foreign agents," and compile frequent, time-consuming financial reports. They can ban foreign funding and anonymous contributions outright and warn domestic businesses not to contribute.

Accusing the opposition of violence. Recognizing the costs of violence, spin dictators limit its use. But why stop there? A next step is to accuse the *opposition* of violence in order to discredit it. When tens of thousands thronged to demonstrations in 2013, Turkey's President Erdoğan attacked them as "looters," "anarchists," and "terrorists."[135] In Russia in 2019, police charged dozens of people with committing "violence against state agents" at several antigovernment rallies. One had thrown an empty paper cup in the air; another had tossed two empty plastic bottles.[136] Provocateurs can also be sent to hurl rocks and engage in real violence so the police can arrest innocent bystanders near them.[137] In 2013, for instance, one Russian operative told journalists he had been hired by an agent for the country's Interior Minister to create mayhem at an anti-Putin rally.[138]

Privatizing the dirty jobs. When leaders cannot resist using force, they may farm out implementation to loosely affiliated agents. The authorities can deny involvement or even knowledge. Spin dictators sometimes co-opt bands of martial arts enthusiasts or soccer hooligans to intimidate the opposition. To combat pro-Europe protesters in 2013–14, Ukrainian president Viktor Yanukovich relied on a 20,000-strong private army of "Adidas-clad thugs" known as *titushki*, after Vadym Titushko, the first to be exposed by the media.[139] Similarly, in Venezuela, Chávez and his successor, Nicolás Maduro, hired gangs of private hoodlums, known as *colectivos*, to terrorize antigovernment activists.[140]

In fact, this is an old technique, often used by twentieth-century fear dictators. Various Latin American autocrats backed semi-independent paramilitaries and death squads. African strongmen dependent on aid from democratic donors have often done the same.[141] For spin dictators, the practice is dangerous and usually employed sparingly. It only works if links to the state can be successfully hidden, which gets harder as society and media grow more sophisticated. In Ukraine, journalists quickly traced the *titushki*'s connections to the government, which accelerated the fall of the regime. It also requires avoiding violence on a scale that would prompt strong international outrage and demands for police investigations.

Zersetzung 2.0. The Internet offers unprecedented opportunities for slandering activists and sowing distrust within their networks. Anonymous posts can accuse them of being state agents. Indeed, most of the old KGB and Stasi techniques can be used online. In the old days, anonymous phone calls harassed dissidents. Now, unidentified trolls insult and threaten them on social networks, bombard them with hostile emails, and "dox" them—that is, post online incitements to attack them, with details of their location. As Sergey Sanovich, Denis Stukal, and Joshua Tucker have shown, the Russian government uses a sophisticated and constantly evolving tool kit of online tactics against the opposition, combining both Internet restrictions and "online engagement" by means of trolls, bots, and hacking-and-shaming operations.[142]

In Ecuador in 2014, opposition journalist Martha Roldós's email account was hacked and her private messages published in the state newspaper *El Telégrafo*. A wave of Internet trolls then mocked her physical appearance, threatened her with rape and murder, and accused her of being a CIA agent. A year later, a supporter of President Correa unmasked the satirical blogger known as "Crudo Ecuador," publishing his address, phone number, parents' names, and photographs of him apparently taken by a stalker. Confronting death threats, the blogger closed all his social media accounts.[143]

The dictator's agents—or private sector proxies—can also hack into the private files of opposition activists and publicize any embarrassing materials they find. Again, there is a pre-Internet analog—the leaking of security service recordings of opposition members' phone calls and the secret filming of them in compromising situations. Shame—and its exploitation by dictators—predates the World Wide Web.

CHECKING THE EVIDENCE

All these examples paint a consistent picture. But how do we know they add up to a broader trend? After all, newspapers still overflow with gruesome accounts of massacres of Rohingya Muslims in Myanmar, torture of activists in Syria, and persecution of Chinese Uighurs. Are these really—as we claim—exceptions to the rule? And were past decades as blood-soaked as we contend?

To check this more systematically, we collected data on political violence by all authoritarian governments since 1946.[144] (We already encountered these data in chapter 1, where they went into calculating the frequencies of spin and fear; recall figure 1.1.) Of course, counting the victims of past autocrats is incredibly hard. Even those who did not deliberately conceal their work rarely kept accurate tallies. Our estimates rely on the painstaking research of human rights activists, historians, journalists, government bodies, international organizations, and other investigators. Sometimes, after a dictatorship crumbled, the new leader created a truth commission to record evidence of its crimes; we examined their reports. In all, we ended up consulting almost a thousand sources.

A key decision was to compare not countries or political regimes but individual leaders. Within a single regime, violence levels can vary dramatically. Soviet communism saw both the genocidal extremes of Stalin and the relative restraint of Gorbachev. Indeed, as already noted, the intensity may vary under a single dictator. To take this into account, we compare the average level of repression under each leader, calculated over all his years in power. Since averages based on very short periods would be noisy, we include only rulers who remained atop a nondemocracy for at least five years.

For each, we recorded our best estimate of the number of state political killings. By this we mean all killings of nonviolent individuals by state agents for political reasons. That includes assassinations and executions of political prisoners, as well as all other deaths of political prisoners and detainees while in custody. (The dictator may blame natural causes, but these often result from mistreatment or at least inadequate medical care.) We also include indiscriminate killings of protesters and other unarmed civilians by the police, armed forces, or security personnel; these often serve the political goal of spreading terror.[145] We interpret "political reasons" broadly, counting members of persecuted sects killed by the state because of their religion and those killed while protesting peacefully for economic demands. We do not include killings in two-sided violence or deaths from state-caused famine.

We also did our best to count the number of political prisoners and detainees. It quickly became clear that we could not obtain reliable figures for every year. So, instead, we focus on the year for each dictator in which the number reported was highest. That is also likely to be the year with the fullest coverage in human rights reports and other sources. Among political prisoners and detainees, we included any people held for more than a few hours for political—rather than ordinary criminal— reasons. They might or might not be convicted of an offense. We did not count those imprisoned for terrorism or other violent acts (unless human rights organizations such as Amnesty International maintained that the detainee was innocent). Finally, we recorded whether any sources alleged the use of torture against political prisoners. As in chapter 1, we sorted leaders into cohorts based on the decade in which they took power. We call the resulting compilation the Authoritarian Control Techniques Database.[146]

Needless to say, one cannot expect completeness and precision in a task like this. Fine-grained comparisons may well be unreliable—and we avoid them. Still, such data are useful for uncovering large differences and identifying general patterns and trends. One can distinguish butchers like Uganda's Idi Amin, who killed tens of thousands of political victims per year, from strongmen like Argentina's General Jorge Videla, with thousands per year, Uzbekistan's Islam Karimov, with hundreds per year, and Hugo Chávez, with fewer than ten per year.

The patterns we found—after months of gloomy reading and investigating sources—confirmed our hunch. Since the 1980s, the extent of violence in successive cohorts of nondemocratic leaders has fallen dramatically. In the cohort taking power in the 1980s—a group that includes Zimbabwe's Robert Mugabe, Panama's General Noriega, and Saudi Arabia's King Fahd—almost two-thirds had more than 10 political killings a year. The proportion with this many killings dropped to 44 percent in the 1990s cohort. By the 2000s cohort, which includes Lee Hsien Loong of Singapore, Rafael Correa of Ecuador, and Vladimir Putin of Russia, the share was down to 28 percent. The proportion of dictators with more than 100 killings a year has decreased since the 1960s. In the 1960s cohort—which includes Muammar Gaddafi of Libya, Ferdinand Marcos of the Philippines, and Leonid Brezhnev of the USSR—about one-quarter had more than 100 killings a year. By the 2000s cohort, this was down to about 9 percent.[147] Figure 2.1 shows the pattern.

In each cohort, some dictators were far less violent. King Sobhuza II of Swaziland reigned from the country's independence in 1967 to 1982 without reports of political killings, as did several of Kuwait's emirs. And some recent autocrats have a bloody record: Bashar al-Assad of Syria, for instance, averaged nearly 1,500 estimated killings a year (in the years up to 2015, when our data end). But the balance has shifted.

We found a similar fall in the proportion of dictators holding large numbers of political prisoners. In the 1970s cohort, 59 percent of dictators held more than 1,000 political prisoners in their peak year. By the

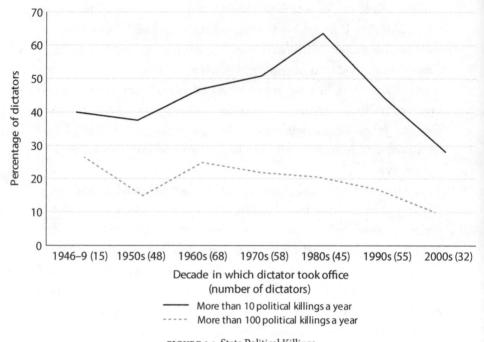

FIGURE 2.1. State Political Killings

Source: Guriev and Treisman, Authoritarian Control Techniques Database.

Note: "Dictators": leaders who were in power for at least 5 years and whose state
had a Polity2 rating of less than 6 in all 5 years.

2000s cohort, this had fallen to just 16 percent. The share holding more
than 100 political prisoners fell from 89 percent in the 1970s cohort to
44 percent in the 2000s cohort (see figure 2.2). As for torture, although
this remains sadly common in authoritarian states, the frequency of allegations in our sources also fell. Among dictators taking power in the
1980s, 95 percent were alleged to have tortured political prisoners or
detainees. In the 2000s cohort, the figure was 74 percent.[148]

Such clear evidence of a fall in violent repression is surprising. Over
time, human rights organizations have developed far greater capacity to
monitor. Their accounts have almost certainly become more comprehensive. That should make it seem as though violence is increasing. And
yet, we see a fall. Could this be somehow influenced by our choice of
thresholds? In fact, we find similar patterns using many alternatives. The

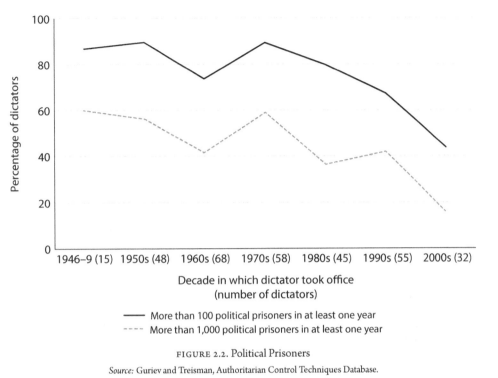

FIGURE 2.2. Political Prisoners

Source: Guriev and Treisman, Authoritarian Control Techniques Database.

Note: "Dictators": leaders who were in power for at least 5 years and whose state
had a Polity2 rating of less than 6 in all 5 years.

proportions of dictators with more than 10 killings a year, more than 100 killings a year, more than 100 political prisoners, and more than 1,000 political prisoners were all much lower in the 2000s cohort than in the 1980s one. The same would be true for one killing a year or 10 political prisoners.[149]

What about other possible problems with the data? Could the pattern somehow reflect change in the tenure of dictators? Those in the 2000s cohort could not have ruled for as long as some earlier dictators such as Kim Il-sung (46 years in power) or King Hussein of Jordan (47 years). If dictators tend to get more violent in their later years, that could distort our comparison. In fact, we find a similar sharp fall in killings and political prisoners if we look at just those dictators who were in power for 5–10 years. In that set, each dictator had a comparable tenure.[150]

Is the pattern driven by some particular part of the world? The late 1980s and early 1990s saw the collapse of communist regimes in Eastern Europe. If the dictators in different periods were concentrated in different parts of the world, that could complicate comparisons. However, it turns out that the downward trend in violence is quite uniform across world regions. We find a similar downward trend in the share of dictators with more than 10 political killings a year in the former Soviet Union and Eastern Europe taken separately, as well as in Latin America and the Caribbean, Sub-Saharan Africa, the Middle East and North Africa, and Asia. All experienced a drop in killings between the 1980s and 2000s cohorts.[151] Across the board, the shift to less violent repression seems robust and broad-based.

Some other data fill out this picture. Jay Ulfelder and Benjamin Valentino compiled a measure of "mass killings" by the state. They defined these as events in which state agents intentionally caused the death of at least 1,000 noncombatants from a particular group.[152] These, too, have become less common in authoritarian states. In 1992, a mass killing was underway in one-third of all nondemocracies. By 2013, this had fallen to about 12 percent.[153] The Varieties of Democracy (V-DEM) project tasks experts with rating the frequency of political killings in countries in particular years. It defines these as "killings by the state or its agents without due process of law for the purpose of eliminating political opponents."[154] The experts do not attempt to actually count the number of such killings, as we did, but give a subjective assessment based on their knowledge of the countries' history. They also assess the extent of torture by the state. The proportion of nondemocracies in which experts judged political killings to be "systematic" or "frequent" fell from a peak of 65 percent in 1974 to 38 percent in 2017. The share of nondemocracies in which state agents were judged to use torture "systematically" or "frequently" fell from 77 percent in 1970 to 50 percent in 2017.[155]

The patterns revealed by different data sets are quite consistent. All confirm that nondemocratic states have, on average, reduced their levels of political violence in recent decades. What permitted this, we argue, was a shift from the dictatorship of fear to the dictatorship of spin. Instead of intimidating citizens with brutal repression and violent rhetoric, rulers were learning how to project a sympathetic image, to appear—in Aristotle's phrase—"not harsh, but dignified." There were several key innovators in the art of political persuasion. But, as with the downgrading of repression, Singapore's trailblazer was out in front—and happy to share his insight.

CHAPTER 3

POSTMODERN PROPAGANDA

On September 19, 1991, Lee Kuan Yew's plane touched down in Almaty, Kazakhstan. It was a strange moment for a visit. Exactly one month earlier, a cabal of military and security officials had tried to seize power throughout the Soviet Union. Now, in the wake of their failed coup, the communist continent was splitting at the seams. In Kazakhstan, Gorbachev's most loyal lieutenant, Nursultan Nazarbayev, still hoped to hold it together—if not as a political union, at least as some kind of economic commonwealth.[1]

But deep down, Nazarbayev must have known it was too late.[2] Soon his country would be independent, vying with its neighbors for the 165th spot in the United Nations. And he needed advice. Singapore's stunning transformation from mosquito-infested backwater to global trade and finance hub had caught his attention. Lee, the architect of that miracle, had retired as prime minister the year before, adopting the title "senior minister." Nazarbayev hoped to learn from him how to lure investment to Kazakhstan.

Lee was known not just for his economic stewardship but also for the tight political grip he had maintained, while still preserving a good reputation in the West. During his five-day visit, he encouraged the Kazakh leadership to break with the past.[3] Communism was over, he told the parliament. In the "information age with TV, satellite, fax, jumbo jet," one could not cut citizens off from the outside world. One could not coerce people as Stalin had done in the 1930s.[4]

And yet, strong central control remained crucial. Lee faulted Gorbachev for starting with glasnost, the policy of free speech and media, rather than using the still powerful Soviet state to push through economic reforms. Nazarbayev listened carefully. Later he summed up what he took to be Lee's credo: "In Asian society discipline and order are more important than democracy, which has to develop over time." He added: "I never concealed the fact that this approach appealed to me."[5]

The son of sheep and cattle herders, Nazarbayev had risen rapidly, advancing from steel worker to Kazakh party chief in just twenty-two years. How could he now impose discipline in an "information age with TV, satellite, fax, jumbo jet" without coercing people as in the 1930s? When, during the August coup, Nazarbayev had phoned the KGB head, Vladimir Kryuchkov, the aging security chief had boasted that he was "re-establishing law and order."[6] That type of order had shattered a couple of days later, accelerating the USSR's implosion. Nazarbayev preferred Lee's approach.

But could it work in Kazakhstan? Rather than an island city-state, Nazarbayev governed a sprawling expanse on the Eurasian steppe, the ninth largest country by area in the world. Instead of a port perched on global trade routes, it was a landlocked enclave, thousands of miles from world markets. Singapore in the 1950s had been shaking off British colonial rule; Kazakhstan was emerging from seventy years of central planning. Lee had managed to rally his population for sacrifice and growth, while squelching what he called "the widespread venting of frustration." How to repeat that experience in such a different setting?

A central point, as Nazarbayev soon realized, was to win over the public—to become and remain popular. People, worldwide, wanted a leader who could make the economy flourish. They wanted jobs, rising incomes, consumer goods. The best way to win support was through effective economic management. But crises and downturns were inevitable, so leaders had to learn how to preserve authority in bad times as well as good. And the key to that was shaping the political discourse, managing the messages citizens received.

RHETORIC OF REPRESSION

Propaganda has always played a role in autocracies. But the characteristic style has changed in recent decades. Here, we explore how. Lee, Nazarbayev, and others adopted a new rhetoric and more sophisticated approach to shaping opinion. Toward the end of the chapter, we will show how spin has come to dominate fear in the public speeches of autocrats. But first, let's look at how old-school dictators worked to control their subjects' speech and thought.

Most sought to monopolize political communication. Some allowed only state-owned media. Others tamed the private press. News and discussion of public affairs then followed the dictator's script. Besides internal controls, many enforced an informational quarantine; we return to this in chapter 6. They banned or censored foreign publications, jammed external broadcasts, and often restricted travel to limit knowledge of the outside world.

A good number imposed an official ideology—that is, a required set of beliefs and social values. All citizens had to publicly adopt this way of thinking. The most elaborate ideologies had been formulated before the dictator and his gang took power. Hitler worked out national socialism in *Mein Kampf*. Stalin and Mao tweaked and twisted Marxism-Leninism. Khomeini built on Shia Islam, adding his own theocratic concept of the "guardianship of the jurist."[7]

A second, usually weaker set of ideologies was devised by dictators already in power. "When one is a leader, one must have a doctrine," Haiti's strongman Papa Doc Duvalier insisted. His "Duvalierism" combined voodoo with celebration of the black masses.[8] Mobutu had Mobutuism. Libya's Gaddafi proposed a "Third International Theory." General Franco forged a version of Catholic corporatism to resist the "Masonic-communist conspiracy."[9]

If one top leader consolidated control, the ideology often evolved into a personality cult.[10] That did not always happen—collective rule survived in some military juntas and one-party regimes. But when a dictator managed to subjugate his colleagues, adherence to a doctrine almost always developed into worship of the leader. Details varied, but most cults shared certain features.

Subordinates competed to flatter the boss. The extravagance of the compliments increased with the severity of terror. Stalin was an "unmatched genius," a "brilliant theoretician," and "the great driver of the locomotive of history," not to mention an expert on Aristotle and Hegel.[11] Ceaușescu was the "Giant of the Carpathians," "the Great Architect," and "the New Morning Star."[12] Idi Amin was "Lord of All the Beasts of the Earth and the Fishes of the Seas."[13] Besides being Syria's president, Hafez al-Assad was also its "premier pharmacist."[14]

Enormous statues of the ruler appeared, often on mountaintops. Mussolini's profile was chiseled into one Italian hillside. Ferdinand Marcos's head topped a ridge in the Philippines. Busts of Stalin capped thirty-eight peaks in Central Asia.[15] In Saddam Hussein's Iraq, replicas of the strongman's forearms thrust up through the earth in Baghdad, brandishing enormous swords. Demand ran so high for dictatorial kitsch that Kim Il-Sung sent a team of Korean sculptors to earn hard currency from despots across Africa.[16]

Smaller images of the dictator also multiplied. Mussolini's face "was on portraits, on medals, in etchings and even on bars of soap. His name adorned newspapers, books, walls and fences."[17] Stalin's likeness was on postage stamps, teacups, and postcards.[18] In Togo, citizens could buy a wristwatch on which the illuminated portrait of President Eyadéma appeared and faded every fifteen seconds.[19] Demand for Mao badges ran so high in the 1960s that China's aircraft industry ran short of aluminum.[20] About 2.5 billion badges are thought to have been produced during the Cultural Revolution—more than three for every Chinese inhabitant.[21]

When not admiring the leader's profile, citizens were expected to study his words. Between 1966 and 1969, an estimated one billion copies of Mao's "little red book" of sayings were printed. The 4,000 tonnes of plastic needed each year for the covers forced cutbacks in output of toys, slippers, and shoes.[22] In case anyone still missed them, Mao's quotations were printed on "towels, pillows, wooden furniture, wine bottles, medicine wrappings, wallets, toys, and candy-paper."[23] Gaddafi had his "little green book," Mussolini his *Breviario mussoliniano*.[24] From 1935, a copy of *Mein Kampf* was presented to each German bride and bridegroom, and it served as a textbook in every school.[25] Saddam's maxims—one pithy example: "Always remember that you might regret being or doing something in some situations, but you will never regret being patient"—were studied in universities and printed on the covers of school notebooks.[26]

And, of course, the dictator's presence was broadcast into all corners of the country by state-controlled radio and later television. In Italy under Mussolini and Germany under Hitler, loudspeakers mounted in town squares amplified announcements and speeches.[27] In China, Mao placed speakers in "courtyards, schools, factories, and government offices" as well as on the streets. They were left continuously on, blasting quotations at high volume.[28]

The broadcasts were supposed to maximize exposure. But they also aimed at something else: the creation of collective experience. In Nazi Germany, "community listening" was strongly encouraged.

> When a speech by a Nazi leader or an important announcement was to be made . . . radio wardens established loudspeakers in public squares, factories, offices, schools, even restaurants. Sirens would howl and professional life throughout the nation would stop for the duration of the "community reception." . . . A leading Nazi radio propagandist compared communal listening with the total experience of worship in a church.[29]

Germans were forbidden to leave their spot before the end of the broadcast. In Spain, Franco's Information Ministry created "tele-clubs" in rural areas for people to watch together. By 1972, these had more than eight hundred thousand members.[30]

The main message propaganda sent was simple: "Be obedient, or else!" The subtext: "We are tough!" The style was usually literal and direct. There was little of the humor, irony, and double meanings that pervade much modern political advertising. Posters and slogans tended toward authoritative exhortations ("Support the assistance program for mothers and children!" "Destroy those who follow the capitalist road!" "Kolkhoznik, exercise!") or abstract statements ("A revolution is not a dinner party," "The Duce is always right!"). Projecting toughness was sometimes combined with feel-good, nationalist messages of self-congratulation ("The glorious future belongs to us!"), exhortations to work harder ("More pigs, more fertilizer, higher grain production!"), or assertions of the ideology's key values ("Country, Religion, Monarchy").

Some dictators—especially the early ones—sought to mobilize the public with rousing appeals. Citizens were to be socialized into loyalty in Nuremberg rallies, Pioneer youth groups, and reeducation camps. Hitler and Stalin hoped to implant devotion at a subrational level by building habits and emotional associations. They married the "conditioned responses" of Ivan Pavlov to the "crowd psychology" of Gustave Le Bon. Their cults of personality clearly packed an emotional punch. Even persecuted victims of Stalin shed spontaneous tears on hearing of his death. Still, should such responses fade, the rational brain was simultaneously treated to a dose of deterrence.

Other dictators—or, often, the same ones in a later phase—aimed at demobilization. Rather than activating people, they sought to envelop them in routine. They addressed the public in a turgid bureaucratese that was hard to follow and alienating. The regime was to be understood as eternal and immutable, to be "taken for granted."[31] Should individuals break through the fog that surrounded politics, the discourse retained plenty of reminders of the state's repressive powers. But violent rhetoric was couched in abstract, familiar formulations that could glide by habitual listeners.

IDIOMS OF INTIMIDATION

If, as we have argued, the old dictators ruled through violent repression, why did they need propaganda, ideology, or a cult of personality? Why bother to control what people said or thought if they had already been terrorized into obedience? Our answer is that all these measures helped make repression more effective. For fear dictators, propaganda was not an alternative to violence: the two worked together.

Most obviously, propaganda was how rulers communicated threats intended to deter opposition. The public executions—"on television," as Gaddafi boasted—showed the fate awaiting those who crossed the dictator. Bloodthirsty speeches conveyed his resolve. Under Hitler, the "use of a violent, exterminatory rhetoric accustomed the public to accept ruthlessness on the part of the regime."[32] Even when rulers were not directly menacing opponents, their propaganda bred anxiety. As social psychologists have shown, people who feel vulnerable tend to rally behind their leader.[33] When reminded of death, they become more attached to the dominant ideology, support harsher penalties for criminals, and show less tolerance toward outsiders.[34] Dictators exploited these tendencies, artificially whipping up a sense of danger while casting themselves as the source of security.

War was a common theme. As we saw in the last chapter, many rulers—even those who had never seen a battlefield—dressed up in khakis, awarded themselves military titles and medals, and employed a martial vocabulary. Posters and films celebrated conflict, even in times of peace. In Spain, Franco championed "crusade cinema" (*cine cruzada*), which glorified his rebellion. Stories of martyrdom were endlessly retold. Stalin's propagandists milked the tale of Pavel Morozov, a peasant boy murdered by outraged villagers after he denounced his father for hoarding grain. Goebbels promoted the myth of Horst Wessel, an SA storm trooper killed by communists in a 1930 street brawl.[35] The discourse of enemies, threats, and sacrifice kept everyone on edge. To the linguist Victor Klemperer, who lived through the Nazi years in Dresden, Hitler's tirades generated a kind of suspense reminiscent of "American cinema and thrillers."[36] This was deliberate. Goebbels aimed to create an atmosphere of tense foreboding, what he called "thick air" (*dicke luft*).[37]

Propaganda and violence came together in the massive pro-government demonstrations many strongmen liked to hold. Castro, Nasser, and Myanmar's generals, among others, staged enormous rallies.[38] These intimidated rivals. Even if many of those waving flags did so out of fear rather than conviction, they showed the dictator's power to mobilize.[39] Mobs of loyalists could justify the regime's aggression—as when Castro summoned a million Cubans to surround his presidential palace and demand the execution of pro-Batista paramilitaries.[40] Or feverish crowds could furnish a striking backdrop for the dictator's militant poses. Nasser used a rally of 1.5 million Egyptians in 1962 to show off two new long-range missiles.[41]

If the desire to spread fear explains the mixing of violence and propaganda, what about the recourse to ideology? Why require adherence to an obscure belief system? One simple view is that the dictators were themselves fervent believers. They imposed Marxism, Maoism, or Ba'athism on their people because, in their view, it solved the riddle of human existence. This was definitely true of many dictators. At some level, all Soviet leaders from Lenin on were sincere Marxists. They used Marxist categories and concepts even in private and probably believed their system was less unjust than those of the capitalist West. Hitler certainly believed the tenets of national socialism. Indeed, the passionate intensity of true believers may have helped them rise to the top in premodern or industrial societies. Still, even in these regimes, ideology had a more practical function.

It helped to organize repression. How can one discipline a vast population? The crucial first step is to publicly define "good" and "bad." Most governments use laws and constitutions to demarcate the permitted from the forbidden. But laws, especially if rooted in judicial precedent, can be rigid and allow power to leak to judges and lawyers. An ideology, by contrast, can be reinterpreted by the ruler at will.[42] Although dictators retained more standard legal mechanisms for ordinary crimes and civil contracts, they used ideologies to define how people should act politically. Their doctrines identified the regime's enemies and justified violence against them.

But that was not all. Besides distinguishing "good" from "bad" and justifying violence, ideologies decentralized repression to ordinary citizens. They inspired loyalty rituals that all could help to enforce. Citizens were required to march in parades, wear party pins, greet each other with stylized salutes, communicate in approved stock phrases, memorize key texts, bow before portraits of the leader, swear oaths (sometimes signed in blood), vote for the ruler, cheer, clap, cry, and yell abuse at "enemies of the people"—and even, under Mao, perform a "loyalty dance" before boarding trains.[43] The more complicated, abstruse, and embarrassing the ritual the better, since the point was to distinguish the truly committed from reluctant compliers.

Such rituals, especially when taught to children, could indoctrinate, adding the force of habit to that of conscious persuasion. More importantly, they enlisted citizens to police each other. Twentieth-century dictators did not have the technology to observe each individual closely. But, by rewarding denunciations of the disloyal, they got ordinary people to do the watching. Mao, for one, aspired to "turn the whole population into 'thought police' who monitored words to detect 'incorrect' thought."[44]

Loyalty to an ideology could protect a party. But to protect an individual leader, a personality cult worked better. That is why, as one leader came to dominate, the cult almost always took precedence. Indeed, excessive devotion to an ideology could at this point prove dangerous. True believers were likely to feel disillusioned at the self-serving reinterpretations of the "great leader."[45] Their loyalty was to ideas, not to a person. Many rulers, therefore, purged their most ideological comrades. Stalin butchered his former allies in the 1930s. Hitler finished off Ernst Röhm in the Night of the Long Knives in June 1934. Mussolini expelled thousands of the more radical members of his party in the 1920s.[46]

Loyalty rituals might seem useless since dissidents could simply mask their true attitudes. They could dance the "loyalty dance" while cursing the dictator under their breath. Yet, even if dissenters continued to dissent in secret, the loyalty machinery kept them from identifying each other and joining forces. As historian Frank Dikötter writes, the cult of personality turned "everyone into a liar"—and when "everyone lied, no one knew who was lying."[47] Or, to use the expression of the Czech dissident playwright and later president Vaclav Havel, all citizens were forced to "live within the lie." That made coordinating opposition much harder.

This view makes sense of some otherwise puzzling features of authoritarian propaganda. As a strategy of persuasion, the approach of fear dictators seems perverse. A good propagandist, one expert writes, will "do his best to appear likeable, humorous, and human." He will empha-

size "what he has in common with his audience."[48] Yet, communist propagandists under Brezhnev were humorless, distant, and cold. They
spoke in opaque jargon, with long strings of nouns piled up around each
verb. Some dictators established more rapport. Mussolini cultivated the
image of a "man of the people, accessible to all," personally answering
thousands of letters from citizens.[49] But the act was highly stylized. He
was "accessible to all" in the way that God is—they both appeared in
rare visions and swooped down to decide citizens' fates. There was
nothing "human" about it.

A smart influencer, the same expert adds, will make his appeals
"simple and memorable."[50] The communists created a discourse that
was boring and arcane. Soviet citizens were expected to cheer to slogans
such as: "We will fulfill the resolutions of the Twenty-Sixth Congress
of the Communist Party of the Soviet Union!" Hungarian news coverage was "ritualistic, repetitive, dull, and extremely boring."[51] Franco's
state media "effectively bored most Spaniards into passivity and acqui-
escence."[52] Throughout Saddam's rule, the Ba'athist press was "one-
dimensional, replete with verbiage, and boring."[53] When they were not
putting listeners to sleep, the regime's propagandists spent their time
fawning over the boss and advancing patently absurd claims. Many leaders, for instance, were said to have wizardly powers. Kim Jong-Il could
teleport himself from place to place. Mussolini could conjure up rain
and stop lava flowing. Mao could swim four times further than the
world record.[54] (Ne Win of Burma was not a wizard himself, but he
consulted one.)[55]

If the goal were to persuade, all this would look odd. But as a tool of
repression, it all makes sense. A "likeable, humorous, and human" leader
with much in common with ordinary citizens is not the ideal choice to
terrorize them into obedience. One prone to violent rants will do better.
To alienate people from politics, boring news colorlessly expressed may
be just what is needed. The more arcane the doctrines, the more useful
for filtering loyalists from opportunists. Only the former will make
the effort to master them. The very absurdity of the propaganda signals
the regime's strength to potential dissidents.[56] It shows its capacity to
force people to repeat nonsense. Demanding slavish flattery and

straight-faced acceptance of ridiculous claims weeds out those with scruples, helping the leader select unscrupulous agents.[57] Rewarding "nauseating displays" of obsequiousness could also enhance the flatterer's loyalty by reducing his appeal to other potential power holders.[58]

And, indeed, available evidence suggests the old model's strength was not in its power to persuade. Fear dictators used to be thought expert in brainwashing. But their reputation has taken some hits. The Nazis did have some success in indoctrinating the young. As economists Nico Voigtländer and Hans-Joachim Voth show, Germans who were schoolchildren under Hitler remained more anti-Semitic throughout their lives than those born either before or after them. Still, the difference is small: only 10 percent of the 1930s generation remained "convinced anti-Semites" in later life, compared to about 5 percent of those born in, say, the 1950s.[59]

Among adults, Nazi messaging seems to have been less effective. One careful study found that Hitler's speeches during his rise to power had a "negligible" impact on his electoral performance.[60] Once in office, the Nazis' radio broadcasts had some influence. They increased anti-Jewish actions by citizens—but only in places that had previously been more anti-Semitic. The broadcasts actually *reduced* such actions where prejudice had historically been weaker. Internal Gestapo reports suggest growing apathy in 1934–35.[61] As one historian notes, "Public receptiveness to press propaganda reached saturation point soon after Hitler came to power, and thereafter went into decline."[62] Circulation of Nazi newspapers fell by a million copies during 1934.[63] And things did not improve. By the middle of the war, radio wardens "were reporting that listeners were so bored that they were switching off."[64] More and more Germans were tuning into foreign broadcasts, even though the announced penalty for doing so was death.[65]

Other authoritarian regimes were also uneven influencers. Franco's propaganda "worked far better when it coincided with people's interests, their hopes and fears, than when it ran against them."[66] In Syria under Hafez al-Assad, political scientist Lisa Wedeen found the public cynical about the regime's appeals. As one member of parliament told her: "No one believes the things they say, and everyone knows that no one believes them."[67] Jokes mocking the leader circulated there, in Romania under Ceauşescu, the USSR under Brezhnev, and even in Kim Jong-Il's North Korea.[68]

In short, although childhood socialization may have reshaped values a bit, authoritarian propaganda seems often to have achieved just compliance among adults.[69] And, in fact, that was the point. What fear dictators care about most is obedience. Whether it is based on sincere commitment or just prudence matters less. As a tool of repression to demobilize citizens, while silencing and isolating dissidents, the old-style propaganda of fear was quite effective.[70]

SPINSPEAK

So what do spin dictators do differently? To get a taste, let's consider one example. For those who share Kim Jong-Il's teleporting powers, the destination is Astana, capital of Kazakhstan, on October 5, 2018—the occasion, President Nazarbayev's annual State of the Nation address. For others, YouTube carries the footage.[71]

On stage, instead of a podium one sees a broad, wooden writing desk, the kind one might find in a chief accountant's office. The president sits behind it in an expensive-looking suit and tie. As he works carefully through his printed pages, he glances up over reading glasses to scan the hall, filled with rows of officials sitting poker-faced in their own conservative suits.

"Today, global and local problems in the world are connecting," Nazarbayev announces. "In these conditions . . . the key to success of the state is the development of the main wealth of our country—its people." Macroeconomic targets do not matter in themselves, he insists. "We achieve them in order to improve life for Kazakhstanis. I ask all governors and ministers to always keep in mind that we will judge their personal effectiveness based on these figures."

The speaker behind the desk looks less a Central Asian strongman than a corporate CFO announcing quarterly results. He sounds like a candidate running in a competitive election. He will raise the minimum wage by 50 percent and create 22,000 new jobs, he promises. He will

increase economic competition, investigate corruption, support manufacturing exports, target credit to small banks, and raise the productivity
of agriculture. His ministers come in for a schoolmasterly scolding.
They are made to stand as he tells them off for not serving the public
better. The world is changing—biomedicine, big data, artificial intelligence, the "Internet of Things," blockchain. Are his ministers up to the
challenge? He seems to doubt it.

"Who is the director of Air Astana? An Englishman. Who's the head
of Nazarbayev University? A Japanese man. If you don't work adequately, I'll invite foreigners to take all your places!"

The chastened officials retake their seats.

As the video makes clear, Nazarbayev's communication style differs
from that of many twentieth-century autocrats.[72] But it resembles that
of other spin dictators. Although each has idiosyncrasies, much is
shared. Rather than harangue citizens with tirades or bore them with
bureaucratese, today's strongmen aim to make a more modern impression. Key elements of their approach include the following.

Instead of fear, project an image of competence. The essential goal is to
replace the rhetoric of violence with one of performance. Rather than
terrify citizens, dictators bid for their support with a show of leadership
skill and dedication. Instead of the old threat—"Be obedient, or else!"—
the new line seems to be: "Look what a great job we're doing!"

Of course, that works better when they are. When they are not, manipulation takes over. In part, the message is visual. Well-pressed business suits suggest professionalism and modernity. So do rulers' publicity photographs, which these days tend to show them at a conference
table or touring a factory rather than addressing a battalion or harangu-
ing a crowd. In his freewheeling TV show, Venezuela's Chávez liked to
appear—like Nazarbayev—sitting behind a desk, the symbol of administrative elbow grease. To simultaneously pantomime engagement with
the public, he had the desk placed somewhere out in the community—
or, in one famous episode, in a field of cows.[73]

Then there is what they say. Rather than conjuring up images of hidden traitors and poisoned daggers, spin dictators evoke peace and prosperity. Instead of demanding blood and sacrifice, they offer comfort and

respect. With his promise-packed speeches, Nazarbayev epitomized this style. When not declaring victories, he was introducing new goals and programs—"Kazakhstan 2030," "100 Concrete Steps to Implement Five Institutional Reforms," "People, Planet, Prosperity, Peace, and Partnership."[74] The titles conveyed the desired mix of vision and technocracy. Others also played the role of national CEO. Alberto Fujimori liked to call himself not a politician but Peru's "manager."[75]

The act is more challenging when performance is clearly bad. But dictators can still project competence by blaming—and firing—subordinates. Indeed, playing the hard taskmaster helps even in good times. Hence Nazarbayev's demonstrative scolding of his ministers. Chávez was famous for axing officials in the middle of his rambling broadcasts.[76]

The aim is not just to show that the incumbent is doing a great job—although that is the main point. In part, the goal is to spread the belief that *others* think he is. Then even citizens who see no improvement in their own life may believe that others do. Conformism kicks in. Just as fear dictators work to spread not just fear but also the belief that others are afraid, spin dictators seek not just admiration but the appearance of being admired.

Instead of ideology, a kaleidoscope of appeals. Many fear dictators use ideology and associated loyalty rituals. They insist on a single, collective truth and enforce it with terror when necessary. The systems this creates are comprehensive but brittle. Any public expression of "incorrect" views—if left unpunished—can signal regime frailty. The risk is not so much that a new "fact" will expose the dictator's lies. Rather, any questioning of these lies with impunity will reveal his weakness.

This ends up a costly trap. As societies modernize, it takes ever more resources—even with the public's help—to track down and punish citizens who skip the loyalty rituals. So spin dictators do not try. They give up on imposing an ideology and enforcing conformity. With no "truth" to defend, they show no weakness when they fail to defend it.

Most have no official doctrine. "We are pragmatists," Lee Kuan Yew insisted. "We are not enamored of any ideology."[77] "Putin," says one Kremlin consultant, "hates the word ideology."[78] Instead, they use a kaleidoscopic mix of images and themes to target multiple audiences at once. The Russian leader blends imperial history, communist tropes, and conservative traditionalism in what political writer Ivan Krastev calls "a Molotov cocktail of French postmodernism and KGB instrumentalism."[79] Nazarbayev's speeches have featured strains of ethnic or civic nationalism, depending on who was listening, combined with Lee Kuan Yew–style developmentalism.[80] At times, Chávez seemed like an old-fashioned leftist. But in fact he did not embrace socialism until six years into his presidency—after reading not Marx but Victor Hugo's *Les Misérables*.[81] His "Chavismo" was—like Putin's rhetoric—more a pastiche of resonant images (Simón Bolívar, Jesus Christ) and varied ideas (socialism, populism, nationalism, anti-imperialism) than any kind of doctrine.[82]

Instead of cult of personality, cultivate celebrity. Among remaining fear dictators, a few still preserve an old-style personality cult. North Korean high school students are forced to slog through a three-year course on the early life of Kim Jong-Un.[83] Turkmenistan's late leader Saparmurat Niyazov changed the names of the months to those of his relatives, put knowledge of his writings on the test for a driver's license, and built a gold statue of himself that revolved to follow the sun.[84]

Some have attributed comparable personality cults to spin dictators such as Chávez and Putin.[85] But, in fact, what these leaders developed were not personality cults but celebrity—of the tacky kind that surrounds Western performers and some U.S. presidents in the Internet age. The classic personality cult involved quasi-religious veneration of the ruler. It was top-down, organized by the dictator and his agents, and imposed on the population.[86] Loyalty rituals—special salutes and greetings, bows before portraits, and so on—enforced conformity. The tone was solemn, and questioning the cult in public was not an option. Citizens had to read the dictator's written works, and the authorities flooded public spaces with his name and image.

Celebrity, by contrast, is mostly decentralized, often spontaneously constructed, and exploited by private actors for profit. Images of the hero are widespread, but they circulate based on demand and market incentives. There are no enforced rituals, although voluntary ones may emerge (public moonwalking, chanting "Yes we can!"). The tone can be serious, but it is often playful, ironic, or even mocking.[87]

With this in mind, consider Putin. Many have marveled at the flood of themed paraphernalia—from matryoshkas, T-shirts, vodka, and cologne to iPhone cases, chocolates, and calendars—that appeared early in his first presidency.[88] His portrait hung in government buildings nationwide; by 2007, twenty-eight slightly different versions were on sale.[89] Songs about him—from the technopop "I Want a Man like Putin" to the rap "My Best Friend Is Vladimir Putin"—became hits.[90] A Putin Avenue appeared in the Chechen capital Grozny, along with a number of Putin streets in rural settlements.[91] The Kremlin website posted photographs of the president in macho poses, hunting, fishing, and—on occasion—riding a horse shirtless. And, periodically, the nightly news featured Putin in heroic adventures—flying a hang glider to guide cranes to their breeding ground, diving in scuba gear to retrieve ancient amphorae from the Black Sea, shooting a wild Siberian tigress with a tranquilizer gun, and fitting a sleeping polar bear with a tracking collar.

All this sparked talk of a classic personality cult. Yet, on examination, the resemblances weaken.[92] There is no Putin salute, dance, or other enforced ritual, no bible of Putinism that all must study and recite. Most Putin merchandise comes not from central propagandists but from street-level hucksters eager to cash in. The Putin Streets turn out to be less a homage than a plea for resources. "If the street is named after Putin," one hopeful resident explained, "then the asphalt will be laid."[93] The songs, rather than worshipful, are slyly ironic. The girls who sing "A Man like Putin" praise not the president's bare-chested machismo but more mundane qualities that stand in humorous contrast with Russian stereotypes. Putin, they sing, "won't drink," "won't hurt" them, and—most important—"won't run away."[94] The TV exploits were almost all quickly exposed as stunts. The polar bear had been drugged.[95] The tigress came from a zoo, not the wild, and later died from an overdose of sedatives.[96] The Greek amphorae had been planted for the president to "find"—as his own press secretary later admitted.[97] The effect, in the end, was more comic than epic.

The classic cults were no laughing matter. One could not poke fun at Stalin's appearance or refuse to give the Hitler salute. By contrast, no Russian is today forced to dance to "A Man like Putin" or slap on Putin cologne. No one is sentenced to a labor camp for mocking the leader's name (as in Mao's China) or wrapping a book in a newspaper with the leader's photograph (as in Kim Il-Sung's North Korea).[98] Entrepreneurs sell not just Putin vodka but Putin dental flossers.[99] In the village of Izborsk, after a presidential visit, locals sold tickets to tour sites where "Putin bought a cucumber" and "Putin took off his jacket."[100] Rather than a personality cult, this resembles a parody of one. If Stalin was a god, Putin has become a trademark.

Although hardly exact, a closer parallel is Barack Obama. He too inspired a catalog of themed merchandise—from wooden eggs to bobble-head dolls, refrigerator magnets, jigsaw puzzles, travel mugs, cocktail glasses, cat collars, nail polish, and even spatulas.[101] Although not usually found in schools, Obama's portrait hung in federal buildings and airports throughout the United States.[102] He, too, was pictured shirtless in the media, attracting comment on his athletic physique.[103] Obama featured in not just one or two popular songs: *Billboard* magazine published a list of the "10 best," including numbers by Mariah Carey, Jay-Z, and Stevie Wonder.[104] As for macho adventures, a quick search of the Internet turns up video of the 44th president eating grizzly bear leftovers in the Alaskan wilds.[105]

Nazarbayev has more elements of a traditional cult: honorific titles, billboards with his portrait, statues, and mountains and towns named after him. In this, he has gone far beyond most spin dictators. Yet, in twenty years at the top the Kazakh leader apparently did not introduce loyalty rituals. In most settings, he still seemed to model a wise manager rather than a fear-inspiring strongman.[106]

Borrow credibility. Rather than monopolizing all media, spin dictators allow some nominally independent press and sometimes even television. They tolerate limited criticism—while, nevertheless, harassing the critics (more on that in the next chapter). This allows them, when needed, to exploit the reputation of non-state outlets for their own purposes. By channeling messages through such media, they borrow credibility.

In 2011, for instance, Nazarbayev faced a political crisis after his police cracked down harshly on rioting workers in the mining town of Zhanaozen. When the authorities censored reports from the scene, wild rumors circulated on Facebook and Twitter.[107] Nobody believed the state media coverage. Finally, to dispel speculation, the government invited six sometimes critical bloggers to tour the area. Their posts quickly reassured readers that shops were well-stocked with food and the morgues not full of corpses.[108]

Keeping one high-credibility channel in reserve, Putin allowed the radio station Ekho Moskvy to broadcast liberal opposition commentary. As political scientist Anton Sobolev shows, Ekho Moskvy's reports on large pro-Putin rallies in early 2012 demoralized opposition supporters more than did the less credible reports on these by pro-Kremlin media.[109] People expected state television to exaggerate the size of pro-Putin crowds. But they believed Ekho Moskvy's estimates.

Like Nazarbayev, the Kremlin also sought to exploit popular bloggers at times—for instance, recruiting one to provide soft-ball coverage of a hydroelectric plant disaster in Siberia in 2009. The blogger was rewarded two months later with an invitation to join the Kremlin press pool.[110] Peru's President Alberto Fujimori also used independent media to convince skeptics of his popularity, as we will see in the next chapter.

A second way to borrow credibility is to conceal the source of propaganda. Old dictators such as Hitler and Mao packed people around loudspeakers to have theses yelled at them. The propaganda of fear was vertical: messages came from on high. Many spin dictators intuited the point, made by scholars such as Jacques Ellul, that the most effective propaganda is horizontal, transmitted in small groups and networks, often via informal conversations.[111] They sought ways to seed their messages into social networks, removing evidence of their origin.

The Internet made this much easier. Propagandists could hire "trolls" to pass as ordinary citizens and infiltrate online conversations. In Russia, one former Kremlin agent recounted in 2015 how he and two partners had simulated genuine debate. First, one would post an anti-Putin comment on an Internet forum. The other two would then jump in to attack the "dissident" with superior arguments, supporting links, and—

if necessary—doctored photographs. Other forum users would observe an "honest" exchange of views but conclude the pro-Putin side was stronger.[112] In Ecuador, Rafael Correa's troll army slavishly retweeted the president's missives.[113] Since his less educated supporters rarely used Twitter, the goal seemed to be to impress the educated opposition with the depth of Correa's support. Malaysia's Najib Razak recruited "keyboard warriors" to plaster opposition Twitter feeds with criticism of antigovernment protesters.[114]

Of course, not only spin dictators use trolls. High-tech fear dictatorships like China and Saudi Arabia also employ them.[115] In 2017, China's authorities were funding about 448 million social media posts a year, according to political scientists Gary King, Jennifer Pan, and Margaret Roberts.[116] Like those in Russia, most aimed to "cheerlead" for the regime, diverting participants away from sensitive topics rather than trying to change their minds. By contrast, Saudi Arabia's trolls threatened and intimidated regime critics, including those outside the kingdom.[117]

Another way to conceal the source of propaganda is to slip it into apparently neutral settings. One technique—the "push poll"—seeks to plant false ideas among respondents by embedding them in seemingly factual survey questions. In 2015, Viktor Orbán polled Hungary's population supposedly to determine public opinion on immigration. "There are some who think that economic migrants jeopardize the jobs and livelihoods of Hungarians," one question asked. "Do you agree?"

Weaponize entertainment. In Peru, Alberto Fujimori weaponized not just news but also entertainment. One popular show, *Magaly Teve*, trafficked in celebrity gossip with a pro-regime slant. Another, *Laura en América*, modeled on Jerry Springer's U.S. talk show, featured screaming guests and tales of infidelity. In between segments, its host, Laura Bozzo, who was close to Fujimori's security chief, Vladimiro Montesinos, shared her admiration for the president.[118] During Fujimori's 2000 reelection campaign, she championed the army's antiterrorist victories and, on one show, featured the illegitimate daughter of Fujimori's opponent, Alejandro Toledo.[119] In Russia, recent years have seen an explosion of talk shows, with attention-grabbing "trash TV" elements such as swearing and on-air brawls.[120] Pro-Kremlin views always seem to end up on top.

Framing and interpreting. Many associate propaganda with the assertion of untrue facts. And, of course, there is a role for "fake news." But interpreting facts is at least as important. Certain realities are difficult to conceal or deny, and a news source that attempts to do so may just lose its audience.[121] Explaining them away is another matter.

For instance, Russia's news producers know they can tell tall tales about foreign events, the details of which are difficult for most viewers to check. But it is hard to persuade people who have been laid off or suffered salary cuts that the country's economy is doing well. Two political scientists, Arturas Rozenas and Denis Stukal, studied 13,000 news reports about the economy broadcast by Russia's main state TV station, Channel One, in 1999–2016. They found that both "good" and "bad" economic facts were reported accurately. What changed was the assignment of credit or blame. "Good" news was attributed to the Kremlin's expert management, "bad" news to external forces such as global financial markets or foreign governments.[122]

Besides redirecting blame for poor performance, spin dictators who cannot conceal bad news try to convince the public that any alternative leader would do worse. One strategy is to contrast the incumbent to a highly unattractive pseudo-alternative. Why does Putin, for instance, keep the controversial ultra-nationalist Vladimir Zhirinovsky and the aging communist Gennady Zyuganov in the parliament decade after decade? The reason is simple: the prospect of either man in the Kremlin horrifies Putin's liberal critics.

At the same time, dictators must prevent attractive alternatives from acquiring a following. Thus, tolerance of criticism and the fringe media runs out when a charismatic individual appears. Huge effort then goes into discrediting the challenger, distorting his record, blocking his communications, and priming the public with negative emotional associations, all while trying to avoid raising his public profile by, for instance, saying his name.[123] In Peru in the 1990s, Fujimori and Montesinos had their tabloids slander rival politicians. Under Hugo Chávez, a late-night talk show, *The Razorblade*, used leaked phone taps and surveillance photographs to humiliate regime opponents.[124]

At times, dictators can discredit unwelcome stories simply by pre-empting them. Nazarbayev's team anticipated that opposition monitors would reveal irregularities in Kazakhstan's 2005 election. So they punched first, accusing the opposition of drawing up lists of alleged violations in advance. "This misinformation, repeated quietly and persistently throughout the press as 'fact,' undercut the opposition's claim."[125]

Nazarbayev's team also knew how to position their boss as a moderate. The secret was to field a more radical proposal that he could shoot down before adopting the one he had favored all along. In 2003–4, Nazarbayev demonstratively rejected restrictions on the media and NGOs that allies had proposed.[126] In 2011, 5.5 million citizens petitioned him to cancel presidential elections and rule until 2020. Posing as a diehard democrat, he refused. Few sophisticated observers were taken in, but such ploys may well work among the politically uninformed.[127] Of course, incumbents in democracies sometimes use similar techniques. But they are far more effective when the incumbent dominates media and completely controls the political agenda.

In short, when the facts are good, a spin dictator trumpets them and takes credit. When they are bad, he co-opts the media to obscure them if possible or redirect blame if not. When his popularity dips, he preserves a relative advantage by casting the choice as between himself and an unappealing pseudo-alternative, while working hard to discredit any genuine rival. Throughout, his aides manage the public agenda to his advantage.

CHECKING THE EVIDENCE

It is easy to find examples of differences in rhetoric between particular fear and spin dictators. But leaders say many things at different times. All sometimes warn of foreign threats and, at other moments, boast of economic performance. So how do we know there has been a systematic change?

To check this, we set out to analyze dictators' speeches. We should right away acknowledge the limits of our evidence. Obviously, we could not examine all the speeches of all modern dictators. And even focusing on a random sample was not possible given the limited availability of appropriate texts. Instead, we focused on a set of speeches by selected leaders of the contrasting types. The results are suggestive rather than definitive.

The leaders we chose came from all over the world; some were from recent years, others from further back. The set included seven fear dictators (Josef Stalin, Adolf Hitler, Benito Mussolini, Francisco Franco, Saddam Hussein, Fidel Castro, and Kim Jong-Un), five spin dictators (Vladimir Putin, Rafael Correa, Hugo Chávez, Nursultan Nazarbayev, and Lee Kuan Yew), and six leaders of democracies (Franklin Delano Roosevelt, Jawaharlal Nehru, and Dwight Eisenhower from the mid-twentieth century, and David Cameron, Nicholas Sarkozy, and Barack Obama from more recent times). We chose these statesmen based on their importance and on the availability of a sufficient number of appropriate speeches. To focus on rhetoric directed at the general public, we used only speeches that had been broadcast nationwide, excluding those made outside the country, during wars, or at party meetings and other special events.

The simplest way to analyze texts is just to count how often the speaker uses words associated with a particular theme. To do this, we compiled lists of words linked to: (a) violence (e.g., "death," "blood," "prison"); (b) economic performance (e.g., "sales," "wages," "inflation," "wealthy"); and (c) public service provision (e.g., "childcare," "hospitals," "funding"). To keep things simple, we combine here the economic performance and public service provision words since both are topics we expect spin dictators to emphasize, unlike fear dictators, who emphasize violence.[128]

So how did the rhetoric of these leaders differ? Figure 3.1 shows this. As expected, the fear dictators (boxed in) used more violent language than almost any of the others. The one exception is President Eisenhower, who—although a democrat—served at an intense moment of Cold War confrontation and so had much to say about missiles and military threats. The democratic leaders (in bold type) rank high in general on economic performance and public service provision words,

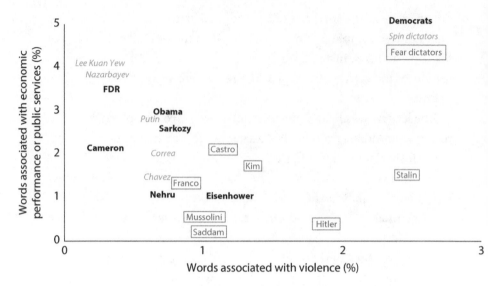

FIGURE 3.1. Rhetoric of Selected Leaders

Source: Guriev and Treisman, "Informational Autocrats."

although communist dictators such as Fidel Castro and Kim Jong-Un also rate quite high on these. What about spin dictators? They (in italics) clearly blend in with the democrats and not the overt dictators. Indeed, Lee Kuan Yew and Nursultan Nazarbayev outdo all others in their economic and public service talk, with only FDR—with his New Deal discourse—close behind.[129]

We also argued that dictators have become less likely to impose an official ideology on their societies. To check this, we collected evidence on whether such an ideology—defined as a social, political, or religious doctrine that was endorsed by top officials and influenced the content of laws—existed in all dictatorships since 1945. More specifically, we classified authoritarian states as Marxist if the government was dominated by a communist party or if the leader publicly said he was a Marxist. We called them Islamist if they privileged Islamic over secular law on a broad range of issues. A residual category, "other ideologies," includes more exotic alternatives, such as Ba'athism, Nasserism, Pancasila, and Kemalism. (Whether these constitute official ideologies at all might be debated.)

Our data reveal a striking change.[130] Largely due to the collapse of communism, official ideologies became much rarer in the 1990s. The share of nondemocracies that had one fell from 42 percent in 1980 to less than 20 percent in 2000. About two-thirds of the official ideologies in 1980 had been some variety of Marxism. The incidence of Islamist dictatorship increased, but only a little—from 3 percent in 1980 to 6 percent in both 2000 and 2015. Other ideologies became slightly rarer, falling from 11 percent in 1980 to 6 percent in 2000.

Having an official ideology, we argued, was a sign of fear—rather than spin—dictatorship. Using our rules of thumb from chapter 1, we confirm this.[131] Among leaders of fear dictatorships, 49 percent imposed an official ideology at some point during their tenure. Among spin dictators, only 15 percent did.

Some other evidence comes from an impressive project of political scientists Erin and Brett Carter. Like us, they distinguish between a kind of deliberately absurd propaganda aimed at demoralizing citizens (the kind we associate with fear dictators) and a more subtle variety that seeks to convince (our spin dictators' approach).[132] They collected nearly 8 million articles from state-run newspapers in autocracies around the world and measured how positive each was toward the regime, using techniques from computational linguistics. They found that articles in state-run newspapers in China, Eritrea, Uzbekistan, and Syria—cases of fear dictatorship—tended to be considerably more positive about the regime in recent years than those in Russia, Venezuela, Ecuador, and Kazakhstan—cases of spin dictatorship.[133] Propaganda in the fear dictatorships intimidated readers with its extreme one-sidedness. That in the spin dictatorships attempted to persuade at least the relatively uninformed, who might be susceptible.

But how to *keep* the poorly informed uninformed? That is a constant challenge. Spin risks falling flat if forced to compete with an independent and vigorous press. Yet, openly censoring or banning the private media—as old-school autocrats do—would undercut a spin dictator's claim to be a democrat, competently and benevolently serving the public. Here, too, various recent dictators have shown creativity. And this time one of the earliest innovators came from South America.

CHAPTER 4

SENSIBLE CENSORSHIP

Around 10:30 p.m. on April 5, 1992, Peru's president, Alberto Fujimori, struck. Tanks surrounded the Congress and Supreme Court, enforcing an *autogolpe*, or "self-imposed coup." In a statement broadcast nationwide, Fujimori suspended the country's constitution and dissolved the parliament. He was introducing emergency rule, he said, to break the political deadlock in a country reeling from corruption, cocaine trafficking, and a murderous Maoist insurgency.

A former agricultural economist, Fujimori had come from behind to win a surprise victory in Peru's 1990 election, riding a wave of frustration with the country's entrenched political class. He had initiated market reforms and managed to curb the country's exploding inflation. But almost immediately, he had found himself squeezed between hostile factions in the parliament, defiant judges, and a restive military. The coup was Fujimori's way out of the conundrum.

As his announcement aired, troops were occupying the offices of the country's newspapers and magazines, television and radio broadcasters. They stopped the presses—literally. Opposition radio stations were pulled from the air. Gustavo Gorriti, an investigative reporter, was at home a few hours later when a gang of plainclothes intelligence officers scrambled over his garden wall, brandishing Heckler & Koch 9mm submachine guns equipped with silencers. He spent the night in solitary confinement in army headquarters, one of twenty-two journalists detained.[1]

That was Sunday. By Tuesday morning, just forty hours after the coup began, the tide had turned. Now, Fujimori was on the defensive. The arrested journalists were being released and soldiers withdrawn from the newsrooms. In an embarrassing climbdown, Fujimori appeared in person at the newspaper *El Comercio*, flanked by the head of the armed forces, to apologize. Sending in military censors had been "an error of my government," he admitted, offering "sincere apologies for any inconvenience caused."[2]

What had changed? Fujimori had made two miscalculations. First, his attack on democracy and the press had provoked the fury of human rights organizations around the world. The U.S., German, and Spanish governments froze all aid except humanitarian assistance. Venezuela and Colombia suspended diplomatic relations and Argentina recalled its ambassador. The Organization of American States began discussing sanctions; some members called for Peru's suspension.[3] Easing up on the press offered a way for Fujimori to break this negative momentum and signal readiness to step back toward democracy.

But, even more important, it turned out gagging the journalists was not necessary. The coup proved overwhelmingly popular. Instant polls showed almost three-quarters of Peruvians supported dissolving the Congress and 89 percent backed Fujimori's plan to restructure the judiciary.[4] Disgusted with the graft and gridlock of previous politics, citizens were ready to rally behind a decisive leader.

Getting this message out could shift the balance of opinion both within Peru's elite and around the world. But who would believe polls published by the regime itself? A realization dawned in Lima's stately Palacio de Gobierno. Rather than ban the opposition press, Fujimori could use it. "For the administration, it was important that the [poll] numbers be taken seriously, both at home and abroad," wrote political scientist Catherine Conaghan. "The pro-coup polls gained credibility because they were published by a free press."[5] And letting small-circulation opposition magazines resume operations, wrote Gorriti, the journalist arrested by intelligence agents, "supported the government's contention that press freedom existed in Peru."[6]

FIGHTING WORDS

For most of the twentieth century, the censor's pencil—typically a blue one—was almost as important to dictators as the AK47. Controlling a country meant controlling the printed page, the radio dial, and the television screen. And leaders devoted enormous energy to doing so. Here, we examine how they went about it—and how spin dictators later redefined the task. Fujimori's experience offers a range of insights and illustrations. We'll touch on censorship of the Internet and end the chapter, as usual, with a glance at some data. But, first, back to the manipulators of fear.

Among them, styles of censorship varied. Still, all shared four key features. First, censorship was *comprehensive*—in ambition, if not always in results. All public communication had to be sanitized. Some dictators— in particular, communists and fascists—aimed to reprogram citizens to think in new ways. Their conservative peers sought to preserve a mindset they thought already prevailed—one favoring hierarchy, patriotism, and tradition. But all sought to block unwelcome ideas.

And most went to extremes to fight them. In the communist world, the information police controlled all media and scrutinized their output, both before and after publication. In 1917, the Bolsheviks imposed censorship on their second day in office. The sheer quantity of the material banned was remarkable. Stalin's agents withdrew more than 16,000 titles from circulation in a single year—1938–39—and pulped 24 million copies of the offending works.[7] In China, Mao's censors worked around the clock. Between 1950 and 1951, one major press had to shrink its offerings from 8,000 to just 1,234 titles.[8] In both countries, minor lapses precipitated crises. When some indiscretion slipped into an agricultural newspaper in Soviet Karelia, the censors raced to track down every copy sold, including 50 already pasted into ersatz wallpaper and 12 used as toilet paper.[9] Not content with just the manuscript of Vasily Grossman's epic novel *Life and Fate*, the KGB even confiscated the carbon paper and typewriter ribbons he had used to write it.[10]

Officially, East Germany had no censors. It did not need them— Party leader Erich Honecker did the job in person. He "dutifully and daily proofread the first few pages of the party central organ, *Neues Deutschland*," correcting punctuation and diction.[11] All major reports were pre-vetted by Honecker, along with his boss of agitprop, Joachim Herrmann. After that, correcting even spelling errors and factual mistakes was forbidden. It was rumored that the general secretary personally selected ties for the anchormen on the evening news show.[12]

Non-communist dictators could also be thorough. In their first fourteen months in power, the Nazis shut down 1,000 newspapers and scared another 350 into closing.[13] By the end of their second year, 40 separate agencies had banned more than 4,000 books.[14] In Spain, until 1966 General Franco required all publications, from newspapers to street posters, to be preapproved.[15] Pop singers had to submit their lyrics before each recording session.[16] Franco's first press minister, José Millán-Astray, summoned "unfortunate journalists with a whistle, shrieking hysterically at any misdemeanors, and threatening with execution any foreign correspondents who criticized the regime."[17] Mussolini found time to check opera librettos and stage productions.[18] Pinochet closed down Chile's left-wing media and posted censors in all newspapers, magazines, radio stations, and television channels. His soldiers raided bookstores. In one case, they impounded art works on Cubism for fear they might be promoting Fidel Castro's revolution.[19]

In Africa, too, rulers fought the printed word. Malawi's Hastings Banda banned 840 books between 1968 and 1975, along with more than 100 magazines and 16 films. Owning George Orwell's *Animal Farm* was prosecuted as treason.[20] The international news magazine *Jeune Afrique* staged a tongue-in-cheek tournament to see which countries would confiscate more of its issues in the first half of 1978. Mobutu's Zaire came first, followed by Egypt and Libya. Algeria, Congo, and Guinea did even better, banning the magazine outright. Its staff took pride in having been censored by both Marxists (as "lackeys of imperialism") and their anticommunist rivals (as "subversive leftists").[21] In apartheid South Africa, agents vetted not just books and newspapers, films and artworks, but even T-shirts, key rings, and shop signs.[22]

What exactly were the censors looking for? First and foremost, messages contradicting the regime's ideology or challenging its political control. But what that meant in practice was often murky. In the late Soviet Union, even the list of proscribed topics—the *perechen*—was itself secret, unavailable to writers and sometimes even censors. Lists that did surface could be surprisingly detailed. Poland's manual in the 1970s forbade mention of statistics on car accidents, fires, drownings, diseases of livestock, food poisoning, foreign debt, and even annual coffee consumption. Positive mention of hippies—including those abroad—was out.[23] For the East Germans, forbidden topics included formaldehyde, lawn bowling, boulevards, bratwurst kiosks, homemade gliders, and Formula 1 racing.[24] In Pinochet's Chile, censors were to remove anything that was "antipatriotic," that concerned "terrorists or communists," or that could pose "a threat to homeland security."[25] This apparently included a photograph of the interior minister with one button unfastened—the magazine guilty of that lapse received a reprimand.[26]

Perhaps deliberately, to spread anxiety, the red lines were left vague. And they changed. Like Winston Smith in Orwell's Ministry of Truth, Stalin's censors rewrote the past as well as the present. Disgraced Bolsheviks were airbrushed out of photographs, their deeds erased from history books. Censors scoured libraries for mentions of discredited officials in order to blot them out with black ink.[27] Others worried that banned photographs might survive in old newspapers used to wrap groceries.[28] Editing the past continued even after Stalin's death, at least for a while. When Stalin's secret police chief Lavrenty Beria was shot in 1953, owners of the *Great Soviet Encyclopedia* received urgent instructions. They were to remove pages 21–24 in Volume V with a razor blade and paste in a newly provided article on the Bering Strait.[29] By the 1971 edition, Beria had vanished without trace.[30]

In the 1930s, Stalin banned ambiguity.[31] Possible double entendres had to be tracked down and liquidated, along with unintentionally suggestive typographical errors and visual resemblances. A certain newspaper photograph of the Bolshevik Mikhail Kalinin was cut at the last minute because he looked too much like Trotsky.[32] Nazi administrators also hunted subversive images. According to Victor Klemperer, officials relandscaped the park in Dresden's Bismarckplatz because the previous radial pattern of paths had resembled the British Union Jack flag.[33] In Franco's Spain and Salazar's Portugal, the censors forbade references to "strikes in Greece, torture in Brazilian jails, [and] demonstrations against the war in Indochina," for fear these might bring to mind domestic parallels.[34]

Second, besides being comprehensive, the process under old-school dictators was quite *public*. Censorship was not just a way to block messages: it *was* a message. Rejecting "bad" ideas became—like the regime's violence—a kind of theater. Goebbels staged book burnings at which students chanting "fire slogans" (*Feuersprüche*) tossed "decadent" literature into the flames. Radio stations broadcast Berlin's auto-da-fé live and movie theaters later screened the newsreel footage.[35] Another 93 book burnings occurred around the country.[36] Other twentieth-century dictators held similar events. Mao's revolutionaries stoked a bonfire in the port of Shantou that burned for three days, devouring 300,000 suspect tomes.[37] Pinochet and his Argentine neighbors were also book burners.[38]

Rather than a surreptitious act, censorship became everyday bureaucratic business. In the USSR, the Main Administration for the Preservation of State and Military Secrets in the Press, known as Glavlit, had about 70,000 employees.[39] There were branches throughout the country, and every newspaper had to provide an office for its in-house censor.[40] Indeed, the agency became so visible and omnipresent that Russians coined a new verb, *litovat*, meaning to obtain formal approval of the censors. Similar arrangements existed across the communist world. In Latin American military regimes, as well, the censor was a familiar face in the newsroom.

Third, censorship under old-style dictators was often *violent* and openly so. Countless artists and writers died in Stalin's and Hitler's camps. And many other regimes also used force. As Pinochet's troops took power in 1973, they bombed the antennas of left-wing radio stations.[41] Mussolini's blackshirts, on entering Rome in 1922, destroyed the printing presses of opposition newspapers.[42] In Iraq under Saddam Hussein, the dictator's older son, Uday, specialized in persecuting journalists. More than five hundred authors, reporters, and artists were executed, and many others mysteriously vanished.[43] One unfortunate journalist was arrested and tortured after writing that the president "cared about every last detail in Iraq, even the toilets."[44] In Malawi, if a critical journalist could not be found, President Banda's goons took it out on his family members.[45] As with violence in general, the point was not just to harm a particular writer but to intimidate all the others.

Finally, although some dictators may have genuinely feared the contents of the books they burned, censorship was more about *demonstrating power and enforcing conformity.* The goal was to keep people not just from knowing the truth but also from saying it. The censorship of fear aimed to demoralize and deter.[46] The extreme reaction to an irreverent word here or there could look like paranoia. But there was a logic to it. Any breach of the rules that went unpunished could signal regime weakness. And breaches in the mass media were witnessed by millions. Worse than that, everyone knew that everyone else had seen them; such lapses created what game theorists call "common knowledge," a key ingredient for coordinated opposition.[47] As a result, blanket censorship became a trap. Once established, it was dangerous to remove.

FUJIMEDIA

Against this background, Fujimori's contrite climbdown at the *El Comercio* office came as something of a surprise. The headstrong leader who had just sent Congress packing was admitting a blunder and offering an olive branch. In subsequent years, he would go further, crafting a new, defter way of managing the press.

Until then, Fujimori had not looked like much of an innovator. Swept to power as Maoist insurgents exploded bombs inside the capital, he had given his generals a free hand to hunt them down. Human rights activists blamed his government for the murder of journalists by right-wing paramilitaries.[48] He called the activists the "legal arm" of terrorism and threatened critics of the military with life sentences for treason.[49]

A previously obscure professor, born to Japanese émigrés, Fujimori had been a complete outsider to Peruvian politics before his surprise electoral victory. But in office he had teamed up with a notorious insider.

Vladimiro Montesinos, whom Fujimori tapped to head the Servicio de Inteligencia Nacional (the National Intelligence Service, or SIN), had connections in the armed forces, the security services, the CIA, and international drug cartels. Trained in Peru's military academy, he had been discharged for selling secrets to the United States. After a couple of years in jail, he resurfaced as a lawyer for Colombian cocaine dealers.[50]

Between the 1992 *autogolpe* and late 2000, when Fujimori's presidency collapsed in scandal, this strange duo dominated Peru's politics. Their strategy was based on knowing everything and shaping what others knew. "The addiction to information," Montesinos once said, "is like the addiction to drugs. We live on information."[51]

He meant the information his agents gathered from tapped phones and surveillance cameras. Images from Congress, the courts, the presidential palace, downtown Lima, and the airport flashed continually on twenty-five screens in Montesinos's office.[52] He even hid a camera in a brothel frequented by Lima's elite.[53] But even more important was managing the information flowing out through both state and private media. Manipulating those currents was crucial to Fujimori's ratings and election victories. By controlling the media, one controlled the ratings. And by controlling the ratings, one controlled politics.

The techniques invented by spin dictators like Fujimori turned the old censorship of fear on its head. Where fear dictators sought comprehensive power, the new approach was *deliberately partial*. In the modern global economy, a complete information monopoly meant settling for backwardness. And, as Fujimori soon realized, a complete monopoly was unnecessary—even undesirable.[54]

In fact, a token opposition media could be useful. It showed the regime was confident in its appeal. It could be held up to the West—and domestic critics—as proof that the authorities respected press freedom. It might even turn up useful information, warning of local crises or looming threats. And, when credibility mattered, it could be used to send messages, just as Nazarbayev used independent bloggers. Amid Fujimori's *autogolpe*, reports of the president's popularity published in the state media would sway few critics. But the same reports, if published by the opposition press, would be more credible.

Fujimori's core base of support lay in the countryside and urban shantytowns. To reach it, he needed to control the main TV stations and tabloid papers. Beyond this underclass, Peru boasted a well-educated, Westernized upper crust. Fourteen percent of adults had a college degree in the early 1990s, about the same proportion as in Israel.[55] Fujimori could not allow this informed stratum to undermine his support. But it had little chance of doing so with its highbrow publications like *El Comercio*, *La República*, and *Caretas*. Such fringe media—ignored by most Peruvians—posed little threat. "What do I care about *El Comercio*?" Montesinos mused at one point. "They have an 80,000 print run. 80,000 newspapers is shit."[56]

Other spin dictators had their own *El Comercios*. Putin had the liberal daily *Novaya Gazeta* and the television channel Dozhd. The Russian authorities harassed both but never quite forced them to close. "There was no mission to shut us down," Dozhd's founder, Natalya Sindeyeva, told journalist Jill Dougherty, "but to make us, let's say, weak—there was that task. They squeezed us."[57] In Venezuela, Chávez "made a tactical decision to keep one opposition TV voice on air. Look at Globovisión, he said. How can anyone say there is not media plurality? It attacks me every day."[58] In Malaysia, English- and Chinese-language media were given freer rein than those in Malay, the language of the regime's base.[59]

As well as deliberately partial, Fujimori's approach was *covert*. Instead of publicly censoring "bad" ideas, it aimed to slant the news without viewers realizing. Overt censorship would suggest the government had something to hide and might send people searching for the missing information.[60] Concealing something can, perversely, increase awareness of it. Scholars call this the "Streisand effect": when the American singer tried to stop a little-known website from posting pictures of her Malibu home, the scandal itself attracted thousands of viewers.[61] "The book that is suppressed today gets twice as much attention tomorrow," wrote South African novelist J. M. Coetzee. "The writer who is gagged today is famous tomorrow for having been gagged."[62] Just as public violence creates martyrs, public censorship creates interest. Research even shows that people are readier to believe information they know to have been censored.[63]

Sensing this, Fujimori set out instead to co-opt the media bosses. In the early 1990s, private businessmen owned six of Peru's seven main television stations. Montesinos bribed them to censor themselves. Officially independent, their broadcasts preserved at least a patina of objectivity. And, working indirectly, the regime benefited from the creativity of the private sector's producers and writers. By the end of the decade, Montesinos was paying more than $3 million a month to the TV stations for sympathetic coverage.[64] All details were specified in formal—but top secret—contracts that the station owners signed. Each day at 12:30 p.m., they huddled with Montesinos to plan the evening's news shows.[65]

As the 2000 presidential election approached, payments increased. One by one, the owners appeared in Montesinos's SIN office to receive stacks of money. We know this because Montesinos videotaped himself bantering with the moguls as they stuffed cash into briefcases and plastic bags. In return, the owners let him direct their news coverage. They closed down investigative shows and benched their star reporters. One channel, América Televisión, received almost $23 million during the two pre-election years.[66] To feign impartiality, Montesinos let one of the stations, Channel 5, invite opposition candidates on air. But their appearances were limited.[67]

Besides bribes in Peruvian soles or U.S. dollars, Montesinos provided other rewards. Sometimes he bartered an exclusive story or a tax write-off for positive coverage.[68] For others, he intervened in court cases and arranged share purchases and debt refinancing. He even offered one TV station a unit of secret policemen to dig up stories. Government publicity contracts helped keep various media companies afloat. Indeed, the state became Peru's largest advertiser, channeling cash to the loyal outlets. When that was not enough, Montesinos prodded private companies to advertise on pro-Fujimori stations.[69]

Nor did he neglect the printed media. Bypassing the snobbish elite, he cultivated the gutter press. The *chicha* papers, named after the corn beer popular with Andean migrants, celebrated the vulgar culture of Lima's streets. Titles such as El Chino ("The Chinaman"—this, despite his Japanese ancestry, was Fujimori's nickname) and El Chato

("Shorty") plastered Lima's kiosks, flashing gaudy headlines above photographs of semi-naked women and crime scenes.

Censorship sometimes shaded into propaganda. In the campaign season, Montesinos dictated the coverage he wanted. A headline on page one cost about $3,000, or slightly more if accompanied by a cartoon.[70] Each evening, SIN agents placed orders for the next day via encrypted fax. Montesinos sometimes wrote the headlines himself.[71] The journalists would then work up stories to go with them.

While Montesinos takes the prize for brazenness, other spin dictators have also co-opted their own media barons. As in Peru, state publicity contracts often served as carrots. In Venezuela, Chávez tripled government advertising spending between 2003 and 2008, directing it to loyal firms.[72] Hungary's Viktor Orbán quadrupled his government's advertising budget to more than $300 million a year.[73] Much of the cash went to friendly outlets, which, in return, reported less about government corruption scandals.[74]

The old censorship had been brutal. The new approach, although hardly gentle, aimed to *avoid violence*. In the twenty-first century, imprisoning journalists prompted denunciations from global human rights groups and foreign governments. Killing them made for PR disasters. Even just suspicion of harming journalists could be dangerous.

In Ukraine, for instance, the brutal murder of the journalist Georgiy Gongadze in 2000 sparked a political crisis. A recording surfaced of the country's president, Leonid Kuchma, apparently asking his security chief to "take care" of the reporter. Kuchma said the tape had been doctored and denied ordering Gongadze's assassination. But the United States and EU denounced Kyiv's failure to investigate properly, and an official from the Organization for Security and Cooperation in Europe (OSCE) called the murder a likely case of "censorship by killing."[75] The scandal helped end Kuchma's hopes of running for a third term.

In Russia, the killing of liberal journalist Anna Politkovskaya in 2006 in an apparent contract hit cast shadows over Putin's administration. Six men were convicted of the crime after complicated and obscure court proceedings. But who ordered it was never proved. Interviewed by Germany's *Süddeutsche Zeitung*, Putin condemned the murder but added that in his view Politkovskaya's influence in Russia had been "negligible." Her killing, he said, had caused "much more damage to the current authorities . . . than her reporting did."[76]

This comment was, rightly, viewed as callous. But it reveals with unintended frankness how spin dictators think. They realize public violence against journalists is counterproductive. Such acts undermine their image as popular leaders far more effectively than do critical articles in fringe publications. Toward the end of the chapter, we will return to this issue and show how spin dictators differ from fear dictators in statistics on violence toward journalists. Spoiler alert: with occasional exceptions, they do less of it.

When coercion is essential, spin dictators like Fujimori try to camouflage it. They prefer to get their way with regulatory pressures or business maneuvers. In Peru, one television magnate, Baruch Ivcher, turned against the government in 1997. His Channel 2 aired embarrassing exposés of Montesinos and the SIN. Montesinos first tried bribery, offering Ivcher $19 million to hand over control of the station's news shows, according to Ivcher. But he refused. Montesinos then defeated him with a legal ploy. He had Ivcher, a naturalized citizen of Israeli origin, stripped of his Peruvian citizenship. By law, only citizens were allowed to own a television station. A pliant judge was therefore "forced" to reassign Ivcher's shares to more loyal holders.[77]

An old-school autocrat might have turned to violence. But not Montesinos. One of his aides suggested making death threats against Ivcher. "Remember why Pinochet had his problems," Montesinos shot back. "We will not be so clumsy. And, besides, what's the purpose of ordering the death of anybody? This is madness." He was not averse to a little blood. A few years earlier, fighting Sendero Luminoso, Montesinos had shown few scruples about sending death squads to intimidate peasants.[78] But he saw that in this case violence would backfire. As it was, the maneuver against Ivcher proved quite costly. In Lima, demonstrators protested his mistreatment. The Catholic Church called his loss of citizenship "illegal and dangerous." The U.S. Congress and the Inter-American Court of Human Rights both denounced the move.[79]

Elsewhere, other spin dictators engineered similar takeovers when co-optation failed. In Russia, the NTV television network attacked Putin and his Unity Party during the 1999–2000 election campaigns. Once in office, the new Kremlin chief detained the station's owner and pressured him to sell out to the state gas company Gazprom. With similar hardball tactics, Putin recovered another oligarch's shares in the main state channel. Eventually, Gazprom's media assets, including NTV, ended up in the hands of Yuri Kovalchuk, an old friend of Putin's, whose media empire was by 2016 worth around $2.2 billion.[80] NTV, the channel that had attacked Putin in 1999–2000, became known for documentaries smearing the president's opponents.

In Hungary, the role of media consolidator fell to one of Prime Minister Orbán's old friends, Lörinc Mészáros. A former small-town gas pipe fitter, Mészáros quickly amassed a fortune of $1.3 billion, according to *Forbes*, a feat he attributed to "God, luck, and Viktor Orbán."[81] Together with two other government-linked businessmen, he snapped up all eighteen of Hungary's regional papers in 2016–17.[82] A company tied to Mészáros bought and closed the country's largest opposition newspaper, *Nepszabadsag*.[83] In Singapore, the company Singapore Press Holdings (SPH) owned almost all of the island's daily newspapers. After Lee Kuan Yew passed a law entitling the government to reassign voting power among members of SPH's board, loyal executives monitored the content themselves.[84]

The old fear dictators felt obliged to censor any criticism to avoid looking weak. Spin dictators, by permitting some independent media and pretending not to censor, free themselves from this trap. Tolerating limited challenges actually makes them look stronger. So long as they remain popular with the general public, they can safely ignore the carping of low-circulation outlets.

Still, tolerating a small, independent press does not mean welcoming it. In Peru, Montesinos found ways to quietly make life difficult for opposition media. At the same time, he sought to interfere with reception of their messages. Again, his favored techniques turn up in many other spin dictatorships.

One powerful weapon is to *sue journalists for libel or defamation*. This ties the victims up in court proceedings and burdens them with crippling fines—or even short jail spells where criminal penalties apply. It also casts them as politically motivated liars. Montesinos, for instance, sued the editor of the opposition magazine *Caretas* in 1991 over an article depicting him as a "Rasputin," influencing Fujimori from the shadows. A judge sentenced the editor to one year in jail (suspended) and ordered him to pay the security chief $40,000.[85] Ecuador's Rafael Correa charged four journalists from the daily *El Universo* with criminal defamation for referring to him as a "dictator." After a trial that lasted less than twenty-four hours, the judge sentenced each journalist to prison for three years and fined the newspaper $40 million.[86]

In Singapore, Lee Kuan Yew repeatedly sued his critics for libel and defamation. As one analyst put it: "forsaken profits and stiff legal penalties have been more effective in fostering self-censorship than earlier methods of intimidation."[87] Turkey's Recep Tayyip Erdoğan sued dozens of individuals for insulting him; in just his first two years in office, he took home $440,000 in damages from the twenty-one cases he won.[88] In Putin's Russia, thousands of defamation lawsuits were filed each year, many against journalists.[89]

Short of such suits, spin dictators harass critical media with *enforcement actions and regulatory fines*. In Venezuela, Chávez's investigators peppered Globovisión with accusations. It had failed to pay taxes, they said (fine: $4.2 million).[90] It had "fueled fear in the citizenry" (i.e., covered a jail riot: penalty: $2.1 million).[91] It had "incited panic and anxiety" by reporting on an earthquake (threatened penalty: seventy-two-hour closure).[92] Its president had illegally stored twenty-four Toyota vehicles to manipulate prices (penalty: up to five years in prison).[93] Government agents searched his house for evidence of illegal hunting but found none.[94] In 2009, Erdoğan's tax ministry slapped a mind-boggling $2.5 billion fine for alleged tax evasion on the Dogan Yayin media group, whose outlets had criticized the government.[95]

Besides fines, regimes sometimes punish publications by restricting their circulation. By avoiding a complete ban, they deflect accusations of censorship. In Singapore, after *Time*, the *Asian Wall Street Journal*, and the *Far Eastern Economic Review* published articles that cast the government in a bad light, it capped their circulation in the country—reducing sales by more than 80 percent in each case.[96] This shrank the companies' advertising revenue. But since some copies still circulated, Lee wrote later, the newspapers "could not accuse us of being afraid to have their reports read."[97]

Regulations are often presented as serving legitimate goals.[98] Russia's authorities filter Internet content to protect citizens from pedophiles and terrorists.[99] To weaken the oligarchy's grasp over the press, Correa amended Ecuador's constitution to prohibit banks from owning media outlets.[100] To fight monopoly, he forbade media owners from holding stock in other types of business. This, of course, prevented cross-subsidization. The owners of *El Universo* had to sell off their highly profitable travel agency.[101]

Such examples suggest an important point. Dictators need not always use *illegal* tools to monopolize power. Often it is enough to misuse legal ones.[102] Libel and defamation laws, judicial discretion, emergency powers, redistricting procedures, voter registration laws, and media regulations can all enhance and preserve democracy—or, in the wrong hands, weaken it. To resist unscrupulous leaders, one needs not just well-crafted laws but citizens with the capacity to monitor, organize, and fight back—in our terms, a robust stratum of *the informed*.

Another, even subtler tactic is to *camouflage interventions as the operation of free markets*. When Russia's opposition TV station Dozhd angered the Kremlin, its private cable providers suddenly canceled contracts, shutting off access to 80 percent of its subscribers.[103] The station was reduced to Internet broadcasts. In Kazakhstan under Nazarbayev, mysterious paper shortages materialized when opposition newspapers sought a printer. The shortages disappeared when the journalists placed orders for an otherwise identical *literary* publication.[104] In Venezuela, too, paper shortages do the censor's work. From 2003, Chávez imposed arcane currency controls that made it hard to get dollars to import vital newsprint and ink. In 2007, some papers had to miss issues or cut pages. The shortages affected primarily publications critical of the government.[105] But the political pretext was hidden in a tangle of technicalities.

Besides harassing opposition media, spin dictators interfere with reception of their messages. One tactic is to disguise censorship as technical constraints—or, in the terms of political scientist Margaret Roberts, "friction."[106] If a blockage can be blamed on technology, governments can avoid political backlash. Roberts studied how Chinese Internet censors slowed down the loading of certain websites. But friction also occurred on pre-Internet media. In Peru, during the 2000 presidential election campaign, one cable channel broadcast embarrassing footage of a hostile crowd jeering Fujimori. Suddenly, that channel's transmission was interrupted by "technical problems."[107]

Another way to neutralize hostile messages is to *discredit the source*. If one can prime readers to distrust a report, there is no need to censor it. Montesinos used the *chicha* tabloids to smear opposition journalists. These bombarded writers with sexist, racist, or homophobic insults. One was a "mental midget," another a "she devil"; others were an "undercover terrorist," a "paid coup provocateur," "communists," "traitors," and "rabid animals."[108] The abuse played on the gap between the street culture of the masses and the snobbery of the elite.

Where Montesinos used the tabloids to insult opposition reporters, others did so directly. Ecuador's Rafael Correa called hostile correspondents "ink-stained hit men" and one well-known newsman a "big fake, a swine, a professional defamer, and a bank employee"—a low blow in a country supposedly run by a grasping oligarchy.[109] Chávez labeled journalists "white collar terrorists" and one media executive a "madman with a cannon."[110]

Yet another tactic is to *divert attention*. To distract the public at critical moments, Montesinos's agents developed a repertoire of sensationalistic stories for tabloids and TV. Among other wonders, the SIN's psyops wizards reported on "a statue of the Virgin Mary that cried real tears, an apparition of Christ," and "a shadowy monster roaming the sand hills of the shanty towns, sowing terror."[111] Chávez was a master of changing the subject. When the facts were unhelpful, he could make the story about his words—as when he called President Bush "Donkey" or "Mr. Danger."[112] His old army friend Francisco Arias Cárdenas marveled at Chávez's ability to trick people into changing their focus:

> On his TV show, he might pick up a carrot and call it a beet. His opponents will begin laughing at him: "What an idiot! He can't even

distinguish a carrot from a beet." But after the show, I guarantee you Chávez will be the one laughing. He'll think to himself, "I can't believe I fooled them into talking about carrots and beets all week."[113]

Besides diverting attention, spin dictators sometimes *drown unwelcome messages in a flood of pro-government content*.[114] The opposition needle then disappears inside a propaganda haystack. Chávez barraged the public with information. Every Sunday, for up to eight hours, he hammered it up in his unscripted television show, *Aló Presidente*. "He would sing, dance, rap; ride a horse, a tank, a bicycle; aim a rifle, cradle a child, scowl, blow kisses; act the fool, the statesman, the patriarch," wrote the journalist Rory Carroll, who appeared in one episode at the comandante's invitation.[115] But mostly he just talked. When he needed still more time, Chávez commandeered the airwaves for urgent announcements or "chains." By the end of a decade, these had taken up 1,300 hours. Still not satisfied, he launched a new website and newspaper column: "I'm going to put a lot of information there. It's going to be a bombardment," he announced.[116] He was not kidding.

Chávez's "excessive verbalization" puzzled his biographer, Alberto Barrera. All those wasted hours, full of repeated jokes and banalities, seemed a "terribly ineffective strategy for governing the country."[117] But there was a point. Chávez occupied the news space so thoroughly, it was hard for much else to sneak in. Correa proved an avid disciple. He would preempt national broadcasting on all channels for his impromptu addresses, known as *cadenas*—observers counted 1,025 of these in less than five years. A close parallel of such flooding is the practice of requiring private media to publish long rebuttals by the government. Correa demanded time on TV channels' news shows to counter their claims.[118] Lee Kuan Yew insisted that foreign publications print unedited replies from the prime minister's office pointing out their mistakes.[119]

In Peru, all these techniques worked for Fujimori for a long time. But he was eventually brought down after the single cable television channel that Montesinos had neglected to neutralize, Canal N, broadcast an explosive piece of footage. The channel screened a leaked video that Montesinos had made of himself paying off an opposition congressman with stacks of dollars. After this bombshell, the other channels—ignoring their agreements with Montesinos—played the video as well. Soon the regime began to implode.

What undermined Fujimori was not the independence of Canal N per se. Leaving one, low-circulation channel was, after all, quite consistent with the spin dictatorship playbook. Canal N had only been launched in July 1999 and, charging a high subscription fee, it had only tens of thousands of viewers.[120] But two things made a difference. First there was the explosive material that Montesinos had, unintentionally, prepared for the channel when he videotaped his acts of corruption. To read in the paper about crooked politicians was one thing. But to see the country's spy chief on screen counting out stacks of dollars and boasting about his influence was something else.[121] To let this material leak was spin dictator malpractice on a legendary scale.

The second key point is that the regime was already weakened. The video was the last straw. Fujimori's liberal economic reforms were seen as failing to create jobs for his poor supporters and economic growth had turned negative in 1998–99. The president's approval ratings had fallen to 44 percent.[122] He was coming under pressure from the United States and some domestic allies to fire Montesinos.[123] The video provoked a final split. Had the duo stuck together, they might have managed to bury the scandal in a long, fruitless investigation, as the team's PR advisor, Daniel Borobio, proposed.[124] But Fujimori lost his nerve, announcing on TV that he would step down early and two months later fleeing to Japan, from where he resigned the presidency by fax.

COMMAND + DELETE

As the Internet took root, some thought it would empower citizens to overthrow dictatorships. However, authoritarian regimes quickly learned how to censor online. Worse, the anonymity of the web enabled them to infiltrate and disrupt opposition groups. All types of dictators turned new information technologies into tools of control. But spin dictators were among the most inventive.

Is the Internet a game changer when it comes to authoritarian manipulation? Does online censorship differ significantly from the traditional kind? Or have dictators merely updated the techniques they developed on twentieth-century media? We see more evidence of the latter.

As with newspapers and TV, spin dictators do not seek total control over the Internet. Although they ban some websites, they tolerate other opposition platforms. Political influence—like that over old media—is often covert and indirect. Where possible, rulers pressure or bribe sites to censor themselves. And they arrange for friends to occupy the online commanding heights. In Russia, the country's largest social network, Vkontakte, helped publicize the 2011–12 mass anti-Putin protests. In 2014, its brilliant but eccentric founder, Pavel Durov, was pressured into selling out to a Kremlin-linked oligarch.[125] When censorship does attract attention, spin dictators pretend to be restricting not political speech but obscenity, extremism, or—most apolitically—copyright violations. Rafael Correa forced documentaries about him off the web by threatening lawsuits for the unauthorized use of his image.[126] He even used a controversial U.S. law to do so.[127]

As in their persecution of print journalists, spin dictators try to avoid violent repression. They do occasionally arrest online activists, but the detentions tend to be rare and short. More often, they tie up their critics with regulations and fines. Since 2014, Russian bloggers who attract more than 3,000 readers a day have had to register with the state Internet oversight agency, publish their names and contact information, and obey all mass media regulations. They can be sued for misinformation posted in comments sections on their websites. Even pro-Kremlin lawmakers have called the rules confusing and difficult to enforce.[128] In Singapore, one blogger was sued for merely sharing an article on Facebook.[129]

Fujimori and his peers interrupted unwelcome TV broadcasts, radio programs, and even phone conversations with "technical problems." Online, spin dictators disrupt with DDoS attacks and hacks.[130] Or they just slow the website down, letting the audience's impatience do the rest.[131] Analog-era leaders commandeered television and radio to bombard viewers with their ramblings. Internet-savvy ones use bots to flood platforms with pro-government messages and distractions. After Russia's 2011 parliamentary election, some 26,000 fraudulent Twitter accounts unleashed a storm of hundreds of thousands of tweets from all around the world. These hijacked the hashtags used by Putin's critics, making it harder to organize protests.[132] On most days in 2014, more than half the tweets about Russian politics posted by active users originated from such bots.[133]

In the past, anonymous phone calls harassed opposition journalists. Montesinos used the *chicha* tabloids for character assassination. Nowadays, government-paid trolls post abuse on the websites of critical journalists and denounce them on social media. In Latin America, the master of such methods was Rafael Correa. His state-funded troll centers savaged opponents, circulating photographs of their children and publishing their hacked emails.[134] Since Twitter reached mostly the educated opposition, Correa could intimidate critics without revealing his brutality to his mass followers.

The early Internet giants—Google, Facebook, and Twitter—are all Western. Some hoped that might prevent authoritarian governments from using them against their citizens. But these companies are vulnerable to losing lucrative markets. According to the newspaper *Vedomosti*, Google began blocking access to websites on the Russian government's blacklist in 2019.[135] Governments pressure such firms to help them with surveillance.[136]

As with old media, China occupies a strange middle ground. On the one hand, it allows some semi-independent content providers, and its censors often hide their fingerprints. On the other hand, some of their interventions are strikingly public. Shenzhen province's Internet censors even have their own endearing cartoon mascots: smiling miniature male and female figures in police uniforms.[137] Under Xi, writes legal scholar Eva Pils, "the Party-State seems intent on advertising its repression."[138] And, at times, its censorship.

CHECKING THE EVIDENCE

As spin dictatorship spreads, we should expect to see overt media controls replaced by less visible ones. Some evidence on this comes from the V-DEM network of experts. For each country and year, they assess whether government censorship was direct or indirect and routine or limited. If our argument is right, recent decades should show a decrease in direct, routine censorship—as favored, for instance, by Kim Il-Sung in North Korea—and an increase in indirect, limited methods—as occurred under Eduard Shevardnadze in Georgia. And we do. The proportion of nondemocracies with direct, routine censorship falls from 68 percent in 1980 to 45 percent in 2018. In the same years, the share with indirect, limited censorship rises from 3 to 19 percent.[139]

Spin dictators' preference for unobtrusive methods extends to control of the Internet. The NGO Freedom House publishes an annual rating of the extent of Internet censorship in about 65 countries. In its 2016 report, the average score for the democracies surveyed was 32 on a scale from 0 (no Internet censorship) to 100 (complete Internet censorship). We use the rules of thumb of chapter 1 to break down the world's nondemocracies into the various types. Spin dictatorships averaged a score of 52; hybrids 59; and fear dictatorships 67. As with other media controls, spin dictators are rated somewhat more restrictive than democracies but much less restrictive than fear dictatorships.[140]

We also claimed that spin dictators are less prone than fear dictators to use violence against journalists. The Committee to Protect Journalists, another NGO, collects information on media workers killed in countries around the world. Since 1992, when the records start, its experts report a total of 892 murders that occurred "in direct reprisal for the journalist's work." (Almost 500 more died in crossfire on battlefields or covering dangerous events such as riots.)[141] In 280 of these murders, agents of the state—government officials, military officers, or paramilitary groups associated with the regime—appear to have participated. Other possible perpetrators include antigovernment parties, insurgents, terrorists, criminal groups, or mobs.

Again using the chapter 1 rules of thumb, we can see how frequently journalists are murdered by state agents under different types of leaders. We calculated the average number of such murders per year under each leader who came to power since 1992—when the data start—and then compared the different types. Both fear dictators and hybrid dictators averaged one such killing every 10 years. Democratic leaders had one every 21 years. (These concentrate in violence-prone democracies such as Turkey in the 1990s, the Philippines, and Colombia.) Spin dictators experienced one such killing every 42 years.[142] Consistent with our argument, state murders of journalists are rare under such leaders.[143]

The goal of manipulating information is to boost the leader's popularity. But does it work? Are spin dictators more popular than other types of leaders? Some evidence on this comes from Gallup, which surveys around 1,000 people every year in more than 120 countries for its World Poll (GWP). We focused on results for 2005–15.[144] Gallup's broad coverage means the sample includes 51 authoritarian states, including both spin and fear dictatorships, as well as more than 90 democracies.

A first, rough cut at an answer is simply to see how leaders' average approval ratings vary with the type of political regime. Each year, Gallup asks respondents: "Do you approve or disapprove of the job performance of the leadership of this country?" Respondents can answer "yes," "no," or "don't know." Averaging the percentages answering "yes" across available years for each leader, we get a measure of that leader's average approval. For spin dictators, this averaged 55 percent in 2005–15. For hybrid dictators, it was 52 percent, and for fear dictators, 51 percent. Democratic leaders, on the other hand, averaged only 41 percent.[145] Of course, this is a very basic test, but it is consistent with the idea that spin dictators tend to be more popular than their democratic counterparts.

But can we believe such polls? Interpreting surveys in free societies is hard enough, but in unfree ones the challenges are huge. Gallup has many decades of experience and its World Poll is widely respected. Still, respondents in authoritarian settings might be afraid to answer surveys frankly, especially on sensitive topics like the performance of the government. The results could suffer from sensitivity bias. Fearing repercussions if they complain, respondents might pretend to be happier than they really are with their self-imposed leader.

One way to check this is to look at how many respondents evade the question. We might expect people who are nervous about expressing negative views to refuse to answer or take the option of saying "don't know." It would be a red flag if such evasions turn out to be more common in authoritarian states than in democracies—and especially common in the fear dictatorships. In fact, that is not the case in the GWP. The percentages saying "don't know" or refusing to answer the leader approval question were 9 percent in spin dictatorships, 7 percent in hybrid ones, 8 percent in fear dictatorships, and 9 percent in democracies—all roughly the same.

Scholars have used a technique called the "list experiment" to assess the extent of sensitivity bias in different settings. Essentially, they slip the sensitive survey question—for example, "Do you think your president is doing a good job?"—in among several other innocuous ones—for example, "Do you prefer tea to coffee?"—and ask respondents to say only *to how many* of the list of questions they would answer "yes." No one can tell from a given respondent's reply whether or not that respondent approves of the president—those with fewer "yes" answers might just be coffee addicts! But if the researchers have information about respondents' average beverage preferences, they can deduce the average level of presidential approval. Comparing this to the results when respondents are asked about approval directly, they can also estimate the extent to which respondents typically "inflate" their support for the leader when asked straightforwardly.

In 2014–15, scholars conducted eight versions of a list experiment to gauge President Putin's popularity in Russia. The estimates of how much people inflated their approval vary—from 6 to 43 percentage points, with an average boost of 18 points.[146] Clearly, we should take the possibility of sensitivity bias seriously. But the main takeaway for our purposes here is that even adjusting for such distortion, Putin's "true" popularity was still very high. Subtracting out the sensitivity bias and averaging across the eight polls, his average approval remained 66 percent.

In spin dictatorships, we have said, violent repression is counterproductive. It undermines the dictator's image as a competent democratic leader. Is there evidence for this in the opinion polls? Note, first, that even if we are right, evidence could be hard to find. Violent repression might scare respondents into giving glowing reports even if it alienates them. In fact, the GWP results suggest that respondents' indignation over state brutality tends to outweigh any anxiety about answering frankly. We used our own data on state political killings to measure violent repression here. Except for those who served during ethnic civil wars—at such times, leaders can get away with considerable brutality against ethnic foes—those with more political killings tended to have *lower* approval.[147] The popularity of less violent dictators ranged widely—after all, there are many other ways to become unpopular. But, except in one case of ethnic civil war, there were no very popular dictators in this period who presided over many state political killings. This is far from conclusive evidence. But it is consistent with the idea that recent dictators have faced a choice between governing through fear or popularity. The two do not go well together.[148]

We already saw evidence that spin dictators tend to be more popular than democratic leaders. We suggested that their high ratings result from manipulation of the media. Again, the GWP offers a source of evidence on this. Every year, Freedom House estimates the extent of media freedom in countries around the world. Using its ratings, we explored whether greater censorship goes along with higher leader approval.[149] Since the GWP contains data for multiple years, we were able to abstract from any factors that are constant over time in a given country and focus on how changes in censorship relate to changes in the leader's popularity.[150] We also controlled for other influences on approval such as economic performance, the electoral cycle, and the level of political repression.

As expected, nondemocratic leaders were more popular when the media was more restricted. To take one example, in Ecuador, Freedom House's estimate of censorship rose by 23 points on a 100-point scale between 2007 and 2014, as Rafael Correa entrenched his control over the country's press. Our statistical model predicted a 9-point rise in Correa's approval because of this—and that was exactly the increase that Gallup registered. We cannot say for sure that censorship increases leaders' ratings; perhaps more popular leaders tend to censor more, so popularity drives censorship rather than the reverse. But the result is consistent with our argument.

We also suggested that spin dictators need to hide their censorship. Their claim to be competent and democratic falls apart if people see them silencing their critics. So they camouflage media controls—and we expect their popularity to fall if citizens nevertheless become aware of them. We use another question in the GWP to check this. It asks whether respondents think the media in their country has "a lot of freedom." From this, we constructed a measure of *perceived censorship*. Holding constant the actual level of censorship as measured by Freedom House, it turns out that approval of the leader falls as more people come to believe the media are restricted. For every 10-percentage-point increase in perceived censorship, the leader's rating drops by about 3 percentage points. To boost a leader's popularity these days, media restrictions do need to be unobtrusive.[151]

Internet censorship is also meant to boost the dictator's appeal. We found some evidence that this works. Internet companies like Google and Twitter report how often foreign governments ask them to take down content from their websites. In 2019, for instance, Google received 30,000 such requests. We took the frequency of these as a measure of the requesting government's effort to censor online materials. In recent years, increases in a nondemocratic government's censorship effort were associated with increases in the leader's approval.[152] Since the data on Internet restrictions are limited, we interpret this cautiously, but, again, it is consistent with our argument.

Other studies have also found that censorship correlates with higher support for incumbents. Political scientists James Hollyer, Peter Rosendorff, and James Vreeland report that less transparent autocracies, which provide little information about economic performance, face fewer mass protests.[153] Political scientists Pippa Norris and Ronald Inglehart studied this question using a different measure of censorship and a different survey. Like us, they found that confidence in the government was higher in countries with more restricted media, such as China and Vietnam, than in those where the press was freer, such as France and Germany.[154]

Some more indirect evidence comes from a study Sergei conducted with the economists Ekaterina Zhuravskaya and Nikita Melnikov.[155] This explored the way that 3G technology—which first brought broadband Internet to mobile phones—was rolled out across countries and subnational regions in 2007–18. The relevant point here is that easy

Internet access allowed people to check the claims of the mainstream media. If censorship previously inflated support for the country's leadership, that support should have fallen as high-speed Internet spread. And, indeed, it did. Moving from no 3G coverage to full coverage led to a drop in government approval of 6 percentage points.[156] Since the geographical reach of 3G technology within countries was unconnected to other politically relevant factors, it seems likely that the increased access to uncensored information neutralized the regime's media manipulation.[157] Indeed, the effect of access to mobile broadband on government approval was stronger in countries with censored media—and was absent when the Internet was itself censored.

Studies of individual countries also confirm that media controls can help incumbents. Economists Ruben Enikolopov, Maria Petrova, and Ekaterina Zhuravskaya examined the effect of the opposition-minded NTV channel in the early Putin era.[158] Recall that NTV's owner was pressured to sell out to Gazprom in 2001, and its editorial line then changed to a pro-Putin position. This study focused on the 1999 parliamentary election, when NTV strongly opposed Putin and supported his main rivals. It found that the Putin-linked Unity Party polled about 9 percentage points lower in areas where NTV was able to broadcast. Access to NTV at that point depended not on censorship but on technology—its signals were only transmitted in certain places. But this gives a sense of the likely impact of subsequent Kremlin censorship of the channel.

In Venezuela, economists Brian Knight and Ana Tribin found that closing the opposition TV station RCTV in 2007 boosted President Chávez's ratings—but only when viewers could not switch to Globovisión, another opposition channel. Losing one critical TV station helped the incumbent—so long as no other was available.[159] In Peru's 2000 election, citizens who reported having watched television coverage of the campaign every day were much more likely to report having voted for Fujimori than those who did not watch it at all—although in that case it is hard to tell whether Fujimori supporters chose to watch more TV or the TV coverage prompted previously undecided voters to support Fujimori.[160]

A final implication of our argument concerns the informed. In spin dictatorships, we suggested, this college-educated, politically savvy segment of society sees through the dictator's lies and opposes him. But a skilled spin dictator's manipulations secure him support among the general public. Is there evidence that dictators are less popular among the informed than among the masses? As a rough proxy for membership in the informed set, we use higher education. It turns out that in all kinds of dictatorships—spin, fear, and hybrid—those with college degrees tend to like the leader less than those without degrees. This is also true of lower-quality democracies (those with Polity2 scores of 6–9.) However, in high-quality democracies—those with perfect Polity2 scores of 10—the highly educated tend to be slightly *more* favorable toward the incumbent than the less well-educated. In flawed political systems, the informed appear more critical of the government than others, while in highly democratic countries they are *less* critical than the general public.[161]

To sum up, in contrast to the fear dictators of the twentieth century, today's spin dictators restrict the press in a way that is deliberately partial, mostly covert or camouflaged, and—although there are exceptions— generally nonviolent. They harass independent media with lawsuits, arbitrary regulations, commercial pressures, and pseudo-technical problems. Rather than ban critical messages outright, they divert viewers from them, drown them in floods of confusing or distracting information, and discredit their sources. They use similar techniques to disrupt online political discussions. Although this approach cannot endlessly offset objectively poor performance, the evidence suggests it can work for a while, sapping the ability of opposition elites to mobilize citizens against the regime. The dictator's goal throughout is to sustain high popularity among the masses, thus isolating and disempowering the informed, who see through the media's lies.

Some see similar tactics at work in flawed democracies.[162] That is not surprising. As we argued in chapter 1, real-world political regimes exist on a spectrum with many shades of gray. Politicians such as Néstor and Cristina Kirchner in Argentina and Silvio Berlusconi in Italy have used some of the same spin techniques to manipulate public opinion. The

Kirchners wooed newspapers with state advertising, apparently trading contracts for softer coverage of corruption.[163] On their watch, spending on such advertising exploded from $16 million in 2000 to $919 million in 2013.[164] Cristina Kirchner's attack on the Clarín media group—with trumped-up tax investigations, personal abuse, and a reelection slogan of "Clarín lies!"—came right out of the spin manual.[165]

In Italy, Berlusconi controlled six out of seven national TV channels for much of his tenure as prime minister—three state owned, and three from his own media empire.[166] A leaked wiretap in 2010 recorded him yelling at the broadcast commissioner and demanding that state TV cancel shows about his corruption cases.[167] When the switch to digital TV suddenly gave viewers access to many independent channels, the vote for Berlusconi's parliamentary coalition fell by 5.5 to 7.5 percentage points—a sign of the impact the Berlusconi-controlled media's slant had been having on public opinion.[168] In the United States, Donald Trump repeatedly tried to discredit the mainstream media in order to undermine its credibility. He verbally assaulted journalists, accusing them of spreading "fake news," and labeled them "enemies of the people."[169]

Still, in democracies—even imperfect ones—disabling the media is harder than in a spin dictatorship. Some attribute this to stronger constitutional protections or norms. Of course, these matter—but they do not act on their own. Journalists, lawyers, judges, and politicians must fight to defend against a destructive populist. Such battles require organizational skills, legal acumen, communication networks, and—usually—financial resources. In addition, there has to be a large enough demand for objective news and media freedom. In short, what is needed is a sizable informed stratum. It helps, too, if there are international organizations and NGOs to add their support. Without such capable and determined defenders, press freedom and all the other institutional features of liberal democracy remain words and diagrams in civics textbooks. But with them, the institutions come to life. Neither the Kirchners nor Berlusconi managed to entrench themselves securely. Both ultimately lost power—in elections.

CHAPTER 5

DEMOCRACY FOR DICTATORS

During the night of February 3, 1992, Lieutenant Colonel Hugo Chávez Frías, a stocky paratrooper in a red beret, began his revolution. With a few tanks, his men surrounded Venezuela's Miraflores Palace, headquarters of the country's president, and opened fire. Yet, within hours, the operation had collapsed. The president, Carlos Andrés Pérez, slipped through the conspirators' fingers and made it to a television studio to broadcast to the nation, still in crumpled pajamas underneath his suit.[1] By midmorning, Chávez had surrendered.

It was a bitter defeat. How could the mutineers have failed? Pérez, a veteran political insider, was deeply unpopular, a symbol of partisan scheming and corruption. When three years earlier, abandoning his electoral promises, he had launched an IMF-backed austerity program, Caracas had exploded into deadly riots. Inflation surged as strikes and protests escalated.[2] Support for change was overwhelming. Yet, the young lieutenant colonel had blundered in his choice of method. His head full of romantic stories of the anticolonial revolutionary Simón Bolívar, he had misread the era, overestimating the power of a few armed men to take and hold a state in the late twentieth century. Pérez's command of TV had trumped the rebels' guns.

Seven years later, Chávez stormed the Miraflores Palace again. This time, he was backed not by tanks but by voters. Running against an assortment of professional politicians and minor celebrities, the charismatic comandante swept through to win the presidency with 56 percent of the ballots. He had found his most powerful weapon. Over the next fourteen years, he would, in the words of Enrique Krauze, a leading historian of modern Latin America, use "democracy to undermine democracy."[3]

Chávez's transformation had not been immediate. After two years in a sewage-ridden prison, he had emerged still dreaming of revolution.[4] Luis Miquilena, a veteran leftist who became Chávez's mentor, set out to disabuse him. If he insisted on armed revolt, Miquilena warned, he would end up just "one more loudmouth yelling on the street corners of Caracas."[5] When Chávez surveyed his supporters, he found Miquilena was right. Most "did not want violent movements." Yet, the same surveys contained a positive message: if he ran for office, he could count on significant support.[6] Chávez "came around to the idea of participating in elections for a simple reason," Miquilena recalled. "He believed that he could win."[7]

First, though, his image had to change. From military fatigues, Chávez switched to what he called some "more or less typical Western-style suits." (With time, his taste would progress to Brioni and Lanvin.)[8] Simultaneously, he retuned his rhetoric. "Chávez often sounded extremely aggressive when he made speeches," wrote his biographers Cristina Marcano and Alberto Barrera. "He also had a tendency to use a confrontational, macabre vocabulary—the word 'death' frequently popped into his speeches, which led people to think of his candidacy as something frightening."[9] His advisors pressed Chávez to adopt a lexicon of hope.

Rafael Céspedes, a Dominican political consultant, was in charge of softening the candidate's rough edges. "His hair was very short, military style, and his face was battered," Céspedes recalled. "He . . . did not know what it means to smile."[10] He got Chávez to appear on the TV show of a female presenter who had been savaging the comandante's record. Instead of the gruff paratrooper she had expected, the host was met by a chivalrous charmer who handed her a bouquet of flowers on air and called her "young lady" (*doñita*). Her barbed questions ricocheted back.[11]

Had he become a democrat? Hardly. "If I get to Miraflores," Chávez had told one friend after leaving jail, "nobody is going to take our power away."[12] And he stuck to this plan after he got there. "The opposition will never return to power, by fair means or foul," he insisted.[13] He spoke of remaining in office "until 2030." The election of 1998 had offered a "tactical window," but he had never intended to "end up with some deputies, some governors, negotiating."[14]

Rather, he used his initial popularity to dynamite the checks and balances of Venezuela's constitutional system. Chávez took office with approval above 90 percent.[15] Aware this could fall, he invested his stratospheric ratings into more durable institutional advantages, networks of supporters, and control over the media. Within three months, a popular referendum had authorized him to call a constituent assembly. Voters gave 93 percent of the seats to Chávez loyalists.[16] Dissolving Congress, this new assembly drafted a constitution that lengthened the president's term to six years, removed the ban on immediate reelection, allowed military servicemen—likely Chávez supporters—to vote, and abolished the Senate, which had previously checked presidential power.[17]

Having elected a pliant new Congress, Chávez used it to expand the Supreme Court from 20 to 32 members and pack it with admirers. At the start of the 2006 session, the robed justices rose "to sing a favored chant of their benefactor: *Uh, ah, Chávez no se va* ('Uh, ah, Chávez is not leaving')."[18] His men took over the national oil company, PDVSA, Venezuela's golden goose. Chávez used its revenues to attack poverty with politically targeted patronage schemes. By 2006, four of the five members of the National Electoral Council were Chávistas, as were the comptroller and the attorney general.[19] To silence critics, Congress passed laws prescribing prison for those who showed "disrespect" to government officials and permitting suspension of media that "promote, defend, or incite breaches of public order or that are contrary to the security of the nation."[20]

When questioned about his commitment to democracy, Chávez was always ready. "I've been elected one, two, three, four times," he said. "Every year, we have elections in Venezuela." Indeed, in the ten years from 1999 to 2008, the country held eight national votes and three regional or local elections.[21] (Chávez suffered only one significant defeat, on a 2007 referendum.) His friend Luiz Inácio Lula da Silva, Brazilian president and a more traditional democrat, even spoke of "an excess of democracy" in Venezuela.[22] Yet, far from constraining the leader, these ballots were weapons he used to re-fire his appeal and discredit opponents.

As for violence, he now recognized its deceptive allure. Rather than employ force himself, he used the aggressiveness of the opposition against it. When in 2002 opponents staged a coup that ousted Chávez for forty-seven hours, the gamble exploded in their faces, as angry crowds demanded the president's release. Chávez emerged empowered. He often baited his critics, almost daring them to radicalize and discredit themselves. "He never answers the way his enemies expect him to . . . with violence," his biographer, Alberto Barrera, explained. In both 1992 and 2002, "Chávez gave up; he gave in. But in giving up, he wins."[23]

ELECTING THE PEOPLE

It is not just Chávez who has used democracy "to undermine democracy." Today's spin dictators are masters of subversion from within. In this chapter, we describe how they use polls and ballots to entrench themselves and consider why, despite high ratings, they typically choose to win their elections with some fraud. We document the trend toward a more sophisticated faking of free government. But first, let's recall the practices that preceded them.

The old fear dictators sometimes claimed to be democratic. To Goebbels, the Nazi regime was "the most ennobled form of a modern European democracy."[24] Fascism, said Mussolini, was an "organized, centralized, and authoritative democracy."[25] Stalin insisted that the Soviet Union had "the most democratic constitution in the world."[26] This document had emerged from a marathon of public consultation. An amazing 623,334 meetings—attended by 80 percent of the electorate—had been held to discuss the draft.[27] Kim Il-Sung even inserted "democratic" into his country's official name.

Yet, what such leaders had in mind was not pluralist democracy, in which different parties represent different groups and ideas and compete in elections. They scorned the "decadent" popular governments of the West. Hitler derided "parliamentary democracy, in which everyone has a voice and nothing can be decided."[28] Chile's Augusto Pinochet mocked the "classic liberal state, naïve and spineless."[29] António Salazar, the long-time Portuguese leader, was, he said, "profoundly antiparliamentarian."[30] "We do not believe in government through the voting booth," scoffed Spain's General Franco.[31]

What they favored was something else: the democracy of unanimity. Like Carl Schmitt, the German legal theorist who attacked liberalism in the 1920s, they rejected the association of democracy with any particular way of electing governments. To them, it meant simply identity of purpose between a leader and his followers.[32] Democracy required a dictator to discern the people's "true" will—and impose it on them.

Some autocrats held no national elections at all. Like Franco, Mao Zedong did not much care for the voting booth. "Revolution has no time for elections," Fidel Castro quipped—although he did later allow one-party ballots for the legislature.[33] Others held votes without competition: only one candidate contested each seat. In the Soviet Union, dissenters could refuse to vote or cross out the candidate's name. Few chose to do so, at least according to official results. In elections to the country's legislature between 1946 and 1984, the single slate received between 99.16 and 99.95 percent on turnout of 99.74 to 99.99 percent.[34] Stalin, running in 1947 for the Moscow City Council, did even better, winning 131 percent after voters from neighboring districts "added their unauthorized support."[35] Elections involved so little uncertainty that the Politburo once approved the communiqué announcing results two days before the polls opened.[36]

Doing one's "civic duty" was not supposed to require much thought. In one joke from the Brezhnev era, an election official scolds a citizen who has stopped to read the ballot paper. "I just wanted to know for whom I'm voting," the voter explains. "Don't you realize," the official retorts, "this is a *secret* ballot!"[37] Saddam Hussein was shocked to learn that only 99.9 percent had supported him in a referendum he called in 1996. He blamed his party's campaigners for failing to win over the few thousand Iraqis who had voted no.[38]

Such elections had nothing to do with choosing leaders. They had other purposes. First, they served, like parades and rallies, to celebrate the regime. They acted out the unity with the people that dictators asserted. Soviet elections were carnivals, occasions for "fireworks, flypasts and festivals."[39] In the provincial city of Rybinsk on election day in 1963 voters could attend no fewer than 135 concerts.[40] In Gabon, the presidential vote quite literally merged with celebration of the incumbent: President Omar Bongo scheduled the election every seven years on his birthday.[41]

Elections also served as propaganda, especially for the regime's more gullible foreign sympathizers. Leading Western intellectuals praised Stalin's 1936 constitutional reforms that introduced universal suffrage and secret voting.[42] To British socialists Sidney and Beatrice Webb, these created "the most inclusive and equalized democracy in the world."[43] Tanzanian leader Julius Nyerere ruled his country for twenty-one years, running four times for president in uncontested, one-party elections, while hundreds of political prisoners languished in his jails.[44] Despite this record, President Bill Clinton called Nyerere "a pioneering leader for freedom and self-government in Africa."[45]

Reversing the democratic logic, phony elections became a way to control citizens. In democratic ballots, the voters grade their country's leaders. In dictatorships of fear, the leaders grade the voters. A citizen who rejected the people's "unanimous choice" became an "enemy of the people" subject to "arrest or annihilation."[46] Surprisingly, a few Soviet voters did scrawl uncomplimentary messages on their ballots such as "You swine," "Bootlicker," "Croak like a dog," and "We want meat, not deputies." Such deviants were tracked down by the KGB's handwriting experts.[47] Later, penalties were reduced, but even under Brezhnev students who failed to register to vote were expelled from university, closing the path to elite careers.[48]

Phony elections could also identify incompetent state agents.[49] They showed how effective local officials were at getting out the vote. Of course, holding an election is an odd and potentially risky way to evaluate bureaucrats. If this were the only goal, we suspect dictators would instead employ nonpolitical competitions. The Chinese, for instance, use regional growth rates and other indicators to rate officials and scan posts on Weibo (the Chinese Twitter) for reports of corruption.[50] Still, if dictators held elections for other reasons, the light they shed on local agents was a bonus.

Whether by accident or design, this sometimes gave citizens temporary leverage. In the communist world after Stalin, voters used pre-election periods to plead for consumer goods, housing renovations, and other services.[51] In some places—Kenya in the 1970s, Egypt under Mubarak—multiple members of the ruling party were allowed to compete against each other in legislative elections. This incentivized candidates to spend on the campaign—including from their own pockets—in order to access the rich fruit higher up the political tree.[52] Even opposition parties were sometimes permitted a token presence in the parliament. Adventurous regimes—for instance, those of Ferdinand Marcos in the Philippines and Mexico's Partido Revolucionario Institucional (PRI)—went one step further and let outside candidates run for president, on the condition that they lose.

Indeed, allowing an opposition candidate or party to run and then crushing them in a landslide helped to demoralize elite rivals. Even if all recognized the incumbent's fat thumb on the scale, the spectacle remained powerful. As political scientist Beatriz Magaloni argues, Mexico's PRI leaders—with their colorful campaigns, massive rallies, and supermajorities—sought to cultivate a "public image of invincibility."[53] Ambitious regional bosses would see that backing the party was the only game in town. Rivals in the military would also think twice about disloyalty. Dictators who hold semi-competitive elections face fewer coup attempts, as Barbara Geddes and her collaborators have shown.[54]

Old-school dictators had no intention of surrendering power. "We are not going to give up our country for a mere X on a ballot," Zimbabwe's dictator Robert Mugabe warned in 2008. "How can a ballpoint fight with a gun?"[55] Still, some—including Mugabe—occasionally took real risks, allowing credible opposition parties to run. Some did so out of desperation, to avert a cutoff of Western aid. Another motive was to forestall rebellion. To opponents planning armed revolts, multiparty elections offered a peaceful—if narrow—alternative path to power. The odds of victory were slim given the incumbent's command of intimidation and fraud. Still, upsets happened. And if challengers faced low penalties for losing at the ballot box, while a failed revolution meant death, the electoral route might seem worth trying.[56]

Like other political phenomena, elections under fear dictators were tied to violence. Stalin's "Great Terror" in the 1930s "proceeded under the slogan of 'expanding democracy.'"[57] As we saw in chapter 2, executing counterrevolutionary "fiends" and "monsters" was considered good for voter morale.[58] Mugabe kept his gun loaded in case the ballpoint pen acted up. Forced into a runoff presidential election in 2008, he launched a campaign of "electoral cleansing" that killed more than 100 opposition officials and supporters.[59] His opponent withdrew.

Most of the time, though, the violence was comfortably under the surface. Elections "anaesthetized" the public, as Philippe Schmitter wrote of Portugal's Salazar dictatorship.[60] The pageant played out, the drinks were drunk and concerts attended, and then everyone went home.

SPINNING THE BALLOT

For spin dictators such as Chávez and Putin, elections took on a new significance. No longer just rituals to honor the ruler or tune the machinery of terror, they became devices to transform popularity into other forms of power. They served as ratings banks, registering the dictator's mass appeal and converting it into institutional and political advantages. For leaders eager to seem nonviolent, the ballot box even replaced coups and revolutions as the preferred route to the presidential palace. Once there, they cultivated their support and harvested it in voting urns.

Hitler, Stalin, and their like had set out to build "new orders"—communism, Aryan empire, corporatist dictatorship, or something else. Spin dictators claim to be committed to democracy. They just seek to adapt it to local conditions or advance toward it gradually. "Full democracy is for us not the start of the road but the end of the road," Kazakhstan's Nazarbayev explained in 2013.[61] Russia, said President Putin, would "decide for itself the pace, terms, and conditions of moving towards democracy."[62] Indeed, they often seem to be saying, as in Saint Augustine's prayer for chastity: "Lord, give me democracy—just not yet!" Unlike their predecessors, spin dictators feign deference toward parliaments and pretend to await election results in suspense. When challenged, they attack the hypocrisy of Western critics, who act liberal purists while suppressing minority voters and rough-handling protesters. Since Gandhi's death, Putin noted acidly, he had found no other leaders pure enough to talk to.[63]

Rather than admitting their authoritarian ways, recent autocrats have stuffed their constitutions full of political rights. Two legal scholars, David Law and Mila Versteeg, set out to measure this. They counted how many of 15 key liberal rights were featured in the constitutions enacted by 188 countries since 1946. These rights included freedom of the press, freedom of assembly, the right to vote, freedom of movement, gender equality in labor relations, and the right not to be tortured. In 1981, the average constitution in a non-military dictatorship contained 7.5 of these; by 2008, the figure had risen to 11.2.[64] Needless to say, these rights are rarely secure in practice. But abusive dictators can point critics to their liberal-sounding commitments.

And, more than their predecessors, spin dictators try to make their elections look competitive.[65] The classic fear dictators banned opposition parties and candidates. By contrast, spin dictators allow some to run. And they sustain the fiction that the outcome is uncertain. Old-school autocrats typically romped home with close to 100 percent of the vote. Spin dictators prefer less implausible landslides, usually in the 60–75 percent range. According to political consultant Vyacheslav Nikonov, the real challenge in Russia's 2004 election was "not to get too much." Too high a Putin vote would tarnish the result. "Seventy-five would be too much," Nikonov explained. "Seventy-two was just right."[66] President Alexander Lukashenka of Belarus claimed to have adjusted *down* the true level of his 2006 victory from 93 to around 80 percent "because more than 90 would not be perceived well psychologically [*psikhologicheski ne vosprinimaetsya*]."[67] He called the new, lower result a "European" figure.[68]

Such large—but less extreme—victories strengthen leaders' control in several ways. In parliamentary elections, landslides can push government seats above the threshold for constitutional amendments. Often a two-thirds vote is needed. Big parliamentary majorities also help fast-track other legislation. At the same time, sweeping victories produce a temporary psychological effect. They mobilize support behind the dictator's projects and allow him to claim a mandate, while demoralizing the opposition.[69]

In democracy, the mandate winners claim is to enact policies. In spin dictatorship, victors often claim voter backing to remove checks on their power. Time and again, elections have opened the door to constitutional reform. Chávez, elected in 1998, immediately called a constituent assembly to expand presidential authority. His left-wing admirers, Rafael Correa and Evo Morales, did the same. After his 2010 victory, Hungary's Viktor Orbán reshaped the constitutional court, retired hundreds of judges, and—one year after his election—adopted a new constitution.[70] His second reelection, in 2018, conferred what he called a "mandate to build a new era," reshaping culture and society.[71] His team took over hundreds of newspapers, rewrote school curricula, and hounded the Central European University, founded by George Soros, out of Budapest.[72]

In Russia, Putin's landslides heralded repeated power grabs. After his 2004 reelection, he abolished gubernatorial elections. In 2008, term limits prevented Putin from running and voters elected his alter ego, Dmitri Medvedev. Within months, the president's term had been lengthened by two years and the parliament's by one.[73] Putin's 2012 victory triggered a barrage of laws to restrict opposition.[74] After his 2018 reelection, anger over an increase in the retirement age forced a delay. But in early 2020, Putin pushed through constitutional amendments that permit him to run again in 2024 and 2030. (Without the amendments, he would have had to step down in 2024.)

Tyrants like Stalin and thugs like Mugabe linked elections to violence. Spin dictators know visible repression undercuts their claim to popularity. Especially around elections, they try to keep their hands clean. Indeed, as noted in chapter 2, they accuse their opponents of violence. Chávez milked the memory of the 2002 coup against him. Putin portrayed his critics as stone-hurling revolutionaries who assaulted policemen and sought to plunge Russia into chaos.[75] When they do use force, the new dictators pretend to be defending free government.

Fujimori's 1992 *autogolpe* was, he insisted, "vital to assure a legitimate and effective democracy."[76]

Rejecting violence, they rely on various alternatives. For spin dictators, election campaigns are, to quote Russian political consultant Gleb Pavlovsky, "special operations using media technologies."[77] Propaganda and censorship, carefully managed at all times, shift into high gear as a vote approaches. Pavlovsky and his colleagues employed many of the dirty tricks developed in Western democracies and added new ones of their own.[78] Still, where possible, they used legitimate methods to avoid provoking opposition. As Sergei Markov, another Kremlin advisor, explained: "those problems that can be solved democratically are solved democratically. Those problems that cannot . . . are resolved by other means."[79]

From the presidential palace, spin dictators first set the rules and then exploit them. While allowing safe opposition politicians to run, they exclude popular candidates on technicalities. Just as they allow some critical press outlets and then harass them, spin dictators register some opposition candidates and then disrupt their canvassing. They pressure media to ignore them and businesses to withhold venues for meetings, while spreading rumors and misinformation to discredit them.

And they gerrymander shamelessly.[80] Through judicious rule-crafting, Chávez transformed 66 percent of the vote for his constituent assembly into 93 percent of the seats. Singapore's electoral system had a similar effect. Even as the ruling PAP's vote share fell to 60 percent in 2011, it still won 93 percent of parliamentary seats.[81] In Hungary, Orbán's bloc got 90 percent of the single-district seats in 2014 with just 45 percent of the vote.[82] (Combined with party-list results, Orbán's alliance received 67 percent of seats on a 45 percent vote share.)[83]

Almost all electoral systems show some disparity between votes and seats. But the gaps in Singapore, Russia, Malaysia, and Hungary are among the largest in recent history.[84] To secure and preserve such advantages, dictators continually overhaul the procedures. In Russia, every parliamentary election from 2003 to 2016 was held under a different set of rules. The only thing that did not change was the victory of Putin's party.

Orbán also pioneered another ploy: padding the electorate with supporters from the diaspora. After he enfranchised Hungarians in territories lost after World War I, more than 90 percent of the new voters gratefully plumped for his bloc.[85] In 2020, Putin offered citizenship to 10 million ethnic Russians in neighboring countries, perhaps hoping for a similar bonus.[86]

Rather than deal with real opposition politicians, dictators sometimes clone their own. In Singapore, Lee Kuan Yew's successor, Goh Chok Tong, appointed "nominated members" to impersonate a parliamentary opposition.[87] The kind of representatives the *voters* might have chosen, Goh said, were "not the kind of people I wanted to do the check and balance."[88] He did not believe, he added, "in constant bickering and struggling for power."[89]

Other spin dictators have co-opted or simply hijacked existing opposition parties. In Kazakhstan, Nazarbayev's people quietly arranged for a loyalist to take over the previously critical Ak Zhol party in 2011. Ak Zhol's former head moved on to a "cushy government job."[90] In Putin's Russia, the co-opted parties even have a special name: the Communists, the Just Russia Party, and the nationalist Liberal Democratic Party are called the "systemic opposition" to distinguish them from oppositionists who actually oppose the government rather than merely pretending to do so while often voting for its legislation.[91]

The power of spin dictators depends on their popularity. So they monitor it closely. Unlike old-school autocrats, who at most dabbled in sociology, the new ones pore over polling data. Each week, for instance, Putin's Kremlin commissions broad-ranging, national surveys from two firms.[92] It periodically adds regionally representative surveys and secret polls on particular topics.[93] At the same time, the Kremlin's security agency, the FSO (Federal Guards Service), conducts its own heterodox soundings of public opinion—roughly five hundred a year, some with as many as fifty thousand respondents.[94] Like Putin, Fujimori developed an "addiction for polls."[95] His secret police, the SIN, conducted numerous "expensive and sophisticated" surveys and hired an Argentine consultant, Saul Mankevich, to do focus groups. Less formally, Fujimori's security chief, Vladimiro Montesinos, sent teams of

SIN agents to pose as taxi drivers and gather insights from chatting with their clients.[96]

As with elections, spin dictators use poll results to justify power grabs. When respondents back some undemocratic or illegal move, leaders act. Putin surveyed both Crimea and Russia before deciding to annex the territory in 2014.[97] Polling also informed Fujimori's 1992 *autogolpe*. Surveys had revealed disenchantment with the Congress, judiciary, and opposition parties.[98] When the troops moved in, pollsters were right behind.[99] The widespread support they uncovered became an instant PR weapon. He had not staged a coup, Fujimori insisted, he had acted democratically. Democracy, he said, meant "respect for public opinion."[100] Many bought it. In later polls, "a majority of Peruvians expressed the view that the Fujimori government was 'democratic.'"[101]

Like opposition newspapers or bloggers, independent pollsters can be exploited for their credibility. Fujimori's critics attacked the methodology of surveys showing his ratings surge, but their efforts "fell flat."[102] Alfredo Torres of the Apoyo firm denounced Fujimori's action. But he "insisted on the accuracy of his polling" that documented the coup's popularity.[103]

Rafael Correa also spun the data expertly. Catherine Conaghan marveled at how quickly Ecuador's leader "mastered the art of mobilizing public opinion via polls, the media, and the streets in order to disorient, demoralize, and disorganize political opponents." Ecuadorians had never "seen a president so obsessed with, and so skillful at, communications and public relations."[104] Like American presidents, Correa boasted that he was running a "permanent campaign."[105]

That spin dictators invest so much in polling suggests they take results at least somewhat seriously. Of course, they pretend to be statesmen focused on the national interest, not populists with a finger to the wind. But occasionally they admit to monitoring their ratings. "Of course, they bring it to me," Putin confessed in 2013. "I take a look, and—in general—I pay attention to it."[106] For several years after coming to power, Putin expected his soaring approval to crash at any moment, according to Pavlovsky, his Kremlin advisor.[107] He did not think it would last. Yet, thanks to good economic performance early on, and manipulation and the Crimean annexation later, he kept his rating above 60 percent for twenty years.

In democracies, politicians use polls to determine what policies the public favors and tailor their programs accordingly. Spin dictators occasionally do the same. After seeing how unpopular it was, Russia's leaders repeatedly declined to remove Lenin's embalmed body from the Red Square mausoleum.[108] But the main way the new autocrats use polls is quite different: to test the effectiveness of their manipulations. According to Aleksei Chesnakov, another former Kremlin consultant:

> When the media are under control, polls can only show how effectively that control is working. It is as if you have a sick person and you infect him with new viruses and take his temperature. The thermometer reveals how the viruses are affecting him. Polls don't provide a reason to change policy. They just show how many people received your signal.[109]

When popular, spin dictators often permit broad publication of polls. But when their ratings fall, they face a dilemma. Allowing reports of this would threaten their image. But if they restrict publication, citizens may infer that their popularity has dipped. Indeed, they may think the decline *bigger* than it actually is. The best strategy—as always—is to censor in a way that does not look like censorship. The Kremlin-connected Public Opinion Foundation stopped publishing Putin's electoral rating in early 2020 because, it said, it was not yet clear who would challenge Putin in the next election.[110] Strangely, that had never bothered the pollster before. The change came at a moment when other surveys showed Putin's approval falling to a historic low.[111] In 2019, the other Kremlin-connected agency, VTSIOM, had changed its methodology in a way that raised its estimate of public trust in Putin, following Kremlin complaints.[112]

In the run-up to Putin's 2020 referendum on a series of constitutional amendments, well-known pollsters mostly avoided publishing anything on voting intentions, or else reported misleading summaries. For instance, one agency announced that 61 percent of respondents favored the amendments, when in fact that figure included 31 percent who were neutral. After the leading business newspaper, *Vedomosti*, was taken over by a Kremlin ally, it stopped printing survey results. In an act of defiance, two individual pollsters managed to finance independent polls by crowdsourcing.[113]

FRAUD AND ABUSE

Interpreting surveys in unfree societies is tricky, as we discussed in chapter 4. But spin dictators like Putin and Chávez were clearly popular—at some moments extremely so. Even their political opponents admitted it. To quote one critic of the Venezuelan president: "Chávez was beloved—genuinely *beloved*—of millions of poor Venezuelans, and won election after election for a decade and a half . . . his power rested not on violence but on genuine popular affection."[114] Or, as the experts on Russian public opinion Samuel Greene and Graeme Robertson wrote in 2019: "Vladimir Putin is a popular man."[115]

With their high ratings, these leaders could have won elections honestly. And yet, they almost always chose to do so with an element of fraud, sometimes barely hidden.[116] This has puzzled observers. It seems perverse. Chávez, Putin, and the others wanted to be considered democratic, legitimately chosen by the public. They invited international observers to certify their victories. So why stuff ballots, massage the count, and engage in other tricks?

Clearly, the purpose was not just to win. Often they won by large margins. As noted already, while avoiding the 99 percent shutouts of past dictators, the new ones still tend to chalk up impressive victories. Political scientist Alberto Simpser examined all elections in nondemocracies between 1990 and 2007 that appeared to have been manipulated. In half, incumbents defeated their closest rival by 30 percentage points or more.[117] In such cases, fraud was not used to win; rather, it magnified the dictator's lead.[118]

Did they rig as an insurance policy? Dictators might not completely trust the polls that showed them ahead. Such surveys had lulled Nicaragua's Daniel Ortega into overconfidence in 1990 before the voters threw him out.[119] And there were other examples. As one Kremlin advisor said of Putin in 2003: "In his mentality every risk should be mini-mized to zero."[120]

This could contribute in some cases. But in general it seems implau-sible. Again, dictators do not use fraud just to win close elections. And fraud often *increases* risk. From the Philippines in 1986 to Yugoslavia in 2000, dirty elections have triggered uprisings that ousted incumbents.[121] If security were the goal, surely dictators would cover their tracks. In fact, the patterns of voting that Russia's officials reported in 2011 were so bizarre that they became an Internet meme. Protesters put pictures of the statistical distributions on their banners to show how mathemati-cally implausible the announced results were. The head of Russia's elec-toral commission, Vladimir Churov, was nicknamed "The Magician" for his "ability to make votes appear and disappear."[122] Before every elec-tion, credible newspapers reported the Kremlin ordering up high votes from its agents. In 2018, for instance, Putin's top political aide assembled the governors and demanded 70 percent of the vote and 70 percent turnout.[123]

Another possibility is that dictators would prefer to win by a respect-ably narrow margin. Yet, their agents compete to report high votes for the boss, producing a fraudulent landslide. Evidence confirms that over-enthusiastic agents have played a role in Russia.[124] Still, if leaders wanted to reduce their margin, they could easily penalize those who stole "too many" votes. In fact, underachievers are the ones punished.[125] And, as noted, orders for large landslides often come from the Kremlin itself. Fraud might aim to convince bureaucrats that the incumbent will win for sure—and will therefore be in a position to reward or punish them later.[126] But when incumbents are known to be very popular, there is little mystery about the election's outcome.

Many scholars believe that dictators commit fraud—and do so blatantly—to demoralize potential challengers. If elections appear free and fair, opponents have an incentive to try to broaden their support and run. But if the incumbent makes clear he will use fraud to cling to power, mounting a campaign may seem pointless to the opposition and its donors. Similarly, anti-regime voters may not bother to vote when they are sure they cannot change the outcome.[127] And, completing the circle, if opposition voters do not bother to vote, then in the end the incumbent does not need to use much fraud.

This may be the explanation at times. Yet, a popular incumbent *should not need* fraud to demoralize the opposition. Its own low poll numbers should suffice. And, as noted, fraud can itself trigger protests. Surveys confirm that Russian voters dislike vote-rigging.[128] Putin survived the demonstrations against falsification that rocked central Moscow after the 2011 parliamentary election. But the scale of these protests clearly alarmed the Kremlin.[129]

If these arguments are at most partly convincing, why *do* spin dictators resort to fraud? We have already mentioned one possibility: inflated margins help incumbents monopolize power. For instance, they may provide the supermajority needed for constitutional amendments. A clear victory, even if padded by ballot-stuffing, can also reduce the bargaining power of the dictator's backers. After a close result, each could claim to have made a crucial difference—and demand more in return. Even the *opposition* elite and media may be easier to co-opt after a large victory. Rousing the public to revolt will seem harder to them than if the incumbent had just squeaked in, so they may be readier to settle.

A second reason is more paradoxical: even if believed to be partly fraudulent, large victories can still increase the incumbent's legitimacy. That might sound strange. Fraud would seem to undercut the dictator's claim to rule. But, in fact, that need not be the case. On the contrary, fraud may actually increase confidence in the election's outcome.

To see this, consider the following example. Suppose people expect the incumbent to inflate his vote by 10 percentage points. If he uses no fraud at all and wins with 55 percent of the vote, citizens may believe he really got only 45 percent and stole the victory. But if he adds the expected 10 percent to his total and reports 65 percent, the public will be sure he is, in fact, the true winner.[130] Bizarrely, fraud in such cases strengthens faith in the reported result. And that may decrease the odds of a voter revolt. This is not because fraud intimidates the voters by demonstrating the regime's determination to win at all costs.[131] It is because the fraud reassures voters that the "right" candidate won.[132]

At the same time, signs of cheating may not undermine incumbents' claims to be democratic because many citizens in autocracies believe that fraud is common *in democracies too*. Spin dictators often take power after periods of chaotic popular government with their own dodgy elections. Compared to these, the dictator's abuses may look normal or even moderate. And his propaganda will claim that Western leaders also manipulate. Western politicians, themselves, sometimes help sell this message. President Trump repeatedly warned of voter fraud in the United States, to the delight of Russia's pro-Kremlin media, which eagerly reported his statements.[133] On its website, Russia's Central Electoral Commission asserts that in American elections the Pentagon ensures "up to 100 percent turnout of military troops," who vote "under the supervision of commanders." Venezuelan officials also like to advertise Washington's weak points. In the 2000 U.S. Florida recount, according to Venezuela's foreign minister, "the whole world could see how a fraud of colossal magnitude was conducted."[134]

Many citizens in dictatorships seem at least partly convinced. Back in October 2000, pollsters asked Russians whether they thought it possible that the next U.S. presidential election would be rigged. (Note that this was *before* the Bush vs. Gore fiasco.) Excluding the 28 percent who answered "don't know," about as many thought rigging definitely or probably could happen as thought it unlikely.[135] In Venezuela in 2011, the average respondent graded democracy in the United States lower than that in Venezuela.[136] Citizens may recognize the flaws in their own countries' practices and yet assume that similar problems occur everywhere.

Fraud is often seen as dangerous to a dictator's international position. It risks provoking condemnation by international observers and sanctions by foreign governments. But, at least when the rigging is moderate, such dangers are probably exaggerated, as we discuss in chapter 6. In fact, monitors often take a soft line for fear of sparking violent protests or because of their countries' strategic interests.[137] And Western governments tend to avert their eyes so long as leaders go through the motions. For most of them, around the turn of the twenty-first century "the new standard was multiparty elections, not democracy."[138]

Fraud can certainly be dangerous to *unpopular* leaders. The perception that desperate incumbents had stolen elections in Georgia, Ukraine, and Kyrgyzstan set off the so-called "colored revolutions" in the 2000s.[139] But dictators who are popular, having successfully manipulated public opinion, face lower risks. Those who could win an honest election are rarely punished for inflating the margin. Indeed, the conventional wisdom on electoral fraud seems to have the logic backward. Such fraud is generally thought useful to unpopular dictators and superfluous to popular ones. In fact, it is useful to popular ones and often dangerous to unpopular ones—who might be better-off negotiating with opposition forces than risking a coordinated revolt.

CHECKING THE EVIDENCE

As usual, various statistics confirm the shift from fear to spin. To start with elections, these have spread steadily across all types of autocracies over the past two hundred years. In 1820, only one in five nondemocracies had held a legislative or presidential election in the previous decade. By the 1870s more than half had, and on the eve of World War I this had risen to two-thirds. By the late 1930s, the figure was up to three-quarters. After dipping during World War II, the share resumed its climb, reaching 85 percent of nondemocracies in 1961 and 93 percent in 2018.[140]

Of course, this includes the kind of ritual elections held by many fear dictators. But the profile of elections was also changing. Multiparty elections spread across the authoritarian world in parallel with the three waves of democracy, which we mentioned in chapter 1. The proportion of nondemocracies that had held at least one legislative or presidential election in the previous ten years in which an opposition party was allowed to run rose steadily from 14 percent in 1820 to two-thirds in 1933. The share dipped in World War II, recovered a little in the postwar "second wave," but then crashed through most of the Cold War, bottoming out at 37 percent in 1983. Finally, multiparty elections surged again in the age of spin, reaching 78 percent of autocracies in 2018.[141]

We argued that while fear dictators like to report vote shares close to 100 percent, spin dictators prefer victories that look less implausibly one-sided. So, as fear gave ground to spin in recent decades, we should see a fall in extremely high results. And we do. In the 1960s, 1970s, and 1980s, more than half of the national elections held in nondemocracies were won with more than 90 percent of the vote. But the frequency of such lopsided victories then plummeted. By the 2000s, winners were pulling in more than 90 percent of the votes in fewer than one-fifth of the presidential elections and fewer than one-tenth of the legislative elections in nondemocracies.[142]

Using our rules of thumb, we can check that spin and fear dictators do differ as suggested in the scale of their victories. They do. Across all presidential elections since 1946, fear dictators won with more than 90 percent of the vote in 57 percent of cases. Spin dictators did so in 26 percent—most of them early on—and democratic leaders in 1 percent. In legislative elections, the winning party won with more than 90 percent of the vote 55 percent of the time under fear dictators, 16 percent of the time under spin dictators, and not once in democracies.[143] While many fear dictators do not wish to make the result seem credible, spin dictators generally do. The average vote for the winner in presidential elections was 85 percent in fear dictatorships and 72 percent in spin ones.

Do spin dictators manage to fool their citizens? Some evidence on this comes from the Gallup World Poll, which we used already in chapter 4. One question asks: "In this country, do you have confidence in the honesty of elections?" Respondents can answer "yes," "no," or "don't know." We averaged the results across all available polls for each country in 2005–15. A first striking feature of the results is that skepticism about elections is strong even in democracies. Only 46 percent of respondents in the average democratic country (with a Polity2 score of 6 or higher) said they had confidence in the honesty of their country's elections. Even in the highest-rated democracies (with Polity2 of 10), the share was only 58 percent. Recall our point earlier that citizens in autocracies often believe that fraud also occurs in democracies. It seems many in democracies agree.

This skepticism is pretty evenly spread across all types of regime— from 36 percent with confidence in the honesty of elections in the average fear dictatorship to 46 percent in the average democracy. Spin dictatorships are right in the middle, with 41 percent expressing confidence in their country's elections.[144] This is slightly higher than the 39 percent confidence recorded in imperfect democracies (Polity2 of 6–9). In a skeptical world, spin dictators manage to sell their elections to citizens about as well on average as democratic incumbents do in countries like Malawi (Polity2 of 6), Georgia (Polity2 of 7), Mexico (Polity2 of 8), and Estonia (Polity2 of 9).

We mentioned a number of ways spin dictators manipulate elections to ensure their dominance, while still appearing somewhat democratic. One technique is gerrymandering constituencies to magnify the impact of victories. A simple measure of malapportionment—which includes gerrymandering and other procedural tricks—is the gap between the shares of parliamentary seats and of votes that the largest party won in the last election. If the dictator's party gets 60 percent of the seats after winning 60 percent of the votes, there is no gap. If it gets 80 percent of the seats, there is malapportionment of 20 percentage points.

We expect more gerrymandering under spin dictators than under fear dictators, who achieve their one-sided victories through more straightforward exclusions and intimidation. So we should see an increase in the average gap in recent decades. And, indeed, the average malapportionment in nondemocracies, after falling between the 1930s and 1960s, ticks up, surging in the 1990s. Since the 1990s, the average gap between the largest party's seats and votes has been around 10 percentage points.[145] Spin dictators take the prize for gerrymandering. Over the whole period 1946–2015, the average gap for fear dictators is only 1 percentage point. Democratic leaders gerrymander somewhat more, averaging a 6.6-percentage-point gap. But spin dictators come out on top with a gap of 11.1 points. Their prowess in malapportionment leaves even the imperfect democracies in the shade.

As they cut back on force, we argued, spin dictators manipulate the media to ensure popularity and electoral victories. Data compiled by political scientists Susan Hyde and Nikolay Marinov cast light on this.[146] They recorded whether in elections worldwide since 1945 the media had been accused of pro-government bias in the run-up to the vote. As expected, alleged pro-government media bias increases in recent decades—from about 30 percent of elections in nondemocracies in the 1980s to more than 60 percent in the 2010s. Such allegations are common against fear dictators—after all, they *publicize* their censorship, so it is not surprising it gets noticed. But, as suggested, such media manipulation is also common among spin dictators: in 40 percent of the multicandidate elections they held, media bias was alleged. This is far higher than the 10 percent of democratic regimes that faced such allegations.[147]

In sum, spin dictators pretend to be dedicated democrats, although sometimes defending their system as a work in progress. Like almost all autocrats these days, they hold elections, and they allow some opposition parties to run. They tend to win by landslides, but not the implausible shutouts that fear dictators favor. These landslides are supported—and magnified—by media manipulation, gerrymandering, and a dose of electoral fraud. When such fraud is expected, fulfilling the expectation may—counterintuitively—enhance confidence that the "right" candidate won. In an age of political skepticism, many in all systems doubt the integrity of their country's elections. But the citizens of spin dictatorships are no more skeptical than those in most imperfect democracies.

At first sight, it seems that apparently competitive elections should reduce the longevity of autocracies. But, in fact, rulers who hold them tend to last at least as long as those who do not.[148] Spin dictators turn the ballot box into a source of strength. They learn how to control the voting, rather than letting votes control them. Imitating democracy reduces the danger of having to accept the real thing. With their domestic position secure, such leaders face one additional key challenge: what to do about the world beyond their borders.

CHAPTER 6

GLOBAL PILLAGE

In 1948, Stalin decided he had had enough of Josip Broz. Four years earlier, the Yugoslav partisan, known by the nom de guerre "Tito," had driven the Nazis out of his country. So far, he had been dependably loyal to the big man of world communism. But he was showing hints of independence—pushing Yugoslav interests in Albania and Greece and resisting Soviet efforts to infiltrate agents into Belgrade's ruling circles.[1] "All I have to do is wiggle my finger, and Tito will be no more," Stalin boasted.[2]

But he must have been wiggling the wrong finger. Despite multiple assassination plots, Tito survived. One plan aimed to mow down the entire Yugoslav Politburo with automatic rifles in the billiard room of Tito's villa. Another involved poisoning him with pneumonic plague.[3] Stalin seems to have considered a military invasion but decided against it.[4] Moscow expelled Yugoslavia from the Cominform, Stalin's club of communist allies, and imposed an economic blockade.[5]

Cut off and dodging the assassins, Tito had to find a new strategy. He settled on a daring form of openness. Although still committed to communism, he appealed for help to his ideological foes in the West. As the Cold War deepened, the United States was eager to block Soviet expansion and happily backed the renegade. Tito's defiance of Stalin won him everything from heavy artillery to fighter jets.[6] By 1955, Western aid to Yugoslavia totaled $1.5 billion.[7]

But Tito did not stop there. Forced into a gray zone between East and West, he sought allies among the postcolonial states of the "Third

World." Together with President Gamal Abdel Nasser of Egypt and Prime Minister Jawaharlal Nehru of India, he forged the "Non-Aligned Movement" of countries that refused to line up behind either Moscow or Washington.[8] Now an international celebrity, he toured the globe, posing in a tribal headdress in Ethiopia and parading through Tunis under clouds of confetti.

As he reached out to the world, Tito opened his country's borders. To earn hard currency and cut unemployment, he let his citizens work in the West. From the late 1950s, thousands of Yugoslav *Gastarbeiter* took the train to Germany, Belgium, or Sweden and returned several years later in cars bought with their earnings.[9] At home, Tito welcomed European tourists to newly built resorts along his country's stunning Adriatic beaches. The number of vacationers rose from 40,000 in 1950 to 3.6 million in 1967.[10] By the end of the 1960s, they brought in 10 percent of Yugoslavia's foreign currency earnings.

With people flooding across the borders, Tito did not bother to erect the usual communist barriers to information. Kiosks in the capital sold the *Frankfurter Allgemeine* and the *New York Times*.[11] Movie theaters played French, British, Italian, and even Hollywood films.[12] Tito, himself, became a kind of kitsch icon.[13] He appeared in a white safari suit and silk cravat and strolled with a pet leopard on a chain.[14] A luxuriously decadent "Blue Train" transported him among his seventeen villas, palaces, and hunting lodges, where he entertained everyone from Charles de Gaulle to Queen Elizabeth.[15] Sofia Loren and Gina Lollobrigida visited him on the island of Brioni, where he made wine and picked tangerines to send to the country's orphanages.[16] Every year, on Tito's birthday, pristine schoolchildren relayed a baton from his birthplace to a packed Belgrade stadium to present to the patriarch on live TV.[17]

It was all great theater. For the young, he allowed in Western rock music. The Jugoton music label released records by the Beatles, David Bowie, and Deep Purple. When, decades later, a popular uprising overthrew the Serbian strongman Slobodan Milošević, a young Serb named Srdja Popović was among the organizers. Growing up, Popović wrote, he and his friends had "barely felt the yoke of dictatorship, busy as we were with great music from around the world."[18]

In some ways, Tito remained a traditional fear dictator. After breaking with Stalin, he sent tens of thousands of Yugoslav Stalinists to be
tortured and "reeducated" on the island of Goli Otok.[19] Back in Moscow's good graces in the 1960s, he became a master of anti-Western
conspiracies, stealing military and industrial secrets, importing banned
technology, and training PLO terrorists.[20] The celebrity shtick sometimes morphed into a full-fledged personality cult. But most of the time,
his act was more Michael Jackson than Mao Zedong. Tito did not aban-
don the violence that underlay old-school autocracy. But he mixed in
elements that twenty-first-century spin dictators would recognize.

WORLD WARY

Any autocrat's top priority is security at home. But to achieve that, he
must heed dangers and opportunities abroad. This chapter explores
how spin dictators approach the outside world. In this they are less distinctive than in their domestic strategies. After all, they face the same
global realities as overt autocrats. Still, they bring different skills and
techniques to bear. We trace how spin dictators manipulate, deceive,
and co-opt their way around the international arena, ending, as usual,
with a glance at some statistical data.

To twentieth-century fear dictators, the outside world posed a complicated challenge. It could not be controlled like their own countries.
Yet, it could not be ignored. To some, the globe was a battlefield. When
feeling confident, they might invade their neighbors, seeking territory
or prestige. To others, it was an arena of ideological contest. Enlisting
allies, they showed the universal appeal of their model. Still others saw
the world as a source of contaminants. Their instinct was to build a
fortress and pull up the drawbridge. The most ambitious entertained
both expansive and defensive impulses at once. Stalin spread Soviet
power westward and into Asia. But he locked his citizens tight inside
the bloc.

Openness had its advantages. As the world integrated and growth
became more international, a closed economy was doomed to fall
behind. It was not just a matter of trade. More and more profit was as-

sociated with flows of people. Tourism exploded as cheap charter flights cut costs. Between 1950 and 2016, global tourism revenues soared from $2 billion to $1.2 trillion.[21] As Tito realized, sending workers abroad could also generate hard currency. Global remittances of migrant laborers rose from $2 billion in 1970 to $656 billion in 2019.[22] And the emerging world media offered new ways to project a positive image.

Yet, at the same time, openness was dangerous. Allowing foreigners in and one's own citizens out could reveal secrets. The world might see the emptiness of the tyrant's boasts and the squalor of life in his supposed utopia. Porous borders could also let in subversive ideas. And migrant workers might refuse to come home. Besides the embarrassment, that could mean a drain of man- and brain power, slowing development.[23]

The old-school dictators struggled with this dilemma. Few went as far as Tito. When it came to letting people out, policies varied. Some rulers opened their borders to expel "enemies." In their first five years, the Bolsheviks encouraged 1.5–2 million opponents of the revolution to flee.[24] They chartered German steamers to ferry the cream of the intelligentsia into exile.[25] For a while, before settling on their "Final Solution," the Nazis pressured German Jews to emigrate.[26] The downside was that such policies strengthened communities of "enemies" abroad.[27] The Bolsheviks soon began to restrict exit visas; by 1922, it was "all but impossible" to get out.[28] The Nazis found their own horrible alternative.

The question was hard to resolve. Was it better to let opponents "exit," to use Albert Hirschman's language, and exercise their "voice" abroad? Or should the dictator lock them in and silence them at home?[29] In the postwar period, many chose the second course. In communist Eastern Europe, attempted emigration was treason. Albania and Romania punished it with death; East German border guards shot those spotted racing to freedom.[30] In Africa, Equatorial Guinea's deranged dictator destroyed fishing boats to prevent his citizens fleeing by sea. He dug hidden trenches on the land borders filled with wooden spikes.[31] Cuba's authorities also regulated fishing boats to prevent "illegal emigration."[32] In Burma under General Ne Win, agreement of the entire cabinet was required for a citizen to obtain a passport.[33] By the mid-1980s, twenty-one dictatorships had tight exit restrictions, according to scholar

Alan Dowty. These included most of the world's communist states as well as Saddam Hussein's Iraq. Another thirty-six imposed partial or occasional restrictions.[34]

There were four main exceptions. First, some in Latin America, Africa, and the Middle East continued to let their enemies "exit." A powerless opponent in a distant capital could make a handy scapegoat. He could be cast as a treacherous extremist, conspiring against his homeland. Some dictators followed the Bolsheviks' early practice and expelled their critics. Pinochet sent many left-wing Chileans on one-way trips across the border.[35] Others just lacked the capacity to police all crossing points.

Second, some regimes allowed short-term travel for propaganda purposes. Khrushchev, in his early, confident phase, sent carefully vetted "tourists" to improve the Soviet Union's image abroad. In the late 1950s, small groups of elite Russians strolled the boulevards of Naples and Capri.[36] Their true mission was not to admire ruins and consume *gelati* but to serve as "ambassadors of socialism." As the Intourist agency's manual put it, each was expected to "talk about . . . the achievements of his great country with love and warmth."[37]

By this point, Moscow was broadcasting 287 hours of radio programming a week to Western Europe, in seven languages.[38] The tourists added a human touch. But it was all a bit comically overdone. As historian Anne Gorsuch describes, the visitors "literally performed on behalf of Soviet socialism: they played the piano, sang opera, read poetry, and danced."[39] Western guides had to rustle up venues for impromptu lectures and recitals.

The third exception was the granting of exit visas for temporary work abroad. Besides Tito's Yugoslavia, authoritarian regimes in Mexico, Tunisia, Morocco, and later Portugal and Spain signed guest worker agreements with rich democracies.[40] Migrants' hard currency remittances financed the purchase of advanced industrial equipment from the West. Opening the gates to labor also helped avoid unemployment, lowering the risk of unrest.

The fourth exception also had a mercenary motivation. Communist leaders learned that some of their citizens could command a ransom.

From the 1960s, East Germany effectively sold thousands of would-be émigrés to Bonn for around $2,500 a head. By the 1980s, East German technocrats were said to factor such payments—now made in bartered copper and oil—into the country's five-year plans.[41] Romania sold off its own German and Jewish citizens. "Oil, Jews, and Germans are our most important export commodities," Ceaușescu crowed, according to his security chief, Ion Pacepa.[42] In the 1970s, the Soviet Union began letting Jewish citizens emigrate to Israel. Emigrants were charged an "exit tax," supposedly to cover the cost of their education. For those with college degrees, the tax could be as high as 12,000 rubles—about $16,000 at the official exchange rate or eighty times the average monthly wage.[43]

The question whether to let foreigners *in* was just as tricky. Visitors could also serve propaganda purposes. The Nazis welcomed tourists to the Third Reich, hoping they would take home positive impressions. Until Hitler's military preparations were complete, convincing "foreigners that Nazi Germany posed no threat to world peace was vital," writes historian Kristin Semmens. To Goebbels, hosting tourists was "peace work in the purest sense."[44] For Franco too, catering to visitors was "a form of propaganda" that could demonstrate the "legitimacy of the Spanish economic model."[45] Guests were expected to report to their friends back home on "the progress, order, and tranquility of Franco's Spain."[46]

From early on, Soviet leaders sought to turn visitors into advocates. Sympathetic writers, intellectuals, and other fellow travelers were invited to Moscow for charm sessions with Stalin. A list of luminaries— from George Bernard Shaw and H. G. Wells to Pablo Neruda and W. E. B. DuBois—left spouting praise for the dictator and his system.[47] For Soviet citizens, contact with such foreigners almost always meant arrest during the purges of the 1930s.[48] Stalin's fear of contamination was so intense that, after the Nazi defeat in 1945, more than 1.5 million repatriated Soviet prisoners of war were either shot or sent to the Gulag.[49] Given heavy wartime losses, the executions were a bizarre sacrifice of manpower that could have helped in economic recovery.

Khrushchev allowed in some Western tourists, and under Brezhnev the flow increased. The main goal was, again, propaganda—to undercut hostile portrayals of Soviet life. Trips were carefully planned. In each city, the KGB trained teams of Young Communist League activists to interact with young visitors.[50] The number of tourists rose from 486,000 in 1956 to more than 6 million in 1988, although two-thirds of these were from other Soviet bloc countries.[51] Yet, fear of foreigners did not disappear: for example, a mass circulation book published in 1963 was titled *Spies Disguised as Tourists*.[52] The West, Brezhnev reminded Soviet youth in 1966, "was and still is a treacherous and dangerous predator."[53]

Besides propaganda opportunities, Western tourists brought profits. Most dictators in warm countries held their noses and admitted rich holiday-makers while defending against ideological or cultural contamination. The conservative colonels who seized power in Greece in 1967 banned miniskirts and sociology lectures.[54] Yet, eager for cash, they tripled the number of inbound tourists between 1966 and 1973. Still, there were limits. Regulations barred entry to "any foreigner, dirty and ragged or wearing long hair."[55]

Besides tourists, another kind of border-crosser was the foreign student. In 1968, fewer than half a million were studying abroad worldwide. By 2017, the number was 5.3 million—and about half were from nondemocracies.[56] Here, too, dictators faced a dilemma. Study in the West meant access to Western technology, knowhow, and even political secrets. Research suggests that countries that send more youngsters to college in advanced economies tend to grow faster, especially if students major in technology-oriented fields.[57] But such students could be turned into revolutionaries or even recruited by foreign intelligence. Back home, they might spread dangerous ideas. Such fears were not unreasonable. Economist Antonio Spilimbergo found that dictatorships that send more young people to study in democracies become more likely to democratize.[58]

Admitting foreign students also had costs and benefits. With well-designed courses, a dictator could shape the thinking of future political elites around the world. The friendships such visitors forged with their hosts could be exploited later. However, students from democracies might spread liberal ideas. And, with their knowledge of the outside world, they could expose the dictator's lies.

In the Soviet Union, Stalin's xenophobia won at first. Fewer than 900 foreigners were studying in the USSR in 1947, the vast majority from North Korea and the Balkans.[59] But later Moscow aspired to educate the postcolonial elite. Khrushchev built the People's Friendship University and named it after Patrice Lumumba, an assassinated Congolese independence leader. Soviet embassies handed out scholarships throughout Africa, Asia, and Latin America. By 1988, there were more than 80,000 foreign students in the USSR.[60] For those who could not come, Moscow helped open universities in Guinea, Mali, Ethiopia, Tunisia, and elsewhere, sending Soviet professors to teach. In 1980, there were 935 such professors working in Algeria alone.[61] Washington, alarmed, stepped up its own efforts.

As he was wooing Third World students, Khrushchev also negotiated an agreement on exchanges with President Dwight Eisenhower in 1958. Under it, Americans were accepted to programs in Soviet universities. But the numbers were small. Even in 1988, only about 1 percent of foreign students in the USSR came from capitalist countries.[62] In return, a few Soviets got to study in the United States. They were all KGB-vetted and often KGB officers themselves. One, Boris Yuzhin, became a double agent for the FBI. Others—including Aleksandr Yakovlev and Oleg Kalugin—later surfaced among reformist supporters of political change under Gorbachev and Yeltsin.

Other authoritarian states also sent students to the United States. In the late 1970s, OPEC dictatorships, flush with oil dollars, invested a few of them in overseas education. The number of Saudis at U.S. universities grew ninefold between 1970 and 1980. The number of Iranians grew even faster, to more than 50,000.[63] However, it was the Iranian students who stayed home who had a bigger impact on their country's history, participating in the 1979 revolution that brought Ayatollah Khomeini to power. Under the Islamic regime, few students made it to the United States.

While ambivalent about foreign tourists and students, almost all fear dictators shared an aversion to foreign media. Most blocked intrusions when they could.[64] The Soviets worked to jam the broadcasts of Radio Liberty, the BBC, and others that beamed programs over the Iron

Curtain. They had limited success: by the end, surveys suggest 50 percent of Soviet citizens were listening to Western broadcasts at least once a week.[65] In Spain, Franco jammed the signals of Radio España Independiente, a station established outside the country by the communist resistance. Pinochet's government in Chile blocked programming from Moscow and Havana. Cuba did its best to drown out Florida radio stations from across the straits.[66] Up until his death in 2016, Uzbekistan's dictator Islam Karimov banned foreign media.

Authoritarian rulers reacted with horror to the satellite TV revolution of the 1980s. Soviet foreign minister Andrei Gromyko threatened to shoot down any Western satellites that tried to broadcast into Soviet territory.[67] (Fifteen years earlier, the KGB had raised alarms about propaganda crossing the border on hot air balloons.)[68] Cuba banned the homemade receivers that were sprouting across Havana in the early 1990s.[69] Iran and Saudi Arabia prohibited satellite dishes in 1994, but enforcement proved difficult. By 1998, 60 percent of Saudis had receivers.[70] Iran managed to slow penetration but could not stop it. In 2003, there were almost 150,000 illegal dishes in just Tehran.[71] But by then the threat from satellite TV had been overtaken by that of the Internet.

Cross-border flows of people and information were of huge concern to twentieth-century dictators. But their most important interactions with the outside world were, of course, military. Some started devastating wars. Hitler marched into Poland; Mussolini invaded Ethiopia; Kim Il-Sung attacked South Korea; Saddam Hussein sent troops against Iran and later Kuwait. Others, however, avoided major external conflicts. For instance, the Duvaliers in Haiti, Robert Mugabe in Zimbabwe, and Augusto Pinochet in Chile did not attack their neighbors. They focused their brutality on their compatriots.

Short of direct military action, powerful dictators fought proxy wars, either supporting other states in aggression or aiding insurgencies.[72] Stalin backed Kim's war in Korea. Later, Moscow helped the North Vietnamese invade the South and Arab states attack Israel. Soviet aid financed insurgents such as the African National Congress in South Africa and the Sandinistas in Nicaragua. Starting under Mao, Beijing championed anti-Western guerrillas around the globe, training an estimated 20,000 insurgents from at least nineteen African countries be-tween 1964 and 1985.[73] Fidel Castro also sent Cuban troops to help guer-rillas in Africa.

Another way dictators struck at their enemies was by supporting ter-rorism. Tito and Ceauşescu both befriended Arafat's PLO. One top KGB general, Aleksandr Sakharovksy, even claimed to be the inventor of airplane hijacking.[74] Moscow and its allies financed, trained, and ad-vised Marxist groups such as the Red Brigades and the German Red Army Faction that attacked Western targets. East Germany, according to its last interior minister, was "an Eldorado for terrorists."[75]

SPINNING THE GLOBE

Compared to their predecessors, spin dictators are much more comfort-able with a world of porous boundaries. In fact, that is also true of most remaining fear dictatorships. Apart from North Korea and Eritrea, few still cling to isolation. But spin dictators turn their openness into a weapon.

Most today embrace international travel. In 2019, 61 million foreign-ers visited Hungary, 26 million Malaysia, 24 million Russia, 19 million Singapore, and 9 million Kazakhstan.[76] And their citizens toured the world: Russians made 45 million trips, Hungarians 25 million, Kazakh-stanis 11 million, and Singaporeans 11 million.[77] Spin dictators are also open to foreign study. In 2018, 84,000 Kazakhstanis, 62,000 Malaysians, 58,000 Russians, 24,000 Singaporeans, and 13,000 Hungarians were en-rolled in universities abroad.[78] Meanwhile, foreign students poured in. In 2018, there were 262,000 of them in degree programs at Russian uni-versities. There were 101,000 in Malaysia and 52,000 in Singapore.[79]

These days, blocking foreign information at the border is extremely hard. Some remaining fear dictators still try, at least to some extent. North Korea does its best to jam radio broadcasts from the South.[80] Access to the Internet is tightly restricted and short-wave radios banned. China blocks the websites of leading Western publications such as the *New York Times*, the *Economist*, the BBC, *Le Monde*, and *Yomiuri Shim-bun*.[81] It is also thought to jam incoming Chinese-language radio broad-casts.[82] Iran tries to block Persian-language satellite programming.[83]

By contrast, spin dictators treat foreign media much as they do domestic publications. They usually tolerate those that appeal only to the intellectual fringe. Rather than ban them, dictators limit their audience. We saw in chapter 4 how Lee Kuan Yew handled Western newspapers and magazines. When these "misreported or slanted stories" about Singapore, he demanded that they publish his reply verbatim. If editors refused, the government capped the number of copies they could sell in the country.[84] "We have to learn to manage this relentless flood of information so that the Singapore government's point of view is not smothered by the foreign media," Lee wrote in his memoir.[85] In poorer countries, expense or language barriers could ration access to foreign news services as effectively as censorship, without reflecting badly on the government. In richer countries, friction—making access to foreign news channels inconvenient—often did the trick.

When it comes to military conflict, some spin dictators have an aggressive image. When the economy falters, they adopt a nationalist tone. Some—including Putin and Chávez—berate the West and portray their country as a "besieged fortress." Yet, with one or two exceptions, data on wars and military disputes suggest the bluster is for show. Most of the wars and military disputes fought in recent decades were initiated by the remaining fear dictators or democracies. We return to this toward the chapter's end.

The relative peacefulness of spin dictators might seem surprising. An external crisis can rally a ruler's base behind him. And such leaders do engage in frequent brinkmanship. Hugo Chávez kept tensions simmering on the border with Colombia, periodically escalating and de-escalating for dramatic effect. He broke off relations with Bogotá four times, only to quietly resume them in return for "very soft concessions."[86] Yet, for obvious reasons, actual military conflict is dangerous. It can end a dictator's rule as easily as prolong it.[87] Militarism also clashes with the technocratic image spin dictators seek. As Putin shows, spin dictators *can* use old-fashioned military force at times. But Putin is the exception that proves the rule. With a massive nuclear arsenal, he knows no country will risk invading to overthrow him. At the same time, sensitive to the rules of spin, he has kept official Russian casualties in Ukraine and Syria low, using proxy forces and mercenaries where possible, and has declared all military deaths a state secret.[88] Most other spin dictators *do* worry about the risk of defeat and prefer other, less dangerous methods of exploiting the outside world.

What methods? Dictators adapt homegrown techniques of manipulation and deception to the international arena. They try to shape public opinion abroad with the kind of modern propaganda they use on their own citizens. And they recruit and corrupt Western elites much as they co-opt their own educated class. They have two key aims: to strengthen their regime at home and to defend against threats from abroad.[89] Let's consider these in turn.

FOREIGN ASSISTANTS

To spin dictators, the outside world is a source of allies, expertise, and other resources to help build their image and spin the news at home. They tap into these in a number of ways.

Collect foreign endorsements. Signs of international respect reinforce the ruler's claim to competence. So spin dictators collect foreign endorsements and display them proudly to their citizens. Lee Kuan Yew's Western visits became occasions for fawning reportage. *Straits Times* correspondents mined dinner speeches and toasts for nuggets of praise. To U.S. president Lyndon Johnson, the paper's readers learned, Lee was "a patriot, a brilliant leader, and a statesman of the new Asia."[90] To British prime minister Margaret Thatcher, he was a "uniquely outstanding" politician with a "supremely fresh approach."[91] To President Reagan, Singapore under Lee was a "dazzling success."[92] "The simple fact is that when you think about Singapore," New Zealand prime minister David Lange was quoted as saying, "you think about Lee Kuan Yew."[93] To drive the point home, Singaporean journalists milked anonymous sources for flattering gossip. "You don't know how glad these people are to talk to a visiting leader like your Prime Minister," one "journalist who covers foreign relations" confided during Lee's 1985 Washington trip. Unlike other leaders, Lee was ready to "go right into the heart of issues."[94] In the Internet age, dictators use websites to advertise such endorsements.

That of Nazarbayev's Presidential Library, for instance, displays complimentary comments from a roster of presidents, prime ministers, and UN secretaries-general.[95]

Another way to show the world's respect is by hosting summits. Putin spent almost $400 million chairing the 2006 G8 meeting in St. Petersburg.[96] The results awed his country's state-controlled TV anchors. The summit was the most important held in Russia since Stalin, Churchill, and Roosevelt met at Yalta, said Channel One. "It is Russia that is setting the economic agenda," NTV gloated.[97] Nazarbayev lobbied hard for Kazakhstan to chair the Organization for Security and Cooperation in Europe (OSCE)—and eventually won. He then used this as validation at home. "Our achievements are being recognized around the world," he told a crowd of students and workers in 2008.[98]

Besides the praise of foreign leaders, dictators seek the approval of international experts. Nazarbayev had a particular penchant for Nobel prize winners. By 2018, twenty laureates had trekked to the Kazakh capital for discussions.[99] Their tactful words were eagerly quoted by domestic media. In 2010, Finn Kydland, an economics laureate, praised Nazarbayev's reaction to the global financial crisis, calling Kazakhstan's situation "much better than in most countries." Fellow prize winner Robert Mundell said Nazarbayev's countermeasures had been "absolutely correct."[100]

A third source of endorsements is celebrities. Of course, many politicians are drawn to entertainers. But spin dictators skillfully cultivate and harvest such relationships. Appearing at rallies or sports events with Western actors and athletes, they deflect criticisms aimed at them by the celebrities' home governments. The message is simple. Western officials might seek to bully the dictator and his country. But the Western public—and its most glamorous representatives—rejects their leaders' attacks.

Tito had hobnobbed with movie stars. Richard Burton and Elizabeth Taylor visited his Adriatic villa. The Welsh actor even portrayed Tito in a World War II adventure film.[101] Today's spin dictators do the same. Putin befriended French actor Gérard Depardieu and action hero Steven Seagal.[102] Hugo Chávez won visits from actors Sean Penn, Danny Glover, Tim Robbins, and Kevin Spacey, as well as model Naomi Camp bell.[103] Singer Harry Belafonte announced in one of Chávez's broad-casts that "not hundreds, not thousands, but millions of the American people ... support your revolution."[104] Diego Maradona, the Argentin-ian soccer star, appeared in a Caracas stadium amid red balloons and fireworks to urge Venezuelans to let Chávez remove term limits and run again.[105] Even Hungary's Viktor Orbán found his own action movie star, Chuck Norris.[106]

Besides presiding at summits, dictators show their international clout by winning the right to host sports events such as the Olympics. As Orbán's global reputation dimmed, his athletics diplomacy went into overdrive. In 2019, Hungary hosted the world championships of table tennis, fencing, canoe sprinting, pentathlon, and Formula 1 racing. "It was one of our main goals to bring as many international sporting events to Hungary as possible," Orbán's foreign secretary explained.[107] As in other overseas endeavors, dictators use corruption to get their way. U.S. prosecutors accused Russia and Qatar of paying millions of dollars in bribes to FIFA officials to secure the 2018 and 2022 World Cup soccer tournaments. Putin later awarded one FIFA official, Gianni Infantino, Russia's Order of Friendship.[108]

Get help from abroad in faking democracy. Having manipulated public opinion, spin dictators hold elections to register their popularity, as we saw in chapter 5. Foreign election observers help to legitimize these votes. But how to keep them from denouncing the fraud that frequently accompanies the balloting?

Sadly, it often does not take much. On various occasions, Western election observers have pulled their punches despite evident irregulari-ties.[109] They may disregard red flags because of a country's geostrategic importance or because they believe it is moving in the right direction. Or observers may be misled by sophisticated deception.

Still, with independent monitors incumbents always face some risk. In the last two decades, dictators have developed a convenient work-around. They create what political scientist Alexander Cooley calls "zombie" election-monitoring groups.[110] The mission of these is pre-cisely to legitimize flawed elections. With official-sounding names and international membership, these groups appear at election time in countries with dubious reputations.[111] After the balloting, they appear on state media certifying the dictator's victory.

The Commonwealth of Independent States-Election Monitoring Organization (CIS-EMO) was founded by a far-right activist, Aleksei Kochetkov, in Nizhny Novgorod, Russia, in 2003. Since then, it has observed dozens of votes in the former Soviet republics plus a few in Turkey, Poland, and France. Its reports almost always endorse the elections of Russia's allies and contradict criticisms of the OSCE observers when both are present.

Some incidents suggest less than total impartiality. Before the 2004 Ukrainian presidential election, one of the group's "observers" spoke at rallies for the Kremlin-favored candidate.[112] In 2005, Kochetkov was arrested in Moldova, where he had gone to observe another election, after he reportedly got into a fight with a local citizen.[113] (He said the case against him was fabricated.) In August 2008, Kochetkov followed Russian troops into Georgia to set up an international press center in occupied South Ossetia.[114]

Kochetkov's group managed to persuade a number of European political bigwigs to serve on its missions, including former prime ministers of Poland and Slovakia and European Parliament members from Italy, Poland, Latvia, France, and Germany.[115] This gave its pronouncements a credibility with domestic audiences that an exclusively Russian team would have lacked. The missions also offered the organizers opportunities to befriend members of the European elite—another tactic we return to below.

Latin America has its own Council of Electoral Specialists of Latin America (CEELA). A shadowy organization, without a website and with unclear funding, CEELA was created in the mid-2000s as a "leftist counterpart to electoral observation agencies sponsored by the Organization of American States (OAS)," in the words of the Nicaraguan publication *El Nuevo Diario*.[116] It was staffed by former electoral officials and judges from various Latin American countries, mostly those with left-wing governments. The group has monitored national elections in Venezuela under Chávez and now Maduro, pronouncing them legitimate.[117] When the Sandinista leader Daniel Ortega rejected OAS observers in 2008, he welcomed those of CEELA, calling them among "the most suitable we could count on."[118] The Nicaraguan opposition disagreed. CEELA, the Liberal Constitutionalist Party charged, was "an instrument of the electoral fraud that the ruling Sandinista National Liberation Front is forging."[119]

Get help from abroad in arresting dissidents—for "nonpolitical" offenses. At home, spin dictators prosecute opposition leaders for nonpolitical offenses to conceal their true motivation. In much the same way, they exploit Interpol—the international police organization—asking it to issue "Red Notices" against their enemies abroad. Circulated globally, these notices request all states to arrest the target and extradite him to the source country.[120]

Interpol's rules require it to reject applications that have a "political character."[121] So, just as they do at home, dictators accuse their enemies of nonpolitical crimes. Hugo Chávez pursued numerous individuals on trumped-up charges. Patricia Poleo, a prize-winning investigative journalist, was granted asylum in the United States after facing threats in Venezuela.[122] Yet, on a trip to Peru she was detained because of a Red Notice charging her with murder. The main witness later confessed he "had been paid to fabricate his evidence."[123] Poleo's father, Rafael, also a well-known journalist, received his own Red Notice for comparing Chávez to Mussolini and suggesting he might share the latter's fate. As the communications minister saw it, Poleo Senior had "asked for an assassination"—a serious crime.[124]

Russia under Putin also exploited this process, hounding opposition members for supposedly nonpolitical offenses.[125] One political activist, Petr Silaev, received a Red Notice for "hooliganism."[126] Another democratic campaigner, Anastasia Rybachenko, was accused of "participating in mass riots," apparently for marching in a pro-democracy protest.[127] Putin also used Red Notices against troublesome foreigners like the investor William Browder, who lobbied Western governments to punish the Kremlin for the death in custody of his lawyer, Sergei Magnitsky.[128] Although Interpol does often reject politicized requests, it may arrest the target first before evaluating such arguments, thus enabling dictators to harass and intimidate their opponents on a global scale.

Cooperate with the West—while denouncing and exploiting it. Tito was a master of playing both sides. For a while, he sold his "communist renegade" image to the United States for generous helpings of military and economic aid. But at the same time he sent spies to pilfer Western intellectual property and help terrorists like Italy's Red Brigades.[129] By the 1970s, he was not so much nonaligned as a double agent, and one dependent on borrowing and stealing from the West. "Without Western money and technology," he told Romania's Nicolae Ceauşescu, "there wouldn't be any Communist society in our countries."[130]

Today's spin dictators turn Tito's double game into an art. They participate in Western institutions in order to extract benefits, exploiting the design flaws and weaknesses of these bodies. They trade with Western countries, while denouncing them. They recruit networks of corrupt partners in the West, simultaneously pursuing concrete goals and eroding Western cohesion. At the same time, they make hypocritical speeches about the West's hypocrisy.[131]

Take Hungary's Viktor Orbán. In the 2010s, he was simultaneously among the European Union's biggest beneficiaries and its harshest critics. As of 2018, only Poland received larger net payments from the European budget.[132] That year, Brussels sent Hungary about 5 billion euros—around 4 percent of the country's GDP.[133] These funds helped Orbán entrench himself. He used the money, according to the *New York Times*, to build a "patronage system that enriches his friends and family, protects his political interests and punishes his rivals."[134]

One pot of cash was tied to land. Brussels allocated agricultural subsidies on the basis of acreage. So the Hungarian leader sold thousands of acres of state land to friends and associates in "cut-rate deals." The owners then received tens of millions of euros in subsidies.[135] One beneficiary was Lörinc Mészáros, the old friend of Orbán's turned billionaire media baron whom we met in chapter 4. Mészáros and his family ended up with more than 3,800 acres of state land.[136] Other EU money made its way to Orbán's cronies "via overpriced procurement contracts."[137]

Yet, even as the funds flooded in, Orbán heaped abuse on his fellow European leaders. Faced with an influx of migrants, they were "like an old woman who is shaking her head in shock."[138] All he heard from

Brussels was "European liberal blah blah."[139] The continent was "staggering towards its own moonstruck ruin."[140] Billboards throughout Budapest urged: "Let's stop Brussels."[141]

For a long time, the EU hardly responded. Having grown from a small club of like-minded West European states, it had few procedures to restrain disruptive members. In the European Parliament, Orbán could exploit his party's importance to the center-right coalition, the European People's Party (EPP). Although Orbán's party, Fidesz, accounted for only 5–7 percent of EPP seats, it could make a crucial difference in close votes.[142] In the European Council, Orbán could simply threaten to veto—as he did in late 2020, blackmailing his colleagues by blocking the continent's vitally needed post-pandemic recovery package until they weakened a proposal to discipline countries like his that abused the rule of law.[143] Defying the EU's principles, Orbán removed democratic checks on his power while deriding the Western politicians who failed to stop him. And he did this with the help of EU money.

In Venezuela, Chávez used the Organization of American States (OAS) as a backdrop for his international grandstanding—while calling for its dissolution. The OAS, he said, was "a corpse that must be buried."[144] Despite the organization's commitment to defending democracy, it did little to oppose Chávez's monopolization of power in Venezuela until 2010, when its Commission on Human Rights issued a critical report.[145] In part, OAS inaction reflected Chávez's use of petrodollars and cheap oil to co-opt a phalanx of small Caribbean island states. These constituted a "diplomatic shield . . . against international criticism" and made it hard to assemble the two-thirds majority necessary to suspend an OAS member for "interruption of the democratic order."[146]

With the United States, Chávez played a similar double game. He baited President Bush pitilessly for the amusement of his base. Bush was a "donkey," "an ignoramus," "a coward," "a killer" "a drunk," "a liar," "a psychologically sick man," or simply "Mr. Danger." He was "more dangerous than a monkey with a razor blade."[147] At the UN in New York in 2006, Chávez claimed to detect a lingering smell of sulfur the day after the U.S. president had spoken.[148] One might get the impression Venezuela's dictator hated the *yanquis*. And yet, throughout Chávez's tenure, it was trade with the United States that kept his country afloat. American importers bought most of Venezuela's oil, paying Caracas billions of dollars.[149] Most of the country's imports came from the United States.[150] As journalist Francisco Toro put it, Chávez "railed against gringo imperialism all morning, then spent all afternoon selling those same gringos oil."[151]

Turkey's President Erdoğan relied on NATO for ultimate deterrence against Russia and Iran. He welcomed NATO Patriot missile batteries along the border with Syria in 2012 to defend against a possible chemical weapons attack.[152] Yet, knowing that the alliance has no mechanism for excluding a member state, he openly defied it, buying an S-400 air defense system from Russia that was incompatible with NATO hardware.[153] He violated the UN's arms embargo against Libya.[154] And he used the right of all NATO members to veto proposals to blackmail his partners, threatening to block the alliance's plans to defend the Baltics and Poland unless it backed his offensive against Kurdish fighters in Syria.[155]

Putin used Russia's seat in the OSCE to try to neuter that organization's pro-democracy mission. The organization's consensus rule-making gave each member leverage. At the organization's 2011 summit in Vilnius, for instance, "Moscow vetoed all the significant year-end documents."[156] Together with Nazarbayev and the leaders of five other former Soviet states, Putin introduced a proposal in 2007 to end the autonomy of the OSCE's election-monitoring group. He threatened to veto proposed OSCE protections for human rights advocates and pro-democracy NGOs.[157] In the end, the Western powers only deflected this challenge by co-opting Nazarbayev with the 2010 OSCE chairmanship.

Get international help with political dirty tricks. A sad fact about spin dictators is how many of the tricks they use originated in Western democracies.[158] Gerrymandering, for instance, got its name from a nineteenth-century governor of Massachusetts, Elbridge Gerry, who approved a peculiarly shaped voting district in 1812. The political use of libel suits surfaced during the U.S. civil rights struggles of the 1950s, as southern leaders deployed them to silence critics.[159] Indeed, the U.S.

South was a hotbed of innovation. Long before Putin or Erdoğan, officials there were harassing activists with ostensibly nonpolitical prosecutions. They charged Martin Luther King Jr. with tax evasion and perjury and arrested others for disturbing the peace, trespass, and disorderly conduct. The state of Virginia pursued the NAACP for alleged violations of legal ethics.[160]

The world's sleazy operators continue to look to the West for inspiration. As the Kremlin's political gurus set about recrafting constituencies for their 2016 election, they studied recent U.S. practice.[161] In the early 2000s, the Kremlin smeared Putin's rivals by claiming they took money from Jews, homosexuals, and a famous Russian Ponzi scheme organizer.[162] Sound familiar? In the 1972 U.S. race for the Republican nomination, Roger Stone, a young aide to Richard Nixon, donated to Nixon's rival, Pete McCloskey, in the name of the "Young Socialist Alliance" and then used the receipt to paint McCloskey as a left-wing stooge.[163]

In Singapore, British colonial practices prefigured much of Lee Kuan Yew's system, from its severe libel law to its Internal Security Act, which permits indefinite preventive detention on national security grounds. The island's Sedition Act, based on a 1948 colonial ordinance, makes it criminal to attempt any act that would "have a seditious tendency," to utter any "seditious words," or to distribute or import any "seditious publication"—all without defining "seditious."[164]

Not just techniques but also expertise often comes from abroad. Orbán's idea to seek votes with vicious attacks on the émigré philanthropist George Soros was the brainchild of two Washington consultants. One of them, Arthur Finkelstein, was a legend in U.S. conservative politics, having started out advising Nixon. Opponents called him the "Merchant of Venom."[165] Finkelstein also worked for a string of Israeli Likud politicians including Ariel Sharon and Benjamin Netanyahu, as well as postcommunist leaders from Albania to Ukraine.

Dictators seeking help with "black operations" can buy assistance from firms based in rich democracies. Hollywood movie mogul Harvey Weinstein hired an Israeli private security firm founded by former Mossad agents to investigate a woman who accused him of rape.[166] Orbán reportedly hired this same firm, Black Cube, to discredit Soros's

NGOs. It secretly recorded conversations with Soros employees and leaked misleading excerpts to the press.[167] Two Black Cube employees were arrested in Romania in 2016 for allegedly staging cyberattacks against that country's anticorruption prosecutor.[168]

Of course, most dictators in economically developed countries have their own, homegrown political tricksters. Putin has gone through a series of them without having to resort to Americans. Indeed, he sends his own "political technologists" or propagandists to help allies fight their own tough elections or protests; recent beneficiaries include Viktor Yanukovych in Ukraine in 2004 and Alexander Lukashenka in Belarus in 2020.[169] Russian political operatives have also been spotted advising candidates throughout Africa.[170] Chávez and Correa hired the best on the Latin American market.[171] And most dictators use their own security services rather than retired Mossad agents to surveil domestic opponents. Still, when they need to, autocrats can find a range of eager helpers in the West.

MAKING FRIENDS AND INFLUENCING PEOPLE

Besides enlisting foreigners to help dominate their own countries, spin dictators adapt homegrown techniques to fend off threats from abroad. The greatest danger is that trigger-happy Western powers might intervene to restore democracy. As the world modernizes, human rights organizations and liberal groups in the West grow more insistent, as we will see in the next chapter. A robust defense requires military preparation and economic resilience. But, at heart, the battle is over ideas. To fight it, spin dictators take their manipulation to the international arena. They work to reshape global public opinion and co-opt Western power brokers.

Shaping global opinion. Most autocrats know Western elites would like to remove them. But leaders in democracies depend on their citizens. They must get public support for military or economic actions to oust a foreign ruler. Spin dictators work to prevent this.

But how? One way is to win over Western publics. If dictators can do that, governments will hesitate to attack. That can be a tall order, especially in well-informed, educated societies. Despite hobnobbing with global celebrities and topping polls at home, most dictators win few Western fans. In 2007, Pew surveyed respondents in 47 countries about their opinions of selected leaders. Among dictators, China's Hu Jintao did best, with 42 percent expressing "some" or "a lot" of confidence in him in the median country. Hugo Chávez came next with 36 percent, then Vladimir Putin with 32, and Iran's Mahmoud Ahmadinejad with 19. In each case, far more respondents expressed "not much" or "no confidence." For comparison, 50 percent had confidence in Germany's Angela Merkel.[172]

A second option, almost as effective, is to turn Western publics against their own governing elites—in particular, those tempted by foreign military action. That means supporting anti-elite movements. Russia's Putin has become the guardian angel of right-wing populists across Europe, providing moral and sometimes financial support.[173] Hugo Chávez also had his network. Three of his former advisors helped set up Spain's left populist Podemos party.[174]

At home, dictators can co-opt or censor critical media, while broadcasting their own messages on state-controlled TV. They have fewer levers to influence public opinion abroad. Although certain ambitious fear dictators attempt to censor media in the West—more on that later—spin dictators are more realistic. What they can do is use their propaganda skills on an international scale. One way is to create their own global TV channels to compete with the BBC and CNN.

In 2005, Putin launched the international station Russia Today, later shortened to RT. It aimed, the Russian president said, to "break the Anglo-Saxon monopoly on . . . global information streams."[175] RT's programming brought together anti-Western gadflies (Julian Assange of Wikileaks had his own show for a while) with established Western journalists (like the former CNN heavyweight Larry King) along with young, bilingual recruits.[176] These included embittered former journalists for Western networks who had been laid off as Western media cut back foreign coverage.[177] By 2015, the channel claimed an audience of 700 million people in 100 countries, although some accused it of inflating its figures.[178]

RT simultaneously seeks to boost Putin's image and to fan populist sentiment in the West. It portrays Putin as a responsive, popular leader.

And it exaggerates—and, where possible, inflames—tensions between Western publics and elites, who are portrayed as cynical and bellicose. Besides targeting Western viewers, the channel also appeals to those in non-Western countries who are angered by U.S. interventions. Its presenters specialize in a kind of anti-imperial pathos.

The station does not pretend to be independent. RT's CEO has a phone on her desk with a direct line to the Kremlin, used, in her words, to "discuss secret things."[179] But the channel enhances its credibility with relatively objective and detailed reporting on matters in which Russia's authorities have no stake. By 2010, the Kremlin claimed to be spending $1.4 billion annually on international propaganda, much of this via RT. Electronic media, Putin said in October 2014 with surprising frankness, had become "a formidable weapon that enables public opinion manipulations."[180]

Venezuela's Hugo Chávez founded his own network, Telesur, with Cuban, Uruguayan, and Argentine backing.[181] By 2015, it was "the largest 24-hour television news channel in Latin America."[182] According to its disillusioned former director, Aram Aharonian, Telesur quickly became a "political instrument," providing "propaganda as rolling news" to serve Chávez's agenda.[183] The central point in that agenda was limiting U.S. intervention in South America. Chávez's communications minister, Andrés Izarra, who later headed Telesur, described the network as resisting "imperialism in any of its expressions."[184]

Telesur sought to cultivate a region-wide, left-wing public opinion that could combat U.S. influence and discourage right-wing coups. The network proved itself when Chávez's ally, President Manuel Zelaya of Honduras, was overthrown in 2009. Telesur broadcast the protests of his supporters and interviewed the deposed leader, helping rally international opinion against the junta.[185] The next year, when protesting police officers imprisoned Ecuador's President Correa in a hospital, killing five people, Telesur filmed Chávez urging Ecuadorians to "neutralize the coup attempt" and the army to rescue Correa.[186] Ecuadorian troops later came to the president's defense.[187]

Unlike the propaganda organs of old-school dictators, these channels do not push an ideological, clearly distorted version of events. Rather, they imitate modern Western programming, with high-quality production and catchy formats.[188] Instead of indoctrinating, they suggest alternative narratives, distract from awkward truths, and spread doubt about the West. "Question more," is RT's marketing slogan.[189] In style, they also differ from the global TV stations of modernized fear dictators such as China's CGTN (formerly CCTV) and Iran's Press TV. Both of these suffer from the censorship and cruder propaganda that characterize these countries' official media at home. A repressive undercurrent mars their patriotic message. Both have broadcast confessions of prisoners extracted through torture.[190]

Spin dictators back up their international programming with other public relations efforts. To buff his image, Chávez set up a Venezuelan Information Office in Washington, headed by Deborah James, an experienced anti-globalization activist.[191] The office placed ads in popular magazines, fielded a "rapid response team" of writers to challenge articles critical of Chávez, and sent employees to conferences, demonstrations, and college campuses to hand out literature.[192] They educated grassroots sympathizers, James said, on "ways they can work against US intervention."[193] Other leaders bought PR services on the market. After Kazakhstan's police killed fourteen striking workers in the mining town of Zhanaozen, President Nazarbayev hired former British prime minister Tony Blair to advise on handling the press.[194] Acknowledge the human rights issue, Blair told him, but insist on the need to go "step by step."[195] Between 2000 and 2016, the Russian authorities spent an estimated $115 million on foreign PR contracts, according to *PRWeek*.[196] Spending increased after the Russian annexation of Crimea and interference in the 2016 U.S. election blackened Putin's image.

To exploit the reputations of Western publications, dictators like to place disguised advertisements in them. Kazakhstan paid CNN International to run infomercials that glamorized the country. In style and format, these were hard at first to distinguish from CNN's own reports.[197] An insert titled "Russia beyond the Headlines" and paid for by the Russian government appeared in Western newspapers such as the *Daily Telegraph*, *Le Figaro*, *Süddeutsche Zeitung*, *La Repubblica*, and the *Washington Post*.[198] In each country, it mimicked the language and design of the host paper.[199]

Another homegrown tactic later used abroad is the manipulation of social media. Russia's Internet Research Agency (IRA) first surfaced in 2013 with a brief to support the pro-Kremlin Moscow mayor, Sergei Sobyanin, and attack his challenger, Aleksei Navalny.[200] In 2016, its trolls used similar techniques on U.S. voters. They posted messages online, set up tens of thousands of bots, bought political ads using invented or stolen identities, and even organized rallies in the United States.[201] In Europe, too, the IRA sought to influence elections, posting in German, French, Spanish, Italian, Estonian, Bulgarian, and Romanian.[202]

Yet another way to influence Western opinion—and foreign policymakers—is to fund think tanks. According to the *New York Times*, Kazakhstan, Hungary, and Singapore have all contributed to the Washington-based Atlantic Council.[203] Kazakhstan also contracted with the Institute for New Democracies, a partner of the Washington-based Center for Strategic and International Studies.[204] The U.S. State Department recently urged U.S. think tanks to "disclose prominently on their websites" any funding received from foreign governments or state-owned companies.[205] Sometimes dictators set up their own deceptively named think tanks in the West. Kazakhstan established a Eurasian Council on Foreign Affairs in Brussels.[206] A Russia-linked Institute of Democracy and Cooperation appeared in Paris in 2008, and another office with the same name opened in New York (it closed in 2015). These denied direct Kremlin involvement but were founded by a Moscow lawyer, Anatoly Kucherena, who served on the public council of the Russian Interior Ministry.[207]

Co-opting Western elites. At home, spin dictators try to co-opt their elite. In a similar way, they set out to win friends in foreign capitals. The methods range from personal charm to financial incentives and operate at multiple levels.

Throughout his career, Lee Kuan Yew worked to befriend influential foreigners. In 1968, while serving as prime minister, he took a "sabbatical" for a month at Harvard. There he got to know opinion makers such as political scholars Richard Neustadt and Henry Kissinger and economists John Kenneth Galbraith and Paul Samuelson.[208] The association lasted all his life. In 2013, Harvard's Belfer Center published a book of deferential interviews with the "grand master." Kissinger wrote an admiring foreword.[209]

Lee appealed with his intellect and good manners. Others offer additional inducements. Putin has actively cultivated present and former European leaders. After Gerhard Schröder stepped down as German chancellor, the Russian president quickly found him a job on the Nordstream gas pipeline consortium. Later, Schröder added the chairmanship of the Russian state oil company Rosneft.[210] Putin offered positions in Russian energy companies to former Italian prime minister and EU Commission president Romano Prodi, former French president Jacques Chirac, and former U.S. commerce secretary Donald Evans, although all declined.[211] The Russian president vacationed in Sardinia with Silvio Berlusconi, the former Italian prime minister. Various members of the British House of Lords had connections to Russian circles.[212] In 2020, the London *Times* reported that fourteen ministers in the British Conservative government and two members of the Parliament's Intelligence and Security Committee, charged with investigating Russian political interference, had themselves "accepted donations linked to Russia."[213]

Such highly placed friends helped Putin in various ways. Berlusconi stood up for him when he was attacked over human rights and the war in Chechnya and even proposed admitting Russia to the EU.[214] Later, he defended Putin's seizure of Crimea and sampled wine with him at a Crimean vineyard—to the outrage of the Ukrainian government.[215] While still Italian prime minister, Prodi helped normalize the scandalous expropriation of the oil company Yukos and the jailing of its owner, backing the purchase of Yukos assets by the Italian energy companies ENI and ENEL.[216] Schröder, who claimed to view Putin as an "impeccable democrat,"[217] helped Gazprom's CEO lobby the German economics minister.[218]

To boost Kazakhstan's image, Nazarbayev formed an International Advisory Board of European political VIPs in 2010. They met in Astana, the Kazakh capital, several times a year.[219] The board included "four former presidents, two former prime ministers, six former foreign ministers (including from the UK, Germany, and Italy), a former European commissioner (Benita Ferrero-Waldner), and other politicians and prominent public figures."[220] According to the German magazine *Der Spiegel*, each was paid an annual fee "in the seven figures."[221]

Another way to buy influence abroad is by funding Western political parties. Generally, this is not legal—which actually makes the contributions *more* effective: the dictator earns not just gratitude but blackmail material. Such funding is not new in itself. The Soviets, for instance, secretly funneled money to communist politicians and parties in the West. What is new is the non-ideological, opportunistic way dictators enlist political allies.

A number of Europe's right-wing parties have been accused of taking Russian funds. In 2014, a small bank with links to the Kremlin loaned 9 million euros to the French National Front party of Marine Le Pen.[222] Shortly afterward, Le Pen publicly endorsed the referendum in which Crimea residents approved Russian annexation. In 2018, an aide to the leader of Italy's populist Lega party discussed with Russians a deal to channel tens of millions of dollars to his party via discounted fuel sales.[223] The deal apparently fell through, but Italian prosecutors opened a corruption investigation. Putin later praised the Lega leader, Matteo Salvini, with whom he claimed to be in "constant contact." Salvini frequently denounced EU sanctions against Russia.[224] An associate of Putin's reportedly pledged 1.5 million euros to Edgar Savisaar, the leader of Estonia's Center Party, in 2010.[225] Savisaar said the contribution was to renovate a Russian Orthodox church.

Short of paying them directly, the simplest way to influence Western politicians is to hire lobbyists. This is completely legal and nothing new. In 2018–19, authoritarian governments spent up to $172 million on lobbying and PR in the United States alone.[226] Putin hired the Washington firm Ketchum, whose staffers, according to Reuters, "urged the State Department to soften its assessment of Russia's human-rights record."[227] Chávez's image was protected by the law firm Patton Boggs.[228] Even as he insulted the *yanqui* imperialists and sheltered Julian Assange in his London embassy, Ecuador's President Correa paid a boutique PR firm $6.5 million to ingratiate him with Washington insiders.[229] The firm's activities included paying "protestors to wave signs and shout slogans" during a shareholders meeting of the oil company Chevron, with which Correa had a dispute.

FEAR VS. SPIN

Many of the techniques spin dictators employ abroad are also used by today's fear dictators—and even by democrats. Indeed, in many ways, foreign affairs have themselves become more a matter of spin, and less of fear, than in the past. The ultimate decider remains military force. But it is used less often. And deception, manipulation, and image—although always important—have become more central.

These days, almost all states have porous borders, crossed each month by staggering flows of people, products, and data. Leaders of all descriptions hire PR firms and lobbyists to protect their interests and reputation in the West. Even during the Cold War, some fear dictators had their man on K Street. Republican operative Paul Manafort hit the news for helping the thuggish leader of Ukraine in the 2000s. But before that he represented so many African strongmen—from Sani Abacha of Nigeria to Mobutu Sese Seko of Zaire—that rivals called his firm the "torturers' lobby."[230]

China, Libya, and most of the Gulf monarchies donate to Washington think tanks.[231] And fear dictators also cultivate foreign leaders, current and former. The Advisory Council of China's sovereign wealth fund counts among recent members one former prime minister of Pakistan, one former Canadian foreign minister, and one former German chancellor—the globetrotting Gerhard Schröder, who, as we saw, has also graced the boards of Russia's state-owned companies.[232] Like spin dictators, high-tech fear mobilizers such as Saudi Arabia's MBS use trolls and Twitter bots to infiltrate social networks and promote their global image.[233]

Still, there are differences. Most follow from the aim of spin dictators to blend in with democracies rather than define an alternative model. Abroad as at home, they act the part of ordinary, democratic leaders. As noted, they tend to be less bellicose than fear dictators. But they are dangerous in their own way. They participate in predominantly Western institutions such as NATO, the EU, and the OECD and exploit these from inside, eroding their cohesion. As "good democrats," they enroll in international forums that promote free government. In Warsaw in 2000, for instance, 106 countries signed a charter to advance democracy worldwide. Almost half the then-existing spin dictators enlisted in this Community of Democracies, compared to only 12 percent of fear dictators. With such a diverse membership, it remained largely inactive.

Some fear dictators try to censor press coverage of themselves worldwide. MBS seems to aspire to this. The murder of *Washington Post* journalist Jamal Khashoggi and the 2017–21 blockade of Qatar, in part to squeeze Al Jazeera, both appear aimed at that goal.[234] Earlier, Iran's clerics asserted global censorship power with the fatwa against Salman Rushdie. China, under Xi Jinping, has used economic leverage to punish tweets about Hong Kong and Tibet and to pressure the publisher of *China Quarterly* to purge articles from its online archive.[235] North Korea hacked into Sony's computers to block the release of an unflattering comedy about its leader.[236]

By contrast, spin dictators do not obsess over foreign coverage. Nazarbayev's team was flustered at first by the 2006 release of Sacha Baron Cohen's comedy *Borat*, which portrayed Kazakhstan as an anti-Semitic, misogynistic backwater. But they soon recovered. As one Astana-based PR specialist put it, officials quickly refocused on "how to exploit such an unexpected spotlight on the country."[237] The foreign minister later thanked the film for boosting tourism: visa applications, he said, had jumped tenfold.[238]

CHECKING THE EVIDENCE

We mentioned that spin dictators fight wars and initiate military disputes far less often than do fear dictators. This is based on data on interstate wars from the Center for Systemic Peace's Major Episodes of Political Violence (MEPV) data set and on militarized interstate disputes from the Correlates of War (COW) project. Let's consider these in turn.

Between 1980 and 2015, the only spin dictatorships to fight wars were Russia, which invaded Georgia in 2008, and Azerbaijan, which fought

Armenia in Nagorno-Karabakh in the early 1990s.[239] During the same period, seven fear dictatorships fought a total of five wars.[240] While the average fear dictator was at war in one out of every 33 years, the average spin dictator was at war in only one out of every 164 years. The rate for spin dictators was actually lower than that for democracies (one out of every 114 years).[241] In some of these wars, a dictator was attacked and so had to fight back. But if we include only wars the country initiated, the frequency for spin dictators is an even smaller fraction of that for fear dictators.[242]

What about military conflicts short of war? Here, we use COW's measure of "militarized interstate disputes," which are defined as "all instances when one state threatened, displayed, or used force against another."[243] Examples include harassing another country's planes with fighter jets, firing warning shots, placing troops on higher alert, violating borders, and threatening military actions.

Between 1980 and 2014, the last year in the data, spin dictators initiated 63 such military disputes, averaging one every 7.7 years. In the same period, fear dictators initiated 421, or one every 2.9 years. Again, the rate was lower for spin dictators than for leaders of democracies, who initiated one dispute every 5.6 years.[244] Putin turns out to be an exception. He initiated more military disputes—21 in all—than any other spin dictator in our data.[245]

We should note one important issue. We are classifying dictators in part by the extent of their domestic repression. But what if it is external military conflict that makes autocrats more repressive at home? In that case, we might see this pattern of results for the opposite reason. Rather than fear dictators adopting aggressive strategies abroad, it might be that autocrats who get drawn into wars, for whatever reason, tend to rule by fear at home.

In fact, a quick look at the seven fear dictators who fought wars during this period suggests this was not generally the case. Six of them—Isaias Afwerki, Ayatollah Khomeini, Deng Xiaoping, Le Duan, Meles Zenawi, and Saddam Hussein—were well-known for repressive policies *before* their countries became involved in the given war, not always at their choosing. The remaining one—Hun Sen—came to power after war had already begun. Still, even if we drop him, that changes the results only very slightly: the average fear dictator was at war in one out of every 35—instead of every 33—years, a rate more than four times higher than that of the average spin dictator.

In short, the evidence suggests that dictatorships have changed not just in how they maintain control at home but also in how they deal with the outside world. As the balance has shifted from fear to spin, dictators have become less bellicose and more focused on subtle manipulation. They seek to influence global opinion, while co-opting and corrupting Western elites. Rather than threatening Western alliances and institutions with frontal attacks, they exploit them from inside. But what explains this global change? We turn to that question in the next chapter.

PART II

WHY IT'S HAPPENING AND WHAT TO DO ABOUT IT

CHAPTER 7

THE MODERNIZATION COCKTAIL

If dictatorship has been changing, that prompts the question why. What has led strongmen around the world to dress up in suits and act like democrats? Why have most stopped executing their rivals in football arenas, packing dissidents by the thousands into prison camps, and terrorizing the public with loyalty rituals and personality cults?

The shift from fear to spin fits into a broader historical trend. For centuries, as Steven Pinker has shown, violence has been receding.[1] Statistics on everything from wars, homicides, and torture to animal abuse show long-term declines. Most explanations focus on slow-moving forces. Sociologist Norbert Elias credited what he called "the civilizing process." From the Middle Ages, as population density rose and commerce spread, norms emerged to reduce interpersonal friction. Pinker, citing historian Lynn Hunt, emphasized Enlightenment ideas and a broadening of empathy fueled by the growth of printing, literacy, and the reading of novels.[2]

All this makes sense. But the reshaping of dictatorship since the 1980s requires a more proximate explanation. In the preceding decades, autocracies had been becoming, if anything, more violent.[3] As we saw in chapter 2, the share of dictators with more than ten political killings a year peaked in the cohort that took power in the 1980s. Then something changed to reverse the dynamic.

One possibility might be the falloff in wars. Both interstate and civil conflicts have become rarer in recent decades.[4] Military conflict has a brutalizing effect, so that could in theory be part of the story. But, in fact, we find a sharp drop in state political killings even among dictators who were *not* involved in any wars at home or abroad.[5]

So what triggered the shift in forms of autocracy? We think the answer lies in a cocktail of interconnected forces related to economic and social modernization combined with globalization. For short, we call this the "modernization cocktail." It makes life harder for violent dictatorships and nudges some into democracy. But others find ways to adapt and survive, substituting deception and manipulation for terror.

The modernization cocktail has three ingredients: the shift from industrial to postindustrial society, the globalization of economies and information, and the rise of a liberal international order. The end of the Cold War—itself partly a result of these forces—catalyzed the process. We will use the rest of this chapter to spell out the details. But first, a note on how the cocktail works.

It operates both within countries and at the international level. The shift to postindustrial society occurs within countries. Work, education, information technology, and social values all change. Sometimes this internal dynamic prompts a dictator to replace terror with manipulation. But as more and more countries modernize, the effect of the cocktail leaps to the international level. It becomes an emergent property of the system. Trade and investment flows knit economies together, while global media link their news cycles and informational fields. International movements and coalitions of states form to promote the new values— most importantly, the respect for human rights. Sometimes these global influences drive even dictators with less advanced economies to replace fear with spin.[6] Table 7.1 summarizes the cocktail's elements.

Our argument adapts—and revises—the "modernization theory" prominent in Western social science since the 1960s. We agree that economic development promotes political change.[7] But we add two key points. First, the global dynamic causes some dictatorships that are less modern to democratize "early" because of pressures generated by modernization elsewhere. The level of development matters not just within countries but worldwide. And, second, the same forces that lead some to democratize prompt others to adapt and preserve their dictatorship in a new guise. Although economic development creates pressures for

TABLE 7.1. The Modernization Cocktail

Shift from industrial to postindustrial society
Increased role of creative, information-rich work
Spread of higher education
Replacement of "survival" by "self-expression" values
Rise of new communications technology
Economic and informational globalization
International integration of trade and finance
Emergence of global media
Rise of a liberal world order
Growth of international human rights movement
Spread of international law and institutions promoting human rights and democracy

genuine democracy, some autocrats manage to delay the transition by faking it. Eventually, further modernization undermines even this option. But, expertly executed, spin dictatorship can delay this reckoning for a while. As a result, although the link from development to democracy still holds, it is less obvious and immediate than simple versions of modernization theory suggest.

Evidence of the modernization cocktail at work can be found in statistical data, historical patterns, and in what dictators themselves have said about the challenges they faced. We turn to these now.

POSTINDUSTRIAL STRENGTH

The first ingredient in our modernization cocktail is *the postindustrial transition*. Since the start of the Industrial Revolution in the eighteenth century, economic life has changed—and, with it, society and politics. People sometimes imagine this as a single, sweeping transformation that, in one blow, turned traditional communities into modern ones. But that is not how it actually happened. In fact, change came in two phases.

In the first, people moved from the countryside to cities, leaving farms and workshops for factories. Subsistence agriculture and crafts gave way to mass production of standardized goods. Societies of small, mostly self-sufficient villages linked up into complex, interdependent

systems. The second phase began after World War II in the more economically advanced countries. In this period, a "postindustrial society"
replaced "industrial society," as manufacturing lost ground to services
and—most importantly—to creating and processing information.

Many writers—from sociologist Daniel Bell to business analyst Peter
Drucker and futurist Alvin Toffler—have described how this second
phase changed life in Western democracies. But fewer have considered its
influence on authoritarian states. Those who did usually assumed modernization would lead straight to democracy. As we have said, it does push
in that direction. Yet, rather than simply giving in, dictators can adapt.

But before getting to that, let's consider what goes into the postindustrial transition. This consists of several elements. First, *the nature of
work changes.* By the late twentieth century, industry was running out
of steam as a driver of economic growth in the West. Further advance
required not just more factories with longer assembly lines. It required
inventing smarter machines and smarter ways to use them, along with
new products that no one yet realized they needed. In short, it called for
innovation.

Industry's share in output was shrinking. By the 1970s, service-sector
jobs outnumbered working-class ones in the United States.[8] In what
remained of industry, fewer worked in factories.[9] Robots were taking
over the rote tasks. Those humans still employed used mostly brain, not
muscle. They were computer operators and technical analysts, process
engineers and programmers, designers and marketers, accountants and
managers.[10] They experimented, problem-solved, gathered data and
interpreted it.

Meanwhile, the growing service sector demanded ever more creativity. Of course, there were plenty of janitors and hamburger cooks. But
they worked alongside hordes of consultants, architects, engineers, doctors, academics, artists, designers, entertainers, athletes, and
journalists—occupations that fall within what urbanist Richard Florida
calls the "creative class."[11] By 2015, this class had 52 million members in
the United States—about one-third of the workforce.[12] In Western Europe, the share ranged from 26 percent in Portugal to 54 percent in
Luxembourg.

From financial products to health treatments and musical performances, the things these professionals produced required deep knowledge and original thinking. Their value came from the information they embodied more than from the materials embodying it. With digitization, informational goods could be reproduced without limit and transported at virtually no cost. That meant enormous economies of scale.[13]

For authoritarian leaders, the changing sources of growth posed a dilemma. In the old days, Stalin and Mao could double GDP by forcing peasants into factories, at great human cost. In that phase, the coerced reallocation of labor was a brutal but effective way to raise output. Despite the inefficient organization of Stalinist industry, labor was still more productive in the factories than on peasant farms.[14] But once progress required imagination, Stalin-style coercion no longer worked. You could not order people to have ideas.[15] Bureaucratic discipline stifled innovation, which almost by definition requires breaking rules. Ideology was even more deadly.

The pioneer of spin dictatorship, Lee Kuan Yew, understood this already in the 1990s. As he told an interviewer:

> With today's high technology you just can't squeeze the maximum productivity out of advanced machinery without a self-motivated and self-governing work force. What is the point of having $100 million worth of machinery in a factory if you can't get 95 percent productivity or more out of it through the use of quality circles, involving engineers in the productivity process, as the Japanese do? . . . One simply cannot ask a highly educated work force to stop thinking when it leaves the factory.[16]

A *highly educated workforce*? That was another issue. As the nature of work changed, so did the importance of education. In the industrial age, capitalists had lobbied the state to set up primary schools.[17] Factory owners needed well-trained workers. Basic literacy and arithmetic came in handy, but character and discipline mattered more. Peasant recruits had to learn to sit still for hours, performing boring, repetitive tasks. They had to become attentive, respectful, "punctual, docile, and sober."[18] Of course, those traits were also politically useful. To please the government, primary school teachers mixed in a dose of deference and patriotism. Even secondary schools helped with socialization.

But higher education is something else. As countries leap to postindustrial production, they need a new kind of human capital. For basic industrial jobs, primary and secondary schooling are sufficient. But competing with the advanced economies requires college-educated workers.[19]

The problem for autocrats is that higher education is intrinsically linked to freedom of thought. College courses are almost impossible to sanitize completely. Critical thinking tends to slip out of control. Those who examine electrodes on Monday may turn to electoral procedures on Tuesday. Analytical, communication, and organizational skills can be used for many purposes—including coordinating antigovernment protests.[20] At the same time, cutting-edge research is by nature international, which means it contains hidden messages about the outside world. All this makes university education much harder for dictators to manage.

Consider one example. The early 1950s in the Soviet Union was a time of intense conformism. Stalin had unleashed a vicious "anti-cosmopolitan campaign," arresting Jewish doctors and executing them as spies. At Moscow State University, the undergraduate course in law consisted mostly of "massive ideological brainwashing," as one alumnus later recalled. Although an idealistic communist, this student found himself plagued by questions about the party line. What sowed these doubts? Some dissident's pamphlet? In fact, the source was the classic texts of Marx, Engels, and Lenin, each of which, he wrote, "contained a detailed criticism of their opponents' theses, a system of counter-arguments and theoretically sustained conclusions."[21] These works did not turn Mikhail Gorbachev into an anticommunist. But—perhaps more dangerous to the old order—they taught him to think.

Why did clear-sighted dictators not simply close the universities? Mao and Pol Pot tried this for a while. Pinochet reduced college admissions by a third.[22] But to others the economic costs seemed too high. To boost growth and defend against military threats, dictators needed graduates—so they churned them out. In 1950, almost no one in the average nondemocracy had a bachelor's degree. By 2010, 6 percent of those aged fifteen and older did. In some authoritarian states, the rate exceeded that in the average democracy (9.5 percent)—and even that in the high-income democracies (14.6 percent).[23] In Singapore by 2010, 30 percent of those fifteen and older had completed higher education. Among Russians, the figure was 25 percent, and among Kazakhs, 14 percent. In all three countries, the proportion in 1950 had been under 2 percent.[24]

As numbers rose, dictators sought to limit the damage. One possibility was to restrict advanced study to technical disciplines. That had been the Soviet plan. "Education," Stalin told British novelist H. G. Wells, "is a weapon the effect of which is determined by the hands which wield it."[25] He and his successors sought to wield it in the interest of stability. Mathematics and physics were developed to world standards, while social sciences were replaced by Marxism-Leninism.[26]

Yet, even in the sciences something still went wrong. In the 1950s, physicist Andrei Sakharov helped to develop the Soviet hydrogen bomb. In the 1960s, he developed a conscience. Again, his doubts came not from some freethinker's pamphlet but from his work itself. In 1961, the Soviet leader, Nikita Khrushchev, decided to resume atmospheric nuclear testing. To Sakharov, that threatened a slide toward thermonuclear war, the horrible consequences of which he understood. Exploiting his international reputation, he published in the West a passionate plea for global cooperation. In it, he warned against the "infection of people by mass myths, which, in the hands of treacherous hypocrites and demagogues, can be transformed into bloody dictatorship."[27] The "Father of the Soviet H-bomb" became the father of the dissident movement.

Even for those who avoided politics, technical education provided skills to circumvent state controls. The Soviet bosses frowned on Western rock music, with its subversive lyrics. But bootleggers made records of foreign hits by cutting grooves into discarded X-ray plates.[28] In the 1970s and 1980s, Estonians bought microchips in Finland that enabled their TVs to receive Finnish programming. A shortage of thermometers broke out after someone found a way to improve TV antennae using mercury.[29] The knowledge that enabled technicians to serve the authorities also helped them cut through censorship.

Old-style repression was ill-suited to these challenges. In the 1930s, Stalin might have denounced Sakharov as a Japanese spy and executed him in the basement of the Lubyanka Building. But then what breakthroughs could be expected from the next generation of nuclear physicists?

In fact, it was even worse. Dictators had to contend with a third, related challenge. The spread of higher education and creative work catalyzed another disruptive development. This one had to do with the *beliefs and values* of citizens.

Since the early 1980s, a team of researchers led by Ronald Inglehart, a professor of political science at the University of Michigan, has been studying how values evolve. Every five years or so, the team polls representative samples of adults in close to 100 countries, containing almost 90 percent of the earth's population. Their World Values Survey, which we encountered already in chapter 1, asks about everything from sexual norms and personality traits to religion and national pride. The results show striking common patterns. As countries develop economically, their citizens undergo dramatic shifts in values and beliefs. These come at somewhat different times and income levels in different places—the onset and speed of change reflect local religious and other historical legacies. Still, the same evolution seems to occur everywhere.

A first change happens as countries industrialize. The traditional culture of the village, centered on religion and customary family roles, gives way to "secular-rational" values, based on man-made laws. Impersonal procedures become more important than personal relationships, which no longer work so well in a society of dense cities and large factories. This need not threaten authoritarian rulers. They are, after all, the ones who make the laws and procedures.

But a truly revolutionary shift occurs in the second phase. In the agricultural and industrial eras, most people struggle to survive. But in the postindustrial age, as affluence spreads, people think less about making ends meet and more about the quality of life. They start to see their social identity as a personal choice rather than an accident of birth—and as something they should "express." People become more tolerant and individualistic, less deferential, and more eager to participate in civic and political settings. In Inglehart's terms, "survival values" give way to "self-expression values."[30]

This does not happen to everyone at the same time. Although industry shrinks in the postindustrial age, it does not disappear. Indeed, for a while, agricultural and industrial workers remain a majority. If their prospects worsen, they may retreat to "survival" and "traditional" values. Often, manual workers resent the information economy professionals with their postmodern perspectives. The early postindustrial era is a time of culture clashes. And these may intensify as the industrial-era majority shrinks toward minority status.

A final aspect of the postindustrial transition concerns *technology*. The new, information-rich work requires novel communications media. The most dramatic example is the emergence of the Internet. To understand its impact, consider how online messaging differs from earlier methods.

The key media of the mid-twentieth century—radio and television— were "one-to-many." A single source broadcast to a large audience. Such media favor centralized politics, whether autocracy or elite-dominated democracy. They helped old-school dictators project strength and spread fear. "It would not have been possible for us to take power or to use it in the ways we have without the radio," Goebbels insisted.[31] One-to-many media are also relatively easy to censor. By controlling a few studios, one controls virtually all broadcasting.

By contrast, the Internet is "many-to-many." Many users can interact simultaneously with many others. At almost no cost, they can create their own content, effectively building their own media. At the same time, the Internet is searchable. Thanks to Google and similar programs, needles leap out of any haystack. And, for those with broadband connections, sending and receiving messages (including photos and videos) is virtually costless even over immense distances.

These features affect politics in several ways. The Internet's many-to-many interface, searchability, and low marginal transmission cost make it uniquely suited to form networks of like-thinkers. Indeed, the networks form themselves as individuals use the web. Meanwhile, the Internet makes blanket censorship difficult. It is no longer enough to control a few central studios. Besides facilitating creative jobs, the Internet incubates the creative class. It is where the informed get to know each other. Fear dictators triumph through divide and conquer, by isolating opponents and crushing them. The Internet brings them together.[32]

These four changes—in the nature of work, education, social values, and communication technology—make it harder for dictators to dominate citizens in the old way. Harsh laws and bureaucratic regulations provoke furious responses from previously docile groups. These groups have new skills and networks that help them resist. At the same time, violent repression and comprehensive censorship destroy the innovation now central to progress. Eventually, the expansion of the highly educated, creative class, with its demands for self-expression and participation, makes it difficult to resist a move to some form of democracy.

But so long as this class is not too large and the leader has the resources to co-opt or censor its members, an alternative is spin dictatorship. At least for a while, the ruler can buy off the informed with government contracts and privileges. So long as they stay loyal, he can tolerate their niche magazines, websites, and international networking events. He can even hire the creative types to design an alternative reality for the masses. This strategy will not work against a Sakharov. But Sakharovs are rare. With a modern, centrally controlled mass media, they pose little threat.

Co-opting the informed takes resources. When these run low, spin dictators turn to censorship, which is often cheaper. They need not censor everything. All that really matters is to stop opposition media reaching a mass audience. And here the uneven dynamics of cultural change help. Early in the postindustrial era, most people still have industrial-era values. They are conformist and risk averse. The less educated are alienated from the creative types by resentment, economic anxiety, and attachment to tradition. Spin dictators can exploit these sentiments, rallying the remaining workers against the "counterculture" while branding the intellectuals as disloyal, sacrilegious, or sexually deviant. Such smears inoculate the leader's base against opposition revelations.[33]

As long as the informed are not too strong, manipulation works well. Dictators can resist political demands without destroying the creative economy or revealing their own brutality to the public. But as the informed become numerous, accumulating skills and resources, developing their media, and spreading their values deeper into the population, it gets harder to prevail even with the help of expert spin. And then there are the cocktail's international effects, which can undercut even a successful domestic strategy.

NETWORK EFFECTS

The second element in the modernization cocktail is *economic and informational globalization*. As more and more countries make the postindustrial transition, connections proliferate among their economies and media. These elevate modernization from a process within individual states to a global force. Contacts among the informed of different countries generate networks of liberal opinion and activism.[34] Such networks coordinate pressures on the remaining dictatorships—including those that are less modern. Old-style autocrats become increasingly vulnerable.

Economic integration has reshaped the world since 1945. Many dictatorships were sucked into this process. As World War II ended, most of these consumed almost all they produced. The median nondemocracy exported just 10 percent of the goods it made and spent just 8 percent of its income on imports. By the mid-2000s, it was exporting 43 percent of output—about twice the pre-World War II peak—and spending 33 percent of GDP on imports.[35] The global production chains of multinational corporations crisscrossed the continents. By 2019, such firms employed 82 million people outside their home countries, many in autocracies.[36]

As they raced into product markets, dictators also plugged into the circuits of global finance. Already in the 1980s, many were borrowing mind-boggling sums. The OPEC oil price hikes showered hundreds of billions of dollars onto a few oil-rich states, which deposited their winnings in Western banks. These then loaned much of the money to developing world dictatorships. Debts ballooned. Between 1971 and 1988, the Soviet Union's debt to Western creditors soared from $2 billion to

$42 billion and Poland's from $1 to $39 billion.[37] In the same period, Brazil's foreign debt surged from $8 to $118 billion, Mexico's from $8 to $99 billion, and Argentina's from $6 to $59 billion.[38] After 1990, it was foreign direct investment (FDI) that soared. The stock of FDI in the median authoritarian state increased from 6 percent of GDP in 1990 to 26 percent in 2010.[39]

Another integrating force was new communication technology. As the Internet connected critics of the government within countries, it simultaneously wove networks across state borders. To censor comprehensively, dictators now had to either block off their country completely or filter a barrage of data. And as the world economy built the Internet into its infrastructure, a total boycott grew increasingly costly. By 2014, 12 percent of global goods trade occurred through e-commerce.[40] In 2017, half of all services exchanged—worth $2.7 trillion—were delivered digitally.[41] By that time, international data flows were having a stronger effect on growth than either trade or FDI, according to the consultancy McKinsey.[42] Old-school censorship—restricting citizens to a few homemade, pro-government broadcasts—was less and less feasible.

As communication technology advanced, media globalized. A symbol of this was the rise of CNN, the first truly international television news network. Founded in 1980, the station had attracted 53 million viewers in 83 countries by 1992. Fifteen years later, it was reaching 260 million households.[43] Its success spawned imitators. In 1994, the BBC started a 24-hour news channel, and the Qatar-based Al Jazeera launched its international news coverage in 1996.[44] In the 2000s, some spin dictators founded their own international channels, as we discussed in chapter 6.

Globalization—in all its dimensions—inspired high hopes. Some imagined international commerce would undermine dictatorship by spreading political knowledge. As U.S. president George H. W. Bush put it in 1991: "No nation on Earth has discovered a way to import the world's goods and services while stopping foreign ideas at the border." Others thought competition for investment would force autocrats to liberalize. The information revolution prompted similar claims. President Clinton thought freedom would "spread by cell phone and cable modem."[45] The Internet was pronounced a "liberation technology" that would free oppressed societies.[46] Some also thought global 24-hour news channels like CNN would expose and isolate human rights abusers. UN secretary-general Boutros Boutros-Ghali called CNN "the sixteenth member of the Security Council."[47]

Such expectations proved exaggerated. The evidence that trade and investment by themselves drive political change is weak.[48] Businessmen are too inconsistent, forgetful, and profit-oriented to act as political umpires. Exporting countries whose trade partners respect human rights do tend to respect them more themselves, but that probably reflects the pressure of governments and human rights organizations rather than trade per se.[49] Foreign direct investors seem to prefer humane democracies, perhaps because they have more checks and balances, more transparent policies, or more educated, innovative workers.[50] Yet, there are glaring exceptions. In the five years after troops massacred students in Beijing's Tiananmen Square, the stock of FDI in China more than quadrupled.[51] It rose from about $21 billion in 1990, the year after Tiananmen, to $1.8 trillion in 2019.[52] When there is money to be made, memories of atrocities fade fast. And banks do not seem to limit their lending on humanitarian grounds.

The Internet's political effects also turned out to be complicated and context-dependent. It both empowers anti-regime protesters and facilitates state surveillance.[53] As for global TV news, the immediacy of CNN footage was offset by a trend after 1980 toward cost-cutting in international reporting. By 2014, the share of international news across all U.S. media was "at an all-time low."[54] And research has failed to find clear evidence for the "CNN effect"—the idea that vivid media coverage prompts Western governments to act.[55]

No single aspect of globalization proved a silver bullet. But they pack more of a punch when combined and mixed with other elements of the cocktail. Footage channeled from social media to global TV weakened dictators at times, especially those already destabilized by economic globalization and domestic modernization. Al Jazeera's coverage of protests in Tunisia in 2011 helped ignite the Arab Spring. Much of that coverage, in fact, "came from cell phone videos, taken by the public on the spot and communicated via Facebook."[56] Tunisia, which had grown richer and more educated under the twenty-four-year rule of dictator Zine el Abidine Ben Ali, tipped into tentative democracy.[57]

Or consider an early, celebrated case—that of Mexico's Zapatista uprising. In January 1994, a band of indigenous guerrillas emerged from the jungle to seize four towns in the Chiapas mountains. For centuries, local people had grown corn and coffee on the rocky hillsides. But the North Atlantic Free Trade Agreement (NAFTA), just signed with the United States and Canada, threatened to flood the market with cheap alternatives. As the guerrillas' spokesman—the ski-mask-sporting, pipe-smoking Subcomandante Marcos—put it: "The free-trade agreement is a death certificate for the Indian peoples of Mexico."[58]

Mexico's President Carlos Salinas sent in 15,000 troops with helicopter gunships to bomb from the air. "We unleashed every possible measure to annihilate the guerrillas," he said later.[59] But then, unexpectedly, he stopped, announcing a unilateral cease-fire and sending a trusted colleague to negotiate. This reversal surprised his supporters. One television tycoon urged him to crush the rebels, just as a previous president had massacred students in 1968.[60] "I told him these were different times, and that instead we had to listen to their valid demands for justice," Salinas recalled.

Why were the times different? First, while past clashes between troops and peasants had attracted little press coverage, this story exploded. Suddenly, unrest in a remote corner of Central America was on the news in capitals around the globe. "It was something new, unexpected, unheard of that it had captured the world's attention," Salinas remembered.[61] In Mexico City, middle-class protesters waved signs that read "Stop the Genocide."[62] Demonstrations of sympathy erupted across North America and Europe.[63]

The rapid global response reflected in part the Internet's new power. A couple of years earlier, local NGOs in Chiapas had bought a web server hoping to cut their fax bills.[64] Soon they were connected to a worldwide coalition of anti-globalists, environmentalists, union organizers, human rights activists, feminists, and advocates of indigenous people. When Salinas's troops struck, this network was ready. As soldiers stormed the villages, pictures and videos filtered out to partners around the world. News stations picked them up.

A second reason for Salinas's reversal was the timing. In 1994, as a crucial presidential election loomed, Mexico's economy was on a knife-edge. A massive inflow of speculative money was boosting the spending of the middle and working classes. Political violence threatened to send investors fleeing. The economy, wrote one analyst, was "an enormous confidence game."[65] Salinas could not risk bursting the bubble. U.S. ambassador James Jones warned him that if he crushed the Zapatistas, Wall Street would drop him "like a hot potato." "About 24 hours of a CNN war" is all it would take, he told the president.[66]

Had they acted earlier, the authorities could have cut the guerrillas' web connections, stemming the flow of news. But Salinas's generals were still fighting the last war. They thought they were up against a classic guerrilla insurgency. In fact, they faced something new. As Mexico's secretary of foreign affairs, José Ángel Gurría, put it, this was not a battle of guns and grenades but "a war of ink, written words, a war on the Internet."[67]

Salinas's regime, already halfway from fear to spin dictatorship, was pushed into a low-violence strategy.[68] What made the difference was the combination of Internet communications, global news media, and financial vulnerability produced by the country's rapid integration into global capital markets. That—and one other element to which we now turn.

THE RIGHTS STUFF

Our cocktail's third ingredient is *the rise of a liberal international order*. An important driver of this was the emergence of a global movement for human rights. From around the world, small groups of educated professionals with progressive values and often legal training linked up in the late twentieth century into a network of liberal NGOs. They used the global media, international law, and a range of innovative tactics to focus pressure on brutal dictators. It was this network that turned the Zapatista rebellion into a cause célèbre.

Such activists created a range of problems for the old-school autocrats. "It's difficult for us to make history," one African strongman lamented in 2009. "We have to carry out our own French Revolution with Amnesty International peering over our shoulder."[69] The strongman in

question, Laurent Gbagbo, had become president of the Ivory Coast
nine years earlier. In April 2011, a mix of rebels, French troops, and UN
blue helmets would pry him out of his presidential bunker. He had refused to accept defeat in an internationally monitored election. Hunker-
ing down in the capital of the world's leading cocoa producer, Gbagbo
had clung to power as his supporters rampaged outside the palace gates.[70]

Not so long before, he had been his country's hope for a better future.
During the thirty-three-year rule of Ivory Coast's postcolonial dictator,
Félix Houphouët-Boigny, Gbagbo had become a dissident demanding
democracy. But once elected president, he had changed. Nicknamed
"the baker"—slang for a crafty manipulator—Gbagbo had terrorized
supporters of his northern rival, Alassane Ouattara. He had canceled the
2005 election. But then in 2010 he had called a national vote, only to find
his supporters outnumbered by the northern opposition. Down to his
last few million dollars, Gbagbo retreated to the bunker as fighting killed
thousands outside.

Back in 1999, Gbagbo had puzzled over the stubbornness of Slobodan Milošević, the Serbian dictator who was defying NATO over
Kosovo. "What does Milošević think he can do with the whole world
against him?" he had asked his aides.[71] But in 2011 it was Gbagbo that
"the whole world" was after. Indicted by the International Criminal
Court for crimes against humanity, he followed the Serbian strongman
to the Hague and spent seven years there in a prison cell. Unexpectedly,
he was acquitted in 2019, after the judge ruled the prosecutor's evidence
inadequate.[72]

Amnesty International (AI)—the group that makes it hard for
modern-day Robespierres to "make history"—was founded in 1961. A
London lawyer, Peter Benenson, read of two Portuguese students who
had been jailed for drinking a toast to freedom.[73] Benenson's idea was
to recruit volunteers to track all those imprisoned for their political beliefs worldwide and barrage their jailers with letters.[74] The organization
has since grown to include 5 million activists, along with 2 million members and supporters.[75]

The ideas behind the modern "human rights revolution" go back to
the Enlightenment.[76] Writings of Locke, Hume, Voltaire, and Rousseau

informed the American and French revolutionaries, with their Bill of Rights and Declaration of the Rights of Man and of the Citizen.[77] Similar language featured in various nineteenth-century campaigns—against slavery and colonial abuses, for women's equality. But only after World War II was much done to incorporate human rights into international law.[78] The five years after 1945 saw the UN created, the Universal Declaration of Human Rights adopted, the Nuremberg and Tokyo trials held, and the Genocide Convention and Geneva Convention signed.

During the Cold War, anticommunism often overshadowed humanitarian goals for Western elites. But the USSR's disappearance lessened the appeal of realpolitik. Human rights became "cool," with artists and popular culture celebrities embracing activism.[79] The term itself invaded public debates. In 1980, the *New York Times* referred to "human rights" in 595 stories. By 2000, that had increased to 1,548 articles. This changed not just in the West. In news programming from around the world monitored by the BBC, "human rights" appeared in 838 stories in 1980, 1,809 in 1990, and 9,193 in 2000. Even China's Xinhua state news agency mentioned human rights more and more often—140 times in 1980 and 1,415 times in 2000.[80]

As more countries democratized, many created "truth commissions" to document past abuses—28 countries had these by 2006.[81] Some set up museums to preserve and exhibit evidence. Meanwhile, lawyers took to prosecuting former dictators and their agents.[82] Some pressed for new international courts and tribunals, while others used domestic courts. The number of prosecutions rose from zero in 1970 to more than 250 worldwide in 2007.[83] Most trials were domestic, but a few notorious offenders faced justice in international bodies. Milošević died in jail in 2006. Bosnian Serb leader Radovan Karadžić, plucked out of a secret second life, was sentenced to life in prison. Liberian rebel leader and president Charles Taylor is serving fifty years.

Besides public opinion and law, human rights activism has influenced international business. No CEO wants to be branded a friend of torturers or an exploiter of penal labor.[84] In the late 1990s, the oil companies Amoco, ARCO, Petro-Canada, and Texaco all withdrew from collaborations with Myanmar's generals.[85] More recently, companies sponsoring the 2021 World Hockey Championship in Belarus pulled out after brutality against peaceful protesters, forcing the tournament's relocation.[86] Firms including H&M and Burberry boycotted cotton from Xinjiang after reports of mistreatment of Muslim Uighurs.[87] When activists publicize abuses in developing countries, research suggests multinationals invest less in them.[88]

For dictators, all this has made overt repression riskier. Brutal violence might discourage investors or halt economic and military aid. Even worse, it could trigger "humanitarian interventions" by foreign armies or international forces, like the UN-French joint operation that bombed Gbagbo out of his bunker. International "shaming" could even embolden rivals at home to challenge the incumbent.[89]

Do these considerations register? Some evidence suggests they do. Of course, dictators are not turning into humanitarians. But they recognize the incentives to reduce visible violence. Political scientist Darius Rejali notes the spread since the 1970s of "clean" torture techniques. These include methods such as forced standing, stress positions, and waterboarding that—although excruciating—leave fewer scars. He attributes this to the global human rights movement. The change has been most pronounced in dictatorships more closely linked to the West—those, that is, with the greatest reason to fear repercussions.[90]

Even Mobutu, Zaire's bloodthirsty tyrant, worried in the 1980s that reports from inside his prisons might offend his two main backers, France and the United States.[91] Efforts increased to conceal the evidence. In 1991, one jailer beating a detainee was reproached by his superior: "It will leave scars and we will get complaints from Amnesty International."[92] The previous year, the U.S. Congress had cut $4 million from military aid to the country to protest human rights abuses and corruption.[93]

Another example comes from Argentina's military dictatorship in the 1970s. The junta hoped to preserve good relations with the United States. But it also wanted to terrorize regime opponents. Street-level officers focused on intimidation while, at the top, General Videla prioritized the junta's reputation. In 1976, to demoralize leftists, police dynamited the bodies of thirty executed subversives in the town of Pilar, scattering body parts throughout the neighborhood. According to a declassified CIA cable, Videla became incensed at the carnage, which, he said, "seriously damages the country's image domestically and abroad." Murdering leftists was fine in his book, but such matters, he thought, "should be dealt with discreetly."[94]

Fear of losing Western aid was apparently what prompted Jerry Rawlings, Ghana's military dictator, to hold competitive elections in the early 1990s. Rawlings had come to office in a 1981 military takeover. No sentimentalist, he had ordered three prior heads of state shot after a previous coup.[95] In the 1980s, he detained and tortured pro-democracy activists.[96] An odd candidate for democratic reformer. But Ghana at the time received the World Bank's biggest lending program in Africa.[97] And Rawlings took seriously—perhaps too seriously—hints that continued aid hinged on political change.[98] "We were forced by the State Department—oh yes, forced—to adopt multiparty democracy," he complained in 2009.[99] He had had to "force democracy down the throats" of his reluctant compatriots, he told political scientist Antoinette Handley, because "the State Department was saying that there'll be no more IMF and World Bank facilities for us."[100]

From the mid-1970s, Western governments had begun emphasizing human rights in their relations with dictatorships. Cold War realism was still usually more powerful. But from 1974, the U.S. Congress started banning assistance to countries guilty of gross abuses.[101] In his inaugural address, President Carter declared that the U.S. commitment to human rights "must be absolute."[102] And in 1978 he blocked loans to Guatemala and Nicaragua to punish violations.[103]

Like Rawlings, various other African dictators were feeling vulnerable as the Cold War wound down. Between 1970 and 1990, total non-military aid to dictatorships grew from $4 billion to $38 billion.[104] By that year, such flows equaled 8 percent of GDP in the median autocracy. Political respectability helped to keep the aid flowing. In 1989, the World Bank pledged to consider "political barriers to economic development" when reviewing programs in Africa.[105] By the late 1990s "nearly 78 percent of conditions imposed by international financial institutions in loan agreements targeted legal reform and the promotion of 'the rule of law.'"[106] One such institution, the European Bank for Reconstruction and Development, created in 1991, specified in the first article of its charter that it would only operate in countries "applying principles of multiparty democracy and pluralism."[107] Research shows that from the mid-1990s—although not before—dictators who held multiparty executive elections received more aid per capita than those who did not.[108] Another study found that countries denounced for abuses by the UN Human Rights Commission suffered a fall in World Bank aid flows.[109]

Regional associations also began insisting on good governance. In 1989, the European Economic Community, predecessor of the European Union, added a clause on human rights to the Lomé Convention, which covers its trade with developing countries. To join the European Union, postcommunist states had to agree to democracy and human rights protections. Commitment to democracy also became a criterion for NATO accession. Further west, the Organization of American States (OAS) pledged in 1991 to preserve democracy in its members. And the Organization of African Unity, later renamed the African Union (AU), agreed in 2000 to suspend any state whose government changed unconstitutionally.[110]

The new focus on human rights and democracy had some success. When Guatemala's President Jorge Serrano dissolved parliament and the supreme court in 1993, the United States, Japan, and the EU halted all non-humanitarian aid and the OAS began discussing a trade embargo.[111] The military quickly forced Serrano out. In 1994, President Clinton sent U.S. troops under UN authorization to depose Haiti's dictator, Raoul Cédras.[112] When a mutinous general tried to replace Paraguay's President Juan Carlos Wasmosy in 1996, quick pressure from the OAS, United States, and EU helped Wasmosy prevail.[113] In 2009, when the Honduran military ousted President Manuel Zelaya, the OAS suspended it.[114] Likewise, the AU suspended ten of the fourteen African countries where coups occurred in 2000–14, often also imposing sanctions.[115] Almost all quickly returned to civilian rule.

Such embargoes and interventions do not always succeed. And Western leaders have hardly been consistent in their protection of human rights. Still, the calculus has changed. Violence and undemocratic behavior tend to be costlier than before. In this new environment, some

dictators end up transitioning to genuine democracy. Rawlings, for instance, eventually stepped down in compliance with term limits. Others
have instead sought salvation in spin dictatorship.

The first line of defense, as we have seen, is disinformation. Already
in the 1970s, Romania's Nicolae Ceauşescu gleefully welcomed President Carter's campaign, telling aides: "If he wants human rights, let's
give him human rights." Romanian agents were told to plant the idea in
Carter's circles that Romanians enjoyed more religious freedom than
others in the communist world.[116]

A second option is to imitate democracy but bend the rules. International organizations may react to visible atrocities and blatant fraud. But
they have a harder time with subtler infractions.[117] When the OAS faces
evidence of electoral rigging, two analysts write, it becomes "a matter of
degree . . . how severe is the fraud, and would a clean election have resulted in a different outcome?"[118] The AU, two others conclude, has
shown an "inability to deal with authoritarian backsliding."[119] A little
simulation can go a long way.

COLD WAR AND AFTER

To recap, the modernization cocktail emerges over time. Its elements
interact. And it operates at two levels: inside countries and internationally. Within countries, the growth of a postindustrial economy increases
the share of people with higher education, creative jobs, and basic income security. Such people tend to be more individualistic, tolerant,
and eager to participate in public life.[120] They also have greater organizational and communication skills. While relatively small at first, this
group is vital to the innovation economy and expands over time. Authoritarian regimes must accommodate its demands or accept slower
development.

As this process spreads to more countries, it reshapes the global setting.
Societies become linked by complex economic flows and global media.
International movements form around the progressive values fostered
by modernization. "Boomerang effects" and feedback loops transfer
information and pressures for change across the levels. For instance,

news smuggled out of autocracies is broadcast back into them over the censors' heads.[121] Dictators' abuses provoke indictments by judges in distant democracies. International courts and tribunals penalize the governments that created them. Stories ricocheting around the globe spark calls for international interventions—even against strongmen in less developed states that might seem poor candidates for liberal democracy. Opposition movements learn to enlist diaspora members worldwide, attracting global attention.[122]

What happens then depends on how sensitive an abusive ruler is to Western pressure. The military context matters, but so do international trade and finance. Dictators who depend on Western markets or owe billions to Western banks are vulnerable—like Mexico's Salinas in 1994. Those who rely on foreign aid—like Ghana's Rawlings—may be nudged from fear to spin, or even further.

One momentous event—the end of the Cold War—both exemplified and, later, catalyzed the cocktail's effects. The Soviet collapse had complex causes. It certainly did *not* follow from a postindustrial revolution; as the West was crafting the first cell phones, Russian plants still cranked out substandard tractors. But the spread of higher education was gradually changing the culture. By 1990, the share of adults with a college degree in Russia was higher than that in the UK or Germany. In Bulgaria, it was higher than in France.[123] Values were evolving. In Russia in 1990, 90 percent of those polled said they approved of the human rights movement, the same percentage as in the United States. Ninety percent of Russians said their government "should be made much more open to the public."[124]

Communist leaders faced these changes at a moment of international weakness. To support living standards, they had borrowed recklessly from Western banks, pushing right to the verge of default. By the late 1980s, economic crisis, stirrings of dissent, and pressures from Western leaders on human rights were inflaming tensions within rigid political systems. Gorbachev's responses combined political misjudgments, economic misconceptions, and his own dose of progressive values. His rejection of political violence—and denial of responsibility when it happened—was part personal morality, part classic spin. Glasnost—

Gorbachev's liberalization of media—was meant to be partial, letting off steam while eliciting useful feedback. But the crisis was too severe and Gorbachev's approach too inconsistent for manipulation to save the regime.

The Soviet extinction accelerated the global trend toward less openly violent politics. While locked in existential battle, Western leaders had backed vicious strongmen so long as they were "on the right side." Moscow, in turn, supported brutal communist regimes. But that changed with the collapse of Moscow's empire. As Soviet aid to client states dried up, the West had more room to condition its assistance on better governance. The Berlin Wall came down just as the human rights movement in the West was hitting its stride.

This might seem like a rosy view of recent history. Of course, the West's role has not always been benign. National interests sometimes hide behind humanitarian appeals, and demands that authoritarian states reform often involve some hypocrisy and posturing.[125] The way these trends unfolded was far from smooth. Still, the emergence of a global movement for political freedom, with significant support in the richest countries and a growing legal infrastructure to back it up, did change things. Compared to previous eras, it is harder for dictators to continue as before.

Despite the momentum toward spin, some dictatorships of fear survive. Their leaders seek to preserve the old model and prove us wrong. Among these are Saudi Arabia, Egypt, Iran, and North Korea. China is a telling case. In some regards, it resembles the Soviet Union in the late 1980s. Like the USSR then, it is still hyperindustrialized, with 40 percent of GDP in industry and construction, compared to an average of 23 percent for high-income countries. But, also as in the Soviet Union under Brezhnev, higher education has been surging, reaching 7 percent of the population aged fifteen and over by 2019.[126] That is still below the 13 percent recorded by Russia in 1990 but close to that of some other Eastern Bloc states.

Xi Jinping's obsession since taking power has been to avoid Gorbachev's fate. And China differs in important ways from the late Soviet Union. Where Brezhnev presided over demoralizing stagnation, decades of explosive growth have boosted the Beijing leadership's support. So far, there is little evidence of a broad cultural shift in China comparable to that in the Soviet Union under Gorbachev.[127] Asked which they would prefer if they had to choose between freedom and security, 93 percent of Chinese respondents in 2018 opted for security. This far exceeds the worldwide average (70 percent), let alone the levels in postindustrial countries such as Australia (47 percent) and Germany (53 percent).[128] The economic struggle continues for many, and few have yet substituted self-expression for survival values. China is not in an economic crisis and does not depend on Western banks or government loans. Western economic leverage is offset by China's own leverage over the West. In short, any effect of the modernization cocktail on China is still weak.

Facing neither strong internal nor external pressure to renounce violent repression, China's rulers need not give up—yet—on the dictatorship of fear. Instead, they have set out to improve it. The last decade has seen rapid innovation in surveillance technology. New tools allow Beijing to track dissidents, both online and in the flesh. Xi's policemen combine these with traditional methods, locking up large numbers of ethnic minority members, Hong Kong democracy activists, and mainland human rights lawyers, among others. While selectively experimenting with elements of spin, they remain committed to intimidation.

What will the coming decades hold for such upgraded regimes of fear? And how will the spin specialists fare? We turn to these questions in the final chapter.

CHAPTER 8

THE FUTURE OF SPIN

The rise of spin dictatorship is one of the most striking political phenomena of the last half century. But will it last? Can the regimes ruling today in Singapore, Russia, Hungary, and Kazakhstan survive into the mid-twenty-first century? Will the violent autocracies that remain switch from terror to deception? Or, conversely, will spin dictators revert to more bloody, overt forms of tyranny?

Taking up the argument of the last chapter, we consider here what it implies for the future of different kinds of political regimes. We explore how the West's approach to its authoritarian rivals changed in the late twentieth century and how it needs to change again. We suggest a few principles that might guide policy in an age of spin. Some make sense in dealing with all types of dictatorship while others are more specific to the newer form.

If our understanding is correct, the balance among autocracies in the coming years will depend on whether modernization and globalization continue. If they do, dictators will face growing pressure to replace violent repression with spin. Some may fall to popular uprisings. However, if the modernization cocktail weakens or even reverses, democracies may backslide and autocracies become more openly repressive.

What happens to spin dictatorships will depend in part on how they emerged. As we saw, these come about in two ways. Some rulers are driven to spin by the modernization of their own societies. In Singapore and Russia, at least one in four adults today has a college degree and many work in creative jobs.[1] In such places, internal factors cause dictators to replace terror with deception. Others change because of pressure from abroad. In Tanzania, the college-educated community is tiny. Two-thirds of the workforce remains in agriculture.[2] And yet, recent leaders have acted democratic, slanting media to boost their popularity, while using— at least until recently—less coercion.[3] Such restraint aimed to please Western governments and donors, on whom the country depends. In 2009, foreign aid equaled 70 percent of central government spending.[4] Let's consider these two routes—and types of spin dictatorship—in turn.

SPINNING UPWARD

In the first type, the driving force is domestic modernization. As the informed stratum expands, it gets expensive to co-opt and difficult to censor. Its members forge links with global human rights networks and foreign governments. At the same time, its economic importance grows. All this makes it harder to deny the informed a say in politics. At first spin dictators just imitate democracy. But eventually some have to accept the real thing.

Lee Kuan Yew saw the logic. Already in 2000, he questioned how long his handiwork could endure. "Will the political system that my colleagues and I developed work more or less unchanged for another generation?" he wondered in his memoir:

> I doubt it. Technology and globalization are changing the way people work and live. Singaporeans will have new work styles and lifestyles. As an international hub of a knowledge-based economy in the information technology age, we will be ever more exposed to external influences.

To survive, his successors would have to "respond to changes in the needs and aspirations of a better-educated people, and to their desire for greater participation in decisions that shape their lives."[5]

Lee's heirs have managed to keep the lid on—so far. But in neighboring Malaysia, spin dictatorship seemed recently to cross into infant democracy. Under Prime Minister Mahathir Mohamad (1981–2003) and his successors, Abdullah Ahmad Badawi (2003–9) and Najib Razak (2009–18), leaders manipulated their way through elections. Yet, as they did so the country was modernizing. Between 1980 and 2018, per capita income rose from under $6,000 to more than $25,000. The share of college-bound school leavers soared from 4 to 45 percent.[6] Employment in industry, after peaking in 1997, fell as the postindustrial transition began. By 2019, Internet penetration, at 84 percent, was higher than in France.[7]

For years, the ruling UMNO party successfully co-opted the elite. But from the late 1990s, the Reformasi movement of young, educated Malaysians began agitating for political reform.[8] In the 2008 election—in part due to growing access to the Internet, which by then featured a "vibrant opposition blogosphere" and independent news outlets—UMNO's coalition lost its two-thirds parliamentary majority as well as control of five of the thirteen state assemblies.[9] Finally, in a stunning upset, the opposition won the 2018 election, ending UMNO's six-decade-long monopoly.[10] The story is not over: amid the 2020 coronavirus crisis, old-order politicians made a comeback.[11] But their grip is more tenuous than before.

Other spin dictators have also faced challenges as their countries developed. In Russia, the 2000s saw striking progress. The average wage rose from under $4,000 a year in 2000 to more than $15,000 in 2011. Personal computer ownership soared from 6 to 75 percent of households and cell phones became ubiquitous.[12] Values also modernized in some key respects. The proportion of Russians who thought having a democratic political system was "very" or "fairly" good grew from 46 percent in 1999 to 67 percent in 2011.[13] This climaxed in the demonstrations of 2011–12, in which massive crowds protested electoral fraud.

One obvious way a dictator can resist is to freeze—or even reverse—modernization. That was Putin's response after 2011.[14] He let cronies gut the high-tech initiatives of the Medvedev interregnum (2008–12), while scaring away Western investment and provoking sanctions with military attacks on Ukraine. Russians faced years of economic stagnation and tightening political controls.

Yet, in the absence of natural or man-made disasters, reversing modernization is hard. Education is not easy to erase. And demand for it does not vanish just because a ruler wants it to. Worldwide, college enrollment has risen consistently in both democracies and dictatorships, surging from 10 to 39 percent of school leavers since 1970.[15] The postindustrial transition is also tough to roll back. Despite populists' promises, reviving obsolete industries in a modern economy is virtually impossible.

In fact, freezing modernization can trigger exactly the political crisis dictators fear. The paradox is that while development threatens dictators, economic growth helps them survive.[16] Halting development usually means slashing growth, which—in all political orders—erodes the leader's popularity.[17] Dictators must then use more repression. Yet, the inadequacy of repression in a modernized society is what led them to spin dictatorship in the first place. We know of no antidote to the modernization cocktail. Choosing stagnation is a desperate move. It may help for a while, but not forever.

In Russia, despite Putin's reactionary turn, aspects of modernization continued. College enrollment rose still further, from 76 percent in 2012 to 85 percent in 2018.[18] Internet penetration deepened and creative-class employment edged up.[19] The proportion of respondents favoring a democratic political system remained as high in 2017—the last year surveyed by the WVS—as in 2011.

In neighboring Belarus, too, recent modernization destabilized what had seemed a relatively secure fear dictatorship. By 2018, 87 percent of high school graduates were attending college—a rate higher than in the UK or Germany.[20] A hugely successful high-tech industry exported $15 billion worth of products in 2019, equal to almost a quarter of GDP.[21] Between 2011 and 2017, the share of respondents who thought having a democratic system was "very good" grew from 33 to 45 percent.[22] As in Russia nine years earlier, Belarusians hit the streets in 2020 to protest a fraudulent election.

Besides long-run trends, short-run crises—economic, military, or medical—can influence the political dynamic. They serve as an excuse for dictators to assume emergency powers and target scapegoats. Hardship may revive values associated with the struggle for survival. But crises can also overwhelm the leader's manipulative techniques, sending his ratings plunging. At such moments, the only option—other than surrendering—may be to retreat to more open repression, hoping it will shock all into submission. Whether that succeeds depends on just how strong and resourceful the informed have become.

Global crises also distract Western governments. During 2020, 38 countries used the coronavirus pandemic as a pretext to harass opposition media, and 158 restricted demonstrations.[23] In the future, climate change might revive violent dictatorship if it causes environmental and economic disruptions or mass migration. Yet, at the same time, crises expose leaders' incompetence. Despite coronavirus restrictions, protests erupted in at least 90 countries in 2020, forcing Kyrgyzstan to rerun a fraudulent election and Nigeria to disband an abusive police unit.[24]

Even in normal times, vast oil reserves change the equation. Petro-states can use mineral revenues to appease or control the public, while avoiding social modernization.[25] Arabian Gulf monarchies like Saudi Arabia and Kuwait achieved some of the world's highest incomes without building manufacturing industries, empowering women, or significantly weakening religious authorities. With society largely unchanged by the income growth, pressures for democracy remained weak. However, some Gulf regimes, fearing the end of oil, have recently tried to modernize and diversify. College enrollment leapt to 71 percent of school leavers in Saudi Arabia in 2019 and 55 percent in Kuwait.[26] In both, more women now study than men. The region's Internet penetration tops the world, with 100 percent online in Bahrain, Kuwait, and Qatar.[27] Time will reveal whether this kind of directed social modernization can—as leaders hope—coexist with continuing fear-based political control. We expect either a shift from fear to spin or intensifying demand for more open politics.

Oil wealth and economic crisis combine in the starkest recent case of authoritarian backsliding. Venezuela has enormous hydrocarbon reserves but imports almost all other goods. Soon after Hugo Chávez died in 2013 the oil price crashed. That left his successor, Nicolás Maduro, to cope with dwindling revenues, crippling shortages, and a legacy of economic mismanagement. He retreated from spin to a more traditional fear dictatorship.[28] The opposition's efforts to force him out with waves of protest prompted growing violence from the police, army, and paramilitaries.[29] That this has worked for eight years suggests the relative weakness of Venezuela's informed stratum. As in the Gulf states, modernization had been shallow. As of 2010, fewer than 3 percent of adults in Venezuela had a college degree, hardly more than in 1980. The economy—still focused on oil—is far from postindustrial.[30]

In short, postindustrial development within dictatorships tends to raise the cost of violent repression. Those previously relying on terror switch to manipulation. Those already manipulating are sometimes pushed into genuine democracy. The timing of transitions is unpredictable and there can be setbacks. There is no magic development threshold at which dictatorship disappears in a puff of smoke. But as pressures mount, the odds of change increase.[31]

OUTSIDE INFLUENCES

But what about nondemocratic leaders in less modern countries? For them, the impetus to retool comes from outside. When Lee Kuan Yew first turned to spin, Singapore was still quite poor. Having trounced the island's communists, Lee faced little pressure from a deferential public. His key concerns were international investment and prestige.

Subsequent modernization sometimes locks in the initial choice. After Singapore's economy took off, overt repression would have alienated entrepreneurs and investors. But other spin dictatorships remain less developed. Think again of Tanzania. There, the years of spin since the 1990s saw no noticeable increase in higher education and no postindustrial transition. In such cases, whether dictators revert to fear depends mostly on the global context.

And that can change. Unlike modernization, which has never reversed worldwide for long, international integration and support for democracy have seen major swings. In the 1930s, world trade imploded amid an upsurge of competitive tariffs. From 1929 to 1935, global goods trade fell from 23 to 11 percent of GDP.[32] Foreign investment dried up as countries stumbled off the gold standard. Politically, many rickety democracies turned fascist.

Are we on the brink of another de-globalization? Some fear one has already begun. Populist politicians attack imports and immigration, blaming them for the dwindling fortunes of unskilled workers. In the United States, President Trump quit trade agreements and slapped tariffs on both adversaries like China and partners like Europe. If deglobalization shreds economic ties between rich and poor countries, many dictators will have less incentive to act democratic.

But that has not happened yet. Today's world differs from that of the 1930s. For one thing, global GDP is more than fifteen times higher and dependence on exports twice as great.[33] In 2019, world goods trade equaled 44 percent of GDP.[34] The Great Depression, which sparked protectionism, was far more brutal than the global financial crisis or the Covid shock: U.S. output contracted then by 32 percent—compared to 4 percent in 2007–9 and 10 percent in 2020.[35] Even as output fell in 2020, financial markets surged, buoyed up by huge liquidity injections.[36] Economic globalization might reverse in the future, but that is far from clear.

Although trade has not collapsed, authoritarian states have become less financially dependent. That could shield them from political pressure. In the median nondemocracy, aid and development assistance fell from 8 percent of GDP in 1990 to 2 percent in 2017.[37] Richer ones built up reserves to ride out short-lived crises. In Singapore, Russia, and Saudi Arabia, among others, gold and currency holdings now exceed 25 percent of GDP. Reducing dependence was quite deliberate. Dictators sometimes de-globalize precisely to protect their regimes. When the West sanctioned Putin for invading Crimea, he added his own ban on EU food imports and ordered elites to bring home assets invested abroad.[38] Still, "de-offshorization" has its limits. And cutting financial ties reduces a dictator's own leverage over Western elites.

Chinese investment and aid has also curbed Western influence. In just 2010–19, Beijing's stock of foreign direct investment (FDI) around the world grew from $317 billion to $2.1 trillion. That is still far below the $7.7 trillion U.S. FDI stock that year.[39] But global lending by China—amounting to $1.5 trillion in credits to more than 150 countries—now dwarfs that of the United States. Indeed, China's lending exceeds that of "all OECD creditor governments combined."[40]

Backed by Beijing, autocrats have less need to pretend. Consider Ethiopia. To please Western donors, that country's leader, Meles Zenawi, a former Marxist guerrilla, toned down his revolutionary rhetoric after taking power in 1991. Yet, by 2014 China had loaned the country $12.3 billion—a sum equal to half its average annual GDP. Less concerned to seem democratic, the regime claimed 99.6 percent of seats in the 2010 parliamentary election. In 2015, its security forces brutally crushed a protest movement, killing 700 people and arresting 23,000. This is not an isolated example. Political scientists Steve Hess and Richard Aidoo found that countries financed relatively more by China and less by the West use harsher political repression.[41] In Tanzania, President John Magufuli stepped up harassment of journalists and activists as money from Beijing poured in.[42] He made a point of thanking China for providing aid with no strings attached.[43]

As we saw in chapter 7, economic ties by themselves rarely cause dictators to change approach. But they can be powerful when combined with international media, human rights campaigns, and Western political pressure. Some fear these other elements of the modernization cocktail are weakening. In the West, traditional media have been struggling as Internet platforms steal their advertisers and audiences fragment. If that leaves Western elites less informed about repressive regimes, dictators will benefit.

But, again, that does not seem to be happening. In fact, compared to the few global TV networks and wire services of the 1980s, today's media overflow with detail about authoritarian societies. And that is precisely because of the intense competition, new technology, and market fragmentation that are undermining old media models. Expensive foreign bureaus are giving way to networks of local stringers, freelancers, and "citizen journalists" with cell phone cameras.[44] Hackers unmask the secrets of high finance and diplomacy, revealing everything from ambassadors' cables to billionaires' tax schemes. Human rights groups set up "pseudo-newsrooms" and dispatch "firemen" to report on disasters.[45] NGO investigators uncover environmental abuses (Global Witness), corruption (Transparency International, the Organized Crime and Corruption Reporting Project), and money laundering (the International Consortium of Investigative Journalists). Even espionage operations, targeted killings, military movements, and radical right-wing militias are exposed by investigative outlets such as Bellingcat. Two decades ago, only the world's top spy services had the kind of information that anyone can now obtain with a smartphone.[46]

The key need today is not more information. It is, first, verification and interpretation, and, second, focus.[47] The first remains a task for traditional media. Major companies, with brands to defend, have incentives to verify reports. If people continue to buy the *New York Times* and watch CNN, it will be not because they break every story but because their reports are reliable. The second task is trickier. Politicians respond to news based on whether voters have seen it. By reaching huge audiences, the old networks created pressure on governments. But the fragmentation and diversity of news feeds today shield officials. In the West, the function of focusing attention has passed from media elites to the algorithms that decide what goes viral.

Here the human rights movement could play an increasing role. Activists have always sought to mobilize public opinion and trigger government action. Since the 1980s, NGOs have become sophisticated influencers, recruiting celebrities to raise awareness and money. As long ago as 1985, 40 percent of the world's population reportedly tuned in to watch the Live Aid concert.[48] These days, social networks direct attention to distant atrocities. Viral videos publicized the crimes of Ugandan warlord Joseph Kony and urged the rescue of Nigerian schoolgirls kidnapped by Boko Haram.[49]

Besides rallying Western opinion, human rights groups like Amnesty International may influence autocrats, as we saw in the last chapter. Dictators now know they are being watched. And this will continue. Amnesty International and Human Rights Watch have dramatically increased their funding, staff, global presence, and reporting. Total U.S. giving to international affairs charities—a category that includes international human rights, development, aid, peace and security, exchange programs, and foreign policy—grew from $2.7 billion in 2000 to $29 billion in 2019.[50]

The final ingredient in the modernization cocktail is the liberal world order. Many see this too as threatened. To Princeton scholar John Ikenberry, it is already "collapsing."[51] Legal experts declare the "age of human rights" to be over, at least for now.[52] It is easy to share the pessimism. In just a few years, President Trump withdrew the United States from treaties or negotiations on arms control (the Iran nuclear deal, Open Skies Treaty), climate change (the Paris Agreement), and trade (NAFTA—which was later replaced, the Trans-Pacific Partnership). On his watch, the United States walked out of the UN Human Rights Council, UNESCO, and the World Health Organization and undermined the World Trade Organization's appellate body. Populists in other countries also reject international cooperation.

As the liberal order weakens, some see a potential rival to liberal democracy in China's technocratic authoritarianism.[53] The "Washington Consensus" of the 1990s, rooted in free markets, is said to face competition from a "Beijing Consensus."[54] According to writer and Asia expert Joshua Kurlantzick, China's governance model poses "the most serious challenge to democratic capitalism since the rise of communism and fascism in the 1920s and early 1930s."[55]

But here too, although dangers are real, the alarm seems premature. Despite Trump, the system of international law and enforcement has not collapsed. The UN tracks the status of twenty-two key human rights treaties, including the conventions against genocide and torture. As of 2010, the average country had ratified eleven of these. By 2020, it had ratified two more. In those ten years, no country withdrew from a single UN human rights treaty.[56] And the UN's monitoring of compliance increased. Since 2008, each state has had its human rights record vetted twice in so-called "Universal Periodic Reviews."[57] These are sometimes criticized as toothless, but in fact they have prompted changes such as the abolition of Fiji's death penalty and protections for activists in Côte d'Ivoire. The share of the UN budget devoted to human rights has increased fivefold since 1992.[58]

In a dramatic departure, all UN members agreed in 2005 that they have a "responsibility to protect" people from atrocities, wherever these occur. The principle has been invoked to justify various diplomatic and military interventions. Some are viewed as successful (the effort to halt ethnic violence after Kenya's 2007 election), others less so (the Western intervention in Libya in 2011). But the doctrine remains a threat to dictators contemplating brutality. So does the increasingly frequent assertion by courts of universal jurisdiction—that is, the right to prosecute crimes committed anywhere in the world. Such prosecutions have soared. Between 2008 and 2017, 815 universal jurisdiction prosecutions began worldwide, compared to 503 in the previous decade and 342 in the decade before.[59] These same years saw the innovative use of personal sanctions—including asset freezes and travel bans—to target human rights abusers abroad, as pioneered in the U.S. Magnitsky Act, which punished Russian officials for the death in prison of the lawyer Sergei Magnitsky. Following the U.S. example, Canada, the UK, and the EU have passed their own Magnitsky Acts. Despite the illiberal tirades and actions of some populist leaders, the infrastructure of international human rights law is not collapsing: it is growing.

That is not surprising because protecting victims is popular. In 2018, large majorities in a range of countries—from 58 percent in Belgium to 90 percent in Serbia—thought legal protections for human rights important. Even in Saudi Arabia, 61 percent agreed.[60] Polls find strong support for the United Nations. Among 14 developed democracies in 2020, a large majority viewed the UN favorably in all except Japan. Even in the United States after three years of the Trump presidency, 62 percent were favorable—14 percentage points *more* than in 2007.[61] International cooperation is also more popular than unilateralism. The Pew Center asked respondents whether their country should "take into account other countries' interests, even if it means making compromises," or instead "follow its own interests even when other countries strongly disagree." In 12 of the 14 countries—all except Australia and Japan—a majority chose compromise. The highest support was in the UK (69 percent) and Germany (65 percent). But even in the United States, respondents chose cooperation over short-term self-interest by 58 to 39 percent.[62]

As for Beijing-style techno-authoritarianism, even the Chinese do not seem sold on it. Among Chinese respondents in 2018, 90 percent said having a democratic political system was "very" or "fairly" good— more than the world average of 84 percent.[63] But only 41 percent said the same of "having a strong leader who does not have to bother with parliament or elections"—a nutshell definition of authoritarianism—

and only 37 percent saw merit in "having experts, not government, make decisions according to what they think is best for the country"—a description of technocracy. Chinese support for each of these was below the world average.[64]

Elsewhere, enthusiasm for China's approach is underwhelming. Even as Beijing plowed hundreds of billions of dollars into its Belt and Road Initiative and promoted its brand with 548 Confucius Institutes around the world, it won few fans.[65] Among 10 Western countries plus Japan and South Korea, *unfavorable* views of China surged from 36 percent of respondents in the median country in the mid-2000s to 73 percent in 2020.[66] That might reflect rivalry. But even in Africa, recipient of massive Chinese aid and investment, few seem taken by Beijing's approach. In 2019–20, the Afrobarometer asked respondents in 18 African countries what other state offered the best model for their own development. Pluralities in 14 of the 18 named the United States. Only in 3—Botswana, Mali, and Burkina Faso—did a larger proportion of respondents favor China.[67] Asked what foreign language young people should learn, 71 percent said English. Only 2 percent said Chinese.[68]

Our point is not that all is rosy in the world of human rights or that Western leaders consistently protect them. Many foreign policy elites hold fast to a cynical version of realpolitik. Washington's post-2001 "War on Terror" motivated extreme abuses—from the waterboarding and "rendition" of suspects to indefinite detentions at Guantanamo. Dictators from Uzbekistan's Islam Karimov to Egypt's Abdel Al-Sisi learned that they could get away with terror if packaged as counterterrorism.[69] Our point is just that the thugs face greater pushback than before from a ramifying international network of activists and lawyers, backed up by global public opinion. And, despite the rhetoric of populists, no other model—including China's—has anywhere near the global appeal today of liberal democracy.[70]

As with economic globalization, the liberal world order could collapse in the future. Yet, despite continuous challenges, that has not happened. More generally, we see little sign the modernization cocktail is finished. It has had a powerful run. Indeed, the recent flare-up of anti-globalism is largely a reaction to the remarkable changes of the last three decades. As countries became postindustrial, educated, and internationally linked, their rulers had to adapt—or, at least, pretend to. Amid the third wave of democracy, liberal norms spread worldwide.

The force of this modernizing onslaught was what eventually caused the losers to rally.[71] Today's nativist populism—in both West and East—unites the economic resentment and obsolescent values of those hurt by the postindustrial transition. Workers and others from dying industrial regions; owners of polluting factories and mines; farmers and rural laborers; the illiberal old, disoriented by value change—all come together in a powerful but gradually shrinking coalition. That coalition furnishes support for populists in advanced democracies and spin dictators in semi-modernized autocracies. Instead of compensating and reintegrating economic losers, such leaders exploit them. Whether they have to do so within democratic constraints depends mostly on the strength of the postindustrial *winners*—our informed stratum.

Countries prematurely swept up and thrust ahead by the third wave have been slipping back down the beach in recent years. Observers have expressed alarm at such backsliding. Troubling as it is, we see it as the ebb of a wave rather than a change in the current. After two steps forward comes one step back.

DIAGNOSING THE THREAT

Today's autocracies pose new challenges to the democracies of the West. To deal with these, we first need to understand them. Let's recall the key features of spin dictators and the international behaviors these motivate.

Unlike the West's Cold War adversaries, spin dictators have no real ideology. Recognizing the appeal of democracy to their citizens, they pretend to embrace it.[72] Many fall for the act, and even those who do not are often demoralized. Paradoxical as it might sound, the hypocrisy of such rulers may weaken faith not so much in them as in democracy itself. When dictators claim to be building communism—or Ba'athism or Mobutuism—their opponents can believe in popular government as a better alternative. But when the incumbent is himself a "democrat," it is easy to think that democracy is always a sham.

Abroad, spin dictators use propaganda to spread cynicism and division. If Western publics doubt democracy and distrust their leaders, those leaders will be less apt to launch democratic crusades around the globe. Whether Russian interference influenced the 2016 U.S. election was—and is—debated. But just the perception that it might have done so cast a shadow on the vote and turned American attention inward. Besides attacking Americans' confidence in their system, Russian social media trolls had a message for viewers back home: U.S.-style democracy leads to polarization and conflict.[73]

A second key tactic is to exploit corruption. At home, spin dictators buy off elites in covert ways. And abroad, as we saw, they do the same. Along with disinformation, they export sleaze. They have two motives. First, they seek to weaken Western governments and block hostile actions. They recruit Western helpers to provide intelligence and lobby their interests. Besides spies—which have always existed—they cultivate friends in the West's political and corporate undergrowth. Such relationships yield concrete payoffs and create opportunities for blackmail. At the same time, the graft that autocrats finance damages the West's reputation. When discovered, it discredits Western elites.[74] This points to dictators' second motive: to shape public opinion in their own countries. By fueling—and sometimes leaking details of—corruption in the West, spin dictators normalize their own unsavory tactics. When reports of dirty dealings in their own governments surface, the dictators' defenders can reply that graft is universal. Their operations abroad help inoculate them against scandals at home.

Focused on personal power and self-interest, today's dictators have trouble forming solid alliances. Stalin forged a stable bloc based on shared ideology. Current autocrats can collaborate with each other on specific projects. But their loyalties realign as new opportunities emerge. Putin and Erdoğan have flipped between friends and enemies so many times it is hard to keep track. Chávez embraced Castro and other Latin leftists. But when Venezuelan oil shipments dipped after the comandante's death, Cuba began angling for détente with Washington.[75]

Rather than unite to oppose the West, spin dictators infiltrate Western alliances and institutions. As we saw in chapter 6, they pretend to share Western goals only to impede them covertly. From inside, they throw sand in the works and retarget such bodies against their enemies. Much as they discredit liberal democracy by imitating it, they embrace liberal internationalism to exploit it.

As we saw, Hungary's Orbán helps decide the policies of NATO, the OECD, and the European Union. Erdoğan is a member of the first two, and Putin joins both in the Council of Europe. Further afield, African dictators consort with British royals at Commonwealth summits. In the United Nations, torturers sit on human rights bodies.[76] Venezuela, Russia, and Qatar were founding members of the so-called Community of Democracies, discrediting that grouping from day one. Of course, such tactics are not new. From the start, the Soviet Union and China exploited their UN positions and African dictators participated in the Commonwealth. But today's authoritarians work systematically to grasp the levers of the liberal world order.

In sum, the challenges are various. Spin dictators are not out to take over the world. They are non-ideological, opportunistic, and uncoordinated. They still use military force at times, seizing territory near their borders, intervening in conflicts, or staging provocations, usually to boost their image at home. More often, they attack the West from inside elite economic and political networks. To protect themselves, they work to erode confidence in liberal democracy, weaken the West's alliances and institutions, and corrupt and exploit its leaders.

HOW TO RESPOND?

Since World War II, two approaches have dominated Western policy toward dictators. In the Cold War, the chief threat came from communist states and guerrilla forces. These sought to conquer territory and spread their ideology, subverting free societies. The cohesion of the international communist movement was often exaggerated. But the danger was real.

The main Western response was containment. In George Kennan's vision, that meant "the long-term, patient but firm and vigilant" rebuffing of Soviet challenges.[77] This mostly worked. Western Europe regained its confidence and economic dynamism in the 1950s. Eventually,

Gorbachev's "New Thinking" eased the Soviet Union into oblivion. But the way containment was implemented also had costs. To combat Moscow, the West allied with anticommunist dictators and extremists, setting aside its commitment to democracy and human rights. The United States armed jihadists in Afghanistan whom it would later have to fight. It waged—and lost—a demoralizing war in Vietnam that was fueled by anticolonial sentiment as much as Soviet ambition.

After 1991, as the global struggle against communism ended, Western policy changed. The key goal became the economic development and integration of authoritarian states into the West. In essence, the idea was to catalyze the modernization cocktail. Policymakers hoped that developing the economies of dictatorships would create demand within them for political reform. Modernization would render them more democratic and cooperative. To help the process along, Western governments and international institutions started pressing dictators to allow more freedom, conditioning aid on political reforms, and sending teams of advisors to help organize elections, set up parties, and support civil society.[78]

This approach is now often criticized as naïve. In fact, it had considerable success. The first two post-Cold War decades saw huge economic and political progress. Between 1990 and 2010, world income per capita grew by 60 percent. Fewer people died in state-based wars than in any previous twenty-year period since World War II.[79] The number of electoral democracies rose from 29 to 53 and that of liberal democracies from 28 to 45.[80] Indeed, it was when Western states went beyond assisting development and integration and used military force to promote regime change that the greatest problems arose. The invasions of Afghanistan and Iraq, while overturning vicious dictatorships, led to long wars with enormous costs in lives, money, and the United States' international reputation.

Although supporting development and integration made sense, as with containment the implementation was problematic. First, the West was hardly consistent in its commitments. Leaders privileged some countries and slighted others, for reasons that had to do with politics back home. They continued to support their favorite dictators, pretending to believe their promises to reform. France remained loyal to some unsavory old friends in Africa such as Congo's Denis Sassou Nguesso and Chad's Idriss Déby, while Britain and the United States soft-pedaled the human rights abuses of clients such as Uganda's Yoweri Museveni.[81]

Second, even when they were sincere, Western governments and institutions were not prepared. They were too easy for opportunistic authoritarians to game. NATO and the EU had grown out of clubs of like-minded Western countries and made decisions based on consensus, with few mechanisms to sanction members who broke rules—especially if they skillfully pretended to follow them. The Western multilateral organizations assumed shared ideals and mutual trust and lacked tools to deter or punish incremental misbehavior.

At the same time, Western leaders did not foresee how integration would affect *their* societies. They thought current and former autocracies could be assimilated without changing the West. But integration is a two-way process. The gains from trade with China after its 2001 WTO entry were considerable. Yet, Chinese competition also created losers, changing the political landscape in Western states in ways their leaders failed to address. Nor did these leaders anticipate how corruption in the East would mesh with their own homegrown sleaze. As they freed capital flows, deregulated business, and opened trade with their former adversaries, Western governments did little to guard against the backflow. Underneath new reformed institutions, many of the old networks remained—and linked up with the West's own. Greater openness should have been accompanied by spring cleaning at home to flush out the exploiters of banking secrecy, tax havens, intelligence networks, and organized crime. But this did not happen—at least, not right away and not on a sufficient scale. Greater integration made the East more like the West. It also made the West more like the East.

This history should inform policies today. Neither containment nor the kind of straightforward development and integration tried in the past quite fit the current challenges. Elements of military containment are still needed to deter opportunistic aggression around Russia's and China's borders. But the West cannot contain China indefinitely, with its massive population, technological proficiency, and GDP overtaking that of the United States. In the medium run, there is no alternative to integrating it and other rivals—and that is fine since the modernization cocktail *does* work. But the West needs to devise a smarter version of integration.

What would that look like? We suggest an approach of *adversarial engagement*. The West must continue to engage. But it should not expect integration to automatically disempower dictators and render them cooperative. Rather, the West should use the leverage of an interconnected world to defend its interests and nudge dictatorships toward free government. The catch is that dictatorships will be doing the same in reverse. They will try to use interdependence to advance their interests and weaken democracy. Western leaders have to be better at this game than they are.

Some believe, by contrast, that the best path would be simply to decouple from authoritarian countries. They advocate protecting markets, sharply limiting immigration, and focusing on domestic tasks. But, in fact, isolation is not feasible. Like it or not, the world will become more interconnected in coming decades. Even if economic globalization stalls, technological advances, environmental threats, and deadly pathogens will crisscross borders. The West can either lead on global issues or be led by others.

So how to succeed at adversarial engagement? Dealing with dictatorships is hard, and we do not pretend to have perfect answers. But thinking from the perspective of fear and spin suggests a few principles that could help guide the search for strategies.

The first is to *be more watchful*. In the last thirty years, spin dictators have slipped under the radar by imitating democracy. The West was slow to recognize their approach and too ready to believe autocrats who claimed to be on the path to free government. Western states need to do a better job of tracking the many links—often covert—that connect their countries to the authoritarian world. As we saw, dictators launder money, steal industrial secrets, corrupt politicians, hack into state computers, and plant propaganda on social networks in the West. Of course, governments try to detect and prevent these activities. Yet, scandals continually reveal massive failures.

So, as we engage, we need to keep watching. That means investing more in financial monitoring, counterintelligence, and cybersecurity.[82] It also means sharing information and coordinating responses, both across seemingly distinct spheres and among democratic allies. Effective monitoring requires a light touch. There are two dangers: first, that the West will not react adequately to political threats, and, second, that it will overreact. Onerous reporting requirements lead to noncompliance and overload state agents with superfluous paperwork. The challenge is to create unobtrusive yet powerful systems that respect privacy.

Agile networks of state investigators are vital. But Western governments also need to engage with the private sector. Groups such as Bellingcat and the International Consortium of Investigative Journalists have shown how much can be gleaned from open source information and leaks. Crowdsourcing and machine learning could enhance Western understanding of ongoing world events. Cutting-edge technology companies—both big and small—need to be part of the mix. Both Western governments and big tech companies share the goal of preserving and deepening liberal democracy. Yet, they have rarely cooperated on this. Setting aside disagreements, they need to create partnerships that use the technical firepower of Silicon Valley against dictators.

The second principle is to *welcome modernization—even in our adversaries.* Economic and social development remains the best hope to transform autocracies first to less violent forms and ultimately to genuine democracy. At the same time, global integration—if managed right—traps dictators in a web of external relationships and incentives. So, although economic sanctions may be necessary at times, they should be targeted and narrow, aimed at individuals and firms. They should not seek to prevent modernization or isolate whole countries from world markets.

Of course, the cocktail works slowly and unevenly. We will not always like how modernizing dictatorships behave. China's integration into global trade coincided with a rise in its assertiveness. This has caused some to question the wisdom of admitting China to the WTO.[83] But if a developing China seems a problem, a China blocked from development would be a bigger one. A dictator unable to satisfy his population with exports and growth has a stronger incentive to turn to violence both at home and abroad.

A third principle is to *put our own house in order*. Spin dictatorships exploit the vulnerabilities of democracies and try to create new ones. So a key defense is to build resilience. Economically, that means continually examining supply chains and trade relationships, identifying emerging monopolies and bottlenecks that could be weaponized. Anti-trust has to be nimble and attentive to global political factors as well as market conditions. Although expensive, the West needs to build redundancy into infrastructure and ensure multiple competing firms exist in strategic sectors, even if the sectors are natural monopolies. All this will require cooperation from business.

Defeating dictatorship also requires the West to stop enabling dictators. Without the help of armies of Western lawyers, bankers, lobbyists, and other elite fixers, autocrats would have a harder time exploiting the West. Measures to disable the enablers have to be sophisticated. They must distinguish the corrupt exchanges that strengthen dictators from the beneficial contacts that gradually nudge them toward democracy. But the West's infrastructure of graft can and should be pruned back. Anonymous shell companies should be banned—within countries, by laws, and, internationally, by a UN convention. Western democracies should strengthen their authority to pursue corruption worldwide (with laws such as the U.S. Foreign Corrupt Practices Act and the OECD Anti-Bribery Convention) and enforce these more energetically.[84] They should increase rewards to whistle-blowers who expose serious banking fraud and broaden the extraterritorial reach of anti-fraud laws.

In this vein, it is time to end the practice of paid lobbying on behalf of authoritarian governments. When Western firms and former officials take money to promote the interests of human rights abusers, it tarnishes the reputation not just of themselves but of their countries. To be clear, broad leeway for the expression of unconventional opinions and for contacts even with odious figures is essential to liberal democracy. Smart integration requires the exchange of ideas at all levels. But contracts to advocate for dictators or their associates do not serve any legitimate interest. States have embassies to communicate their positions.

The West's reputation also suffers when its firms sell technologies to dictators that are then used to control their citizens. European firms have sold surveillance equipment to Azerbaijan, Egypt, Kazakhstan, Saudi Arabia, Ethiopia, Syria, and Libya.[85] Israel's private tech sector has supplied spy software to the dictators of Bahrain, Azerbaijan, Uzbekistan, Kazakhstan, Ethiopia, South Sudan, Uganda, Ecuador, and the United Arab Emirates, among other countries.[86] Of course, Chinese and other companies will fill the gap. But the damage to the West's reputation from making such sales outweighs the limited commercial benefit. More generally, the West needs to thoroughly investigate the current practices of firms providing security and legal services to the world's dictators and debate what is and what is not appropriate. Law associations might want to discourage members from helping abusive rulers pursue dissidents and journalists by means of frivolous suits in Western courts.

Most important of all, the West needs to put its *political* house in order, repairing government institutions and restoring confidence in them. Political polarization has reached extreme levels in some countries, creating opportunities that dictators exploit. Some see this as endangering democracy by weakening citizens' attachment to it. This seems to us a bit exaggerated. Western citizens appear more disillusioned with current incumbents than with democracy itself. In the 2017–20 round of the World Values Survey and European Values Study, for instance, 93 percent of respondents in the median country in Western Europe and North America said that having a democratic political system was "very" or "fairly" good—a higher percentage than in any of the four preceding rounds (1995–99, 2000–2004, 2005–9, and 2010–14).[87] Yet, while the ideal of liberal democracy remains robust, confidence that governments are respecting it in practice is weaker. Asked to rate how democratically their country was being governed on a scale from 1 ("not at all democratic") to 10 ("completely democratic"), only 58 percent of U.S. respondents and 61 percent of Italians chose a number in the top half of the scale.

Under President Trump, the image of U.S. democracy took a hit not just at home but around the world. In 2018, Pew asked respondents in

25 countries whether they thought "the government of the US respects the personal freedom of its people." In 40 percent of countries—including France, Germany, and the UK—a majority said no. (When Pew asked the same question back in 2008, that was true in none of the 23 countries then included.) Pew also sometimes asks respondents whether they like or dislike "American ideas about democracy." The share of countries where a majority liked the American concept fell from 58 percent in 2002 to 35 percent in 2017.[88]

All this suggests not a rejection of democracy but increasing doubts about the West's—and, in particular, the United States'—commitment to it. The Trump presidency brought the weak points in U.S. politics into sharp focus. Like a hacker hired to detect flaws in a security system, he exposed loopholes and gaps unnoticed under more ethical administrations. These relate to financial disclosure, nepotism, conflicts of interest, improper pressure on courts, civil servants and law enforcement, the politicized declaration of emergencies, misallocation of budget funds, corrupt use of pardons, and war powers. Even before Trump, U.S. elections were notorious for extreme gerrymandering, voter suppression, and dark money.[89] As already noted, illiberal actions in the "War on Terror"—the indefinite detentions at Guantanamo Bay and "enhanced interrogation" methods—weakened U.S. moral authority worldwide. Other policies—from the invasion of Iraq to remove nonexistent weapons of mass destruction to the NSA's secret mass surveillance programs—allow spin dictators to paint Western governments as hypocritical.

And that's not all. Recent economic failures have further sapped faith in Western leadership. The remarkable performance of China's economy gave some the impression that authoritarianism accelerates growth. In fact, economists find that the opposite is true: if a country moves from autocracy to democracy, some recent research suggests that its growth rate tends to increase by about 1 percentage point a year.[90] In each decade from the 1950s to the 1990s, democracies grew faster on average than authoritarian states.[91] However, in the 2000s authoritarian states did outpace democracies. They were less affected by the bursting of the dotcom bubble in 2001–2, the global financial crisis in 2009, and the Eurozone debt crisis in 2011–12—all of which were triggered by

Western regulatory or policy failures. Dictatorships still produce only a fraction of world GDP. But their share is rising.[92]

Rebuilding confidence in the integrity, competence, and liberalism of democratic governments is the surest way to combat authoritarian propaganda. The great virtue of democracy is its ability to admit and correct errors. "If we wish to fulfill the promise that is ours," said President Harry Truman in 1948, "we must correct the remaining imperfections in our democracy."[93] After Watergate, the U.S. Congress passed a plethora of laws to address the flaws that scandal revealed. As Trump left office, many were calling for a new package of comparable reforms.[94] Similar measures are needed in other Western countries to attack corruption and revive faith in their leaders.

Spin dictators seek to weaken Western alliances and international organizations. Our fourth orienting principle is to *defend and reform the institutions of the liberal world order*. The EU and NATO must avoid being blackmailed by leaders such as Orbán and Erdoğan. The rules that worked when these were small clubs need to be adapted to the broader membership of today. NATO must also change from a body focused almost entirely on military threats—although those remain—to one defending against the full spectrum of attacks today's dictators favor. Article 5 of the North Atlantic Treaty could be amended or interpreted to include collective defense against cyber-interference in the elections of any member country. Members could define specific actions all would take in response to the hacking of polling stations or major disinformation offensives. The EU also needs to develop and enforce more stringent controls on corruption and influence peddling.

Then there are the multilateral organizations with global membership. Western governments must prevent these from being co-opted or abused. For instance, they should stop autocrats from using Interpol to harass opponents. At the UN, the world's liberal democracies must defend human rights law and enforcement. A majority of states may still favor protecting abusers. China and Russia have sought to build such a coalition, with some success: China's foreign minister Wang Yi claimed in 2021 that eighty countries on the UN Human Rights Council had expressed solidarity with Beijing over Xinjiang, an astounding figure if true.[95] Still, if they work together—and enlist help from regional institutions like the Organization of American States, the European Union, and the African Union—the genuine liberal democracies may be able to purge human rights bodies of the worst abusers.

This points to our fifth and final principle: *support democracy democratically.* There is little evidence that military interventions to spread democracy work—and the West should avoid them.[96] Instead, it should use democratic practices to promote popular government worldwide. Several practices are key: appeal to public opinion, forge coalitions, identify and build on areas of agreement, and accept periodic defeats without walking out.

Promoting democracy by force is not just self-defeating. It neglects the key resource that adherents could bring to bear: global public opinion. The vast majority of people worldwide already believe in democracy. As we saw in chapter 1, among 83 countries polled in 2017–20, 84 percent of respondents on average thought having a democratic government was "very" or "fairly" good. In no country did a majority *not* favor democracy. The global appeal of democracy is a weapon the West should use. It should confront dictators with the evidence that their citizens want popular government.

A key activity in democracies is forging coalitions. The free countries of the world should forge one to support freedom. At present, many countries have their own programs of democracy promotion, sometimes combined with others on human rights, governance, or economic development. Together, they create a labyrinth of bureaucracies with overlapping remits. Some agencies are associated with the Cold War and mix support for free government with a history of pursuing military interests or partisan missions.

It is time to found an alliance of liberal democracies to defend democracy. A united, international coalition, governing itself by democratic procedures, would have greater moral authority than any individual state.[97] Dictators can accuse any particular country's programs of being a Trojan horse for strategic interference. To make that stick against a broad-based, global coalition of liberal democracies would be much harder.[98] Besides having greater moral authority, an alliance of democracies, backed by independent analysts and coordinating with global human rights organizations, would be more effective than a myriad of agencies operating separately. It could coordinate efforts, pool resources, decide on common positions, and divide up concrete tasks.

Reducing redundancy, such a coalition could establish global programs on all the key elements—from party-building, election administration and monitoring, human rights, and independent media to rule of law and democracy-supporting information technology. It could work out norms to govern electoral observation, codify these, and establish an accreditation system that would expose zombie monitors. It could negotiate an international convention on transparency in political financing, establishing standards for the disclosure of sources of campaign contributions. It could set up exchange programs for young people, police, judges, and others in member and non-member states to spread knowledge about modern democracies and counter the relativizing propaganda of spin dictators. At the same time, such a multilateral forum could coordinate with NGOs and journalists to document electoral fraud, monitor human rights worldwide, report rapidly on abuses, and maintain registers of political prisoners and torturers.

Of course, dictatorships would try to divide and conquer, turning democracies against each other, exploiting particular interests and cultural affiliations. To resist this, a coalition of democracies should focus on areas of agreement, bracketing points of dispute. Understandings of democracy and policy priorities vary across countries. That can inform the division of tasks. Still, disagreements could threaten cohesiveness, especially since an alliance of democracies would also need to address the practices of its members. So internal procedures have to be not just democratic but crafted to privilege points of agreement and de-escalate conflicts.

Finally, just as in democratic government itself, members would have to be ready to tolerate periodic defeats. This has been an issue for the United States in the past. From the beginning, U.S. support for global democracy has combined soaring rhetoric with reluctance to commit. From Woodrow Wilson to George W. Bush, presidents have proposed to make the world "safe for democracy" and spread a "global democratic revolution," while refusing to join the League of Nations, hesitating for almost forty years before ratifying the Genocide Convention, and declining to be bound by the International Criminal Court.[99] Most recently, the United States walked out of the UN's Human Rights Council. A key aspect of democracy is accepting losses. It is time to retire U.S. exceptionalism and unilateralism—at least as they apply to the struggle for democracy.

A POWERFUL IDEA

The West today faces a complicated challenge. In the world wars of the twentieth century and the Cold War, the enemies of freedom wore no disguise. Their military tunics, impassioned speeches, and public executions left little doubt about their true nature. The geopolitical dividing lines were drawn in black and white.

These days, the map is mainly shaded in gray. Except for a few strongmen like Kim Jong-Un and Bashar al-Assad who oblige by playing the villain, most are harder to place. They blend in and erode international society from within. Western observers have not known how to describe these new autocrats. Either they equate them to the old—labeling Putin a tsar, Chávez another Castro—or they endorse their democratic act, as some accept Orbán's bona fides. In fact, these leaders are neither classic twentieth-century tyrants nor wayward members of the Western club. They are something else—something we have tried to characterize in this book.

Many today fear Western states will become more like *their* regimes— that our democracies will sink into spin. Some opportunistic politicians try for exactly that. They forge television and social media links to the unsophisticated and unhappy, while co-opting elite helpers. Such politicians have destabilized some fragile third wave democracies and even some more established ones—like Venezuela's—where the educated class was narrow and compromised. There is no need to exaggerate the danger. Today's backsliding is more likely to end in the spin of a Bolsonaro than the carnage of a Pinochet. Although the former is troubling, the latter is clearly worse. The first two "reverse waves" produced Hitler and Franco, Mobutu and Idi Amin. The third has given us Correa and Erdoğan.

In more developed, highly educated societies, what holds back aspiring spin dictators, we have argued, is the resistance of networks of lawyers, judges, civil servants, journalists, activists, and opposition politicians. Such leaders survive for a while, lowering the tone and eroding their country's reputation. But so far they have all been voted out of office to face possible corruption prosecutions. That was the outcome for Silvio Berlusconi and Donald Trump. No one can be sure this will always be the case. But if it is, the credit will go less to institutions per se than to those who defend them.

Internationally, Western societies are now linked to the dictatorships of the world by multiple capillaries. There is no safe way to opt out of the global system. A better goal is to make that system healthier and ensure it works in the West's interest, along the lines suggested in this chapter. This is a contest that can be won. Spin dictators would like their citizens to trust them and distrust the West. They thrive in a world of cynicism and relativism. But the West has something they do not: a powerful idea around which it can unite, the idea of liberal democracy.

This idea—although some today see it as tarnished—is, in fact, the West's strongest weapon. Reinforcing the commitment to it is good policy both at home and abroad, which is why autocrats are so eager to stand in the way. Indeed, concern that the West may reinvigorate its democracy and set a strong example animates today's fear and spin dictators alike. Both will throw up obstacles. But the only way to defeat an idea is with a better idea, and they do not have one. That spin dictators pretend to be democrats proves they have no vision to offer. They can only delay and discourage us for a while—if we let them.

NOTES

PREFACE

1. This is based on the Varieties of Democracy data set, version 10. We count both "electoral" and "liberal" democracies, using the "regimes of the world" variable. The number of these hit 98 in 2010.

CHAPTER 1: FEAR AND SPIN

1. On how the ruling People's Action Party dominates in Singapore, see, for instance, Freedom House, *Freedom in the World 2021*: "Singapore's parliamentary political system has been dominated by the ruling People's Action Party (PAP) and the family of current prime minister Lee Hsien Loong since 1959. The electoral and legal framework that the PAP has constructed allows for some political pluralism, but it constrains the growth of credible opposition parties and limits freedoms of expression, assembly, and association." In September 2020, Prime Minister Lee Hsien Loong seemed to cast doubt on the possibility of another party successfully governing the country: "Is it really true that one day if there is a change of government, a new party can run Singapore equally well . . . ? This is like saying anybody can be the conductor for the New York Philharmonic Orchestra" (Loong, "PM Lee Hsien Loong at the Debate"). For other characterizations of the system as less than democratic, see Morgenbesser, *Behind the Façade*, 146–47, and George, *Singapore, Incomplete*, 115–22. On Orbán's dismantling of democracy, see Ash, "Europe Must Stop This Disgrace"; Beauchamp, "It Happened There"; and *Economist*, "How Viktor Orbán Hollowed Out Hungary's Democracy." Among classifiers of political regimes, Varieties of Democracy (V-DEM) rates both Singapore and Hungary as nondemocracies in recent years and Freedom House rates both as only "partly free." Polity rates Singapore a nondemocracy but Hungary (in 2018) as still a democracy.

2. In earlier works (Guriev and Treisman, "Informational Autocrats," "A Theory of Informational Autocracy," and "The Popularity of Authoritarian Leaders"), we used the term "informational autocracy" for this model of rule. We refer to the same model as "spin dictatorship" here. For an excellent survey of some recent cases, see Dobson, *The Dictator's Learning Curve*.

3. For details, see Barry, "Economist Who Fled."

4. This might sound strange coming from someone who faced security service scrutiny for something he helped to write. But what got the Kremlin's attention in Sergei's case was not criticism of Russia's authorities in the press—such criticism remains quite common—but that he had, in their eyes, interfered in a politically sensitive court case.

5. In February 2015, Boris Nemtsov, a leader of the anti-Putin opposition, was assassinated outside the Kremlin. A Chechen former security officer was sentenced to prison for the murder, along with four accomplices. But who ordered the killing has never been proven (see Nechepurenko, "Five Who Killed"). Opposition politician and activist Vladimir Kara-Murza was twice poisoned while in Russia and almost died on both occasions (Eckel and Schreck, "FBI Silent on Lab Results in Kremlin Foe's Suspected Poisoning"). Then, in 2020, opposition leader Aleksei Navalny was also poisoned with a form of the rare nerve agent Novichok (Bennhold and Schwirtz, "Navalny Awake and Alert"). In all these cases, the Kremlin denied any responsibility.

6. Attacks like those against Nemtsov, Kara-Murza, and Navalny send a clear message to anti-Kremlin activists. But do ordinary people feel fear? Of course, it is hard to be sure. Still, various evidence suggests not—at least until recently. Asked in 2019 by the independent and respected Levada Center which of a list of feelings they had experienced more strongly recently, only 7 percent of respondents included "fear." Asked which they thought *other* people around them had experienced in the previous year—perhaps a less sensitive question—only 13 percent said "fear." The most popular answer, chosen by 36 percent, was "weariness, indifference." Polled repeatedly in 2003–17 on whether they feared a "return to mass repression," at most 30 percent said yes (in 2013), fewer than confessed that year to fear of world war, criminal attacks, natural disasters, unemployment, and AIDS. However, the percent fearing mass repression has risen since 2017, reaching 52 percent in 2021—quite possibly indicating the end of Putin's experiment with spin (see Levada Center, "Kharakter i struktura massovoy trevozhnosti v Rossii"). In chapter 4, we provide evidence that in general in spin dictatorships most of the public is not afraid to express critical views when polled.

7. In 2020–21, as we were writing this book, the use of harsh measures against the anti-Putin opposition—and even some who just expressed opposition views—increased. The number of political prisoners rose from 45 at the end of 2014 to 81 in August 2021, according to the human rights organization Memorial, and others were apparently imprisoned for their religious beliefs (Memorial, *Annual Report, 2013–14*, 20; Memorial, *Spisok lits, preznannykh politicheskimi zaklyuchennymi*). Protests were suppressed, with thousands detained. As we discuss in chapter 8, spin dictatorships like that of Putin in his early years may revert to violent repression when severe economic crisis or social modernization renders spin no longer viable. Such tactics are unlikely to work for long but may still be the ruler's best bet at the time.

That may be what is happening now in Russia. However, although higher than before, the tally of political prisoners remains in the dozens, not the thousands. Political killings occur much more rarely than under most of the "fear dictators" we discuss throughout the book, and state involvement is concealed—albeit sometimes ineptly. The Kremlin continues to pretend the elections it holds are free and fair and that peaceful demonstrations are permitted. YouTube remains largely uncensored. Although increasingly embattled, independent media such as *Novaya Gazeta* and pollsters such as the Levada Center continue to publish. Those punished for political crimes are accused of extremism, terrorism, or nonpolitical offenses. Navalny was finally jailed in 2021 over the alleged defrauding of a cosmetics company. In April 2021, the authorities labeled his political network "extremist-linked," forcing it to disband (Sauer, "'End of an Era'"; Roth, "Russian State Watchdog Adds Navalny"). We see Russia as of early 2021 as on the border between spin and fear, and moving in the direction of the latter.

8. As we discuss later in this chapter, there are some resemblances to populist politicians in democracies such as Silvio Berlusconi and Donald Trump.

9. Safire, "Essay: The Dictator Speaks."

10. The Isle of Man, the Cook Islands, and New Zealand all permitted women to vote in national elections before 1900, but each was a colony, protectorate, or dependency of Britain rather than an independent state (Teele, *Forging the Franchise*, 1–3). In some other places, property-owning women could vote, usually in local elections. All women had the vote in certain U.S. states (e.g., Wyoming, Colorado, Utah, and Idaho).

11. They are France, Belgium, Switzerland, Greece, and Canada (we use the Lexical Index of Electoral Democracy; see Skaaning, Gerring, and Bartusevicius, "A Lexical Index").

12. Huntington, *The Third Wave*; Markoff, *Waves of Democracy*.

13. This is based on the Varieties of Democracy (V-DEM) database, v.10, using the "Regimes of the World" index, which classified 23.5 percent of countries as liberal democracies in 2015. See Coppedge et al., "V-Dem Codebook V.10." In fact, the proportion of democracies is even higher than this as V-DEM does not include a number of small Caribbean and Asian island democracies.

14. See Aron, "The Future of Secular Religions."

15. Pinto, "Fascism, Corporatism and the Crafting of Authoritarian Institutions."

16. See, for instance, Wiarda, *Corporatism and Comparative Politics*.

17. On Marcos, see Hutchcroft, "Reflections on a Reverse Image." On Bendjedid, see Stone, *The Agony of Algeria*, 64–65.

18. There were some exceptions with relatively little brutal repression, such as the Kenyan independence leader Jomo Kenyatta and several Gulf emirs. But, compared to recent decades, low violence strategies were rare, as we document in chapter 2. Even those, such as the Argentine populist Juan Péron, whose rule saw few political killings, often imprisoned thousands of dissidents (see, e.g., Blankstein, *Péron's Argentina*, 204).

19. French, "Anatomy of an Autocracy."

20. Natanson, "Duvalier, Terror Rule Haiti, Island of Fear."

21. FBIS Daily Report, "Saddam Speech Marks Revolution's 22nd Anniversary."

22. Franco, "End of Year Address to the Spanish People."

23. Torpey, "Leaving: A Comparative View," 24.

24. Davidson, *Black Star*.

25. Daniszewski and Drogin, "Legacy of Guile, Greed, and Graft." An exception here was some Latin American military juntas, which promised to restore democracy after they had rid the country of subversives. Mexico's Institutional Revolution Party leaders also claimed, like later spin dictators, to be governing democratically.

26. See Chacon and Carey, "Counting Political Prisoners in Venezuela."

27. Rachman, "Lunch with the FT."

28. Morgenbesser, *Behind the Façade*, 138; Fernandez, "GE2020."

29. Amnesty International, *Singapore*. The teenager, Amos Yee, was sentenced to four weeks' imprisonment.

30. Guriev and Treisman, "Informational Autocrats," "A Theory of Informational Autocracy," and "The Popularity of Authoritarian Leaders." The online supplement can be accessed via: https://press.princeton.edu/books/spin-dictators.

31. Two of many important works are Geddes, Wright, and Frantz, *How Dictatorships Work*, and Svolik, *The Politics of Authoritarian Rule*. For a review of formal models of authoritarian politics, see Gehlbach, Sonin, and Svolik, "Formal Models of Nondemocratic Politics."

32. Huang, "Propaganda as Signaling."

33. A foundational work is Kuran, "Now out of Never." Other articles that focus on preventing public coordination include Kricheli, Livne, and Magaloni, "Taking to the Streets"; King, Pan, and Roberts, "How Censorship in China Allows Government Criticism but Silences Collective Expression"; Edmond, "Information Manipulation, Coordination, and Regime Change"; and Chen and Xu, "Information Manipulation and Reform."

34. Other important works explore how dictators avoid the other main danger besides revolution—being overthrown in a coup (Svolik, *The Politics of Authoritarian Rule*; Myerson, "The Autocrat's Credibility Problem"; Boix and Svolik, "The Foundations of Limited Authoritarian Government"; Egorov and Sonin, "Dictators and Their Viziers")—or how they co-opt fellow insiders by sharing the spoils of office. In the latter case, the key question is how large a set of insiders to co-opt (Bueno de Mesquita et al., *The Logic of Political Survival*). We have little to add here on those questions.

35. We return to the question of how one can judge people's true feelings in an authoritarian society in chapter 4.

36. Levitsky and Way, *Competitive Authoritarianism*. See also Gandhi and Lust-Okar, "Elections under Authoritarianism," and Kendall-Taylor and Frantz, "Mimicking Democracy to Prolong Autocracies." In practice, our distinction between spin and fear dictatorships corresponds only weakly with Levitsky and Way's between "competitive authoritarian" and "fully authoritarian" regimes (see the online supplement, table OS1.5). Only 34 percent of the country-years that we classify as occurring in spin dictatorships are classified by Levitsky and Way as competitive authoritarian. Similarly, only 33 percent of the competitive authoritarian country-years in Levitsky and Way's sample were spin dictatorships. Many competitive authoritarian regimes use significant violent repression to spread fear and so are not spin dictatorships (e.g., Zimbabwe under Robert Mugabe, Kenya under Daniel arap Moi). And many spin dictatorships hold elections that are not at all competitive and so are not competitive authoritarian regimes (e.g., Singapore under Lee Kuan Yew and his successors, Kazakhstan under Nazarbayev).

37. On the post-Soviet states, see Wilson, *Virtual Politics*; on South-East Asia, Morgenbesser, *Behind the Façade*, "The Menu of Autocratic Innovation," and *The Rise of Sophisticated Authoritarianism in Southeast Asia*; George, *Singapore, Incomplete*; and Rajah, *Authoritarian Rule of Law*. On Egypt, see Blaydes, *Elections and Distributive Politics in Mubarak's Egypt*; on Latin America, inter alia, Schedler, "The Menu of Manipulation"; on Africa, inter alia, Cheeseman and Klaas, *How to Rig an Election*, and Cheeseman and Fisher, *Authoritarian Africa*.

38. For instance, Kendall-Taylor, Frantz, and Wright, "The Digital Dictators"; Dragu and Lupu, "Digital Authoritarianism."

39. Aristotle, *The Politics*, 145–47 (Book 5, Chapter 11).

40. Montesquieu, *The Spirit of the Laws*, 22 (Book 3, Chapter 3).

41. Ibid., 28 (Book 3, Chapter 9).

42. See Boesche, *Theories of Tyranny from Plato to Arendt*, chap. 10.

43. Aristotle, *The Politics*, 147–50 (Book 5, Chapter 11). Aristotle defines six main types of government, distinguished on the basis of who rules and in whose interest. A single ruler who governs in the common interest is a king, while one who rules in his own interest is a tyrant. (The other types are: aristocracy: rule by the few in the common interest; oligarchy: rule by the few in their own interest; *politeia* or constitutional government: rule by the many in the common interest; democracy: rule by the many in their own interest.) See ibid., Book 3, Chapter 7.

44. Machiavelli, *The Prince*, 74.

45. Ibid. See also Machiavelli, *The Discourses*, 175, 310.

46. Machiavelli, *The Prince*, 49. For Machiavelli, deception can never completely replace violence. A prince has to be a lion as well as a fox (74). In a democratic age, however, violence is hard to combine with the image of benevolence that spin dictators cultivate.

47. Guriev and Treisman, "The Popularity of Authoritarian Leaders."

48. Geddes and Zaller ("Sources of Popular Support for Authoritarian Regimes") also argued that in authoritarian societies the most educated and politically aware would be less susceptible to government propaganda. Note that the informed, although rich in human capital, need not have high wealth or income. This segment generally overlaps with the middle class—often seen as a driver of democratization, most recently by Fukuyama (*Political Order and Political Decay*, 436–51)—but is not equivalent to it. We are also not making any moral argument that the informed should or should not dominate. We just make the factual claim that they play an important role in postindustrial politics.

49. Even in old-style dictatorships, censorship was rarely 100 percent in practice. Fringe opposition publications sometimes existed but usually because authorities lacked the capacity to eliminate them all. This was true, for instance, of some Latin American and African dictatorships. In spin dictatorships, permitting some opposition press—to make the regime look democratic and to provide a channel for credible communication when necessary—is a deliberate part of the strategy.

50. In the 83 countries polled in the latest round of the World Values Survey (2017–20), the proportion of respondents saying that having a democracy was either "very" or "fairly" good ranged from 58 percent in Iraq to 98 percent in Iceland. The cross-national average was 84 percent (World Values Survey, online analysis). See the online supplement, table OS1.1.

51. See, e.g., Iqbal, Hossain, and Mathur, "Reconciliation and Truth in Kashmir."

52. Amnesty International, *Russian Federation*, 1.

53. Central Asia Report, "Oppositionists Claim Government behind Rape Charge."

54. Aristotle, *The Politics*, 219–22.

55. Wolf, *France, 1814–1919*, 243. Napoleon used his personal popularity to consolidate power via plebiscites and preserved a democratic facade. However, he combined this with considerable repression, for instance exiling 15,000 regime opponents to foreign countries and colonies such as Algeria and French Guiana after his coup. His press censorship was also strict and overt.

56. In fact, the end date for Nazarbayev is not clear. Although he stepped down as president in 2019, he has continued to dominate from behind the scenes (see, e.g., *Economist*, "The People of Kazakhstan Wonder"). In constructing our data set on authoritarian control techniques, we used the codings of the Polity IV project to distinguish nondemocracies from democracies.

However, since spin dictators imitate democracy, there are—not surprisingly—some problematic cases. Polity codes Hungary under Orbán after 2010 as a perfect democracy (Polity2 = 10). However, we agree with Timothy Garton Ash ("Europe Must Stop This Disgrace") that Orbán's consolidation of control over media, courts, and electoral administration turned the country quite quickly into a nondemocracy. Polity also codes Turkey as a democracy until 2014. We believe that Erdoğan had reshaped it into a spin dictatorship some years before that. In statistical classifications and figures, like figure 1.1, we still follow the Polity codings to avoid making ad hoc changes and place Hungary and Turkey among democracies in the relevant years. So our count of spin dictatorships is, if anything, conservative.

57. Peru's Truth and Reconciliation Commission estimated that state agents were responsible for more than 400 killings and disappearances in each year from 1990 to 1992; the number fell to 17 in 1999 and 5 in 2000 (Lerner, *Informe Final de la Comisión de la Verdad y Reconciliación*, 84).

58. For instance, where Orbán antagonized Muslims and posed as a defender of "Christian Europe," Nazarbayev regularly hosted a "Congress of Leaders of World and Traditional Religions" to encourage interconfessional dialogue and tolerance (Tharoor, "Hungary's Leader Says He's Defending Christian Europe"; Stevens, "Kazakhstan").

59. Our spin dictators are close to what Joel Simon, the executive director of the Committee to Protect Journalists, calls "democratators." The main difference is that Simon includes extremely violent dictators such as Paul Kagame of Rwanda, whereas we view a strategy based on overt violence and fear as inconsistent with the goal of projecting an image of democratic, competent leadership. See Simon, *The New Censorship*, 32–34. Some aspects of spin dictatorship are also highlighted in Morgenbesser, "The Menu of Autocratic Innovation" and *The Rise of Sophisticated Authoritarianism*.

60. Item (a) is based on the Polity IV classification: a nondemocracy is a country with a Polity2 score of less than 6 on the 21-point Polity2 scale, on which −10 represents a pure dictatorship and +10 a pure democracy. Items (b) and (c) come from the Varieties of Democracy (V-DEM) database, version 10; (b) is met when the variable *v2elmulpar_ord* ≥ 2 in at least one year of the leader's tenure; (c) is met when *v2mecrit* ≥ 1 in all years of his tenure. Items (d) and (e) come from our own Authoritarian Control Techniques (ACT) database, which we introduce in more detail in chapter 2.

61. Item (a) is met when Polity2 < 6. Item (b) is from V-DEM; it is met when *v2mecrit* ≤ 1 in at least one year of the dictator's tenure. Items (c) and (d) are, again, from our ACT database. We do not include a condition on the existence of opposition parties in the definition of fear dictatorships since even some regimes that terrorize citizens allow token opposition.

62. The indicators of censorship and multiparty elections are available in annual form, so in the online supplement we also show an annualized estimate of the proportion of spin and fear dictators (figure OS1.1). In each year, this represents the proportion of dictators who meet the censorship and elections criteria that year and the violent repression criteria (in their tenure as a whole). The pattern is similar to that for leader cohorts, but there is a slight lag as the characteristics of each new cohort mix with those remaining from older ones. The proportion of fear dictators peaks around 1980 before falling sharply. The proportion of spin dictators rises from a low point around 1980, overtaking fear dictators around 2000.

63. In Zimbabwe, for instance, Robert Mugabe interspersed outbursts of brutal violence with periods of respite, during which previous thuggery continued to intimidate. After burning down an opponent's house, one can secure compliance for a while by merely "shaking the matchbox." Of course, one still needs to refresh memories periodically with new brutality (Cheeseman and Klaas, *How to Rig an Election*, 116–17). Mugabe's Zimbabwe was definitely a fear dictatorship, not a spin dictatorship.

64. In the online supplement to chapter 2, we discuss whether omitting short-tenure dictators might distort the patterns in violence. It appears not.

65. See the online supplement for more on how the fear-spin dictatorship categorization corresponds to other regime classifications, including that of Geddes, Wright, and Frantz, *How Dictatorships Work* (table OS1.4) and Levitsky and Way, *Competitive Authoritarianism* (table OS1.5).

66. Levitsky and Way, *Competitive Authoritarianism*, 58.

67. Dragu and Lupu, "Does Technology Undermine Authoritarian Governments?"; Dragu and Przeworski, "Preventive Repression"; Dimitrov and Sassoon, "State Security, Information, and Repression," 3.

68. Frantz, Kendall-Taylor, and Wright, *Digital Repression in Autocracies*.

69. Bradshaw and Howard ("The Global Organization of Social Media Disinformation Campaigns") explore formally organized social media manipulation campaigns in 29 countries around the world and find evidence of extensive use of social media by governments in both spin and fear dictatorships.

70. Data accessed online September 20, 2021. http://www.worldvaluessurvey.org/WVSOnline .jsp. This is based on comparing country means. See the online supplement, table OS1.6.

71. Data accessed online September 20, 2021. http://www.worldvaluessurvey.org/WVSOnline .jsp. Results for Turkey were available for this question but not the previous one. See the online supplement, tables OS1.7 and OS1.8.

72. Coonan, "Democracy Not for China."

73. Roberts, *Censored*. We return to this in chapter 4.

74. Amnesty International, *"Changing the Soup"*; deHahn, "More than 1 Million Muslims."

75. Davies, "President Xi Jinping Vows."

76. Saunders, "Xi Jinping's Threats."

77. This is according to activists' lists. See Hong Kong Watch, *Political Prisoners Database*.

78. Blanchard and Miles, "China Tries to Spin."

79. Myers, "How China Uses Forced Confessions"; Singer and Brooking, *LikeWar*, 99.

80. Zhao, "Xi Jinping's Maoist Revival."

81. Tong, "The Taming of Critical Journalism," 80; Lorentzen, "China's Strategic Censorship." Leaked instructions to the censors suggest adoption of a more selective approach in 2008–12 (Tai, "China's Media Censorship").

82. Man, "Who Wants to Watch CCTV's Xinwen Lianbo Program?"

83. Ma and Thomas, "In Xi We Trust."

84. Tong, "The Taming of Critical Journalism," 88; Committee to Protect Journalists, "Journalists Attacked in China since 1992."

85. Carter and Carter, *Propaganda in Autocracies*, 141.

86. Ibid., 150–51.

87. MBS also rejects democracy while nevertheless courting Western investors and government. In his words: "There is an advantage to quickness of decision-making, the kind of fast change that an absolute monarch can do in one step that would take a traditional democracy 10 steps" (Hubbard, *MBS*).

88. The Saudi government later acknowledged responsibility, blaming a "rogue operation." See BBC, "Jamal Khashoggi"; and Rappeport, "Saudi Crown Prince Calls Khashoggi's Death 'Heinous.'"

89. Islamic Human Rights Commission, "IHRC's UPR Report on Saudi Arabia"; Human Rights Watch, "Saudi Arabia"; *Guardian*, "Saudi Blogger Receives First 50 Lashes of Sentence for 'Insulting Islam.'"

90. Hubbard, *MBS*.

91. Waisbord, "All-Out Media War"; *Economist*, "AMLO's War against the Intelligentsia."

92. See Zakaria, *The Future of Freedom*, and Mukand and Rodrik, "The Political Economy of Liberal Democracy."

93. Meng, *Constraining Dictatorship*.

94. Levitsky and Way, *Competitive Authoritarianism*.

95. By "the informed," we mean those who understand the nature of the regime and have the skills and resources to organize society against it. Members may or may not have high incomes and wealth. For a similar argument, see Acemoglu, "We Are the Last Defense against Trump."

96. Indeed, a number of countries around the world have constitutions similar to that of the United States and yet have suffered from political instability and undemocratic politics. According to Law and Versteeg ("The Declining Influence of the US Constitution"), the five countries with constitutions most similar to the U.S. Constitution are Liberia, Tonga, the Philippines, Kiribati, and Uganda.

97. Of course, in the long run this segment may grow to include most of the population, rendering democracy even more secure.

98. Besides our own Authoritarian Control Techniques Database, we use political data from the Center for Systemic Peace (Polity IV, Major Episodes of Political Violence), Correlates of War (Militarized Interstate Dispute Database), V-DEM, Archigos (see Chiozza and Goemans, "International Conflict and the Tenure of Leaders"), the Mass Killings Database (see Ulfelder and Valentino, *Assessing Risks of State-Sponsored Mass Killing*), the Committee to Protect Journalists (on killings of journalists), NELDA (Hyde and Marinov, "Which Elections Can Be Lost?"), and Freedom House (Freedom of the Press, Freedom on the Net). We use public opinion survey data from the World Values Survey and the Gallup World Poll and economic data from the World Bank, IMF, and Fouquin and Hugot, "Two Centuries of Bilateral Trade and Gravity Data."

CHAPTER 2: DISCIPLINE, BUT DON'T PUNISH

1. *Straits Times*, "The Clean-Up: Act Two"; Wong, "Subversion or Protest," 191.

2. Lee, *The Singapore Story*, 249; Mauzy and Milne, *Singapore Politics*, 15.

3. Lee, *The Singapore Story*, 251; Barr, *Singapore*, 112.

4. Lee, *The Singapore Story*, 63.

5. Ibid., 472–73; Jones, "Creating Malaysia."

6. Mydans, "Lee Kuan Yew"; Ibrahim and Ong, "Remembering Lee Kuan Yew."

7. Lee, *The Singapore Story*, 77.

8. *Straits Times*, "Midnight Bomb Attack on Gimson."

9. Lee, *The Singapore Story*, 251.

10. Ibid., 250.

11. Gardels, "The Sage of Singapore."

12. Lee, *From Third World to First*, 676, 681–82.

13. Elliott, Abdoolcarim, and Elegant, "Lee Kuan Yew Reflects."

14. George, "Consolidating Authoritarian Rule."

15. George, *Singapore, Incomplete*, 119.

16. Morgenbesser, "The Autocratic Mandate"; George, *Singapore, Incomplete*, 108–9.

17. Even critics conceded that Lee had "genuine popular support" (George, *Singapore, Incomplete*, 44).

18. Hodos, *Show Trials*, 96; Thompson, *Nordic, Central, and Southeastern Europe*, 525. On the ruthless crushing of dissent in postwar Eastern Europe, see Applebaum, *Iron Curtain*, especially chap. 12.

19. Johnson, "Who Killed More." Here, and in the following paragraphs, we can offer only highly approximate figures. Most mass killers leave no completely reliable tally of the victims. Still, the estimates indicate the scale of the violence.

20. Meng, Qian, and Yared, "The Institutional Causes of Famine in China, 1959–61"; Kung and Chen, "The Tragedy of the Nomenklatura."

21. Mydans, "Death of Pol Pot."

22. Kim, "Forgotten War, Forgotten Massacres," 532–35.

23. Rosenbaum and Kossy, "Indonesia's Political Prisoners," 36; Amnesty International, *Indonesia*, 12.

24. Fagen, "Repression and State Security," 54; Pereira, *Political (In)justice*, 21.

25. Heilbrunn, "Equatorial Guinea and Togo," 236.

26. Metz, *Egypt*, 341.

27. Derfler, *Political Resurrection in the Twentieth Century*, 93.

28. Kershaw, *To Hell and Back*; Blanke, *Orphans of Versailles*, 96.

29. Fayet, "1919"; Bodó, "Paramilitary Violence in Hungary."

30. Cheeseman and Fisher, *Authoritarian Africa*.

31. See, for instance, Trevizo, *Rural Protest*, 171; Green, *A History of Political Murder*, 256; Calderón and Cedillo, *Challenging Authoritarianism in Mexico*.

32. Foucault, *Discipline and Punish*.

33. See Pinker, *The Better Angels of Our Nature*, for a detailed account of the trend toward less violent punishment.

34. Johnson and Zimring, *The Next Frontier*, 362.

35. Miller, "Sudan Publicly Hangs an Old Opposition Leader."

36. Preston, *Franco*, 42.

37. Preston, *The Spanish Holocaust*.

38. Rauschning, *The Voice of Destruction*, 80–81.

39. Carver, *Where Silence Rules*, 47.

40. Ibid., 41.

41. Amnesty International, *Annual Report 1988*, 247–48.

42. Almoina, *Una Satrapía en el Caribe*, 113.

43. Roucek, "Yemen in Geopolitics," 312–13.

44. Shapiro, *Invisible Latin America*, 77.

45. Torres, "Bloody Deeds/Hechos Sangrientos."

46. Talbot, *Pakistan*, 250; International Commission of Jurists, *Pakistan*, 84.

47. National Commission on the Disappearance of Persons, "Nunca Más (Never Again)."

48. Service, *Stalin*, 548. Franco and Trujillo had been high-ranking military officers before taking power. Stalin and Tito had not, although Tito had been a successful partisan commander.

49. Fedorova, "Dressing Like a Dictator."

50. Willson, "The Nation in Uniform?" 242–43.

51. Pfaff, *The Bullet's Song*.

52. Willson, "The Nation in Uniform?" 242.

53. Dikötter, *How to Be a Dictator*, 21.

54. Pfaff, *The Bullet's Song*, 40.

55. Germino, *The Italian Fascist Party in Power*, 72.

56. Falasca-Zamponi, *Fascist Spectacle*, 102; Dikötter, *How to Be a Dictator*.

57. Dikötter, *How to Be a Dictator*, 112.

58. Egorov, "Why Soviet Children Were Prepared for War."

59. Sassoon, *Saddam Hussein's Ba'th Party*, 181.

60. Coolidge and Segal, "Is Kim Jong-Il Like Saddam Hussein and Adolf Hitler?"

61. On these and other cases, see Ludwig, *King of the Mountain*, 249–51.

62. Witte, "Violence in Lenin's Thought and Practice," 146, 174.

63. Holquist, "State Violence as Technique."

64. Witte, "Violence in Lenin's Thought and Practice," 150, 159.

65. Quotes are from Ebner, *Ordinary Violence*, 8–14.

66. Ibid., 2.

67. Applebaum, *Gulag*, 63–65.

68. Overy, *The Dictators*, 177, 178.

69. Green, *A History of Political Murder*, 19.

70. As quoted in Noman, "Pakistan and General Zia," 33.

71. Mao, "Remarks at the Small Group Meeting."

72. Quoted in Heller and Nekrich, *Utopia in Power*, 308.

73. Koestler, *The Invisible Writing*, 395.

74. Heller and Nekrich, *Utopia in Power*, 305.

75. Loushnikova, "Comrade Stalin's Secret Prison."

76. Slezkine, *The House of Government*, 852.

77. Orwell, *1984*, 266.

78. Koestler, *Darkness at Noon*, 198.

79. Davies, *Mission to Moscow*. See also Hollander, *From Benito Mussolini to Hugo Chávez*, 128.

80. Davies, *Popular Opinion in Stalin's Russia*, 131–32, 118–19.

81. Abrahamian, *Tortured Confessions*, 114–16.

82. Ibid., 4, 13.

83. Ibid., 143.

84. Ibid., 154.

85. For instance, see Feldman and Stenner, "Perceived Threat and Authoritarianism."

86. Young, "The Psychology of State Repression."

87. Nicolaevsky, *Power and the Soviet Elite*, 18–19.

88. Osiel, *Mass Atrocity*, 86.

89. Taussig, *Defacement*, 2–5.

90. George, *Singapore, Incomplete*, 118–19.

91. Lee had stepped down as prime minister by this point but remained as "senior minister."

92. Today Online, "The Evolution of Singapore's Speakers' Corner"; Kampfner, *Freedom for Sale*, 25.

93. Lee, *From Third World to First*, 151–52; Andrews, "'Soft' Repression."

94. This fact was announced during court proceedings by Singapore's attorney general, Chan Sek Keong. See Emmerson, "Singapore and the 'Asian Values' Debate," 98.

95. Human Rights Watch, "Singapore."

96. Ibrahim and Lim, "Lee Kuan Yew." Government leaders strongly denied using defamation and libel suits for political purposes. But Amnesty International accused the Singapore government of "resorting to defamation suits as a politically-motivated tactic to silence critical views and curb opposition activity" (Amnesty International, *Singapore J B Jeyaretnam*).

97. Ng, "Lee Kuan Yew."

98. Bolat, "Distinguished Fellow Lee Kuan Yew Awarded by President of the Republic of Kazakhstan."

99. Urazova, "Nazarbayev about Lee Kuan Yew."

100. Gabuev, "Lee Kuan Yew and Russia."

101. BBC Summary of World Broadcasts, "Thailand's Thaksin."

102. Morgenbesser, *The Rise of Sophisticated Authoritarianism*; Varol, "Stealth Authoritarianism," 1696; Champion, "Call the Prime Minister a Turkey, Get Sued."

103. Zamyatina, "Speakers' Corners in Moscow." However, the one in Gorky Park was closed in 2015. The other received sporadic use—including for a celebration of Muammar Gaddafi's birthday and an event to prepare therapy dogs for work in orphanages—but did not catch on with opposition politicians (Bondarenko, "Stolichnie Gayd-Parky Umerli").

104. Sharlet, "Dissent and Repression," 776.

105. Scammell, "Pride and Poetry."

106. See the account in Soldatov and Borogan, *The Compatriots*, 87.

107. Rubenstein, "Introduction," 4.

108. Andrew and Mitrokhin, *The Sword and the Shield*, 312.

109. Mlechin, *Yuri Andropov*.

110. Popov, "What Kind of Minister Was Shchelokov?"

111. From 11,856 in 1967 to 23,106 in 1981. See Dimitrov, "The Case of the Soviet Union," 335–36. The KGB reports Dimitrov cites are from the Dmitrii Antonovich Volkogonov Papers in the Library of Congress.

112. Dimitrov, "The Case of the Soviet Union," 335–36.

113. Sharlet, "Dissent and Repression."

114. Ibid., 783.

115. Ibid., 782–83.

116. Rubenstein, "Introduction," 41–42.

117. Pingel-Schliemann, *Zersetzen*, 288–94. See also Harding, *Mafia State*.

118. Pingel-Schliemann, *Zersetzen*, 196.

119. As quoted in Pacepa, *Red Horizons*, 144–45.

120. Lillis, *Dark Shadows*, 27–28, 58, 66.

121. MacFarquhar and Nechepurenko, "Aleksei Navalny, Viable Putin Rival."

122. RBC, "Lidery oppozitsii."

123. Gokoluk, "Turkey Arrests Pro-Kurdish Party Leader," 7.

124. Yoong, "Singapore's Lee Has Anwar Opinion."

125. Yee, "Malaysia's Ex-Police Chief Admits to Beating Anwar."

126. Amnesty International, *Report 2012*, 121–22.

127. Seddon, "'Why Don't They Come and Sit in Jail with Me?'"

128. *Economist*, "J. B. Jeyaretnam."

129. Rodan, "Singapore 'Exceptionalism'?" 26; Rodan, "The Internet and Political Control in Singapore," 68; Rodan, "Singapore in 1997."

130. *Moscow Times*, "Russian Protest Fines Surge."

131. Klishin, "How Putin Is Bankrupting the Russian Opposition"; Rudnitsky and Arkhipov, "Russia Turns Trampled Grass into Weapon against Opponents."

132. *Moscow Times*, "Russia Freezes Bank Accounts."

133. *Economist*, "The Media and the Mouth."

134. *Moscow Times*, "Opposition Meeting Point Likened to Concentration Camp."

135. *Guardian*, "Recep Tayyip Erdoğan Dismisses Turkey Protestors as Vandals." He would, in fact, face genuinely violent opponents in a failed coup attempt in 2016. But that was not who was demonstrating to protect Gezi Park from the developers in 2013.

136. Charges were dropped against the first participant after he had spent a month in pre-trial detention. See Associated Press, "Russian Crackdown on Protesters Seen as Intimidation Tactic."

137. This technique has been around since at least the nineteenth century. But it is particularly effective today, given the greater stigma that many potential opposition supporters place on violence.

138. Kravtsova, "Former 'Provocateur' Blames Police."

139. Salem and Stack, "Streetfighting Men."

140. Corrales, "Authoritarian Survival."

141. Roessler, "Donor-Induced Democratization."

142. Sanovich, Stukal, and Tucker, "Turning the Virtual Tables."

143. Nyst and Monaco, *State-Sponsored Trolling*, 29–31.

144. As in chapter 1, we classify governments as authoritarian if their Polity2 score is less than 6.

145. Of course, these subtypes of political killings differ. But we sought an aggregate measure of all the violent repression used by dictators to maintain their power.

146. The latest version is available via https://press.princeton.edu/books/spin-dictators.

147. See Guriev and Treisman, "Informational Autocrats." All the figures given in this section refer to cohorts of those who remained in power for at least five consecutive years in a nondemocracy (i.e., a country with Polity2 score below 6). It might seem that one should focus on the number of killings per capita rather than the absolute number. In fact, since populations have soared in recent decades, doing so would yield an even more striking fall in the level of political violence than the one we show. However, comparing countries' per capita rates of political killing implicitly assumes that, for instance, a massacre of 1,000 dissidents in China has the same effect as the killing of one in Trinidad and Tobago. We believe that political killings get harder to conceal as their absolute number rises, regardless of the size of the country. So we use the absolute number but pay attention only to large cross-national differences.

148. See the online supplement, figure OS2.1.

149. See ibid., figures OS2.2, OS2.3.

150. Ibid., figure OS2.4. In the online supplement (chap. 2, section II) we discuss whether the data could be distorted by the exclusion of leaders who served for less than five years and show that this is unlikely to have changed the pattern.

151. Ibid., figure OS2.5.

152. Ulfelder and Valentino, Assessing Risks.

153. Online supplement, figure OS2.6.

154. Coppedge, "V-Dem Codebook V.10," 162.

155. Online supplement, figure OS2.7. Our calculations using the data from V-DEM V.10. We code as nondemocratic states with a Polity2 score of less than 6.

CHAPTER 3: POSTMODERN PROPAGANDA

1. Aitken, Nazarbayev and the Making of Kazakhstan, 106–8.

2. He wrote later that, witnessing the interactions in the post-coup days between Gorbachev, Yeltsin, and Ukrainian leader Leonid Kravchuk, "it was becoming increasingly clear to everyone that there was no way that these three sides could agree on anything" (quoted in ibid., 108).

3. Kay, "Kazakhstan President Lauds Lee Kuan Yew's Contribution."

4. Lee, "Address by Mr. Lee Kuan Yew."

5. Nazarbayev, The Kazakhstan Way, 26.

6. Aitken, Nazarbayev and the Making of Kazakhstan, 101.

7. Shadmehr, "Ideology and the Iranian Revolution."

8. Dikötter, How to Be a Dictator, 160–61. Duvalierism, which built on Papa Doc's extensive earlier research into voodoo and noirisme, reached full expression with the publication of his Essential Works in 1966.

9. Folch-Serra, "Propaganda in Franco's Time"; Hodges, Franco.

10. One exception was Pol Pot, who avoided public appearances. Fidel Castro also sought to avoid a personality cult. For a fascinating examination of twentieth-century personality cults, see Dikötter, How to Be a Dictator.

11. Ibid., 81–83; Lyons, Stalin, 216.

12. Quoted in Márquez, "A Model of Cults of Personality," 1.

13. Cheeseman and Fisher, *Authoritarian Africa*.

14. Wedeen, *Ambiguities of Domination*, 1, 12.

15. Dikötter, *How to Be a Dictator*, 91.

16. Winter, "Mansudae Art Studio, North Korea's Colossal Monument Factory."

17. Dikötter, *How to Be a Dictator*.

18. Lyons, *Stalin*, 215.

19. Lamb, *The Africans*, 48.

20. Dikötter, *How to Be a Dictator*, 117.

21. Leese, *Mao Cult*, 215.

22. Ibid., 108; Dikötter, *How to Be a Dictator*, 116.

23. Leese, *Mao Cult*, 213.

24. Koon, *Believe, Obey, Fight*, 11.

25. Manning, *When Books Went to War*, 6.

26. Sassoon, *Saddam Hussein's Ba'th Party*, 176–79.

27. Dikötter, *How to Be a Dictator*, 16, 48.

28. Ibid., 116.

29. Welch, *The Third Reich*, 42.

30. Gunther, Montero, and Wert, "The Media and Politics in Spain," 37.

31. Yurchak, *Everything Was Forever*.

32. Overy, *The Dictators*, 180.

33. Landau et al., "Deliver Us from Evil."

34. Greenberg, Pyszczynski, and Solomon, "Terror Management Theory"; Florian, Mikulincer, and Hirschberger, "An Existentialist View on Mortality Salience Effects."

35. Baird, "Goebbels, Horst Wessel, and the Myth of Resurrection and Return."

36. Klemperer, *Language of the Third Reich*, 28.

37. Fritzsche, *Hitler's First Hundred Days*.

38. Skidmore and Wilson, *Dictatorship, Disorder and Decline in Myanmar*, 40.

39. Hellmeier and Weidmann, "Pulling the Strings?"

40. Guerra, *Visions of Power in Cuba*, 46–48.

41. Podeh, *The Politics of National Celebrations*, 78.

42. On why authoritarian leaders might nevertheless want to enact constitutions, see Ginsburg and Simpser, introduction.

43. In the "loyalty dance" (*zhongzi wu*), the performer clasped his hands to his heart, stretched his arms to the sky, and clenched his fist in homage to the revolution. Nguyen-Okwo, "Hitler Had a Salute, Mao Had a Dance."

44. Ji, *Linguistic Engineering*, 2.

45. Bauer, Inkeles, and Kluckhohn, *How the Soviet System Works*, 37.

46. Dikötter, *How to Be a Dictator*. Of course, ideologues were not the *only* victims of dictators' purges, but they were seen as particularly dangerous.

47. Dikötter, *How to Be a Dictator*, xii.

48. Taylor, *Brain Washing*, 346.

49. Dikötter, *How to Be a Dictator*, 1–2.

50. Taylor, *Brain Washing*, 345.

51. Sükösd, "Democratic Transformation and the Mass Media in Hungary," 132.

52. Gunther, Montero, and Wert, "The Media and Politics in Spain," 38–39.

53. Bengio, *Saddam's Word*, 9.

54. Crabtree, Kern, and Siegel, "Cults of Personality, Preference Falsification, and the Dictator's Dilemma"; Pike, *Empires at War*, 347.

55. Lamb, "Burmese Leader Ne Win."

56. Huang, "Propaganda as Signaling." Little ("Propaganda and Credulity") discusses how absurd propaganda can discourage protest even among those who do not believe it.

57. Crabtree, Kern, and Siegel, "Cults of Personality, Preference Falsification, and the Dictator's Dilemma."

58. Shih, "'Nauseating' Displays of Loyalty"; Márquez, "Two Models," 274.

59. Voigtländer and Voth, "Nazi Indoctrination and Anti-Semitic Beliefs in Germany."

60. Selb and Munzert, "Examining a Most Likely Case."

61. Adena et al., "Radio and the Rise of the Nazis in Prewar Germany."

62. Bankier, *Germans and the Final Solution*, 21.

63. Ibid., 162, 24.

64. Welch, *The Third Reich*, 43.

65. Doob, "Goebbels' Principles of Propaganda," 429.

66. Cazorla-Sánchez, *Franco*, 5.

67. Wedeen, *Ambiguities of Domination*, 3.

68. Márquez, "A Model of Cults of Personality," 5–6.

69. There is some evidence that living in communist societies leaves people less supportive of markets and democracy. Ten years after German unification, even those former East Germans who had moved to the West remained more favorable toward state economic intervention than native West Germans (Alesina and Fuchs-Schündeln, "Goodbye Lenin"). Pop-Eleches and Tucker (*Communism's Shadow*) found that additional years living under communism correlated with more negative attitudes later toward both markets and democracy—and the effect for additional years as an adult was often greater than that for additional years as a child. This could indicate that communist propaganda in Eastern Europe was effective. It could also reflect the cumulative influence of other aspects of living under communism besides propaganda. (For instance, support for democracy in consolidated democracies is somewhat higher among the old, who have been exposed to it for longer, but it is not clear that this is because of political messaging by the state; see, e.g., Wuttke, Gavras, and Schoen, "Have Europeans Grown Tired of Democracy?") In a more recent case of communist propaganda, one study found that a reform of Chinese school curricula in the early 2000s left students more skeptical about Western-style free markets and "unconstrained democracy," even some years later (Cantoni et al., "Curriculum and Ideology").

70. Carter and Carter (*Propaganda in Autocracies*) argue that Chinese state media under Xi Jinping aim less to persuade citizens than to intimidate them into obedience. They show, using a list experiment in a 2020 survey, that reading pro-government coverage from the official media caused respondents to upgrade their estimates of the regime's strength and durability—but did not increase their approval of the Communist Party or Xi Jinping. Huang ("The Pathology of Hard Propaganda") reports similar results.

71. Tengri TV, "Nazarbayev vystupil"; *Total*, "Nazarbayev poruchil."

72. It has to be said, there are also a few echoes of late Soviet socialism mixed in with the corporate vibe. Brezhnev-era bosses promised bumper harvests and scolded their officials in public. However, they did not threaten to replace subordinates with English managers or trumpet global technologies in which they lagged. The boasts were phrased in Marxist jargon and often accompanied by talk of nuclear missiles and international threats. Their suits were baggier and weighed down by military medals.

73. Nolan, "The Realest Reality Show"; Carroll, "Government by TV."

74. Omelicheva, "Authoritarian Legitimation," 487–88; Zhussupova, "Kazakhstan to Present Its First Report."

75. Conaghan, *Fujimori's Peru*, 4. We do not mean that spin dictators never play up foreign threats to rally the public—on the contrary, some, such as Putin, do so vigorously when they need to divert attention from domestic failures. Still, they tend to do so less—and in less blood-curdling terms—than did the old-school autocrats.

76. Carroll, "Government by TV."

77. *New York Times*, "Excerpts from an Interview with Lee Kuan Yew." Tan ("The Ideology of Pragmatism") argues that pragmatism was itself an ideology embraced by Lee's PAP. We agree that Lee used a rhetoric of pragmatism but would not call this an ideology—and definitely not an official one enforced on all Singaporeans.

78. Taylor, *The Code of Putinism*, 9.

79. Krastev, "New Threats to Freedom," 58.

80. Kudaibergenova, "Compartmentalized Ideology."

81. Anderson, "Postscript: Hugo Chávez, 1954–2013."

82. Frajman, "Broadcasting Populist Leadership," 512.

83. Richardson, "North Korea's Kim Dynasty."

84. *Guardian*, "The Personality Cult of Turkmenbashi"; BBC, "Turkmen Drivers Face Unusual Test."

85. James, "Absent but Omnipresent, Chávez a Powerful Symbol"; Arutunyan, *The Putin Mystique*.

86. In a study of the personality cults of eight dictators—Mussolini, Hitler, Stalin, Mao, Kim Il-Sung, Duvalier, Ceaușescu, and Mengistu—Dikötter notes that "every one made all the key decisions that led to his own glorification" (*How to Be a Dictator*, xii).

87. On celebrity, see, for instance, Marshall, *Celebrity and Power*.

88. E.g., Luxmoore, "Putin Mania."

89. Glasser, "Putin's Cult of Personality," A3.

90. Ibid. Luxmoore, "Putin Mania."

91. Podrez and Prikhodina, "Znak pochtenia, znak otchayania."

92. Cassiday and Johnson, "Putin, Putiniana and the Question of a Post-Soviet Cult of Personality," 695.

93. Ibid.

94. Russmus.net, "Takogo kak Putin." To be fair, he is also described as "full of strength."

95. Harding, "Vladimir Putin Hugs Polar Bear."

96. Kirilenko and Sindelar, "Sleeping Tiger, Hidden Agenda?"; Elder, "Putin's Fabled Tiger Encounter."

97. Batty, "Vladimir Putin's Chief Spokesman Admits Greek Urn Find Was Staged."

98. Dikötter, *How to Be a Dictator*.

99. "In 2004, a St. Petersburg company named Prosperiti began marketing dental flossers in packets with the President's portrait emblazoned on the front" (Cassiday and Johnson, "Putin, Putiniana and the Question of a Post-Soviet Cult of Personality," 692).

100. Goscilo, "Russia's Ultimate Celebrity," 12.

101. White House Gift Shop, "Barack Obama Collectibles"; Cochrane, "Obama Merchandising Madness."

102. Rein, "Federal Offices Are Still Waiting to Hang Trump's Picture."

103. Warner, "A Hot Time in Washington"; Associated Press, "Shirtless Images of Obama Cause Stir Online." In fact, quite a list of presidents—Kennedy, Nixon, Ford, and Reagan—have been featured shirtless in U.S. publications (O'Rourke, "Chronicle Covers"; *Daily Beast*, "Shirtless Presidents"; Beggs, "Pumped-Up Presidents").

104. Ramírez, "Barack Obama."

105. IMDB, "Running Wild with Bear Grylls: President Barack Obama."

106. Adams and Rustemova, "Mass Spectacle and Styles of Governmentality."

107. Lewis, "Blogging Zhanaozen," 426–27.

108. Ibid., 427.

109. Sobolev, "Dictators in the Spotlight."

110. Soldatov and Borogan, *The Red Web*, 117.

111. Ellul, *Propaganda*, 80–84. See also Murphy and Shleifer, "Persuasion in Politics."

112. Volchek and Sindelar, "One Professional Russian Troll Tells All." See also Sobolev, "Dictators in the Spotlight," for evidence of trolls' success in diverting netizens from politically charged topics.

113. Mackey, "All the President's Trolls."

114. Johns and Cheong, "Feeling the Chill," 7.

115. Pomerantsev, *This Is Not Propaganda*.

116. King, Pan, and Roberts, "How the Chinese Government Fabricates Social Media Posts."

117. Mackey, "All the President's Trolls."

118. Bowen and Holligan, *The Imperfect Spy*, 330–31.

119. Ibid., 331–32.

120. Tolz and Teper, "Broadcasting Agitainment," 221.

121. Gehlbach and Sonin, "Government Control of the Media."

122. Rozenas and Stukal, "How Autocrats Manipulate Economic News." Another strategy is to ignore bad news but not deny it. Melnikov ("Censorship, Propaganda, and Political Popularity") finds that Russian official media are more likely to discuss the ruble's exchange rate in weeks when it strengthens than in those when it weakens. He shows that this strategy boosts the regime's popularity in regions with lower Internet penetration.

123. Walker, "'This Gentleman.'"

124. Carroll, *Comandante*, 38.

125. Schatz, "Transnational Image Making," 54.

126. Schatz, "The Soft Authoritarian Tool Kit," 211.

127. Kucera, "No One Rigs an Election Quite Like Kazakhstan."

128. For details, see Guriev and Treisman, "Informational Autocrats." Among speeches, we included televised call-in or town-hall meetings, radio addresses (Obama, FDR), and leaders' signature TV shows (Chávez's *Aló Presidente* and Correa's *Enlace Ciudadano*), always cutting out parts not spoken by the leader. We used official English translations when we could find them and, as recommended by Lucas et al. ("Computer-Assisted Text Analysis," 260), the renditions of Google Translate in the few cases where we could not (Franco in Spain, Chávez in Venezuela, Correa in Ecuador). While the best machine translation programs remain imperfect for most tasks, word-count text analysis is arguably an exception. When estimating word frequencies, the order of words, punctuation, grammar, and so on do not matter, so the "software needs only to correctly translate the significant terms in the original document."

To check that our word lists pick up relevant differences, we first tried them out on documents we knew would focus on the three topics in question. For instance, we used the violence list on the closing statements of prosecutors in trials for war crimes or terrorism. As expected, these texts recorded unusually high concentrations of the violence words (2.5–4.7 percent). The economic performance and public service word lists also gave high readings in test runs on, respectively, IMF briefings on the world economy and budget speeches of democratic finance ministers. Since some words have more than one meaning, we scanned the speeches for usages of words with the "wrong" meaning. (For instance, "spending" money is relevant to economic performance and public service provision; "spending" time is not.) When we found more than two non-germane uses, we excluded the word from the dictionary.

129. The differences between the spin dictators and fear dictators are statistically significant; those between spin dictators and democrats are not (see Guriev and Treisman, "Informational Autocrats").

130. See figure OS3.1 in the online appendix.

131. Note that our rules of thumb do not refer to ideology, so this is not circular.

132. Carter and Carter (*Propaganda in Autocracies*). They argue that what determines the choice is whether the country has formally democratic institutions: electoral constraints lead to subtler propaganda. We agree that seemingly democratic institutions go along with subtler propaganda—both are part of what we call the spin dictatorship approach. Where they see electoral institutions as the ultimate cause of the propaganda strategy, we see both pseudo-competitive elections and sophisticated propaganda as elements in a broader package of tactics to sustain spin dictatorship. We argue that this package is chosen in response to pressures from modernization and globalization (see chapter 7).

133. See Carter and Carter, *Propaganda in Autocracies*, figure 4.1, especially the comparison for article valence.

CHAPTER 4: SENSIBLE CENSORSHIP

1. Bowen and Holligan, *The Imperfect Spy*, 125–26; Kerr, "Fujimori's Plot."
2. Wood, "The Peruvian Press under Recent Authoritarian Regimes," 23.
3. Cash, "Peru Chief Orders New Mass Arrests."
4. Lane, "The 'Self Coup' That Rocked Peru."

5. Conaghan, *Fujimori's Peru*, 34.

6. Gorriti, "Living Dangerously," 239.

7. Overy, *The Dictators*, 368.

8. Dikötter, *How to Be a Dictator*, 190.

9. Plamper, "Abolishing Ambiguity," 531.

10. Chandler, introduction.

11. Boyer, "Censorship as a Vocation," 525.

12. Ibid., 526.

13. Overy, *The Dictators*, 370.

14. Battles, *Library*, 168.

15. Diéguez, "Spain's Golden Silence," 93.

16. Ibid., 98.

17. Hodges, *Franco*, 108.

18. Bonsaver, *Censorship and Literature in Fascist Italy*, 74.

19. Edwards, "Books in Chile," 20.

20. Carver, *Where Silence Rules*, 70.

21. Gaillard, "Jeune Afrique."

22. Coetzee, "Emerging from Censorship," 36.

23. Kott, "Controlling the Writing on the Wall."

24. Boyer, "Censorship as a Vocation," 528.

25. Long, "Living in Fear."

26. Spooner, *Soldiers in a Narrow Land*, 89.

27. Overy, *The Dictators*, 368.

28. Plamper, "Abolishing Ambiguity," 529.

29. L. L., "Stalinism in the Post-Stalin Regime."

30. Gwertzman, "Beria Is Ignored in Soviet Volume."

31. Plamper, "Abolishing Ambiguity."

32. Ibid., 532.

33. Klemperer, *I Shall Bear Witness*, 291.

34. Carvalho and Cardoso, "Press Censorship in Spain & Portugal," 55.

35. Manning, *When Books Went to War*, 3.

36. Ibid., 4.

37. Dikötter, *How to Be a Dictator*, 190.

38. Edwards, "Books in Chile," 20; Jones, *Censorship*, 91.

39. Vladimirov, "Glavlit," 41. More recently, China's authorities revealed that they employed 2 million people to monitor and censor just the Internet (Hunt and Xu, "China 'Employs 2 Million to Police Internet'").

40. Dobbs, "Soviet Censorship Dead but Showing Signs of Life."

41. Skarpelos, "Communication Breakdown," 147.

42. Dikötter, *How to Be a Dictator*.

43. Isakhan, "Read All about It."

44. Ibid.

45. Carver, *Where Silence Rules*, 81.

46. Roberts, "Resilience to Online Censorship," 406.

47. See Chwe, *Rational Ritual.*

48. Inter Press Service, "Peru."

49. Golden, "Maoist Rebels Now Are Worst Offenders"; Bowen and Holligan, *The Imperfect Spy,* 121.

50. See the fascinating account of the Fujimori-Montesinos partnership in McMillan and Zoido, "How to Subvert Democracy."

51. Ibid., 74.

52. Ibid., 75.

53. Ibid., 84.

54. Bennett and Naím, "21st-Century Censorship."

55. Education statistics from Barro and Lee, "A New Data Set."

56. McMillan and Zoido, "How to Subvert Democracy," 84.

57. Dougherty, "How the Media Became One of Putin's Most Powerful Weapons." See also Gehlbach, "Reflections on Putin and the Media" on Putin's partial approach.

58. Carroll, *Comandante,* 186.

59. George, "Journalism and Authoritarian Resilience," 545.

60. Roberts, *Censored,* 23.

61. *Economist,* "What Is the Streisand Effect?"

62. Coetzee, "Emerging from Censorship," 45.

63. Cialdini, *Influence,* 205.

64. McMillan and Zoido, "How to Subvert Democracy," 81–82.

65. Ibid., 83.

66. Castro, "Venta de Línea."

67. Bowen and Holligan, *The Imperfect Spy,* 329.

68. Ibid., 311–13.

69. McMillan and Zoido, "How to Subvert Democracy," 83.

70. Bowen and Holligan, *The Imperfect Spy,* 333.

71. Bentin, "The Politics of Illusion."

72. Mander, "Advertisers Feel Squeeze from Chávez." Populist leaders in democracies, such as the Kirchners in Argentina, have also used the discriminatory allocation of state advertising to influence media bosses. More generally, leaders co-opt media companies to secure favorable coverage at times in democracies as well—although on a smaller scale (see Besley and Pratt, "Handcuffs for the Grabbing Hand?").

73. *Economist,* "How Viktor Orbán Hollowed Out Hungary's Democracy."

74. Szeidl and Szucs, "Media Capture through Favor Exchange."

75. Tyler, "New Tapes Appear"; BBC, "Ukraine's 'Censorship Killing.'"

76. President of Russia, "Interview with the German Newspaper *Suddeutsche Zeitung.*"

77. McMillan and Zoido, "How to Subvert Democracy," 85.

78. Ibid.

79. Ibid.

80. Lipman, Kachkaeva, and Poyker, "Media in Russia," 165; Rusyaeva and Surganova, "Mediakompaniu Kovalchuka i Mordashova otsenili v 150 mlrd. rub."

81. Forbes, "Profile Lorinc Meszaros"; Talley and Hinshaw, "U.S. Keeps Sanctions at the Ready Even as Trump Courts Hungarian Leader"; Mutler, "Pro-Orbán Media Moguls Who Destroyed Hungary's Media Now Targeting European Outlets."

82. Reporters Without Borders, "Hungary."

83. *Economist*, "How Viktor Orbán Hollowed Out Hungary's Democracy"; Mutler, "Pro-Orbán Media Moguls Who Destroyed Hungary's Media Now Targeting European Outlets."

84. George, *Singapore, Incomplete*, 139–40.

85. Long, "Journalism."

86. Lauría, "Confrontation, Repression in Correa's Ecuador."

87. Rodan, "The Internet and Political Control in Singapore," 69.

88. Champion, "Call the Prime Minister a Turkey, Get Sued."

89. Varol, "Stealth Authoritarianism," 1696.

90. Mander, "Venezuelan Private Media Fear Fresh Assault."

91. Human Rights Watch, "Venezuela."

92. Toothaker, "Last Anti-Chávez TV Station Faces Probe, Shutdown."

93. Wallis, "Chávez Turns up Heat on Globovisión in Venezuela."

94. Brice, "Venezuela Opens New Probe against TV Station."

95. Arsu and Tavernise, "Turkish Media Group Is Fined $2.5 Billion."

96. Lee, *From Third World to First*, 219–22.

97. Ibid., 219.

98. Legal scholar Ozan Varol calls such use of seemingly legitimate legal devices to limit democracy "stealth authoritarianism." See Varol, "Stealth Authoritarianism," 1673.

99. Davidoff, "Duma Masks Internet Crackdown by Citing 'iPhone Pedophiles.'"

100. De la Torre and Ortiz Lemos, "Populist Polarization and the Slow Death," 233.

101. Southwick and Otis, "Ecuador's U-turn away from Media Repression."

102. Varol, "Stealth Authoritarianism."

103. Roth, "Independent News Station, Feeling Kremlin's Wrath, Asks 'Why?'"

104. Lillis, *Dark Shadows*, 64.

105. García, "Los Periódicos Venezolanos, sin Papel."

106. Roberts, *Censored*, 56–80.

107. Bowen and Holligan, *The Imperfect Spy*, 337. Of course, such discretionary interventions require a certain level of state capacity that not all dictators have.

108. McMillan and Zoido, "How to Subvert Democracy," 84–85; Alonso, "The Impact of Media Spectacle on Peruvian Politics"; Simon, *The New Censorship*, 47.

109. Conaghan and De la Torre, "The Permanent Campaign of Rafael Correa," 279; Lauría, "Confrontation, Repression in Correa's Ecuador."

110. Mander, "Venezuelan Private Media Fear Fresh Assault"; Toothaker, "Last Anti-Chávez TV Station Faces Probe, Shutdown."

111. Bowen and Holligan, *The Imperfect Spy*, 311.

112. Anderson, "Postscript: Hugo Chávez, 1954–2013."

113. Foer, "The Talented Mr. Chávez."

114. Roberts, *Censored*, 80–91.

115. Carroll, *Comandante*, 23.

116. Ibid., 184.

117. Barrera, "Interview Alberto Barrera."

118. Lauría, "Confrontation, Repression in Correa's Ecuador."

119. Lee, *From Third World to First*, 219.

120. Conaghan, *Fujimori's Peru*, 157.

121. McMillan and Zoido, "How to Subvert Democracy," 90.

122. Faiola, "Army Played 'A Key Role.'"

123. Bowen and Holligan, *The Imperfect Spy*, 383–84; Conaghan, *Fujimori's Peru*, 228–30.

124. Bowen and Holligan, *The Imperfect Spy*, 389.

125. Enikolopov, Makarin, and Petrova, "Social Media and Protest Participation"; Toor, "How Putin's Cronies Seized Control of Russia's Facebook."

126. Ball and Hamilos, "Ecuador's President"; Ruiz, "Ecuador."

127. This was the Digital Millennium Copyright Act, which was intended to protect intellectual property.

128. Birnbaum, "Russian Blogger Law Puts New Restrictions on Internet Freedoms."

129. Reuters, "Singapore PM Files Defamation Suit." It does not help that the law on this in leading democracies is evolving and sometimes highly restrictive. In 2020, the Supreme Court of Switzerland ruled that "liking and sharing posts can potentially amount to punishable defamation" (Müller and Häsler, "Liking or Sharing Defamatory Facebook Posts").

130. For instance, DDoS attacks have targeted Malaysian opposition groups and media (Johns and Cheong, "Feeling the Chill," 6).

131. Roberts, *Censored*.

132. Thomas, Grier, and Paxson, "Adapting Social Spam Infrastructure for Political Censorship." There is no proof that the Russian government was the contractor, but it certainly had the motive.

133. Stukal et al., "Detecting Bots on Russian Political Twitter."

134. Mackey, "All the President's Trolls." "He knew how to get into your mind and heart," one expert told journalist Danielle Mackey. "The principal tool for Correa wasn't public works, but instead communications."

135. Boletskaya, "Google nachal udalyat iz poiska zapreshchennie v Rossii sayty"; Luxmoore, "Google Censors Search Results after Russian Government Threat, Reports Say."

136. Hakim, "Once Celebrated in Russia, Programmer Pavel Durov Chooses Exile."

137. George and Liew, *Red Lines*, 96.

138. *ChinaFile*, "Rule by Fear."

139. See the online supplement, figure OS4.1. We do not show evidence on how the types vary across spin and fear dictators since our rules of thumb for spin and fear dictators themselves include another V-DEM measure of media control, rendering such a demonstration somewhat circular. Of course, direct, routine censorship is rarer—and indirect, limited censorship more common—among spin dictators than among fear dictators.

140. The average for spin dictatorships was significantly higher than that for democracies and lower than that for fear dictatorships at $p < .05$.

141. Committee to Protect Journalists, "1396 Journalists Killed."

142. The differences between the averages for fear and spin dictators and between those for spin and hybrid dictators are both statistically significant at $p < .05$. The difference between spin dictators and democratic leaders is not statistically significant—as we would expect.

143. This should not really seem strange since we classify regimes as spin dictatorships based in part on a low level of state killings in general. What these data show is that—despite the poor reputation of some of these states with regard to the press—killings of journalists are not an exception to the general pattern. Russia under Putin is an outlier among spin dictatorships in this regard. Out of 36 spin dictators in the years since 1992, 31 had no confirmed murders of journalists by state agents at all. Under Putin, between 2007 (the first year Polity classified Russia as a nondemocracy) and 2015, CPJ recorded 5. Four of these were in the North Caucasus.

144. Guriev and Treisman, "The Popularity of Authoritarian Leaders."

145. The difference between spin dictators and democratic leaders is statistically significant at $p < .01$.

146. The 6 percent is the lowest result from Frye et al., "Is Putin's Popularity Real?" The 43 percent is the highest result from Kalinin, "Exploring Putin's Post-Crimean Supermajority"; see his table A1. The 18-percentage-point average figure is the mean of four estimates of the inflation of Putin's approval in Frye et al., "Is Putin's Popularity Real?" and four estimates in Kalinin, "Exploring Putin's Post-Crimean Supermajority." On this, see also Blair, Coppock, and Moor, "When to Worry about Sensitivity Bias," which examined these and other poll results to assess sensitivity bias. They found similar sensitivity bias on government approval in China, but Russia was the only spin dictatorship included.

147. See the online supplement, figure OS4.2. The correlation between the average approval of the dictator and the average number of state political killings under him (logged) is $r = -.30$. If we include leaders who served during ethnic wars (as classified by the Center for Systemic Peace's Major Episodes of Political Violence Database), there is one outlier: under the presidency of Mahinda Rajapaksa, in 2005–15, tens of thousands of Sri Lankan civilians were killed by government troops in the heat of an ethnic civil war (UN, *Report of the Secretary-General's Panel of Experts*). Yet, Rajapaksa remained very popular—clearly with his co-ethnics, rather than the victims.

148. This is all the more striking given the possibility that fear would inflate approval for violent dictators. Gallup did not poll in Syria or North Korea, where respondents might indeed have been terrorized into reporting high approval.

149. Guriev and Treisman, "The Popularity of Authoritarian Leaders."

150. In more technical language, we analyzed dynamic models in a panel, controlling for country and year fixed effects.

151. Again, we cannot be sure about causation. It could be that respondents who lose faith in the government for other reasons also come to believe it is censoring the media.

152. Guriev and Treisman, "The Popularity of Authoritarian Leaders."

153. Hollyer, Rosendorff, and Vreeland, *Transparency, Democracy, and Autocracy*.

154. Norris and Inglehart, "Silencing Dissent." They used the 2005–6 wave of the World Values Survey, which polled representative samples of the population in 44 countries, and an index of media freedom constructed by the organization Reporters Without Borders.

155. Guriev, Melnikov, and Zhuravskaya, "3G Internet and Confidence in Government."

156. Average approval was 51 percent.

157. While this study focuses on the impact of mobile broadband Internet on government approval, there is also evidence on the importance of the pre-3G Internet as well. In Malaysia, expansion of Internet penetration in 2004–8 resulted in a 6.6-percentage-point decrease in the ruling party's vote share; see Miner, "The Unintended Consequences of Internet Diffusion."

158. Enikolopov, Petrova, and Zhuravskaya, "Media and Political Persuasion."

159. Knight and Tribin, *Opposition Media, State Censorship, and Political Accountability*. Chávez's approval was falling during this period, but it fell about 5 percentage points less in places without access to Globovisión.

160. Boas, "Television and Neopopulism in Latin America," 35–36, 44. Survey respondents might also misremember their previous TV-watching habits or for whom they had voted (Prior, "The Immensely Inflated News Audience").

161. See the online supplement, table OS4.4.

162. Kellam and Stein, "Trump's War on the News Media."

163. Di Tella and Franceschelli, "Government Advertising and Media Coverage of Corruption Scandals."

164. Kopel, "Argentina's Free Press Is in Grave Danger."

165. Romero and Schmall, "Battle between Argentine Media Empire and President Heats Up."

166. See Durante and Knight, "Partisan Control, Media Bias, and Viewer Responses" for evidence on the pro-Berlusconi bias that emerged in the three state channels after Berlusconi came to power.

167. Kington, "Silvio Berlusconi Faces Inquiry over Bid to Block 'Hostile' TV Show"; Day, "Silvio Berlusconi Caught Out Trying to Stifle Media."

168. Barone, D'Acunto, and Narciso, "Telecracy."

169. Samuels, "Trump Ramps Up Rhetoric."

CHAPTER 5: DEMOCRACY FOR DICTATORS

1. Carroll, *Comandante*, 36; Marcano and Barrera Tyszka, *Hugo Chávez*.
2. Marcano and Barrera Tyszka, *Hugo Chávez*.
3. Krauze, "The Shah of Venezuela."
4. Anderson, "The Revolutionary."
5. Da Corte, "Miquilena."
6. Ibid.
7. Foer, "The Talented Mr. Chávez."
8. Harnecker, "Hugo Chávez Frías."
9. Marcano and Barrera Tyszka, *Hugo Chávez*.
10. López Hurtado, "Rafael Céspedes."
11. Ibid.
12. Said to Nedo Paniz, quoted in Marcano and Barrera Tyszka, *Hugo Chávez*.
13. Quoted in Krauze, "The Shah of Venezuela."
14. Marcano and Barrera Tyszka, *Hugo Chávez*.

15. Ibid.

16. Corrales and Penfold, *Dragon in the Tropics*, 19.

17. Zambrano, "The Constitutional Path to Dictatorship in Venezuela"; Corrales and Penfold, *Dragon in the Tropics*, 19.

18. Foer, "The Talented Mr. Chávez"; Marcano and Barrera Tyszka, *Hugo Chávez*.

19. Marcano and Barrera Tyszka, *Hugo Chávez*.

20. Foer, "The Talented Mr. Chávez."

21. Reuters, "Factbox: Hugo Chávez's Record in Venezuelan Elections."

22. Weisbrot, "Changes in Latin America."

23. Barrera, "Interview Alberto Barrera."

24. *Hamburger Fremdenblatt*, No. 78, March 20, 1934 (evening edition), quoted in Marx, "Propaganda and Dictatorship," 211.

25. Mussolini, "The Political and Social Doctrine of Fascism," 10, quoted in Marx, "Propaganda and Dictatorship," 211.

26. Overy, *The Dictators*, 55.

27. Ibid., 56.

28. Rauschning, *Hitler Speaks*, 199.

29. Constable and Valenzuela, *A Nation of Enemies*, 71.

30. Whitman, "Antonio Salazar."

31. Abjorensen, *Historical Dictionary of Democracy*, 146.

32. Schmitt, *Crisis of Parliamentary Democracy*, 29.

33. Quoted in Hermet, "State-Controlled Elections," 12.

34. To give the appearance that the deputies would represent even non-party members, the slate was officially referred to as the "unbreakable bloc of communists and non-party members." Of course, the "non-party members" were carefully selected by the party. See "Bloc of Communists and Non-Party Members," in *The Great Soviet Encyclopedia*, 3rd ed. (1970–79). In the Brezhnev era, citizens could also avoid voting by obtaining an "absentee certificate," allowing them to vote outside their home district—and then not using it. The turnout statistics were calculated as the percentage of voters who had not obtained such certificates. See Zaslavsky and Brym, "The Functions of Elections in the USSR," 365–66.

35. Overy, *The Dictators*, 55.

36. White, Rose, and McAllister, *How Russia Votes*, 10–11.

37. Zlobin, "Humor as Political Protest."

38. Sassoon, *Saddam Hussein's Ba'th Party*, 176.

39. Overy, *The Dictators*, 55.

40. Merl, "Elections in the Soviet Union, 1937–1989," 293.

41. Lamb, *The Africans*, 56.

42. Jessen and Richter, "Non-Competitive Elections in Twentieth Century Dictatorships," 20.

43. Quoted in Getty, "State and Society under Stalin," 18.

44. Power, *Amnesty International*, 104–11.

45. Clinton, "Statement on the Death of Former President Julius Nyerere of Tanzania."

46. Merl, "Elections in the Soviet Union, 1937–1989," 281.

47. Ibid., 302–3.

48. Zaslavsky and Brym, "The Functions of Elections in the USSR," 368.

49. Simpser, *Why Governments and Parties Manipulate Elections*; Zaslavsky and Brym, "The Functions of Elections in the USSR," 369.

50. Kendall-Taylor, Frantz, and Wright, "The Digital Dictators," 110.

51. Jessen and Richter, "Non-Competitive Elections in Twentieth Century Dictatorships," 29; Zaslavsky and Brym, "The Functions of Elections in the USSR," 367.

52. In Kenya, "elections were frequently seen as a kind of bargaining game between voters and candidates, in which the candidate may be awarded a license to improve his personal fortunes by becoming an MP in return for pledges and tokens of his intention to help improve the fortunes of his constituents" through campaign spending and pork-barrel projects if elected (Hyden and Leys, "Elections and Politics in Single-Party Systems," 402–3). On Egypt, see Blaydes, *Elections and Distributive Politics in Mubarak's Egypt*. Another case in which multiple candidates from the ruling party have competed is communist Vietnam; see Malesky and Schuler, "Nodding or Needling." See also Geddes, Wright, and Frantz, *How Dictatorships Work*.

53. Magaloni, *Voting for Autocracy*, 8–9.

54. Geddes, Wright, and Frantz, *How Dictatorships Work*, 181.

55. Tran, "Zimbabwe Election." This was actually an old theme for Mugabe; in 1976, he had warned that "the gun, which provides the votes, should remain its security officer, its guarantor" (Bratton and Masunungure, "Zimbabwe's Long Agony," 49).

56. Treisman, "Authoritarian Elections as Inoculation."

57. Heller and Nekrich, *Utopia in Power*, 308. See also Goldman, "Stalinist Terror and Democracy."

58. Heller and Nekrich, *Utopia in Power*, 308.

59. Bratton and Masunungure, "Zimbabwe's Long Agony," 41, 50. See also Hafner-Burton, Hyde, and Jablonski, "When Do Governments Resort to Election Violence?"

60. Schmitter, "The Impact and Meaning of 'Non-Competitive, Non-Free and Insignificant' Elections in Authoritarian Portugal, 1933–74."

61. Lillis, *Dark Shadows*, 86.

62. BBC, "Putin Deplores Collapse of USSR."

63. Reuters, "I'm the World's Only True Democrat, Says Putin."

64. Law and Versteeg, "Constitutional Variation among Strains of Authoritarianism," 184.

65. Sometimes, they actually *are* competitive (Levitsky and Way, *Competitive Authoritarianism*). We believe that is generally—although not always—by mistake rather than design. The competition is usually supposed to be apparent rather than real.

66. Quoted in Baker and Glasser, *Kremlin Rising*, 322.

67. Gusman, "Alexander Lukashenka." Overall, Lukashenka was too violent to be considered a spin dictator. But at times he followed the playbook.

68. Maksymiuk, "Belarus." In Rwanda before the 2003 elections, according to a fascinating report by Africa expert Michela Wrong, President Paul Kagame's political minders met to debate how big a splash to make. Kagame's urbane intelligence chief, Patrick Karegeya, argued for the kind of restrained rigging consistent with rule by spin: "'We should get 65 percent,' he said. 'We need an opposition, and we need the electoral process to have credibility.'" But the hard-line general James Kabarebe disagreed: "'You're talking nonsense,' he told Patrick. '*Affande*'—the

boss—'should get 100 percent.'" In the event, Kagame, who had already turned Rwanda into a tightly surveilled police state with frequent recourse to state violence, opted to stick with fear. The RPF share officially announced was 95.1 percent (Wrong, *Do Not Disturb*, 346–47).

69. Magaloni, *Voting for Autocracy*.

70. Lendvai, *Orbán*, 101–6.

71. Than, "Hungary's Government Plans to Tighten Control over Theaters."

72. Dunai, "Hungarian Teachers Say New School Curriculum Pushes Nationalist Ideology."

73. Dyomkin and Faconbridge, "Russia Medvedev Proposes Presidential Term of 6 Years."

74. Barry, "Russian Lawmakers Aim at Foreign Cars, Films and Schooling in Patriotic Purge."

75. For instance, when asked about protesters imprisoned after the Bolotnaya demonstration in 2012, Putin answered: "You cannot call for beatings or bodily injuries of the police, try to gouge out eyes, call for hitting people on the head, or rip off their epaulettes. . . . The authorities must respond accordingly" (President of Russia, "Meeting of the Valdai International Discussion Club"). On another occasion, he said: "As for mass protests, I would like to draw your attention to the following. Certainly, everyone participating in these mass events has the right to do so, and the government must secure these rights. But there is a third issue: the people themselves must abide by the law. If they attack members of the police force, if they cause them any harm, if they throw stones at them, etc.—that kind of activity must, without any doubt, be stopped, and it must be stopped as early as possible" (President of Russia, "Seliger 2012 National Youth Education Forum").

76. Conaghan, *Fujimori's Peru*, 29–30.

77. Krastev, *Eksperimentalnaya rodina*, 114.

78. Cheeseman and Klaas, *How to Rig an Election*; Wilson, *Virtual Politics*.

79. Avenarius, "'Manipulieren, aber geschickt."

80. Wong, "Gerrymandering in Electoral Autocracies."

81. Tan, "Manipulating Electoral Laws in Singapore," 638.

82. Lendvai, *Orbán*, 129; Pivarnyik, "László Kövér Is Heard Justifying Gerrymandering on Leaked Recording."

83. Mudde, "The 2014 Hungarian Parliamentary Elections."

84. Malapportionment sometimes results not from gerrymandering per se but from setting a very high threshold to receive any legislative seats in a proportional system, which results in many votes being "wasted." For instance, to get any seats in Kazakhstan's legislature a party must win at least 7 percent of the nationwide vote.

85. Mudde, "The 2014 Hungarian Parliamentary Elections."

86. *Moscow Times*, "Russia Passes Dual Citizenship Law, Hoping to Add 10M Citizens."

87. Peh, *Tall Order*.

88. Ibid.

89. Rodan, "Goh's Consensus Politics of Authoritarian Rule," 63; Rodan, *Participation without Democracy*, chap. 4.

90. Lillis, *Dark Shadows*, 82.

91. On Kremlin co-optation of the so-called opposition, see Wilson, *Virtual Politics*, chap. 8.

92. For more on this, see Frye, *Weak Strongman*.

93. Rogov and Ananyev, "Public Opinion and Russian Politics," 204.

94. Meduza, "What Putin Reads."

95. Schmidt, "Peru," 685.

96. Bowen and Holligan, *The Imperfect Spy*, 325.

97. Alpert and Rousek, "Vladimir Putin"; BBC, "Putin Reveals Secrets of Russia's Crimea Takeover Plot."

98. Conaghan, *Fujimori's Peru*, 31–32.

99. Ibid., 33.

100. Ibid.

101. McClintock, "Peru's Fujimori," 112.

102. Conaghan, *Fujimori's Peru*, 35.

103. Ibid.

104. Conaghan, "Ecuador," 47.

105. Ibid. On "permanent campaigns," see Blumenthal, *The Permanent Campaign*.

106. NTV, "Odin den iz zhizni Putina," about fifteen minutes in.

107. BBC, "Pavlovsky."

108. Valery Fyodorov, director of VTSIOM, interview by Treisman, January 2016.

109. Aleksei Chesnakov, interview by Treisman, January 27, 2016.

110. FOM, "Vladimir Putin."

111. Levada Center, "Indikatory." The Levada Center is an independent pollster that was designated as a "foreign agent" by the Russian government. As a result, it is forbidden to publish Putin's electoral ratings, but it can still publish his approval ratings.

112. RBC, "Kreml otsenil novuyu metodiku oprosa VTsIOMa o doverii Putinu."

113. Yudin, "In Russia, Opinion Polls Are Being Used."

114. Toro, "Chávez Wasn't Just a Zany Buffoon."

115. Greene and Robertson, *Putin v. the People*, 1.

116. On fraud under Chávez, see, e.g., Corrales, *Electoral Irregularities*; and Jiménez and Hidalgo, "Forensic Analysis of Venezuelan Elections."

117. Simpser, *Why Governments and Parties Manipulate Elections*. See also Lehoucq, "Electoral Fraud."

118. Another motive was to boost turnout at times of public apathy.

119. Guillermoprieto, "Letter from Managua."

120. Quoted in Baker and Glasser, *Kremlin Rising*, 325. The quote might sound strange given Putin's later propensity to take major risks—such as in invading Crimea and intervening in Syria. But in his first two terms he did appear quite cautious.

121. Tucker, "Enough! Electoral Fraud, Collective Action Problems, and Post-Communist Colored Revolutions."

122. Frye, *Weak Strongman*.

123. *Moscow Times*, "Kremlin 'Aiming for 70% Victory' in 2018 Presidential Election."

124. Rundlett and Svolik, "Deliver the Vote! Micromotives and Macrobehavior in Electoral Fraud."

125. Reuter and Robertson, "Subnational Appointments in Authoritarian Regimes."

126. Gehlbach and Simpser, "Electoral Manipulation as Bureaucratic Control."

127. See Simpser, *Why Governments and Parties Manipulate Elections*; Magaloni, *Voting for Autocracy*; and Egorov and Sonin, "Elections in Nondemocracies."

128. Szakonyi and Reuter, "Electoral Manipulation and Regime Support."

129. Vinokurova, "To chto na ulitsu vydut desyatki tysyach lyudey, ne ozhidal nikto."

130. The logic is similar to that of political business cycles, as modeled by Rogoff and Sibert, "Elections and Macroeconomic Policy Cycles." See also Little, "Fraud and Monitoring," for a related argument.

131. This is argued, for instance, by Simpser, *Why Governments and Parties Manipulate Elections*.

132. Opinion polls published before the election could also increase the credibility of the outcome by showing that 55 percent did, indeed, support the incumbent. Fraud might then seem redundant. But, in fact, if the voters strongly expect the incumbent to fraudulently inflate his vote, they may conclude that the opinion poll must have been wrong rather than that the election was clean. So fraud—inflating the incumbent's vote to 65 percent—would still increase confidence that he had, in fact, won.

133. TASS, "'Mertvie dushi' po-amerikanski."

134. *Granma*, "Canciller venezolano auguro ingreso a Consejo de Seguridad."

135. FOM, "'Penta' Poll No. 43," October 28–29, 2000, 1,446 respondents. Available at http://sophist.hse.ru/.

136. The average grade for the United States was 7.1 on a 10-point scale; that for Venezuela was 7.3. See Latinobarometro, *Informe Latinobarómetro 2011*, 44.

137. Cheeseman and Klaas, *How to Rig an Election*, 182–206.

138. Levitsky and Way, *Competitive Authoritarianism*, 19.

139. Tucker, "Enough! Electoral Fraud, Collective Action Problems, and Post-Communist Colored Revolutions."

140. Data from V-DEM. See the online supplement, figure OS5.1.

141. See ibid.

142. Online supplement, figure OS5.2.

143. Online supplement, table OS5.1. These are the proportions looking across all elections. But even looking at just the multiparty elections held by fear dictators, the winner got more than 90 percent in 34 percent of cases (presidential) and 17 percent of cases (legislative), compared to 19 percent (presidential) and 11 percent (legislative) for spin dictators. Of course, holding multiparty elections is one of our rule-of-thumb criteria for spin dictatorship.

144. Online supplement, table OS5.2. The difference between spin and fear dictators is only significant at $p = .07$.

145. Online supplement, figure OS5.4.

146. Hyde and Marinov, "Which Elections Can Be Lost?"

147. Online supplement, figure OS5.5, table OS5.4. The difference between the frequency for spin dictators and democracies is significant at $p < .01$.

148. Geddes, "Why Parties and Elections in Authoritarian Regimes"; Kendall-Taylor and Frantz, "Mimicking Democracy." However, Brownlee (*Authoritarianism*) finds that multicandidate elections have no independent impact on authoritarian survival.

CHAPTER 6: GLOBAL PILLAGE

1. For a recent review of what is known about the motives for the Soviet-Yugoslav split, see Perović, "The Tito-Stalin Split." On Tito's resistance to Stalin's infiltration, see Andrew and Mitrokhin, *The Sword and the Shield*, 356.

2. This is according to Khrushchev, *Memoirs of Nikita Khrushchev*, 532. Perović is not convinced that Stalin actually said this.

3. Andrew and Mitrokhin, *The Sword and the Shield*, 357.

4. Perović, "The Tito-Stalin Split."

5. Lees, *Keeping Tito Afloat*, 51.

6. Ognjenović, Mataušić, and Jozelić, "Yugoslavia's Authentic Socialism," 9, 17–18.

7. Rajak, "The Cold War in the Balkans," 215.

8. Roberts, "Tito—Personal Reflections."

9. West, *Tito and the Rise and Fall of Yugoslavia*, 285–86.

10. Tchoukarine, "The Yugoslav Road to International Tourism," 120–21.

11. Calic, *Tito*, 198–99.

12. Ibid., 211.

13. The Czech film director Jiří Menzel recalled that socialist Yugoslavia had been perceived in communist bloc countries as the "America of the East." Menzel, *Moja Hrvatska*.

14. Barnett, *Tito (Life and Times)*, 140.

15. Calic, *Tito*, 246.

16. Barnett, *Tito (Life and Times)*, 138.

17. Ognjenović, introduction, 2.

18. Popovic and Miller, *Blueprint for Revolution*, 68–69.

19. Ognjenović, Mataušić, and Jozelić, "Yugoslavia's Authentic Socialism," 16.

20. CIA, "Yugoslavia: PLO Ties and Terrorism"; Pacepa, *Red Horizons*, 346.

21. UN World Tourist Organization, *Tourism Highlights, 2017 Edition*, 2.

22. World Bank, "Personal Remittances, Received (Current US$)."

23. On this trade-off, see Miller and Peters, "Restraining the Huddled Masses." Before the East Germans built the Berlin Wall, hundreds of thousands were fleeing to the West each year (Applebaum, *Iron Curtain*, 432).

24. Light, "What Does It Mean to Control Migration?"

25. Chamberlain, *Lenin's Private War*.

26. Dowty, *Closed Borders*, 79–80.

27. Light, "What Does It Mean to Control Migration?"; Dowty, *Closed Borders*, 81.

28. Dowty, *Closed Borders*, 69.

29. Hirschman, *Exit, Voice, and Loyalty*. For a formal analysis of the choice, see Gehlbach, "A Formal Model of Exit and Voice."

30. Dowty, *Closed Borders*, 117.

31. Kenyon, *Dictatorland*, 263.

32. Potter, "Cuba Cracks Down on Illegal Emigration."

33. Liang, *Burma's Foreign Relations*, 47.

34. Dowty, *Closed Borders*, 186.

35. Roniger et al., *Exile, Diaspora, and Return.*

36. Gorsuch, *All This Is Your World*, 11.

37. Ibid., 106.

38. Ibid., 113.

39. Ibid., 114.

40. Chilton and Posner, "Why Countries Sign Bilateral Labor Agreements."

41. Markham, "Germany's Trafficking in People."

42. Pacepa, *Red Horizons*, 73.

43. Shabad, "Soviet Waives Its Exit Tax for Five Leaving for Israel." The 1975 Jackson-Vanik Amendment that introduced trade sanctions for countries without free emigration was applied to all communist countries except Poland and Yugoslavia. These two countries also had emigration restrictions but were exempted for other reasons (see Pregelj, "The Jackson-Vanik Amendment").

44. Semmens, *Seeing Hitler's Germany*, 130.

45. Pi-Sunyer, "Tourism in Catalonia," 237.

46. Pack, *Tourism and Dictatorship*, 11.

47. Hollander, *From Benito Mussolini to Hugo Chávez*, 122–35.

48. Conquest, *The Great Terror*, 271.

49. Heller and Nekrich, *Utopia in Power*, 452.

50. Hornsby, "The Enemy Within?" 258.

51. Arefyev and Mieczkowski, "International Tourism in the Soviet Union."

52. Mieczkowski, "Foreign Tourism in the USSR," 119.

53. Hornsby, "The Enemy Within?" 237.

54. Judt, *Postwar*, 507.

55. Nikolakakis, "The Colonels on the Beach," 432..

56. Data from UNESCO Institute for Statistics, UIS.Stat Database, and UNESCO, *Statistics of Students Abroad, 1962–1968.* This gives a total for 1968 of 428,883 people studying abroad.

57. Kim, "Economic Analysis of Foreign Education and Students Abroad," 360.

58. Spilimbergo, "Democracy and Foreign Education." Study in other dictatorships had no clear effects.

59. Babiracki, "Imperial Heresies," 205.

60. Perraton, "Foreign Students in the Twentieth Century," 174.

61. Katsakioris, "Creating a Socialist Intelligentsia."

62. Perraton, "Foreign Students in the Twentieth Century," 174.

63. Bevis, *International Students in American Colleges and Universities*, 173.

64. Some Latin American dictatorships aligned with Washington allowed some sales of English-language newspapers, confident that only a tiny share of the population would be able to read them.

65. Stoner and McFaul, "The Soviet Union and Russia," 44.

66. Berg, *Broadcasting on the Short Waves*, 47.

67. Shanor, *Behind the Lines*, 167.

68. Office of the Federal Commissioner for the Stasi Records (BStU), *Stasi Note on Meeting with KGB Officials.*

69. Kalathil and Boas, *The Internet and State Control in Authoritarian Regimes*.

70. Sakr, "Frontiers of Freedom," 96.

71. Rahimi, "Cyberdissent."

72. The United States also supported insurgents such as the Nicaraguan contras, Afghan mujahideen, and Tibetan Buddhist fighters in the attempt to combat communist expansion (Byman et al., *Trends in Outside Support for Insurgent Movements*, 1).

73. Zakaria, "The New China Scare," 56.

74. Lockwood, "How the Soviet Union Transformed Terrorism."

75. Andrew and Mitrokhin, *The Sword and the Shield*, 298.

76. World Bank, "International Tourism, Number of Arrivals."

77. The latest figure for Malaysians—from 2017—was 12 million trips (European Travel Commission, *South-East Asian Outbound Travel Market*). Data for Russia, Hungary, Kazakhstan: World Bank, "International Tourism, Number of Departures."

78. UNESCO Institute for Statistics, UIS.Stat Database.

79. Ibid. More than 60 percent of those in Russia were from other former Soviet republics, but up to 113,000 were from further away. See Potapova and Trines, "Education in the Russian Federation." This source gives a higher figure for total foreign students in Russia than UNESCO because it also includes non-degree students.

80. Williams, "South Korea Adjusts Some Radio Frequencies to Escape Jamming."

81. Davis, "China Bars Access to Nearly a Quarter of Foreign News Websites."

82. VOA, "VOA, BBC Protest China Broadcast Jamming."

83. Human Rights Watch, "World Report 2014."

84. Lee, *From Third World to First*, 219.

85. Ibid., 225.

86. Corrales and Penfold, *Dragon in the Tropics*, 128.

87. Chiozza and Goemans ("International Conflict and the Tenure of Leaders," 617) found that the tenure of leaders of autocratic and mixed regimes is reduced by military defeat and not increased by victory.

88. Luhn, "Vladimir Putin Declares All Russian Military Deaths State Secrets."

89. For a comprehensive account of how recent authoritarians have manipulated their public image abroad, see Dukalskis, *Making the World Safe for Dictatorship*.

90. *Straits Times*, "LBJ Gives Lee Red Carpet Welcome."

91. Drysdale, "A Chat with Maggie."

92. *Straits Times*, "Singapore 'A Dazzling Success.'"

93. Daniel, "Lange Pays Tribute to PM Lee."

94. Liak, "Concern, Warmth . . . a Touch of Eloquence."

95. Biblioteka Pervogo Prezidenta Respubliki Kazakhstana, "Mir o Nursultane Nazarbayeve."

96. Agence France Presse, "G8 Summit Cost Russia 400 Million Dollars."

97. BBC, "Russian TV Sees G8 Summit as Recognition of Success of Putin Presidency."

98. Aitken, *Nazarbayev*, 217.

99. Kazinform, "Kazakh Capital to Host."

100. Kazinform, "V ramkakh III Astaninskogo ekonomicheskogo foruma."

101. Feron, "Burton Elicits Tips from Tito for Film."

102. Hauser, "From Putin's Hands."

103. Reuters, "Sean Penn Joins Chávez on Campaign in Venezuela"; Markowicz, "Hollywood's Chávez-Cheering Stars"; Gallego, "Hugo Chávez Collects A-List Friendships"; *El País*, "Chávez Conquista a Robbins"; Associated Press, "Kevin Spacey Visits Hugo Chávez."

104. Associated Press, "Belafonte."

105. *El País*, "Maradona rompe una lanza."

106. Cockburn, "Hollywood Star Meets Hungary Prime Minister."

107. Hungary Today, "Hungary Prepared to Host 'Just About Any' Sporting Event, Says Govt."

108. Panja and Draper, "US Says FIFA Officials Were Bribed." But note that Infantino was not at FIFA when the 2018 and 2022 locations were decided.

109. Cheeseman and Klaas, *How to Rig an Election*, 182–94.

110. Cooley, "Authoritarianism Goes Global," 55; Cheeseman and Klaas, *How to Rig an Election*, 200–202.

111. Hyde, *The Pseudo-Democrat's Dilemma*.

112. Ilko, "Na vybori v Ukraine opredelen smotryashchy ot Kremlya?"

113. RIA Novosti, "Aleksei Kochetkov nameren podat isk"; Lenta.ru, "Moldavia gotova osvobodit vtorogo rossiiskogo nablyudatelya."

114. CIS-EMO.net, "Aleksei Kochetkov."

115. CIS-EMO.net, "Monitoring Missions' Participants."

116. Pantoja, "CEELA fue creado por Chávez."

117. Gaytan, "Who Are the Council of Electoral Specialists of Latin America (CEELA)?"

118. EFE Newswire, "Ortega dice que observadores que vigilarán comicios son los más idóneos."

119. EFE Newswire, "Liberales califican de 'non gratos' a observadores CEELA en campaña Nicaragua."

120. Lemon, "Weaponizing Interpol."

121. Interpol, *About Notices*.

122. Committee to Protect Journalists, "Attacks on the Press 2006: Venezuela."

123. Fair Trials, "Patricia Poleo."

124. Human Rights Watch, *Tightening the Grip*; Padgett, "Red Alert."

125. Aslund, *Russia's Interference*.

126. *Economist*, "Rogue States."

127. Mineev, "'Krasnaya metka' dlya Interpola."

128. See Browder, *Red Notice*.

129. Pacepa, *Red Horizons*, 354.

130. Ibid., 349.

131. Putin is a regular critic of the West's "double standards." See, for instance, Anderson, "Putin Accuses the West."

132. Ross, "Which Countries Are the Biggest Boost or Drag on the EU Budget?"

133. Europa.eu, "Hungary."

134. Gebrekidan, Apuzzo, and Novak, "The Money Farmers."

135. Ibid.

136. Ibid.

137. *Economist*, "The EU Is Tolerating."

138. Diekmann, "Hungary's Prime Minister Says Accepting Syrian Refugees 'Also Means Importing Terrorism, Criminalism, Anti-Semitism and Homophobia.'"

139. Lendvai, *Orbán*, 202.

140. Ibid., 203.

141. Ibid.

142. Eventually, facing mounting criticism, Orbán's Fidesz party left the EPP in March 2021 (Hopkins, "Hungary's Fidesz Finalizes EPP Divorce").

143. Rohac, "A European Compromise Not Worth Making."

144. Venezuela Analysis, "Venezuelan President Chávez."

145. Carroll, "Chávez Furious as OAS Rights Watchdog Accuses Him of Endangering Democracy."

146. Corrales and Penfold, *Dragon in the Tropics*, 133; Martin, "Chávez, the Organization of American States, and Democracy."

147. Campbell, "Chávez Makes a Monkey of Bush."

148. BBC, "Hugo Chávez."

149. Foer, "The Talented Mr. Chávez."

150. Frontline, "Interview: Teodoro Petkoff."

151. Toro, "What Fidel Taught Hugo."

152. Gordon, "NATO Backs Defense Plan for Turkey."

153. Gall, "Turkey Gets Shipment."

154. Erlanger, "Turkish Aggression."

155. Waldman, "Turkey, Not Trump."

156. Socor, "Russia Blocks Consensus."

157. Ibid.

158. Cheeseman and Klaas, *How to Rig an Election*; Morgenbesser, "The Menu of Autocratic Innovation," 1055–56.

159. Varol, "Stealth Authoritarianism."

160. Ibid., 1708.

161. Frye, *Weak Strongman*; Kozlov, "V Kremle izuchayut amerikanskie tekhnologii."

162. Wilson, *Virtual Politics*, 70.

163. Toobin, "The Dirty Trickster." The same Roger Stone would be sentenced to jail in 2020 for various felonies committed while an advisor to President Trump. Trump later commuted the sentence (Gambino, "Roger Stone Sentenced to 40 Months in Prison").

164. Human Rights Watch, *"Kill the Chicken to Scare the Monkeys."*

165. Grassegger, "The Unbelievable Story of the Plot against George Soros"; Schudel, "Arthur Finkelstein."

166. Feuer, "Federal Prosecutors Investigate Weinstein's Ties to Israeli Firm."

167. Bayer, "Israeli Intelligence Firm."

168. Wootliff, "Israelis Arrested for Spying."

169. Gould-Davies, "Putin and the Belarusian Question."

170. Rozhdestvensky, Rubin, and Badanin, "Chef i povar."

171. Barnes, "Brazilian Advisers Spin Elections in Venezuela and Beyond."

172. These percentages exclude those who did not answer or said they did not know. U.S. president George Bush was also widely disliked, with only 29 percent confidence in the median country. See Pew Research Center, *Global Unease with Major World Powers*. By 2020, with the change from Hu to Xi, confidence in China's top leader had fallen to 19 percent (Pew Research Center, *US Image Plummets*).

173. Klasa et al., "Russia's Long Arm Reaches to the Right in Europe."

174. Roman, "How Hugo Chávez Helped Inspire Spain's Far-Left Podemos Movement."

175. RT, "Putin Talks NSA, Syria, Iran, Drones in RT Interview."

176. Stanley, "Julian Assange Starts Talk Show on Russian TV"; Rutenberg, "Larry King, the Russian Media and a Partisan Landscape."

177. Gatov, "Research the Revenge."

178. Shuster, "Inside Putin's On-Air Machine"; Richter, "RT: A Low-Grade Platform for Useful Idiots."

179. Shuster, "Inside Putin's On-Air Machine."

180. President of Russia, "Russia Today TV Channel Starts Broadcasting in Argentina."

181. Marthoz, *Venezuela's Foreign Policy*.

182. Bennett and Naím, "21st-Century Censorship."

183. Quoted in Carroll, *Comandante*, 195.

184. Reardon, "Latin America's TeleSUR Now Available to U.S. Viewers."

185. Daniel, "Chávez-Funded Telesur Flourishes in Honduras Coup."

186. Pearson, "Venezuela"; Romero, "Ecuador Leader Confounds Supporters and Detractors."

187. Singapore also founded its own international all-news TV station, Channel News Asia, in 1999 to offer an "Asian viewpoint"—which turned out to be remarkably close to that of the Singapore government. See Atkins, *The Politics of Southeast Asia's New Media*, 157; National Archives of Singapore, "Speech by DPM Lee Hsien Loong."

188. Painter, "The Boom in Counter-Hegemonic News Channels," 54.

189. Dougherty, "How the Media Became One of Putin's Most Powerful Weapons."

190. Gambrell, "Report: Iran TV Airs 355 Coerced Confessions over Decade"; Sadr, "Documenting the Perpetrators amongst the People"; Mozur, "Live from America's Capital, a TV Station Run by China's Communist Party."

191. Foer, "The Talented Mr. Chávez."

192. Forero, "Venezuela's New Campaign."

193. Bogardus, "Venezuela Head Polishes Image with Oil Dollars."

194. Mendick, "Tony Blair Gives Kazakhstan's Autocratic President Tips on How to Defend a Massacre"; Tynan, "Kazakhstan."

195. Mendick, "Tony Blair Gives Kazakhstan's Autocratic President Tips on How to Defend a Massacre."

196. Gerden, "Can Russia Reengage the West."

197. Smith, "Kazakhstan."

198. Gerden, "Can Russia Reengage the West."

199. Shafer, "Hail to the Return of Motherland-Protecting Propaganda!"

200. Garmazhapova, "Gde zhivut trolli."

201. See Golovchenko et al., "Cross-Platform State Propaganda"; and U.S. House of Representatives Permanent Selection Committee on Intelligence, "Exposing Russia's Effort to Sow Discord Online."

202. Dawson and Innes, *The Internet Research Agency in Europe*.

203. *New York Times*, "Foreign Government Contributions to Nine Think Tanks."

204. Lipton, "Feud in Kazakh President's Family Spills into U.S."

205. Pompeo, "On Transparency."

206. Gardner, "From Astana to Brussels, via Eurasia"; Green, "Jack Straw Criticised for Accepting Part-time Job Paid for by Kazakhstan."

207. MVD Rossii, "Sostav Obshchestvennogo soveta pri MVD Rossii sozyva 2011–2013 g."; Krastev, "In the Heart of New York, Russia's 'Soft Power' Arm Gaining Momentum"; Corporate Europe Observatory, *Spin Doctors to the Autocrats*.

208. Lee, *From Third World to First*, 511–13.

209. Allison, Blackwill, and Wyne, *Lee Kuan Yew*.

210. BBC, "Anger as German Ex-chancellor Schroeder Heads up Rosneft Board."

211. Dempsey, "Gazprom Courts Prodi as Pipeline Chief"; Zygar, *All the Kremlin's Men*, 122–23.

212. Fisher and Greenwood, "Tory Peers Told to Come Clean about Russian Links." According to this 2018 article, Lord Barker of Battle "is chairman of En+, the Russian energy giant majority-owned by the oligarch Oleg Deripaska, a close ally of President Putin. En+ and Mr Deripaska have been subject to sanctions since the Salisbury nerve agent attack in March."

213. Greenwood et al., "Conservative Party Ministers Bankrolled." The sources of donations were generally Russian émigrés with British citizenship, some with a history of high-level Kremlin contacts.

214. Castle, "Berlusconi Causes New EU Rift with Chechnya Remarks"; Arbatova, "Italy, Russia's Voice in Europe?" 14.

215. Friedman, "Silvio Berlusconi and Vladimir Putin."

216. Kramer, "Italians Win Yukos Units, but Gazprom Is to Benefit."

217. Dempsey, "Gazprom Courts Prodi as Pipeline Chief."

218. Von Salzen, "Wie Gerhard Schröder als Türöffner für Gazprom agiert."

219. Corporate Europe Observatory, *Spin Doctors to the Autocrats*, 40.

220. Gardner, "From Astana to Brussels, via Eurasia."

221. Mayr, "European Politicians Shill for Kazakh Autocrat."

222. Gatehouse, "Marine Le Pen."

223. Nardelli, "Revealed."

224. Parodi, "Italian Prosecutors Probe Allegations of League Oil Deal."

225. *Moscow Times*, "Yakunin in Estonia Deal"; ERR, "KAPO Declassifies Savisaar Files"; Filatova and Bushuev, "Sanctioned Putin Ally Vladimir Yakunin Granted German Visa."

226. Dukalskis, *Making the World Safe for Dictatorship*, 59. And this is just the amount officially reported.

227. Sullivan, "U.S. Public-Relations Firm Helps Putin Make His Case to America."

228. O'Grady, "Winning Hearts and Minds inside the Beltway."

229. Vázquez-Ger, "What Can Tens of Millions of Dollars Buy Ecuador in the Empire?"

230. Maza, "Here's Where Paul Manafort Did Business with Corrupt Dictators"; Rawnsley, "How Manafort's Work for the 'Torturer's Lobby' Came Back to Haunt Him."

231. *New York Times*, "Foreign Government Contributions to Nine Think Tanks."

232. China Investment Corporation, "International Advisory Council."

233. *Haaretz*, "Report: Israeli Company Sold Surveillance Equipment to Iran"; Brewster, "Manhole Covers That Spy?"; Benner et al., "Saudis' Image Makers"; Hajizade, "ANALYSIS: Unveiling Iranian Pro-government Trolls and Cyber-Warriors."

234. Al Jazeera, "Saudi Arabia's Purge."

235. Rachman, "Chinese Censorship Is Spreading beyond Its Borders"; Dunn, "How Chinese Censorship Became a Global Export"; Denyer, "In Reversal, Cambridge University Press Restores Articles after China Censorship Row."

236. Sanger and Benner, "U.S. Accuses North Korea."

237. Askarbekov, "What Kazakhstan Really Thought of Borat."

238. Ibid.

239. As usual, we use the chapter 1 rules of thumb to distinguish spin, fear, and hybrid dictatorships, and we focus on the period since 1980 when spin dictatorships became more common. The MEPV data set defines wars as "episodes of interstate violence that cause at least 500 directly-related deaths" (Center for Systemic Peace's Major Episodes of Political Violence version 2018, http://www.systemicpeace.org/inscr/MEPVv2018.xls). For comparison, the COW data include only wars that result in at least 1,000 combatant deaths within a twelve-month period. We prefer the more comprehensive accounting with the lower fatalities threshold. Another disadvantage of the COW war data is that they end in 2007, whereas the MEPV data continue through the end of our measures of dictator type (2015). Azerbaijan is coded as at war in 1993–94. In fact, the war began in 1991, but in 1991–92 the country could not be classified as a spin or fear dictatorship since in those years it had two leaders who did not last the five years required to evaluate the level of violent repression. The Karabakh war flared up again in 2020.

240. These were Vietnam, Cambodia, China, Ethiopia, Eritrea, Iraq, and Iran. The wars were between Vietnam and China, Vietnam and Cambodia, Ethiopia and Eritrea, Iraq and Iran, and Iraq and Kuwait plus the United States and its allies. Some additional years of war occurred under dictators such as Argentina's General Galtieri whom we could not classify since they were not in power for five years or under hybrid regimes.

241. See the online supplement, table OS6.2. This is all the more surprising since spin dictators are often "personalistic" autocrats, a type that research suggests is particularly prone to foreign aggression (Weeks, "Strongmen and Straw Men").

242. We coded as initiators: Armenia (vs. Azerbaijan), Cambodia (vs. Vietnam), China (vs. Vietnam), Eritrea (vs. Ethiopia), Iraq (vs. Iran), Iraq (vs. Kuwait), Russia (vs. Georgia), Israel (vs. Lebanon), Argentina (vs. the UK), and the United States (vs. Iraq).

243. We use the Correlates of War project's Dyadic Militarized Interstate Dispute Data, v.4.01 (https://correlatesofwar.org/data-sets/MIDs).

244. See the online supplement, table OS6.3.

245. And Russia is only coded here as a spin dictatorship from 2007 on, since Polity classifies it as a marginal democracy from 2000 to 2006. From 2000 through 2014, Russia under Putin

initiated 35 militarized disputes, averaging more than two a year. Even if we reclassified Russia in 2000–2006 as a spin dictatorship, spin dictatorships would still only initiate militarized disputes once every 6.5 years on average, compared to one every 2.9 years for fear dictatorships.

CHAPTER 7: THE MODERNIZATION COCKTAIL

1. Pinker, *The Better Angels of Our Nature*.

2. See also Pinker, *Enlightenment Now*.

3. Guriev and Treisman, "Informational Autocrats."

4. Between 1982 and 2018, the number of ongoing interstate wars—defined, as in chapter 6, as "episodes of interstate violence that cause at least 500 directly-related deaths"—fell from 8 to 0. The number of ethnic or civil wars peaked in 1992 at 30, before falling to 15 in 2018 (Center for Systemic Peace, Major Episodes of Political Violence; see the online supplement, figure OS7.1).

5. Among dictators whose tenure did not coincide with insurgencies, civil wars, or interstate wars, the proportion with more than 10 state political killings a year fell from 50 percent in the 1980s cohort to 17 percent in the 2000s cohort. See the online supplement, figure OS7.2.

6. Levitsky and Way ("International Linkage and Democratization") divide these international influences between Western leverage (deliberate pressure exerted by Western governments) and linkage to the West (economic and diplomatic ties to Western countries and institutions). They argue that these, when strong, lead to competitive authoritarianism or—when stronger—prompt competitive authoritarian regimes to democratize. We agree with the general point that global influences usually support political liberalization. However, we think these often lead not to competitive authoritarianism but to the kind of uncompetitive, simulated democracy that we call spin dictatorship, as, for instance, in Singapore. Global influences also tend, in the post-Cold War setting, to reduce violent repression (which is not necessarily lower in competitive authoritarian states). And—another point not noted by Levitsky and Way—the effect of globalization depends in part on the modernization levels of the given states and the world as a whole.

7. For a contrary view, see Acemoglu et al., "Income and Democracy." We agree with their analysis that shows that short-run increases in countries' income do not cause systematic short-run changes in their political systems. But a range of subsequent papers have shown that a longer-run relationship between economic development and democracy does exist, and that the timing of political changes is triggered by other variables such as leader turnover. The failure to find an effect of income in Acemoglu et al.'s panel estimations probably reflects the short time coverage of most regressions (just 1960–2000) and the narrow country coverage of the 25-year panel that they do include. It may also reflect that they do not adjust for the fact that countries with a top score on the Polity2 scale cannot move any higher no matter how high their income rises. For references, see Treisman, "Economic Development and Democracy." Acemoglu and Robinson (*Economic Origins*) argue that dictatorships give up power and become democracies when exogenous shocks mobilize the masses behind revolution.

8. Florida, *The Rise of the Creative Class Revisited*, 46.

9. Today, manufacturing accounts for only 8 percent of U.S. employment (U.S. Bureau of Labor Statistics, "Employment by Major Industry Sector").

10. Pinchot and Pinchot, *The End of Bureaucracy*, 30.

11. Florida, *The Rise of the Creative Class Revisited*.

12. This is based on the 32.6 percent share of the creative class in 2015 reported in Florida, Mellander, and King, *The Global Creativity Index, 2015*, 59, and an estimate of the total U.S. labor force of 160 million (from World Bank, "Labor Force, Total").

13. We do not mean to suggest this change was beneficial to all—in fact, the fall in industrial employment and its only partial replacement by creative-class jobs left many in poorly paid, insecure, and tedious services jobs. It coincided in the United States with an increase in income and wealth inequality, along with a rise in crime and declining trust in government (Fukuyama, *The Great Disruption*, 4–5). Our focus here is on how this—quite general—trend in advanced economies affects the options for dictatorial rulers.

14. See Acemoglu and Robinson, *Why Nations Fail*; and Cheremukhin et al., "The Industrialization and Economic Development of Russia."

15. Pinchot and Pinchot, *The End of Bureaucracy*, 32.

16. Gardels, "The Sage of Singapore."

17. See, e.g., Galor, *Unified Growth Theory*, 31–37.

18. Mokyr, "The Rise and Fall of the Factory System," 10.

19. Vandenbussche, Aghion, and Meghir, "Growth, Distance to Frontier and Composition of Human Capital."

20. Glaeser, Ponzetto, and Shleifer, "Why Does Democracy Need Education?"; Dahlum and Wig, "Chaos on Campus."

21. Gorbachev, *Memoirs*, 45.

22. Bautista et al., "Chile's Missing Students."

23. We use data from Barro and Lee, "A New Dataset," and the 2010 World Bank income class classification. See https://datahelpdesk.worldbank.org/knowledgebase/articles/906519.

24. Barro and Lee, "A New Data Set."

25. Wells, "H. G. Wells."

26. One of us, Sergei, witnessed this bifurcation firsthand while studying in an elite Soviet technical university. This institution—the Moscow Institute of Physics and Technology—was created to prepare cadres for careers in defense-related research. Physics, mathematics, and engineering had to be taught well—but history, economics, and philosophy were refracted through an ideological prism. (Sociology and political science were simply banned.) The contrast between the state-of-the-art training in science and the stale rereading of Leninist texts itself sent a message about the intellectual bankruptcy of the regime's political narrative.

27. American Institute of Physics, "The Opening Paragraphs of Sakharov's Reflections."

28. Loudis, "The Art of Escaping Censorship."

29. Ibid.

30. Inglehart and Welzel, *Modernization, Cultural Change, and Democracy*.

31. Goebbels, "Der Rundfunk als achte Großmacht."

32. Of course, as we mention elsewhere, the Internet also creates opportunities for surveillance and propaganda that dictators can use to offset the empowerment of society.

33. Exactly the same strategy often works for populist leaders in democracies; see Guriev and Papaioannou, "The Political Economy of Populism."

34. On transnational pro-democracy networks, see Bunce and Wolchik, *Defeating Authoritarian Leaders*, 300–304.

35. Calculated from data of Fouquin and Hugot, "Two Centuries of Bilateral Trade and Gravity Data," as reproduced in Ortiz-Ospina and Beltekian, "Trade and Globalization." See the online supplement, figure OS7.3.

36. UNCTAD, *World Investment Report 2020*, 22.

37. Zloch-Christy, *Debt Problems of Eastern Europe*, 34; Gaidar, *Collapse of an Empire*, 128.

38. World Bank, "External Debt Stocks, Total (DOD, current US$)," https://data.worldbank.org/indicator/DT.DOD.DECT.CD?locations=BR.

39. Statistics from UNCTAD, authoritarian defined as Polity2 < 6. See the online supplement, figure OS7.5.

40. Manyika et al., "Digital Globalization."

41. UNCTAD, "Digital Service Delivery Shows Potential for Developing World."

42. Manyika et al., "Digital Globalization," 74.

43. Williams, *International Journalism*, 74.

44. McPhail, *Global Communication*, 245.

45. *New York Times*, "Full Text of Clinton's Speech on China Trade Bill."

46. Diamond and Plattner, *Liberation Technology*.

47. Gilboa, "The CNN Effect," 28.

48. Milner and Mukherjee, "Democratization and Economic Globalization."

49. Cao, Greenhill, and Prakash, "Where Is the Tipping Point?"

50. Asiedu and Lien, "Democracy, Foreign Direct Investment, and Natural Resources"; Li and Resnick, "Reversal of Fortunes"; Hollyer, Rosendorff, and Vreeland, *Transparency, Democracy, and Autocracy*; Jensen, "Political Risk, Democratic Institutions, and Foreign Direct Investment"; Harms and Ursprung, "Do Civil and Political Repression Really Boost Foreign Direct Investments?"; Blanton and Blanton, "What Attracts Foreign Investors?"

51. From $17 billion in 1989 to $74 billion in 1994 (UNCTAD statistics).

52. UNCTAD statistics.

53. Morozov, *The Net Delusion*; Tucker et al., "From Liberation to Turmoil."

54. McPhail, *Global Communication*, 2.

55. Gowing, "Real-Time Television Coverage of Armed Conflicts"; Gilboa, "The CNN Effect."

56. Gurri, *The Revolt of the Public*, 48.

57. The number of Tunisian college graduates had soared in the preceding decades (Fukuyama, *Political Order and Political Decay*, 50).

58. Golden, "Old Scores."

59. *1994*, Netflix, 2019.

60. See Malkin, "50 Years after a Student Massacre, Mexico Reflects on Democracy."

61. Interviewed in *1994*.

62. Henck, *Subcommander Marcos*, 221.

63. E.g., Sánchez, "San Diego Rally Backs Mexican Indian Revolt"; Casa, "Sacramento Protesters Shut Down Mexican Consulate."

64. Martínez-Torres, "Civil Society, the Internet, and the Zapatistas," 350–51.

65. Ibid., 348.

66. Association for Diplomatic Studies & Training, "Trouble in Chiapas."

67. Martínez-Torres, "Civil Society, the Internet, and the Zapatistas," 352.

68. Mexico's PRI has the reputation of being relatively nonviolent—and, if compared to the most brutal dictatorships, it was. Still, the security services regularly murdered activists, peasants, and students—and not just in the well-known Tlatelolco massacre of 1968. Over the terms of the four Mexican presidents preceding Salinas—from Díaz Ordaz to de la Madrid—the state political killings for which we found evidence added up to a rate of sixty-four a year.

69. Smith, "The Story of Laurent Gbagbo," 10–12.

70. This paragraph and the next draw on ibid.

71. Konan, "In Ivory Coast, Democrat to Dictator."

72. Searcey and Karasz, "Laurent Gbagbo, Former Ivory Coast Leader, Acquitted of Crimes against Humanity."

73. Power, *Like Water on Stone*, 119–20.

74. Ibid., xi.

75. Amnesty International, "Get Involved."

76. Sikkink, *The Justice Cascade*, 16.

77. Iriye and Goedde, "Introduction," 3.

78. Cmiel, "The Recent History of Human Rights."

79. Pruce, *The Mass Appeal of Human Rights*.

80. Based on a search of Nexis Uni. We extend the count of Ron, "Varying Methods of State Violence."

81. Kim, "Why Do States Adopt Truth Commissions after Transition?" 1490.

82. Sikkink, *The Justice Cascade*, 24.

83. Fariss and Dancy, "Measuring the Impact of Human Rights," 289.

84. Spar, "Foreign Investment and Human Rights."

85. Ottaway, "Reluctant Missionaries."

86. Walker, "Belarus Axed as Host."

87. Standaert, "Nike and H&M Face Backlash in China."

88. Barry, Clay, and Flynn, "Avoiding the Spotlight."

89. Wright and Escribà-Folch, "Are Dictators Immune to Human Rights Shaming?"

90. Rejali, *Torture and Democracy*, 13.

91. Rosenblum, "Prison Conditions in Zaire."

92. Rejali, *Torture and Democracy*, 14.

93. Krauss, "U.S. Cuts Aid to Zaire, Setting Off a Policy Debate."

94. National Security Archive, "Inside Argentina's Killing Machine."

95. Nugent, "Nkrumah and Rawlings," 50.

96. Handley, "Ghana," 224.

97. Ibid., 231.

98. Ibid., 232.

99. Polgreen, "Ghana's Unlikely Democrat Finds Vindication in Vote."

100. Handley, "Ghana," 232.

101. Huntington, *The Third Wave*, 91–92.

102. Avalon Project, "Inaugural Address of Jimmy Carter."

103. Hancock, *Human Rights and US Foreign Policy*, 47.

104. Calculated from World Bank figures as the sum of net official aid received plus net official overseas development assistance received.

105. Handley, "Ghana," 233.

106. Varol, "Stealth Authoritarianism," 1728.

107. Basic Documents of the EBRD, "Agreement Establishing the European Bank for Reconstruction and Development."

108. Geddes, Wright, and Frantz, *How Dictatorships Work*, 139.

109. Lebovic and Voeten, "The Cost of Shame."

110. Legler and Tieku, "What Difference Can a Path Make?" 470.

111. Halperin and Lomasney, "Guaranteeing Democracy," 137.

112. Ibid., 136–37.

113. Ibid., 137.

114. Landau, "Abusive Constitutionalism," 251–54.

115. Legler and Tieku, "What Difference Can a Path Make?" 475; Nathan, *A Survey of Mediation in African Coups*, 10.

116. Pacepa, *Red Horizons*, 220

117. Varol, "Stealth Authoritarianism," 1727.

118. Arceneaux and Pion-Berlin, "Issues, Threats and Institutions," 16.

119. Legler and Tieku, "What Difference Can a Path Make?" 475.

120. Within democracies, many blame elements of the modernization cocktail for an increase in economic inequality and political polarization in recent decades. Class divisions have sharpened between the highly educated creative professionals and remaining industrial and clerical workers, who are threatened by outsourcing and automation. See, for instance, Boix, *Democratic Capitalism at the Crossroads*. Populists in democracies exploit the anxieties of the threatened classes, publicly attacking the educated elite in much the way spin dictators do (see Guriev and Papaioannou, "Political Economy of Populism"). Again, our point is not to debate whether these trends are desirable or undesirable, per se. In fact, we believe that postindustrial modernization both increases the chances of transition from the dictatorship of fear to spin dictatorship or democracy *and* exacerbates social divisions within spin dictatorships and democracies.

121. Sosin, "Censorship and Dissent."

122. For instance, the Malaysian "Bersih" movement for clean elections in 2007–8 used Facebook and Google Groups to organize rallies in 85 cities in 35 countries (Johns and Cheong, "Feeling the Chill").

123. See Barro and Lee, "A New Data Set." We refer to proportion with completed higher education among those aged 15 and older. The rates in 1990 were: 13 percent in Russia, 9 percent in the UK, 8 percent in Germany, 8 percent in Bulgaria, and 6 percent in France.

124. World Values Survey, online analysis, www.worldvaluessurvey.org/WVSOnline.jsp.

125. Some notorious fear dictators continue to get large amounts of aid from the West. Egypt in 2019 under General Sisi received $1.47 billion in U.S. aid (USAID, "Foreign Aid Explorer").

126. Based on National Bureau of Statistics of China, *China Statistical Yearbook 2020*, tables 2.14 and 2.9 (http://www.stats.gov.cn/tjsj/ndsj/2020/indexeh.htm). In the 2019 National Sample Survey, 63,739 out of 908,609 people aged 15 and older completed undergraduate studies.

127. Aron, *Roads to the Temple*.

128. World Values Survey, 7th Wave, "Online Data Analysis." The figure for Hong Kong was 76 percent—closer to the world average.

CHAPTER 8: THE FUTURE OF SPIN

1. As of 2010, the proportion of citizens aged 15 and higher with bachelor's degrees was 25 percent in Russia and 30 percent in Singapore (fifth- and second-highest levels in the world, respectively) (Barro and Lee, "A New Data Set"). In Richard Florida's latest estimates from 2015, the "creative class" made up 47 percent of the workforce in Singapore and 39 percent in Russia (third and nineteenth in the world, respectively) (Florida, Mellander, and King, *The Global Creativity Index, 2015*).

2. World Bank data for 2020, https://data.worldbank.org/indicator/SL.AGR.EMPL.ZS ?locations=TZ.

3. Repression became somewhat more overt under President John Magufuli, in power from 2015 to 2021 (Human Rights Watch, *Tanzania*).

4. World Bank, "Net ODA Received."

5. Lee, *From Third World to First*, 157.

6. GDP per capita in 2011 dollars, from Maddison Project Database 2020 (see Bolt et al., *Rebasing "Maddison"*). Gross enrollment rates in tertiary education, from the World Bank, https://data.worldbank.org/indicator/SE.TER.ENRR?locations=MY.

7. World Bank data, https://data.worldbank.org/indicator/SL.IND.EMPL.ZS?end =2020&locations=MY&start=1991; https://data.worldbank.org/indicator/IT.NET.USER.ZS ?locations=MY.

8. Beng, "Malaysia's Reformasi Movement"; Slater, "Malaysia's Modernization Tsunami."

9. Miner, "The Unintended Consequences of Internet Diffusion."

10. Rogin, "In Malaysia, a Victory for Democracy." Polity V, for instance, coded Malaysia as a democracy in 2018, with a Polity2 score of 7, up from 5 in 2017.

11. Paddock, "Democracy Fades in Malaysia."

12. Wage in rubles from Rosstat, converted to dollars at purchasing power parity using World Bank's PPP conversion factor. Rosstat, *Rossia v tsifrakh 2020*, 134; Rosstat, *Rossia v tsifrakh 2013*, 143.

13. World Values Survey and European Values Study, www.worldvaluessurvey.org /WVSOnline.jsp.

14. See Treisman, "Introduction."

15. World Bank data.

16. Treisman, "Economic Development and Democracy."

17. Guriev and Treisman, "The Popularity of Authoritarian Leaders."

18. World Bank data.

19. World Bank data, https://data.worldbank.org/indicator/IT.NET.USER.ZS?locations =RU; Florida, Mellander, and Stolarick, *Creativity and Prosperity*; Florida, Mellander, and King, *The Global Creativity Index, 2015*.

20. World Bank data, https://data.worldbank.org/indicator/SE.TER.ENRR?locations=BY.

21. See Kozlov, "Belarus Emerges as Europe's Leading High Tech Hub." GDP data at market exchange rates, from IMF, *World Economic Outlook Database*, https://www.imf.org/en/Publications/WEO/weo-database/2020/October.

22. World Values Survey, online data, http://www.worldvaluessurvey.org/WVSOnline.jsp.

23. *Economist*, "No Vaccine for Cruelty."

24. Ibid.

25. Ross, *The Oil Curse*.

26. World Bank data.

27. World Bank data.

28. Corrales, "Authoritarian Survival."

29. Amnesty International, "Venezuela 2019."

30. That said, the educated opposition did have the experience of four decades of democratic—but increasingly corrupt—party competition to draw on (1958–98), as well as a tradition of competitive media, much of it arrayed against the regime. And the opposition came close on several occasions to defeating first Chávez and later Maduro, successfully mobilizing demonstrations of hundreds of thousands of protesters (e.g., Berwick, "Back to the Streets").

31. Reforms are also more likely amid leadership successions and during regional or global waves of political change; see Treisman, "Income, Democracy, and Leader Turnover."

32. Fouquin and Hugot, "Two Centuries of Bilateral Trade and Gravity Data."

33. The Maddison Database 2020 (see Bolt et al., *Rebasing "Maddison"*) gives a total world GDP in 1920 of 4 trillion international dollars at 2011 prices, 7 trillion in 1940, and 114 trillion in 2018. Fouquin and Hugot ("Two Centuries of Bilateral Trade and Gravity Data") put world merchandise trade at 49 percent of GDP in 2014, compared to 23 percent in 1929.

34. World Bank Data, https://data.worldbank.org/indicator/TG.VAL.TOTL.GD.ZS. WTO forecasts in early 2021 were for a 9.2 percent fall in world merchandise trade in 2020 alongside a 4.8 percent fall in global GDP, before a rebound in 2021. These would imply a drop in world goods trade from 44 to 42 percent of GDP in 2020 (World Trade Organization, "Trade Shows Signs of Rebound").

35. Wheelock ("Comparing the COVID-19 Recession with the Great Depression") notes that "at its low point in the first quarter of 1933, real GNP was just 68 percent of its 1929 peak." (GDP figures were not calculated until 1947.) Data from the Federal Reserve Bank of St. Louis (https://fred.stlouisfed.org/series/GDPC1) show a fall from a seasonally adjusted annual GDP of $19.3 trillion in the fourth quarter of 2019 to $17.3 in the second quarter of 2020, a drop of 10 percent. The same source shows a fall from $15.8 trillion in the fourth quarter of 2007 to $15.1 in the second quarter of 2009, a drop of about 4 percent.

36. The *Financial Times* All-World Index of stocks in 47 countries surpassed its previous peak in September 2020 and continued to rise.

37. World Bank data.

38. Hille, "Russian Tax Law Aims to Coax Businesses Back Home."

39. UNCTAD statistics.

40. Horn, Reinhart, and Trebesch, "How Much Money Does the World Owe China."

41. Hess and Aidoo, "Democratic Backsliding in Sub-Saharan Africa."

42. *Economist*, "Another Critic of President John Magufuli Is Silenced."

43. *Economist*, "China Is Thinking Twice."

44. Sambrook, *Are Foreign Correspondents Redundant?* 20–21.

45. Cooper, "When Lines between NGO and News Organization Blur."

46. Sambrook, *Are Foreign Correspondents Redundant?* 27.

47. Powers, "Hello World."

48. Jones, "Live Aid 1985."

49. Taylor, "Was #Kony2012 a Failure?"; Holpuch, "Stolen Daughters."

50. Figures from *Giving USA*, https://blog.candid.org/post/charitable-giving-in-2019-up-4 -2-percent-giving-usa-finds/; Lewin, "Gifts to Charity in US."

51. Ikenberry, "The Next Liberal Order." Ikenberry did, nevertheless, see it as potentially savable.

52. Wuerth, "International Law in the Post-Human Rights Era."

53. Kato, "A Conversation with Francis Fukuyama." Fukuyama called China "the most important challenge to the idea of the end of history" that he had advanced in 1989. He doubted that China's model would prove sustainable, given the social pressures of modernization. But if it did, it would constitute "a real alternative to liberal democracy."

54. Halper, *The Beijing Consensus*.

55. Kurlantzick, "Why the 'China Model' Isn't Going Away."

56. See table OS8.1, based on UN treaty data at https://treaties.un.org/. Jana von Stein examines a broader set of human rights-related instruments in "Exploring the Universe of UN Human Rights Agreements." She uncovers a similar dynamic. The Philippines did withdraw from the Rome Statute establishing the International Criminal Court in 2011 (the UN classifies this under "Penal Matters" rather than "Human Rights"). Among non-UN human rights bodies, Venezuela withdrew from the American Convention on Human Rights in 2013 and from the OAS Charter in 2017 (Inter-American Commission on Human Rights, *Annual Report 2019*, 489).

57. Alston and Mégret, introduction, 2.

58. Hegarty and Fridlund, "Taking Stock."

59. Langer and Eason, "The Quiet Expansion of Universal Jurisdiction," 785.

60. Ipsos, *Human Rights in 2018*.

61. Bell et al., *International Cooperation Welcomed*.

62. Ibid.

63. World Values Survey, online analysis, March 25, 2021, https://www.worldvaluessurvey .org/WVSOnline.jsp.

64. Chinese respondents might be influenced by what they think the authorities *want* them to say. But what that would be is not completely clear here. On the one hand, the authorities sometimes call their system a "socialist democracy" or "people's democracy." On the other hand, they distinguish it sharply from Western-style democracies. Xi, whose popular nickname is Xi Da Da, or "Big Xi," is promoted by Communist Party ideologists as a "strong leader," and there are no popular elections for top leaders (Reuters, "No Cult of Personality").

65. Jakhar, "Confucius Institutes."

66. Silver, Devlin, and Huang, *Unfavorable Views of China*.

67. Appiah-Nyamekye Sanny and Selormey, "Africans Regard China's Influence." The United States and China were tied in Tunisia.

68. Note that this vote of confidence in the U.S. model came after four years of Trump's crude denigration of the African continent. The latest World Values Survey wave included only four sub-Saharan African countries—Ethiopia, Kenya, Nigeria, and Zimbabwe—but respondents there also seemed unimpressed by authoritarian technocracy. Among the four countries, the median percent judging democratic government to be "very" or "fairly" good was 89 percent. By contrast, the median share saying the same of rule by a "strong leader" was 48 percent and of rule by "experts" 63 percent.

69. Standish, "Where the War on Terror Lives Forever."

70. Is the notion of the one-party, developmental state a popular alternative? Polling on this is meager. But the Afrobarometer asks respondents whether they agree more with: (a) "Political parties create division and confusion; it is therefore unnecessary to have many political parties in [this country]" or (b) "Many political parties are needed to make sure that [this country's citizens] have real choices in who governs them." In only 2 of the 18 African countries did a majority think having many political parties was unnecessary in 2019–20 (M'Cormack-Hale and Dome, "Support for Elections Weakens among Africans"). Few apparently prefer a single party to democratic competition.

71. Norris and Inglehart, *Cultural Backlash.*

72. Some try to distinguish their version from that in the West. Viktor Orbán, for instance, endorses "illiberal democracy." But, in this, he is at odds with most Hungarians. In fact, large majorities of Orbán's citizens specifically favor *liberal* freedoms—from religious freedom (70 percent), freedom of the press (76 percent), and Internet freedom (77 percent) to gender equality (85 percent), freedom of speech (87 percent), and equality before the law (95 percent). These figures are from a 2020 Pew Global Attitudes survey (Pew Research Center, "Attitudes towards Democratic Rights and Institutions").

73. Not all are this ambitious, seeking to discredit Western liberalism. Lee Kuan Yew, for instance, just insisted that "Asian values" fit his citizens better.

74. Zelikow et al., "The Rise of Strategic Corruption." As Javier Corrales and Michael Penfold write, Venezuela's Chávez "exported a particular form of corruption" throughout Latin America. "Billed as investment in social services, it in fact consisted largely of unaccountable financing for political campaigns, unelected social movements, business deals, and political patronage by state officials" (*Dragon in the Tropics,* 108).

75. *Economist,* "Why the US and Cuba Are Cosying Up."

76. Vreeland, "Corrupting International Organizations."

77. George F. Kennan, "X, the Sources of Soviet Conduct," *Foreign Affairs* 25, no. 4 (July 1947): 566–82.

78. Of course, supporting democratic development was not the only or always dominant Western motive. Economic and short-run strategic interests continued to matter.

79. GDP per capita from Maddison Project Database 2020 (see Bolt et al., *Rebasing "Maddison"*). Data on battle-related deaths in state-based conflicts are from PRIO (see Roser, "War and Peace").

80. Using the V-DEM classifications.

81. Farge, "Echoes of 'Francafrique' Haunt Central African Democracy"; Burnett, "Uganda."

82. Galeotti, "Trump Was Right."

83. Donnan, "US Says China WTO Membership Was a Mistake."

84. OECD, *OECD Convention on Combating Bribery*; Brewster and Dryden, "Building Multilateral Anticorruption Enforcement," 221, 239; OECD Working Group on Bribery, *2018 Enforcement*.

85. Godfrey and Youngs, "Toward a New EU Democracy Strategy."

86. Shezaf and Jacobson, "Revealed: Israel's Cyber-Spy Industry Helps World Dictators."

87. Online analysis of WVS data and EVS data, see https://www.worldvaluessurvey.org/WVSOnline.jsp.

88. Our calculations are from: Pew Research Center, *What the World Thinks in 2002*; Wike et al., *Trump's International Ratings Remain Low*; Pew Research Center, *Global Economic Gloom*; Wike et al., *US Image Suffers*.

89. Olmsted, "Watergate Led to Sweeping Reforms."

90. Papaioannou and Sirounis, "Democratisation and Growth"; Acemoglu et al., "Democracy Does Cause Growth."

91. See table OS8.2. We use the Penn World Tables 9.1 data to calculate average annual growth rates of GDP per capita in each decade for democracies (states with Polity2 ≥ 6) and authoritarian states (Polity2 < 6). The strong relative performance of democracies in these decades is impressive as they tend to be more economically developed than autocracies, and richer countries generally grow more slowly than poor ones.

92. At purchasing power parity, authoritarian states (with Polity2 < 6) produced 18 percent of world GDP in 2000, 28 percent in 2007, and 33 percent in 2017 (Penn World Tables 9.1, using rgdpo).

93. Quoted in McFaul, *Advancing Democracy Abroad*, 149.

94. Making the U.S. system fairer and more competitive will help restore America's global reputation. But it will not please Trump's populist supporters. Concentrated in rural areas and the South, they are the main beneficiaries of current disproportions, gerrymandering, and voter suppression efforts. Dark money has funded the campaigns of the Republican right. Strengthening U.S. democracy will weaken the populist base.

95. Ministry of Foreign Affairs of the People's Republic of China, "Wang Yi."

96. McFaul, *Advancing Democracy Abroad*, 156–60.

97. Essentially, this was the idea for establishing the Community of Democracies that was formed twenty years ago on the basis of the Warsaw Declaration. But, with low funding, it has remained mostly symbolic. And the list of signatories includes such authoritarian states as Azerbaijan, Egypt, Russia, and Venezuela, which undercuts its ability to act credibly as a promoter of democracy (https://community-democracies.org/app/uploads/2016/10/2000-Warsaw-Declaration-ENG.pdf). In the last two decades, various foreign policy experts have proposed different versions of such a grouping of democracies (e.g., Daalder and Lindsay, "Democracies of the World, Unite"; Ikenberry and Slaughter, "Democracies Must Work in Concert")—an idea that appears to have bipartisan support in the United States, although it also has critics (Miller and Sokolsky, "An 'Alliance of Democracies' Sounds Good"). Ikenberry ("The New Liberal Order," 140) proposes the formation of a "D10, a sort of steering committee of the world's ten leading democracies." We would suggest a broader coalition of established liberal democracies to reduce the perception of U.S. dominance.

98. A key point is that such an alliance should include only genuine liberal democracies and not spin dictatorships pretending to be democratic.

99. Chayes, "How American Treaty Behavior Threatens National Security."

REFERENCES

ABC News. "Putin: Russian Opposition Provoked Summer Police Violence." February 26, 2020. https://abcnews.go.com/International/wireStory/putin-russian-opposition-provoked-summer-police-violence-69224868.

Abjorensen, Norman. *Historical Dictionary of Democracy*. Lanham, MD: Rowman and Littlefield, 2019.

Abrahamian, Ervand. *Tortured Confessions: Prisons and Public Recantations in Modern Iran*. Berkeley: University of California Press, 1999.

Acemoglu, Daron. "We Are the Last Defense against Trump." *Foreign Policy*, January 18, 2017. https://foreignpolicy.com/2017/01/18/we-are-the-last-defense-against-trump-institutions/.

Acemoglu, Daron, Simon Johnson, James A. Robinson, and Pierre Yared. "Income and Democracy." *American Economic Review* 98, no. 3 (2008): 808–42.

Acemoglu, Daron, Suresh Naidu, Pascual Restrepo, and James A. Robinson. "Democracy Does Cause Growth." *Journal of Political Economy* 127, no. 1 (2019): 47–100.

Acemoglu, Daron, and James Robinson. *Economic Origins of Dictatorship and Democracy*. Cambridge: Cambridge University Press, 2006.

———. *Why Nations Fail: The Origins of Power, Prosperity, and Poverty*. New York: Crown, 2012.

Adams, L. L., and A. Rustemova. "Mass Spectacle and Styles of Governmentality." *Europe-Asia Studies* 61, no. 7 (September 2009): 1249–76.

Adena, Maja, Ruben Enikolopov, Maria Petrova, Veronica Santarosa, and Ekaterina Zhuravskaya. "Radio and the Rise of the Nazis in Prewar Germany." *Quarterly Journal of Economics* 130, no. 4 (November 2015): 1885–1939.

Agence France Presse. "G8 Summit Cost Russia 400 Million Dollars: Official." July 14, 2006. https://advance.lexis.com/api/document?collection=news&id=urn:contentItem:4KDH-3NG0-TWMD-626S-00000-00&context=1516831.

Aitken, Jonathan. *Nazarbayev and the Making of Kazakhstan*. New York: Continuum, 2009.

Al Jazeera. "The Listening Post." https://www.aljazeera.com/program/the-listening-post/.

———. "Saudi Arabia's Purge: A Quest for Media Control?" November 19, 2017. https://www.youtube.com/watch?v=mi-74WdFYao.

Alesina, Alberto, and Nicola Fuchs-Schündeln. "Goodbye Lenin (or Not?): The Effect of Communism on People's Preferences." *American Economic Review* 97, no. 4 (2007): 1507–28.

Allison, Graham, Robert D. Blackwill, and Ali Wyne. *Lee Kuan Yew: The Grand Master's Insights on China, the United States, and the World*. Cambridge, MA: Belfer Center Studies in International Security, MIT Press, 2013.

Almoina, José. *Una Satrapía en el Caribe.* Santo Domingo: Letra Gráfica Breve, 2007.

Alonso, Paul. "The Impact of Media Spectacle on Peruvian Politics: The Case of Jaime Bayly's *El Francotirador.*" *Journal of Iberian and Latin American Studies* 21, no. 3 (2015): 165–86.

Alpert, Lukas I., and Leos Rousek. "Vladimir Putin: Decision to Annex Crimea Based on Secret Polling." *Wall Street Journal*, April 10, 2014. https://www.wsj.com/articles/vladimir-putin -decision-to-annex-crimea-based-on-secret-polling-1397133677.

Alston, Philip, and Frédéric Mégret. Introduction to *The United Nations and Human Rights: A Critical Appraisal,* edited by Philip Alston and Frédéric Mégret, 1–38. New York: Oxford University Press, 2020.

American Institute of Physics. "The Opening Paragraphs of Sakharov's Reflections on Progress, Peaceful Coexistence & Intellectual Freedom." https://history.aip.org/exhibits/sakharov /reflections.html.

Amnesty International. "Get Involved." https://www.amnesty.org/en/get-involved/join/.

———. *Indonesia: An Amnesty International Report.* New York: Amnesty International, 1977. https://www.amnesty.org/en/wp-content/uploads/2021/06/asa210221977en.pdf.

———. *Annual Report 1988.* London: Amnesty International, 1988.

———. *Singapore J B Jeyaretnam: The Use of Defamation Suits for Political Purposes.* October 15, 1997. https://www.amnesty.org/en/wp-content/uploads/2021/06/asa360041997en.pdf.

———. *Russian Federation: What Justice for Chechnya's Disappeared?* New York: Amnesty International, 2007. https://www.amnesty.org/en/wp-content/uploads/2021/07/eur46026 2007en.pdf.

———. *Report 2012: The State of the World's Human Rights.* New York: Amnesty International, 2012.

———. *"Changing the Soup but Not the Medicine?" Abolishing Re-Education through Labour in China.* New York: Amnesty International, 2013. https://www.amnesty.at/media/1206 /amnesty-international-changing-the-soup.pdf.

———. *Singapore: Free 16-Year-Old Prisoner of Conscience Amos Yee.* New York: Amnesty International, 2015. https://www.amnesty.org/en/wp-content/uploads/2021/05/ASA362014 2015ENGLISH.pdf.

———. *Report 2015/16: The State of the World's Human Rights.* New York: Amnesty International, 2016.

———. "Venezuela 2019." https://www.amnesty.org/en/countries/americas/venezuela/report -venezuela/.

Anderson, Emma. "Putin Accuses the West of 'Double Standards' on Catalonia and Kosovo." *Politico*, October 19, 2017. https://www.politico.eu/article/vladimir-putin-catalonia-accuses -eu-of-double-standards-on-catalonia-and-kosovo/.

Anderson, Jon Lee. "The Revolutionary: The President of Venezuela Has a Vision, and Washington Has a Headache." *New Yorker*, September 10, 2001. https://www.newyorker.com /magazine/2001/09/10/the-revolutionary.

———. "Postscript: Hugo Chávez, 1954–2013." *New Yorker*, March 5, 2013. https://www .newyorker.com/news/news-desk/postscript-hugo-chvez-1954-2013.

Andrew, Christopher, and Vasili Mitrokhin. *The Sword and the Shield: The Mitrokhin Archive and the Secret History of the KGB.* New York: Basic Books, 1999.

Andrews, Sally. "'Soft' Repression: The Struggle for Democracy in Singapore." *The Diplomat*, February 6, 2015. https://thediplomat.com/2015/02/soft-repression-the-struggle-for -democracy-in-singapore/.

Appiah-Nyamekye Sanny, Josephine, and Edem Selormey. "Africans Regard China's Influence as Significant and Positive, but Slipping." *Afrobarometer Dispatch*, No. 407, November 17, 2020. https://afrobarometer.org/sites/default/files/publications/Dispatches/ad407 -chinas_perceived_influence_in_africa_decreases-afrobarometer_dispatch-14nov20 .pdf.

Applebaum, Anne. *Gulag: A History*. New York: Doubleday, 2003.

Applebaum, Anne. *Iron Curtain: The Crushing of Eastern Europe, 1944–1956*. New York: Double-day, 2012.

Arbatova, Nadezhda. "Italy, Russia's Voice in Europe?" Paris: IFRI, 2011. https://www.ifri.org /sites/default/files/atoms/files/ifrirussieitaliearbatovaengsept2011.pdf.

Arceneaux, Craig, and David Pion-Berlin. "Issues, Threats and Institutions: Explaining OAS Responses to Democratic Dilemmas in Latin America." *Latin American Politics and Society* 49, no. 2 (2007): 1–31.

Arefyev, V., and Z. Mieczkowski. "International Tourism in the Soviet Union in the Era of Glasnost and Perestroyka." *Journal of Travel Research* 29, no. 4 (1991): 2–6.

Aristotle. *The Politics and the Constitution of Athens*. Edited by Stephen Everson. New York: Cambridge University Press, 1996.

Aron, Raymond. "The Future of Secular Religions." In *The Dawn of Universal History*, edited by Yair Renier and translated by Barbara Bray, with an introduction by Tony Judt, 177–201. New York: Basic Books, 1944.

Aron, Leon. *Roads to the Temple: Truth, Memory, Ideas, and Ideals in the Making of the Russian Revolution, 1987–1991*. New Haven: Yale University Press, 2012.

Arsu, Sebnem, and Sabrina Tavernise. "Turkish Media Group Is Fined $2.5 Billion." *New York Times*, September 9, 2009. https://www.nytimes.com/2009/09/10/world/europe /10istanbul.html.

Arutunyan, Anna. *The Putin Mystique: Inside Russia's Power Cult*. Northampton: Interlink Publishing, 2014.

Ash, Timothy Garton. "Europe Must Stop This Disgrace: Victor Orbán Is Dismantling Democracy." *Guardian*, June 20, 2019. https://www.theguardian.com/commentisfree/2019/jun/20 /viktor-orban-democracy-hungary-eu-funding.

Asiedu, Elizabeth, and Donald Lien. "Democracy, Foreign Direct Investment, and Natural Resources." *Journal of International Economics* 84, no. 1 (2011): 99–111.

Askarbekov, Yerlan. "What Kazakhstan Really Thought of Borat." BBC, October 28, 2016. http:// www.bbc.com/culture/story/20161028-what-kazakhstan-really-thought-of-borat.

Aslund, Anders. *Russia's Interference in the US Judiciary*. Washington, DC: Atlantic Council, 2018.

Associated Press. "Belafonte: Bush 'Greatest Terrorist in the World.'" January 8, 2006. https:// www.nbcnews.com/id/wbna10767465#.Xz_21MhKg2w.

———. "Kevin Spacey Visits Hugo Chávez." September 25, 2007. https://www.cbsnews.com /news/kevin-spacey-visits-hugo-chavez/.

———. "Shirtless Images of Obama Cause Stir Online." December 23, 2008. https://www.denverpost.com/2008/12/23/shirtless-images-of-obama-cause-stir-online/.

———. "Russian Crackdown on Protesters Seen as Intimidation Tactic." September 2, 2019. https://apnews.com/article/4ba50a8a75664b91aeb6caa522e112d2.

Association for Diplomatic Studies & Training. "Trouble in Chiapas: The Zapatista Revolt." May 13, 2016. https://adst.org/2016/05/trouble-chiapas-zapatista-revolt/.

Atkins, William. *The Politics of Southeast Asia's New Media*. London: Routledge, 2013.

Avalon Project. "Inaugural Address of Jimmy Carter." Yale Law School. https://avalon.law.yale.edu/20th_century/carter.asp.

Avenarius, Tomas. "'Manipulieren, aber geschickt'; Wie Demokratie 'gelenkt' wird." *Süddeutsche Zeitung*, December 2, 2003.

Babiracki, Patryk. "Imperial Heresies: Polish Students in the Soviet Union, 1948–1957." *Ab Imperio* 2007, no. 4 (2007): 199–236.

Baird, Jay W. "Goebbels, Horst Wessel, and the Myth of Resurrection and Return." *Journal of Contemporary History* 17, no. 4 (October 1982): 633–50.

Baker, Peter, and Susan Glasser. *Kremlin Rising: Vladimir Putin's Russia and the End of Revolution*. New York: Simon and Schuster, 2005.

Ball, James, and Paul Hamilos. "Ecuador's President Used Millions of Dollars of Public Funds to Censor Critical Online Videos." *Buzzfeed*, September 24, 2015. https://www.buzzfeednews.com/article/jamesball/ecuadors-president-used-millions-of-dollars-of-public-funds.

Bankier, David. *Germans and the Final Solution: Public Opinion under Nazism*. New York: Oxford University Press, 1996.

Barnes, Taylor. "Brazilian Advisers Spin Elections in Venezuela and Beyond." *Public Radio International*, October 4, 2012. https://www.pri.org/stories/2012-10-04/brazilian-advisers-spin-elections-venezuela-and-beyond.

Barnett, Neil. *Tito (Life and Times)*. London: Haus Publishing, 2006.

Barone, Guglielmo, Francesco D'Acunto, and Gaia Narciso. "Telecracy: Testing for Channels of Persuasion." *American Economic Journal: Economic Policy* 7, no. 2 (May 2015): 30–60.

Barr, Michael D. *Singapore: A Modern History*. London: I. B. Tauris, 2018.

Barrera, Alberto. "Interview Alberto Barrera." *PBS Frontline*, November 19, 2008. https://www.pbs.org/wgbh/pages/frontline/hugochavez/interviews/barrera.html.

Barro, Robert, and Jong-Wha Lee. "A New Data Set of Educational Attainment in the World, 1950–2010." *Journal of Development Economics* 104 (2013): 184–98.

Barry, Colin M., K. Chad Clay, and Michael E. Flynn. "Avoiding the Spotlight: Human Rights Shaming and Foreign Direct Investment." *International Studies Quarterly* 57, no. 3 (September 2013): 532–44.

Barry, Ellen. "Russian Lawmakers Aim at Foreign Cars, Films and Schooling in Patriotic Purge." *New York Times*, January 13, 2013. https://www.nytimes.com/2013/01/13/world/europe/russian-lawmakers-move-to-purge-foreign-influences.html.

———. "Economist Who Fled Russia Cites Peril in Politically Charged Inquiry." *New York Times*, May 31, 2013. https://www.nytimes.com/2013/06/01/world/europe/economist-sergei-guriev-doesnt-plan-return-to-russia-soon.html.

Battles, Matthew. *Library: An Unquiet History*. New York: W. W. Norton, 2004.

Batty, David. "Vladimir Putin's Chief Spokesman Admits Greek Urn Find Was Staged." *Guardian*, October 5, 2011. https://www.theguardian.com/world/2011/oct/06/vladimir-putin-spokesman-urns-staged.

Bauer, Raymond Augustine, Alex Inkeles, and Clyde Kluckhohn. *How the Soviet System Works*. Cambridge, MA: Harvard University Press, 1956.

Bautista, María Angélica, Felipe González, Luis R. Martínez, Pablo Muñoz, and Mounu Prem. "Chile's Missing Students: Dictatorship, Higher Education and Social Mobility." IE-PUC Working Paper, no. 542, 2020.

Bayer, Lili. "Israeli Intelligence Firm Targeted NGOs during Hungary's Election Campaign." *Politico*, July 6, 2018. https://www.politico.eu/article/viktor-orban-israeli-intelligence-firm-targeted-ngos-during-hungarys-election-campaign-george-soros/.

BBC. "Ukraine's 'Censorship Killing.'" February 14, 2001. http://news.bbc.co.uk/2/hi/europe/1169896.stm.

———. "Turkmen Drivers Face Unusual Test." August 2, 2004. http://news.bbc.co.uk/2/hi/asia-pacific/3528746.stm.

———. "Putin Deplores Collapse of USSR." April 25, 2005. http://news.bbc.co.uk/2/hi/4480745.stm.

———. "Russian TV Sees G8 Summit as Recognition of Success of Putin Presidency." *BBC Monitoring of the Former Soviet Union*, July 17, 2006.

———. "Hugo Chávez: Memorable Moments." March 6, 2013. https://www.bbc.com/news/world-latin-america-20712033.

———. "Pavlovsky: Realnost otomstit Kremlyu i bez oppozitsii." December 31, 2014. https://www.bbc.com/russian/russia/2014/12/141231_pavlovsky_putin_interview.

———. "Putin Reveals Secrets of Russia's Crimea Takeover Plot." March 9, 2015. https://www.bbc.com/news/world-europe-31796226.

———. "Anger as German Ex-chancellor Schroeder Heads Up Rosneft Board." September 29, 2017. https://www.bbc.com/news/world-europe-41447603.

———. "Jamal Khashoggi: All You Need to Know about Saudi Journalist's Death." July 2, 2019. https://www.bbc.com/news/world-europe-45812399.

BBC Summary of World Broadcasts. "Thailand's Thaksin, Singapore's Lee Kuan Yew Hail Close Bilateral Relations." December 16, 2003.

Beauchamp, Zack. "It Happened There: How Democracy Died in Hungary." *Vox.com*, September 13, 2018. https://www.vox.com/policy-and-politics/2018/9/13/17823488/hungary-democracy-authoritarianism-trump.

Beggs, Alex. "Pumped-Up Presidents: The Most Athletic Presidents of All Time." *Vanity Fair*, September 12, 2012. https://www.vanityfair.com/news/2012/09/most-athletic-presidents-of-all-time.

Bell, James, Jacob Poushter, Moira Fagan, Nicholas Kent, and J. J. Moncus. *International Cooperation Welcomed across 14 Advanced Economies*. Washington, DC: Pew Research Center, September 21, 2020. https://www.pewresearch.org/global/2020/09/21/international-cooperation-welcomed-across-14-advanced-economies/pg_2020-09-21_un-multilateralism_2-01/.

Beng, Ooi Kee, "Malaysia's Reformasi Movement." Heinrich Böll Stiftung, June 1, 2018. https://www.boell.de/en/2018/06/01/malaysias-reformasi-movement-lives-its-name.

Bengio, Ofra. *Saddam's Word: Political Discourse in Iraq.* New York: Oxford University Press on Demand, 2002.

Benner, Katie, Mark Mazzetti, Ben Hubbard, and Mike Isaac. "Saudis' Image Makers: A Troll Army and a Twitter Insider." *New York Times,* October 20, 2018. https://www.nytimes.com /2018/10/20/us/politics/saudi-image-campaign-twitter.html.

Bennett, Philip, and Moisés Naím. "21st-Century Censorship." *Columbia Journalism Review* 53, no. 1 (2015). https://archives.cjr.org/cover_story/21st_century_censorship.php.

Bennhold, Alison, and Michael Schwirtz. "Navalny, Awake and Alert, Plans to Return to Russia, German Official Says." *New York Times,* September 14, 2020. https://www.nytimes.com /2020/09/14/world/europe/navalny-novichok.html.

Bentin, Sebastián Calderón. "The Politics of Illusion: The Collapse of the Fujimori Regime in Peru." *Theatre Survey* 59, no. 1 (January 2018): 84–107.

Berg, Jerome S. *Broadcasting on the Short Waves, 1945 to Today.* Jefferson, NC: McFarland, 2008.

Berger, Miriam. "Saudi Arabia Listed Feminism, Atheism, and Homosexuality as Forms of Extremism. Then They (Sort of) Took It Back." *Washington Post,* November 12, 2019. https:// www.washingtonpost.com/world/2019/11/12/feminism-homosexuality-atheism-are-forms -extremism-according-saudi-arabia/.

Berwick, Angus. "Back to the Streets: Venezuelan Protests against Maduro Draw New Crowd." Reuters, January 24, 2019. https://www.reuters.com/article/us-venezuela-politics-protesters /back-to-the-streets-venezuelan-protests-against-maduro-draw-new-crowd-idUSKCN1PI391.

Besley, Timothy, and Andrea Prat. "Handcuffs for the Grabbing Hand? Media Capture and Government Accountability." *American Economic Review* 96, no. 3 (2006): 720–36.

Bevis, Teresa. *International Students in American Colleges and Universities: A History.* New York: Springer, 2007.

Biblioteka Pervogo Prezidenta Respubliki Kazahkstana. "Mir o Nursultane Nazarbayeve [The World on Nursultan Nazarbayev]." https://presidentlibrary.kz/ru/world-about-elbasy.

Birnbaum, Michael. "New Blogger Law Puts New Restrictions on Internet Freedoms." *Washington Post,* July 31, 2014. https://www.washingtonpost.com/world/russian-blogger-law -puts-new-restrictions-on-internet-freedoms/2014/07/31/42a05924-a931-459f-acd2 -6d08598c375b_story.html.

Blair, Graeme, Alexander Coppock, and Margaret Moor. "When to Worry about Sensitivity Bias: A Social Reference Theory and Evidence from 30 Years of List Experiments." *American Political Science Review* 114, no. 4 (2020): 1297–1315.

Blanchard, Ben, and Tom Miles. "China Tries to Spin Positive Message to Counter Criticism of Xinjiang Policies." October 1, 2018. https://www.reuters.com/article/us-china-xinjiang /china-mounts-publicity-campaign-to-counter-criticism-on-xinjiang-idUSKCN1MCoI6.

Blanke, Richard. *Orphans of Versailles: The Germans in Western Poland, 1918–1939.* Lexington: University Press of Kentucky, 2014.

Blankstein, George. *Péron's Argentina.* Chicago: University of Chicago Press, 1953.

Blanton, Shannon Lindsey, and Robert G. Blanton. "What Attracts Foreign Investors? An Examination of Human Rights and Foreign Direct Investment." *Journal of Politics* 69, no. 1 (2007): 143–55.

Blaydes, Lisa. *Elections and Distributive Politics in Mubarak's Egypt*. New York: Cambridge University Press, 2010.

Blumenthal, Sidney. *The Permanent Campaign*. New York: Touchstone Books, 1982.

Boas, Taylor C. "Television and Neopopulism in Latin America: Media Effects in Brazil and Peru." *Latin American Research Review* 40, no. 2 (2005): 27–49.

Bodó, Béla. "Paramilitary Violence in Hungary after the First World War." *East European Quarterly* 38, no. 2 (Summer 2004): 129–72.

Boesche, Roger. *Theories of Tyranny from Plato to Arendt*. University Park: Penn State University Press, 1995.

Bogardus, Kevin. "Venezuela Head Polishes Image with Oil Dollars." Center for Public Integrity, September 22, 2004. https://publicintegrity.org/environment/venezuela-head-polishes -image-with-oil-dollars/.

Boix, Carles. *Democratic Capitalism at the Crossroads: Technological Change and the Future of Politics*. Princeton: Princeton University Press, 2019.

Boix, Carles, and Milan Svolik. "The Foundations of Limited Authoritarian Government: Institutions, Commitment, and Power-Sharing in Dictatorships." *Journal of Politics* 75, no. 2 (2013): 300–316.

Bolat, Aigerim. "Distinguished Fellow Lee Kuan Yew Awarded by President of the Republic of Kazakhstan." National University of Singapore. https://lkyspp.nus.edu.sg/news /distinguished-fellow-lee-kuan-yew-awarded-highest-honour-by-president-nursultan-a -nazarbayev-of-the-republic-of-kazakhstan/.

Boletskaya, Kseniya. "Google nachal udalyat iz poiska zapreshchennie v Rossii sayty." *Vedomosti*, February 6, 2019. https://www.vedomosti.ru/technology/articles/2019/02/06/793499 -google.

Bolotnaya Square Case. "Anastasia Rybachenko." https://bolotnoedelo.info/en/activists/3814 /anastasia-rybachenko.

Bolt, Jutta, Robert Inklaar, Herman de Jong, and Jan Luiten van Zanden. *Rebasing "Maddison": The Shape of Long-Run Economic Development*. Working Paper 10, Maddison Project, 2018.

Bondarenko, Lyubov. "Stolichnie Gayd-Parky Umerli, ne Uspev Roditsya." *Moskovsky Komsomolets*, June 23, 2016. https://www.mk.ru/moscow/2016/06/23/stolichnye-gaydparki -umerli-ne-uspev-roditsya.html.

Bonsaver, Guido. *Censorship and Literature in Fascist Italy*. Toronto: University of Toronto Press, 2007.

Bowen, Sally, and Jane Holligan. *The Imperfect Spy: The Many Worlds of Vladimiro Montesinos*. Lima: Peisa, 2003.

Boyer, Dominic. "Censorship as a Vocation: The Institutions, Practices, and Cultural Logic of Media Control in the German Democratic Republic." *Comparative Studies in Society and History* 45, no. 3 (July 2003): 511–45.

Bradshaw, Samantha, and Philip N. Howard. "The Global Organization of Social Media Disinformation Campaigns." *Journal of International Affairs* 71, no. 1.5 (2018): 23–32.

Bratton, Michael, and Eldred Masunungure. "Zimbabwe's Long Agony." *Journal of Democracy* 19, no. 4 (October 2008): 41–55.

Brewster, Rachel, and Christine Dryden. "Building Multilateral Anticorruption Enforcement: Analogies between International Trade & Anti-Bribery Law." *Virginia Journal of International Law* 57, no. 2 (Spring 2017): 221–62.

Brewster, Thomas. "Manhole Covers That Spy? Saudi Surveillance Cities Are Being Built with American and British Tech." *Forbes*, December 4, 2018. https://www.forbes.com/sites/thomasbrewster/2018/12/04/manhole-covers-that-spy-meet-the-westerners-helping-saudis-build-surveillance-cities/?sh=590f1cd5eb13.

Brice, Arthur. "Venezuela Opens New Probe against TV Station." CNN, June 16, 2009. https://www.cnn.com/2009/WORLD/americas/06/16/venezuela.broadcaster/index.html.

Browder, Bill. *Red Notice: A True Story of High Finance, Murder, and One Man's Fight for Justice.* New York: Simon and Schuster, 2015.

Brownlee, Jason. *Authoritarianism in an Age of Democratization.* New York: Cambridge University Press, 2007.

Bueno de Mesquita, Bruce, Alastair Smith, Randolph M. Siverson, and James D. Morrow. *The Logic of Political Survival.* Cambridge, MA: MIT Press, 2003.

Bunce, Valerie J., and Sharon L. Wolchik. *Defeating Authoritarian Leaders in Postcommunist Countries.* New York: Cambridge University Press, 2011.

Burnett, Maria. "Uganda: Museveni's 10,000 Days in Power." *Human Rights Watch,* June 18, 2013. https://www.hrw.org/news/2013/06/18/uganda-musevenis-10000-days-power.

Byman, Daniel, Peter Chalk, Bruce Hoffman, William Rosenau, and David Brannan. *Trends in Outside Support for Insurgent Movements.* Santa Monica, CA: Rand Corporation, 2001.

Calderón, Fernando Herrera, and Adela Cedillo, eds. *Challenging Authoritarianism in Mexico: Revolutionary Struggles and the Dirty War, 1964–1982.* New York: Routledge, 2012.

Calic, Marie-Janine. *Tito: Der ewige Partisan.* Munich: C. H. Beck, 2020.

Campbell, Duncan. "Chávez Makes a Monkey of Bush." *Guardian,* February 3, 2007. www.guardian.co.uk/world/2007/feb/03/venezuela.usa.

Cantoni, Davide, Yuyu Chen, David Y. Yang, Noam Yuchtman, and Y. Jane Zhang. "Curriculum and Ideology." *Journal of Political Economy* 125, no. 2 (2017): 338–92.

Cao, Xun, Brian Greenhill, and Aseem Prakash. "Where Is the Tipping Point? Bilateral Trade and the Diffusion of Human Rights." *British Journal of Political Science* 43, no. 1 (2013): 133–56.

Carrión, Julio F. "Public Opinion, Market Reforms, and Democracy in Fujimori's Peru." In *The Fujimori Legacy: The Rise of Electoral Authoritarianism in Peru,* edited by Julio F. Carrión, 126–49. University Park: Penn State University Press, 2006.

Carroll, Rory. "Government by TV: Chávez Sets 8-Hour Record." *Guardian,* September 25, 2007. https://www.theguardian.com/media/2007/sep/25/venezuela.television.

———. "Chávez Furious as OAS Rights Watchdog Accuses Him of Endangering Democracy." *Guardian,* February 25, 2010. https://www.theguardian.com/world/2010/feb/25/oas-report-chavez-human-rights.

———. *Comandante: Hugo Chávez's Venezuela.* New York: Penguin, 2013.

Carter, Erin, and Brett Carter. "Propaganda in Autocracies." Unpublished book manuscript, University of Southern California.

Carvalho, A. A. de, and A. M. Cardoso. "Press Censorship in Spain & Portugal." *Index on Censorship* 1, no. 2 (1972): 53–64.

Carver, Richard. *Where Silence Rules: The Suppression of Dissent in Malawi.* New York: Human Rights Watch, 1990.

Casa, Kate. "Sacramento Protesters Shut Down Mexican Consulate." United Press International, January 10, 1994. https://www.upi.com/Archives/1994/01/10/Sacramento-protesters-shut-down-Mexican-Consulate/2937758178000/.

Cash, Nathaniel C. "Peru Chief Orders New Mass Arrests." *New York Times*, April 8, 1992. https://www.nytimes.com/1992/04/08/world/peru-chief-orders-new-mass-arrests.html?pagewanted=all&src=pm.

Cassiday, Julie A., and Emily D. Johnson. "Putin, Putiniana and the Question of a Post-Soviet Cult of Personality." *Slavonic and East European Review* 88, no. 4 (October 2010): 681–707.

Castle, Stephen. "Berlusconi Causes New EU Rift with Chechnya Remarks." *Independent*, November 8, 2003. https://www.independent.co.uk/news/world/europe/berlusconi-causes-new-eu-rift-with-chechnya-remarks-77283.html.

Castro, Jonathan. "Venta de Línea Editorial de Canal 4TV en Tiempos de Crousillat-Montesinos." *La République*, May 2, 2011. https://larepublica.pe/politica/537828-venta-de-linea-editorial-de-canal-4tv-en-tiempos-de-crousillat-montesinos/.

Cazorla-Sánchez, Antonio. *Franco: The Biography of the Myth.* New York: Routledge, 2013.

Central Asia Report. "Oppositionists Claim Government behind Rape Charge against Journalist." *Central Asia Report* 2, no. 42 (November 7, 2002). https://www.rferl.org/a/1342278.html.

Central Intelligence Agency (CIA). "Political Murders in Cuba—Batista Era Compared with Castro Regime." January 21, 1963. https://www.cia.gov/readingroom/docs/CIA-RDP79T00429A000300030015-8.pdf.

———. "Zaire: President Mobutu's Visit." July 28, 1983. Central Intelligence Agency Directorate of Intelligence. https://www.cia.gov/readingroom/docs/CIA-RDP85T00287R000402030001-4.pdf.

———. "Yugoslavia: PLO Ties and Terrorism." March 3, 1986. https://www.cia.gov/readingroom/docs/CIA-RDP86T01017R000403500001-8.pdf.

Chacon, Guillermo Amaro, and John Carey. "Counting Political Prisoners in Venezuela." *Latin America Goes Global*, March 23, 2017. https://theglobalamericans.org/2017/03/political-imprisonment-venezuela/.

Chamberlain, Lesley. *Lenin's Private War: The Voyage of the Philosophy Steamer and the Exile of the Intelligentsia.* New York: Macmillan, 2007.

Champion, Marc. "Call the Prime Minister a Turkey, Get Sued." *Wall Street Journal*, June 7, 2011. https://www.wsj.com/articles/SB10001424052702304563104576357411896226774.

Chandler, Robert. Introduction to *Life and Fate*, by Vasily Grossman. New York: NYRB Classics, 2012.

Chayes, Antonia. "How American Treaty Behavior Threatens National Security." *International Security* 33, no. 1 (2008): 45–81. http://www.jstor.org/stable/40207101.

Cheeseman, Nic, and Jonathan Fisher. *Authoritarian Africa: Repression, Resistance, and the Power of Ideas.* New York: Oxford University Press, 2019.

Cheeseman, Nic, and Brian Klaas. *How to Rig an Election.* New Haven: Yale University Press, 2018.

Chen, Jidong, and Yiqing Xu. "Information Manipulation and Reform in Authoritarian Regimes." *Political Science Research and Methods* 5, no. 1 (2017): 163–78.

Cheremukhin, Anton, Mikhail Golosov, Sergei Guriev, and Aleh Tsyvinski. "The Industrialization and Economic Development of Russia through the Lens of a Neoclassical Growth
Model." *Review of Economic Studies* 84, no. 2 (2017): 613–49.

Chilton, Adam, and Eric Posner. "Why Countries Sign Bilateral Labor Agreements." *Journal of
Legal Studies* 47, no. S1 (2018): 45–88.

Chilton, Adam, Eric Posner, and Bartek Woda. "Bilateral Labor Agreements Dataset." Cambridge, MA: Harvard Dataverse, V1, 2017. https://dataverse.harvard.edu/dataset.xhtml
?persistentId=doi:10.7910/DVN/14YF9K.

Chin, Josh, and Clément Bürge. "Twelve Days in Xinjiang: How China's Surveillance State
Overwhelms Daily Life." *Wall Street Journal*, December 19, 2017. https://www.wsj.com
/articles/twelve-days-in-xinjiang-how-chinas-surveillance-state-overwhelms-daily-life
-1513700355.

ChinaFile. "Rule by Fear." February 18, 2016. https://www.chinafile.com/conversation/rule-fear.

China Investment Corporation. "International Advisory Council." http://www.china-inv.cn/china
inven/Governance/InternationalAdvisoryCouncil.shtml.

China Statistics Press. "China Statistical Yearbook 2019." 2019. http://www.stats.gov.cn/tjsj/ndsj
/2019/indexeh.htm.

Chiozza, Giacomo, and Hein E. Goemans. "International Conflict and the Tenure of Leaders: Is
War Still Ex Post Inefficient?" *American Journal of Political Science* 48, no. 3 (2004): 604–19.

Chwe, Michael Suk-Young. *Rational Ritual: Culture, Coordination, and Common Knowledge.*
Princeton: Princeton University Press, 2013.

Cialdini, Robert B. *Influence: Science and Practice.* New York: Harper Collins, 1993.

CIS-EMO.net. "Aleksei Kochetkov." http://www.cis-emo.net/ru/sotrudniky/aleksey-kochetkov.

———. "Monitoring Missions' Participants." https://www.cis-emo.net/en/category/monitoring
-missions-participants.

Clinton, William J. "Statement on the Death of Former President Julius Nyerere of Tanzania."
American Presidency Project, October 14, 1999. https://www.presidency.ucsb.edu
/documents/statement-the-death-former-president-julius-nyerere-tanzania.

Cmiel, Kenneth. "The Recent History of Human Rights." *American Historical Review* 109, no. 1
(2004): 117–35.

CNN. "Cuba Cracks Down on Illegal Emigration." July 26, 1999. https://www.cnn.com
/WORLD/americas/9907/26/cuba.smugglers/.

Cochrane, Lauren. "Obama Merchandising Madness: Where Will It End?" *Guardian*, March 27,
2012. https://www.theguardian.com/world/shortcuts/2012/mar/27/obama-merchandising
-madness.

Cockburn, Harry. "Hollywood Star Meets Hungary Prime Minister Viktor Orbán and Gets
Guided Tour of Budapest." *Independent*, November 29, 2018. https://www.independent.co
.uk/news/world/europe/chuck-norris-viktor-orban-hungary-meeting-guided-tour
-budapest-facebook-video-watch-a8658771.html.

Coetzee, J. M. "Emerging from Censorship." *Salmagundi* 100 (Fall 1993): 36–50.

Committee to Protect Journalists. "Anna Politkovskaya." https://cpj.org/data/people/anna
-politkovskaya/.

———. "Attacks on the Press 2006: Venezuela." February 5, 2007. https://cpj.org/2007/02
/attacks-on-the-press-2006-venezuela/.

———. "Journalists Attacked in China since 1992." https://cpj.org/asia/china/.

———. "1396 Journalists Killed." https://cpj.org/data/killed/?status=Killed&motiveConfirmed %5B%5D=Confirmed&type%5B%5D=Journalist&start_year=1992&end_year=2020&group _by=year.

Conaghan, Catherine M. *Fujimori's Peru: Deception in the Public Sphere*. Pittsburgh: University of Pittsburgh Press, 2005.

———. "Ecuador: Correa's Plebiscitary Presidency." *Journal of Democracy* 19, no. 2 (2008): 46–60.

Conaghan, Catherine, and Carlos De la Torre. "The Permanent Campaign of Rafael Correa: Making Ecuador's Plebiscitary Presidency." *International Journal of Press/Politics* 13, no. 3 (July 2008): 267–84.

Conquest, Robert. *The Great Terror: A Reassessment*. Oxford: Oxford University Press, 2008.

Constable, Pamela, and Arturo Valenzuela. *A Nation of Enemies: Chile under Pinochet*. New York: W. W. Norton, 1993.

Cooley, Alexander. "Authoritarianism Goes Global: Countering Democratic Norms." *Journal of Democracy* 26, no. 3 (2015): 49–63.

Coolidge, Frederick L., and Daniel L. Segal. "Is Kim Jong-Il Like Saddam Hussein and Adolf Hitler? A Personality Disorder Evaluation." *Behavioral Sciences of Terrorism and Political Aggression* 1, no. 3 (2009): 195–202.

Coonan, Clifford. "Democracy Not for China, Says Xi Jinping." *Irish Times*, April 2, 2014. https://www.irishtimes.com/news/world/asia-pacific/democracy-not-for-china-says-xi -jinping-1.1747853.

Cooper, Glenda. "When Lines between NGO and News Organization Blur." *Nieman Journalism Lab* 21, no. 410 (2009): 515–28.

Coppedge, Michael, John Gerring, Carl Henrik Knutsen, Staffan I. Lindberg, Jan Teorell, David Altman, Michael Bernhard, et al. "V-Dem Codebook V.10," Varieties of Democracy (V-Dem) Project, 2020. https://www.v-dem.net/media/filer_public/28/14/28140582-43d6-4940 -948f-a2df84a31893/v-dem_codebook_v10.pdf.

Corporate Europe Observatory. *Spin Doctors to the Autocrats: How European PR Firms White-wash Repressive Regimes*. Brussels: Corporate Europe Observatory, 2015. https:// corporateeurope.org/sites/default/files/20150120_spindoctors_mr.pdf.

Corrales, Javier. "Hugo Boss." *Foreign Policy*, February 19, 2006. https://foreignpolicy.com/2006 /02/19/hugo-boss/.

———. *Electoral Irregularities: A Typology Based on Venezuela under Chavismo*. Amherst, MA: Amherst College, February 6, 2018. https://www.amherst.edu/system/files/media/Corr ales%2520Venezuelan%2520Electoral%2520Irregularities%2520Feb%25206%25202018_0 .pdf.

———. "Authoritarian Survival: Why Maduro Hasn't Fallen." *Journal of Democracy* 31, no. 3 (2020): 39–53.

Corrales, Javier, and Michael Penfold. *Dragon in the Tropics: Hugo Chávez and the Political Economy of Revolution in Venezuela*. Washington, DC: Brookings Institution Press, 2011.

Cox, Gary W. "Authoritarian Elections and Leadership Succession, 1975–2004." Unpublished manuscript, University of California-San Diego, 2009.

Crabtree, Charles, Holger L. Kern, and David A. Siegel. "Cults of Personality, Preference Falsi-fication, and the Dictator's Dilemma." *Journal of Theoretical Politics* 32, no. 3 (July 2020): 409–34.

Croke, Kevin, Guy Grossman, Horacio Larreguy, and John Marshall. "Deliberate Disengage-ment: How Education Can Decrease Political Participation in Electoral Authoritarian Re-gimes." *American Political Science Review* 110, no. 3 (2016): 579–600.

Crutsinger, Martin. "US Economy Shrank 3.5% in 2020 after Growing 4% Last Quarter." AP, January 28, 2021. https://apnews.com/article/us-economy-shrink-in-2020-b59f9be06dcf1d a924f64afde2ce094c.

Daalder, Ivo, and James Lindsay. "Democracies of the World, Unite." *Public Policy Research* 14, no. 1 (2007): 47–58.

Da Corte, María Lilibeth. "Miquilena: 'No valió la pena sacar a Chávez del camino del gol-pismo.'" *Opinión y Noticias*. http://www.opinionynoticias.com/entrevistas/58-politica/838 -miquilena-qno-valio-la-pena-sacar-a-chavez-del-camino-del-golpismoq.

Dahlum, Sirianne, and Tore Wig. "Chaos on Campus: Universities and Mass Political Pro-test." *Comparative Political Studies* 54, no. 1 (2021): 3–32.

Daily Beast. "Shirtless Presidents: Barack Obama, Ronald Reagan & More." July 13, 2017. https://www.thedailybeast.com/shirtless-presidents-barack-obama-ronald-reagan-and -more.

Daniel, Frank Jack. "Chávez-Funded Telesur Flourishes in Honduras Coup." Reuters, July 14, 2009. https://www.reuters.com/article/idUSN13209584.

Daniel, Patrick. "Lange Pays Tribute to PM Lee." *Straits Times*, November 7, 1988. https:// eresources.nlb.gov.sg/newspapers/Digitised/Article/straitstimes19881107-1.2.6?ST=1&AT =filter&K=Lee%20Kuan%20Yew%20statesman&KA=Lee%20Kuan%20Yew%20 statesman&DF=&DT=&Display=0&AO=false&NPT=&L=&CTA=&NID =straitstimes&CT=&WC=&YR=1988&QT=lee,kuan,yew,statesman&oref=article.

Daniszewski, John, and Bob Drogin. "Legacy of Guile, Greed, and Graft." *Los Angeles Times*, May 17, 1997. https://www.latimes.com/archives/la-xpm-1997-05-17-mn-59597-story.html.s.

Davidoff, Victor. "Duma Masks Internet Crackdown by Citing 'iPhone Pedophiles.'" *Moscow Times*, July 5, 2014. https://www.themoscowtimes.com/2014/07/05/duma-masks-internet -crackdown-by-citing-iphone-pedophiles-a37053.

Davidson, Basil. *Black Star: A View of the Life And Times of Kwame Nkrumah*. New York: Praeger, 1975.

Davies, Guy. "President Xi Jinping Vows Chinese Separatists Will Be 'Smashed to Pieces' as US-Themed Protests Begin in Hong Kong." ABC News, October 14, 2019. https://abcnews .go.com/International/president-xi-jinping-vows-chinese-separatists-smashed-pieces /story?id=66260007.

Davies, Joseph E. *Mission to Moscow*. New York: Simon and Schuster, 1941.

Davies, Sarah. *Popular Opinion in Stalin's Russia: Terror, Propaganda and Dissent, 1934–1941*. Cambridge: Cambridge University Press, 1997.

Davis, Rebecca. "China Bars Access to Nearly a Quarter of Foreign News Websites." *Variety*, October 24, 2019. https://variety.com/2019/digital/news/china-foreign-news-websites -censorship-1203381682/.

Dawson, Andrew, and Martin Innes. *The Internet Research Agency in Europe: 2014–2016*. Cardiff: Crime & Security Research Institute, Cardiff University, 2019. https://www.protagon.gr/wp -content/uploads/2019/05/TheInternetResearchAgencyInEurope2014-2016.pdf.

Day, Michael. "Silvio Berlusconi Caught Out Trying to Stifle Media." *Independent*, March 18, 2010. https://www.independent.co.uk/news/world/europe/silvio-berlusconi-caught-out -trying-to-stifle-media-1923147.html.

deHahn, Patrick. "More than 1 Million Muslims Are Detained in China—but How Did We Get That Number?" *Quartz*, July 4, 2019. https://qz.com/1599393/how-researchers-estimate-1 -million-uyghurs-are-detained-in-xinjiang/.

De la Torre, Carlos, and Andrés Ortiz Lemos. "Populist Polarization and the Slow Death of Democracy in Ecuador." *Democratization* 23, no. 2 (2016): 221–41.

Dempsey, Judy. "Gazprom Courts Prodi as Pipeline Chief." *New York Times*, April 28, 2008. https://www.nytimes.com/2008/04/28/business/worldbusiness/28iht-gazprom.4 .12404427.html.

Denyer, Simon. "In Reversal, Cambridge University Press Restores Articles after China Censorship Row." *Washington Post*, August 21, 2017. https://www.washingtonpost.com/news /worldviews/wp/2017/08/21/cambridge-university-press-faces-backlash-after-bowing-to -china-censorship-pressure/.

Derfler, Leslie. *Political Resurrection in the Twentieth Century: The Fall and Rise of Political Leaders*. New York: Springer, 2012.

Diamond, Larry, and Marc F. Plattner. *Liberation Technology: Social Media and the Struggle for Democracy*, A Journal of Democracy Book. Baltimore: Johns Hopkins University Press, 2012.

Diéguez, Diego. "Spain's Golden Silence." *Index on Censorship* 2, no. 1 (March 1973): 91–100.

Diekmann, Kai. "Hungary's Prime Minister Says Accepting Syrian Refugees 'Also Means Importing Terrorism, Criminalism, Anti-Semitism and Homophobia.'" *Business Insider*, February 24, 2016. https://www.businessinsider.com/viktor-orban-interview-refugee-migrant-hungary-2016-2.

Dikötter, Frank. *The Tragedy of Liberation: A History of the Chinese Revolution, 1945–1957*. London: Bloomsbury Publishing, 2015.

———. *How to Be a Dictator: The Cult of Personality in the Twentieth Century*. London: Bloomsbury Publishing, 2019.

Dimitrov, Martin K. "What the Party Wanted to Know: Citizen Complaints as a 'Barometer of Public Opinion' in Communist Bulgaria." *East European Politics and Societies* 28, no. 2 (2014): 271–95.

———. "The Case of the Soviet Union during the Brezhnev Era." *Russian History* 41, no. 3 (2014): 329–53.

Dimitrov, Martin K., and Joseph Sassoon. "State Security, Information, and Repression: A Comparison of Communist Bulgaria and Ba'thist Iraq." *Journal of Cold War Studies* 16, no. 2 (2014): 3–31.

Di Tella, Rafael, and Ignacio Franceschelli. "Government Advertising and Media Coverage of Corruption Scandals." *American Economic Journal: Applied Economics* 3, no. 4 (October 2011): 119–51.

Dobbs, Michael. "Soviet Censorship Dead but Showing Signs of Life." *Washington Post*, August 2, 1990. https://www.washingtonpost.com/archive/politics/1990/08/02/soviet -censorship-dead-but-showing-signs-of-life/debedb49-f44f-42b0-a335-b076a64c911d/.

Dobson, William J. *The Dictator's Learning Curve: Inside the Global Battle for Democracy.* New York: Random House, 2012.

Donnan, Shawn. "US Says China WTO Membership Was a Mistake." *Financial Times,* January 19, 2018. https://www.ft.com/content/edb346ec-fd3a-11e7-9b32-d7d59aace167.

Doob, Leonard W. "Goebbels' Principles of Propaganda." *Public Opinion Quarterly* 14, no. 3 (Fall 1950): 419–42.

Dougherty, Jill. "How the Media Became One of Putin's Most Powerful Weapons." *Atlantic,* April 21, 2015. https://www.theatlantic.com/international/archive/2015/04/how-the-media -became-putins-most-powerful-weapon/391062/.

Dowty, Alan. *Closed Borders: The Contemporary Assault on Freedom of Movement.* New Haven: Yale University Press, 1989.

Dragu, Tiberiu, and Yonatan Lupu. "Does Technology Undermine Authoritarian Governments?" Unpublished manuscript, New York University, 2017.

———. "Digital Authoritarianism and the Future of Human Rights." Unpublished manuscript, New York University, 2020.

Dragu, Tiberiu, and Adam Przeworski. "Preventive Repression: Two Types of Moral Hazard." *American Political Science Review* 113, no. 1 (2019): 77–87.

Drysdale, John. "A Chat with Maggie: The Iron Lady Looks East." *Straits Times,* March 31, 1985.

Dukalskis, Alexander. *Making the World Safe for Dictatorship.* New York: Oxford University Press, 2020.

Dunai, Marton. "Hungarian Teachers Say New School Curriculum Pushes Nationalist Ideology." Reuters, February 4, 2020. https://www.reuters.com/article/us-hungary-politics -teachers-protests/hungarian-teachers-say-new-school-curriculum-pushes-nationalist -ideology-idUSKBN1ZY28Y.

Dunn, Will. "How Chinese Censorship Became a Global Export." *New Statesman,* October 21, 2019. https://www.newstatesman.com/world/asia/2019/10/how-chinese-censorship -became-global-export.

Durante, Ruben, and Brian Knight. "Partisan Control, Media Bias, and Viewer Responses: Evidence from Berlusconi's Italy." *Journal of the European Economic Association* 10, no. 3 (2012): 451–81.

Dyomkin, Denis, and Guy Falconbridge. "Russia Medvedev Proposes Presidential Term of 6 Years." Reuters, November 5, 2008. https://www.reuters.com/article/us-russia-medvedev -president/russia-medvedev-proposes-presidential-term-of-6-years-idUSTRE4A46 TB20081105.

Ebner, Michael R. *Ordinary Violence in Mussolini's Italy.* Cambridge: Cambridge University Press, 2010.

EBRD. "Agreement Establishing the European Bank for Reconstruction and Development." http://www.ebrd.com/documents/comms-and-bis/pdf-basic-documents-of-ebrd-2013 -agreement.pdf.Eckel, Mike, and Carl Schreck. "FBI Silent on Lab Results in Kremlin Foe's Suspected Poisoning." Radio Free Europe Radio Liberty, October 26, 2018. https://www.rferl .org/a/fbi-silent-on-lab-results-in-kremlin-foe-s-suspected-poisoning/29564152.html.

Economist. "J. B. Jeyaretnam: Joshua 'Ben' Jeyaretnam, an Opposition Politician in Singapore, Died on September 30th, Aged 82." October 9, 2008. https://www.economist.com/obituary /2008/10/09/jb-jeyaretnam.

————. "The Media and the Mouth." March 3, 2012. https://www.economist.com/the-americas/2012/03/03/the-media-and-the-mouth.

————. "What Is the Streisand Effect?" April 16, 2013. https://www.economist.com/the-economist-explains/2013/04/15/what-is-the-streisand-effect.

————. "Rogue States: Cross-Border Policing Can Be Political." November 16, 2013. https://www.economist.com/international/2013/11/16/rogue-states.

————. "Why the US and Cuba Are Cosying Up." May 29, 2015. https://www.economist.com/the-economist-explains/2015/05/29/why-the-united-states-and-cuba-are-cosying-up.

————. "The EU Is Tolerating—and Enabling—Authoritarian Kleptocracy in Hungary." April 5, 2018. https://www.economist.com/europe/2018/04/05/the-eu-is-tolerating-and-enabling-authoritarian-kleptocracy-in-hungary.

————. "The People of Kazakhstan Wonder Who Their Next President Will Be." April 11, 2019. https://www.economist.com/asia/2019/04/11/the-people-of-kazakhstan-wonder-who-their-next-president-will-be.

————. "China Is Thinking Twice about Lending to Africa." June 29, 2019. https://www.economist.com/middle-east-and-africa/2019/06/29/china-is-thinking-twice-about-lending-to-africa.

————. "Another Critic of President John Magufuli Is Silenced." August 1, 2019. https://www.economist.com/middle-east-and-africa/2019/08/01/another-critic-of-president-john-magufuli-is-silenced.

————. "How Viktor Orbán Hollowed Out Hungary's Democracy." August 20, 2019. https://www.economist.com/briefing/2019/08/29/how-viktor-Orbán-hollowed-out-hungarys-democracy.

————. "AMLO's War against the Intelligentsia." September 24, 2020. https://www.economist.com/the-americas/2020/09/24/amlos-war-against-the-intelligentsia.

————. "No Vaccine for Cruelty: The Pandemic Has Eroded Democracy and Respect for Human Rights." October 17, 2020, 50–52. https://www.economist.com/international/2020/10/17/the-pandemic-has-eroded-democracy-and-respect-for-human-rights.

Edmond, Chris. "Information Manipulation, Coordination, and Regime Change." *Review of Economic Studies* 80 (2013): 1422–58.

Edwards, Jorge. "Books in Chile: How the Censorship of Books Has Evolved since 1973." *Index on Censorship* 13, no. 2 (April 1984): 20–22.

EFE Newswire. "Liberales califican de 'non gratos' a observadores CEELA en campaña Nicaragua." October 10, 2008. https://advance.lexis.com/api/document?collection=news&id=urn:contentItem:4TN4-WWW0-TXNM-40SB-00000-00&context=1516831.

————. "Ortega dice que observadores que vigilarán comicios son los más idóneos." November 9, 2008. https://advance.lexis.com/api/document?collection=news&id=urn:contentItem:4TWB-6TH0-TXNM-40GV-00000-00&context=1516831.

Egorov, Boris. "Why Soviet Children Were Prepared for War Better than Anybody Else." Russia Beyond the Headlines, June 26, 2019. https://www.rbth.com/history/330570-soviet-children-were-prepared-war.

Egorov, Georgy, and Konstantin Sonin. "Dictators and Their Viziers: Endogenizing the Loyalty-Competence Trade-Off." *Journal of the European Economic Association* 9, no. 5 (2011): 903–30.

————. "Elections in Nondemocracies." *Economic Journal* 131, no. 636 (2021): 1682–1716.

Elder, Miriam. "Putin's Fabled Tiger Encounter Was PR Stunt, Say Environmentalists." *Guardian*, March 15, 2012. https://www.theguardian.com/world/2012/mar/15/putin-tiger-pr-stunt.

Elliott, Michael, Zoher Abdoolcarim, and Simon Elegant. "Lee Kuan Yew Reflects." *Time*, December 5, 2005. http://content.time.com/time/subscriber/article/0,33009,1137705-1,00.html.

Ellul, Jacques. *Propaganda: The Formation of Men's Attitudes*. New York: Knopf, 1965.

Emmerson, Donald K. "Singapore and the 'Asian Values' Debate." *Journal of Democracy* 6, no. 4 (1995): 95–105.

Enikolopov, Ruben, Alexey Makarin, and Maria Petrova. "Social Media and Protest Participation: Evidence from Russia." *Econometrica* 88, no. 4 (2020): 1479–1514.

Enikolopov, Ruben, Maria Petrova, and Ekaterina Zhuravskaya. "Media and Political Persuasion: Evidence from Russia." *American Economic Review* 101, no. 7 (December 2011): 3253–85.

Epstein, Helen C. "The US Turns a Blind Eye to Uganda's Assault on Democracy." *Nation*, July 20, 2018. https://www.thenation.com/article/archive/us-turns-blind-eye-ugandas-assault-democracy/.

Erlanger, Steven. "Turkish Aggression Is NATO's Elephant in the Room." *New York Times*, August 3, 2020. https://www.nytimes.com/2020/08/03/world/europe/turkey-nato.html.

ERR. "KAPO Declassifies Savisaar Files." December 21, 2010. https://news.err.ee/98700/kapo-declassifies-savisaar-files.

Europa.eu. "Hungary." July 2, 2020. https://europa.eu/european-union/about-eu/countries/member-countries/hungary_en.

European Travel Commission. *South-East Asian Outbound Travel Market*. Brussels: ETC, 2019. https://etc-corporate.org/uploads/2019/09/SOUTH_EAST_ASIAN_OUTBOUND_TRAVEL_MARKET_REPORT_SHORT.pdf.

Fagen, Patricia Weiss. "Repression and State Security." In *Fear at the Edge: State Terror and Resistance in Latin America*, edited by Juan E. Corradi and Patricia Weiss Fagen, 39–71. Berkeley: University of California Press, 1992.

Faiola, Anthony. "Army Played 'A Key Role' in Departure of Fujimori." *Washington Post*, September 18, 2000. https://www.washingtonpost.com/archive/politics/2000/09/18/army-played-a-key-role-in-departure-of-fujimori/a19e190c-87c1-4b64-aee8-666e9fe655e5/.

Fair Trials. "Patricia Poleo." April 5, 2018. https://www.fairtrials.org/case-study/patricia-poleo.

Falasca-Zamponi, Simonetta. *Fascist Spectacle: The Aesthetics of Power in Mussolini's Italy*. Berkeley: University of California Press, 1997.

Farge, Emma. "Echoes of 'Francafrique' Haunt Central African Democracy." Reuters, November 12, 2015. https://www.reuters.com/article/us-africa-france/echoes-of-francafrique-haunt-central-african-democracy-idUSKCN0T02LD20151112.

Fariss, Christopher J., and Geoff Dancy. "Measuring the Impact of Human Rights: Conceptual and Methodological Debates." *Annual Review of Law and Social Science* 13 (2017): 273–94.

Fayet, Jean-Francois. "1919." In *The Oxford Handbook of the History of Communism*, edited by Stephen A. Smith, 109–24. New York: Oxford University Press, 2014.

FBIS Daily Report. "Saddam Speech Marks Revolution's 22nd Anniversary." Baghdad Domestic Service in Arabic. Translation by the Foreign Broadcast Information Service. FBIS-NES-90–137, July 17, 1990.

Fedorova, Inna. "Dressing Like a Dictator: Stalin's Distinctive Military Chic." *Russia Beyond*, August 20, 2014. https://www.rbth.com/arts/2014/08/19/dressing_like_a_dictator_stalins _distinctive_military_chic_39137.html.

Feldman, Stanley, and Karen Stenner. "Perceived Threat and Authoritarianism." *Political Psychology* 18, no. 4 (1997): 741–70.

Fernandez, Warren. "GE2020: PAP Returns to Power with 83 Seats, but Loses Sengkang and Aljunied GRCs in Hard-Fought Covid-19 Election." *Straits Times*, July 11, 2020. https://www .straitstimes.com/politics/ge2020-pap-returns-to-power-with-83-seats-but-loses-sengkang -and-aljunied-grcs-in-hard.

Feron, James. "Burton Elicits Tips from Tito for Film." *New York Times*, October 4, 1971. https:// www.nytimes.com/1971/10/04/archives/burton-elicits-tips-from-tito-for-film.html.

Feuer, Alan. "Federal Prosecutors Investigate Weinstein's Ties to Israeli Firm." *New York Times*, September 6, 2018. https://www.nytimes.com/2018/09/06/nyregion/harvey-weinstein -israel-black-cube.html.

Filatova, Irina, and Mikhail Bushuev. "Sanctioned Putin Ally Vladimir Yakunin Granted German Visa." DW.com, August 21, 2018. https://www.dw.com/en/sanctioned-putin-ally -vladimir-yakunin-granted-german-visa/a-45162025.

Fisher, Lucy, and George Greenwood. "Tory Peers Told to Come Clean about Russia Links." *Times* (London), October 24, 2018. https://www.thetimes.co.uk/article/tory-peers-told-to -come-clean-about-russia-links-gskcs3tw9.

Florian, Victor, Mario Mikulincer, and Gilad Hirschberger. "An Existentialist View on Mortality Salience Effects: Personal Hardiness, Death-Thought Accessibility, and Cultural Worldview Defence." *British Journal of Social Psychology* 40, no. 3 (September 2001): 437–53.

Florida, Richard. *The Rise of the Creative Class Revisited*. New York: Basic Books, 2011.

Florida, Richard, Charlotta Mellander, and Karen King. *The Global Creativity Index, 2015*. Toronto: Martin Prosperity Institute, University of Toronto's Rotman School of Management, 2015. https://budstars.com/martinprosperity/Global-Creativity-Index-2015.pdf.

Florida, Richard, Charlotta Mellander, and Kevin Stolarick. *Creativity and Prosperity: The Global Creativity Index*. Toronto: Martin Prosperity Institute, University of Toronto's Rotman School of Management, 2011. https://tspace.library.utoronto.ca/bitstream/1807/80125/1 /Florida%20et%20al_2011_Creativity%20and%20Prosperity.pdf.

Foer, Franklin. "The Talented Mr. Chávez." *Atlantic*, May 2006. https://www.theatlantic.com /magazine/archive/2006/05/the-talented-mr-ch-vez/304809/.

Folch-Serra, Mireya. "Propaganda in Franco's Time." *Bulletin of Spanish Studies* 89, no. 7–8 (2012): 227–40.

FOM. "'Penta' Poll No. 43." October 28–29, 2000. http://sophist.hse.ru/.

———. "Vladimir Putin: Otsenki raboty, otnoshenie." *Fom.ru*, November 20, 2020. https://fom .ru/Politika/10946.

Forbes. "Profile Lorinc Meszaros." https://www.forbes.com/profile/lorinc-meszaros /#61ffc24d4868.

Forero, Juan. "Venezuela's New Campaign." *New York Times*, September 30, 2004.

Foucault, Michel. *Discipline and Punish*. New York: Pantheon Books, 1977.

Fouquin, Michel, and Jules Hugot. "Two Centuries of Bilateral Trade and Gravity Data: 1827–2014." CEPII Working Paper, no. 2016–14, May 2016. http://www.cepii.fr/cepii/en/bdd_modele/presentation.asp?id=32.

Frajman, Eduardo. "Broadcasting Populist Leadership: Hugo Chávez and Aló Presidente." *Journal of Latin American Studies* 46, no. 3 (August 2014): 501–26.

Franco, Francisco. "End of Year Address to the Spanish People." December 31, 1955. http://www.generalisimofranco.com/Discursos/mensajes/00008.htm.

Frantz, Erica, Andrea Kendall-Taylor, and Joseph Wright. *Digital Repression in Autocracies*. VDEM Working Paper, 2020. https://www.v-dem.net/media/filer_public/18/d8/18d8fc9b-3ff3-44d6-a328-799dc0132043/digital-repression17mar.pdf.

Freedom House. *Freedom in the World 2021*. https://freedomhouse.org/country/singapore/freedom-world/2021.

French, Howard. "Anatomy of an Autocracy: Mobutu's 32-Year Reign." *New York Times*, May 17, 1997. https://partners.nytimes.com/library/world/africa/051797zaire-mobutu.html.

Friedman, Alan. "Silvio Berlusconi and Vladimir Putin: The Odd Couple." *Financial Times*, October 2, 2015. https://www.ft.com/content/2d2a9afe-6829-11e5-97d0-1456a776a4f5.

Fritzsche, Peter A. *Hitler's First Hundred Days: When Germans Embraced the Third Reich*. New York: Basic Books, 2020.

Frontline. "Interview: Teodoro Petkoff." PBS.org, February 25, 2008. https://www.pbs.org/wgbh/pages/frontline/hugochavez/interviews/petkoff.html.

Frye, Timothy. *Weak Strongman: How We Get Russia Wrong and How to Get It Right*. Princeton: Princeton University Press, 2021.

Frye, Timothy, et al. "Is Putin's Popularity Real?" *Post-Soviet Affairs* 33, no. 1 (2017): 1–15.

Fukuyama, Francis. *The Great Disruption: Human Nature and the Reconstitution of Social Order*. New York: The Free Press, 1999.

———. *Political Order and Political Decay: From the Industrial Revolution to the Globalization of Democracy*. New York: Macmillan, 2014.

Gabuev, Alexander. "Lee Kuan Yew and Russia: Role Model for Hire?" Carnegie Moscow Center, March 27, 2015. https://carnegie.ru/commentary/59512.

Gaidar, Yegor. *Collapse of an Empire: Lessons for Modern Russia*. Washington, DC: Brookings Institution Press, 2010.

Gaillard, Philippe. "Jeune Afrique: Censorship Sweepstakes." *Index on Censorship* 1 (1979): 55–56.

Gall, Carlotta. "Turkey Gets Shipment of Russian Missile System, Defying US." *New York Times*, July 12, 2019. https://www.nytimes.com/2019/07/12/world/europe/turkey-russia-missiles.html.

Galeotti, Mark. "Trump Was Right: NATO Is Obsolete." *Foreign Policy* 20 (2017). https://foreignpolicy.com/2017/07/20/trump-nato-hybrid-warfare-hybrid-defense-russia-putin/.

Gallego, Sonia. "Hugo Chávez Collects A-List Friendships." ABC News, October 30, 2008. https://abcnews.go.com/International/story?id=6147631&page=1.

Galor, Oded. *Unified Growth Theory*. Princeton: Princeton University Press, 2011.

Gambino, Lauren. "Roger Stone Sentenced to 40 Months in Prison despite Request for New Trial." *Guardian*, February 20, 2020. https://www.theguardian.com/us-news/2020/feb/20/roger-stone-sentence-judge-refuses-new-trial-request.

Gambrell, Jon. "Report: Iran TV Airs 355 Coerced Confessions over Decade." Associated Press, June 25, 2020. https://abcnews.go.com/International/wireStory/report-iran-tv-airs-355-coerced-confessions-decade-71442899.

Gandhi, Jennifer. *Political Institutions under Dictatorship*. New York: Cambridge University Press, 2008.

Gandhi, Jennifer, and Ellen Lust-Okar. "Elections under Authoritarianism." *Annual Review of Political Science* 12, no. 1 (2009): 403–22.

García, Jaime L. "Los Periódicos Venezolanos, sin Papel." *Elmundo.es*, December 12, 2007. https://www.elmundo.es/elmundo/2007/12/12/internacional/1197427483.html.

Gardels, Nathan. "The Sage of Singapore: Remembering Lee Kuan Yew through His Own Words." *Noema*, March 23, 2015. https://www.noemamag.com/the-sage-of-singapore-remembering-lee-kuan-yew-through-his-own-words/

Gardner, Andrew. "From Astana to Brussels, via Eurasia." *Politico*, November 24, 2014. https://www.politico.eu/article/from-astana-to-brussels-via-eurasia/.

Garmazhapova, Aleksandra. "Gde zhivut trolli: I kto ikh kormit." *Novaya Gazeta*, September 7, 2013. https://novayagazeta.ru/articles/2013/09/07/56253-gde-zhivut-trolli-i-kto-ih-kormit.

Gatehouse, Gabriel. "Marine Le Pen: Who's Funding France's Far Right?" BBC News, April 3, 2017. https://www.bbc.com/news/world-europe-39478066.

Gatov, Vasily. "Research the Revenge: What We're Getting Wrong about Russia Today." *Open Democracy*, August 15, 2018. https://www.opendemocracy.net/en/odr/what-we-are-getting-wrong-about-russia-today/.

Gaytan, Victoria. "Who Are the Council of Electoral Specialists of Latin America (CEELA)?" *Theglobalamericans.org*, October 17, 2017. https://theglobalamericans.org/2017/10/council-electoral-specialists-latin-america-ceela/.

Gebrekidan, Selam, Matt Apuzzo, and Benjamin Novak. "The Money Farmers: How Oligarchs and Populists Milk the E.U. for Millions." *New York Times*, November 3, 2019. https://www.nytimes.com/2019/11/03/world/europe/eu-farm-subsidy-hungary.html.

Geddes, Barbara. "Why Parties and Elections in Authoritarian Regimes?" Paper presented at the Annual Meeting of the American Political Science Association, 2005.

Geddes, Barbara, Joseph Wright, and Erica Frantz. "Autocratic Breakdown and Regime Transitions: A New Data Set." *Perspectives on Politics* 12, no. 2 (2014): 313–31.

———. *How Dictatorships Work: Power, Personalization, and Collapse*. New York: Cambridge University Press, 2018.

Geddes, Barbara, and John Zaller. "Sources of Popular Support for Authoritarian Regimes." *American Journal of Political Science* (1989): 319–47.

Gehlbach, Scott. "A Formal Model of Exit and Voice." *Rationality and Society* 18, no. 4 (2006): 395–418.

———. "Reflections on Putin and the Media." *Post-Soviet Affairs* 26, no. 1 (2010): 77–87.

Gehlbach, Scott, and Alberto Simpser. "Electoral Manipulation as Bureaucratic Control." *American Journal of Political Science* 59, no. 1 (2015): 212–24.

Gehlbach, Scott, and Konstantin Sonin. "Government Control of the Media." *Journal of Public Economics* 118 (2014): 163–71.

Gehlbach, Scott, Konstantin Sonin, and Milan W. Svolik. "Formal Models of Nondemocratic Politics." *Annual Review of Political Science* 19 (2016): 565–84.

George, Cherian. "Consolidating Authoritarian Rule: Calibrated Coercion in Singapore." *Pacific Review* 20, no. 2 (2007): 127–45.

———. *Singapore, Incomplete: Reflections on a First World Nation's Arrested Political Development.* Singapore: Ethos Books, 2017.

———. "Journalism and Authoritarian Resilience." In *The Handbook of Journalism Studies*, edited by Karin Wahl-Jorgensen and Thomas Haznitsch, 538–54. Milton Park: Routledge, 2019.

George, Cherian, and Sonny Liew. *Red Lines: Political Cartoons and the Struggle against Censorship.* Cambridge, MA: MIT Press, 2021.

Gerden, Eugene. "Can Russia Reengage the West through Public Relations?" *PRWeek*, November 1, 2016. https://www.prweek.com/article/1414179/russia-reengage-west-public -relations.

Germino, Dante L. *The Italian Fascist Party in Power: A Study in Totalitarian Rule.* Minneapolis: University of Minnesota Press, 1959.

Getty, John Archibald. "State and Society under Stalin: Constitutions and Elections in the 1930s." *Slavic Review* 50, no. 1 (Spring 1991): 18–35.

Gilboa, Eytan. "The CNN Effect: The Search for a Communication Theory of International Relations." *Political Communication* 22, no. 1 (2005): 27–44.

Ginsburg, Tom, and Alberto Simpser. Introduction to *Constitutions in Authoritarian Regimes*, edited by Tom Ginsburg and Alberto Simpser. New York: Cambridge University Press, 2013.

Glaeser, Edward L., Giacomo A. M. Ponzetto, and Andrei Shleifer. "Why Does Democracy Need Education?" *Journal of Economic Growth* 12, no. 2 (2007): 77–99.

Glasser, Susan B. "Putin's Cult of Personality: From Portraits to Toothpicks, Russian Leader Captures the Day." *Wall Street Journal (Europe)*, March 16, 2003.

Godfrey, Ken, and Richard Youngs. "Toward a New EU Democracy Strategy." *Carnegie Europe*, September 17, 2019. https://carnegieeurope.eu/2019/09/17/toward-new-eu-democracy -strategy-pub-79844.

Goebbels, Joseph. "Der Rundfunk als achte Großmacht." *Signale der neuen Zeit. 25 ausgewählte Reden von Dr. Joseph Goebbels.* Munich: Zentralverlag der NSDAP, 1938. Translated at https://research.calvin.edu/german-propaganda-archive/goeb56.htm.

Gokoluk, Selcuk. "Turkey Arrests Pro-Kurdish Party Leader." Reuters, December 18, 2007. https://www.reuters.com/article/us-turkey-kurdish-arrest-idUSL1873279620071218.

Golden, Arthur. "Maoist Rebels Now Are Worst Offenders, Peru Rights Group Says." *San Diego Union-Tribune*, October 19, 1991.

Golden, Tim. "Old Scores; Left Behind, Mexico's Indians Fight the Future." *New York Times*, January 9, 1994. https://www.nytimes.com/1994/01/09/weekinreview/old-scores-left -behind-mexico-s-indians-fight-the-future.html?searchResultPosition=10.

Goldman, Wendy. "Stalinist Terror and Democracy: The 1937 Union Campaign." *American Historical Review* 110, no. 5 (December 2005): 1427–53.

Golovchenko, Yevgeniy, Cody Buntain, Gregory Eady, Megan A. Brown, and Joshua A. Tucker. "Cross-Platform State Propaganda: Russian Trolls on Twitter and YouTube during the 2016 US Presidential Election." *International Journal of Press/Politics* 25, no. 3 (2020): 357–89.

Gorbachev, Mikhail. *Memoirs.* New York: Doubleday, 1996.

Gordon, Michael. "NATO Backs Defense Plan for Turkey." *New York Times,* December 4, 2012. https://www.nytimes.com/2012/12/05/world/middleeast/nato-backs-defensive-missiles -for-turkey.html?_r=0.

Gorriti, Gustavo. "Living Dangerously: Issues of Peruvian Press Freedom." *Journal of International Affairs* 47, no. 1 (Summer 1993): 223–41.

Gorsuch, Anne E. *All This Is Your World: Soviet Tourism at Home and Abroad after Stalin.* New York: Oxford University Press, 2011.

Goscilo, Helena. "Russia's Ultimate Celebrity." In *Putin as Celebrity and Cultural Icon,* edited by Helena Goscilo, 6–36. New York: Routledge, 2013.

Gould-Davies, Nigel. "Putin and the Belarusian Question." *Moscow Times,* September 2, 2020. https://www.themoscowtimes.com/2020/09/02/russia-and-the-belarusian-question-a71318.

Gowing, Nik. "Real-Time Television Coverage of Armed Conflicts and Diplomatic Crises: Does It Pressure or Distort Foreign Policy Decisions?" Joan Shorenstein Barone Center on the Press, Politics and Public Policy, John F. Kennedy School of Government, Harvard University, 1994.

Granma. "Canciller venezolano auguro ingreso a Consejo de Seguridad." June 22, 2006. http://www.granma.cu/granmad/2006/06/22/interna/artico8.html.

Grassegger, Hannes. "The Unbelievable Story of the Plot against George Soros." *Buzzfeed,* January 20, 2019. https://www.buzzfeednews.com/article/hnsgrassegger/george-soros -conspiracy-finkelstein-birnbaum-orban-netanyahu.

The Great Soviet Encyclopedia. 3rd ed. Edited by A. M. Prokhorov. New York: Macmillan, 1970.

Green, Chris. "Jack Straw Criticised for Accepting Part-time Job Paid for by Kazakhstan." *Independent,* February 19, 2015. https://www.independent.co.uk/news/world/politics/jack -straw-criticised-accepting-part-time-job-paid-kazakhstan-10057426.html.

Green, W. John. *A History of Political Murder in Latin America: Killing the Messengers of Change.* Albany: State University of New York Press, 2015.

Greenberg, Jeff, Tom Pyszczynski, and Sheldon Solomon. "Terror Management Theory of Self-esteem and Cultural Worldviews: Empirical Assessments and Conceptual Refinements." *Advances in Experimental Social Psychology* 29 (1997): 61–141.

Greene, Samuel A., and Graeme B. Robertson. *Putin v. the People: The Perilous Politics of a Divided Russia.* New Haven: Yale University Press, 2019.

Greenwood, George, Emanuele Midolo, Sean O'Neill, and Lucy Fisher. "Conservative Party Ministers Bankrolled by Donors Linked to Russia." *Times* (London), July 23, 2020. https:// www.thetimes.co.uk/edition/news/conservative-party-ministers-bankrolled-by-donors -linked-to-russia-2hm5jhwpx?wgu=270525_54264_16063301342446_843a63bd6c&wgexpiry =1614106134&utm_source=planit&utm_medium=affiliate&utm_content=22278.

Guardian. "The Personality Cult of Turkmenbashi." December 21, 2006. https://www .theguardian.com/world/2006/dec/21/1.

———. "Recep Tayyip Erdoğan Dismisses Turkey Protesters as Vandals." June 9, 2013. https://www.theguardian.com/world/2013/jun/09/recep-tayyip-erdogan-turkey-protesters-looters-vandals.

———. "Saudi Blogger Receives First 50 Lashes of Sentence for 'Insulting Islam.'" January 10, 2015. https://www.theguardian.com/world/2015/jan/09/saudi-blogger-first-lashes-raif-badawi.

Guerra, Lillian. *Visions of Power in Cuba: Revolution, Redemption, and Resistance, 1959–1971.* Chapel Hill: University of North Carolina Press, 2012.

Guillermoprieto, Alma. "Letter from Managua." *New Yorker*, March 26, 1990, 83–93.

Gunther, R., J. R. Montero, and J. I. Wert. "The Media and Politics in Spain." In *Democracy and the Media: A Comparative Perspective*, edited by R. Gunther and A. Mughan, 28–84. Cambridge: Cambridge University Press, 2000.

Guriev, Sergei, Nikita Melnikov, and Ekaterina Zhuravskaya. "3G Internet and Confidence in Government." June 30, 2019. https://ssrn.com/abstract=3456747 or http://dx.doi.org/10.2139/ssrn.3456747.

Guriev, Sergei, and Elias Papaioannou. "The Political Economy of Populism." *Journal of Economic Literature*. Forthcoming.

Guriev, Sergei, and Daniel Treisman. "Informational Autocrats." *Journal of Economic Perspectives* 33, no. 4 (2019): 100–127.

———. "The Popularity of Authoritarian Leaders: A Cross-national Investigation." *World Politics* 72, no. 4 (October 2020): 601–38.

———. "A Theory of Informational Autocracy." *Journal of Public Economics* 186 (2020): 104–58.

Gurri, Martin. *The Revolt of the Public and the Crisis of Authority in the New Millennium.* 2nd ed. San Francisco: Stripe Press, 2018.

Gusman, Mikhail. "Alexander Lukashenka: My Elections Were Falsified." *Izvestia*, August 26, 2009. https://iz.ru/news/352332.

Gwertzman, Bernard. "Beria Is Ignored in Soviet Volume." *New York Times*, January 31, 1971. https://www.nytimes.com/1971/01/31/archives/beria-is-ignored-in-soviet-volume-latest-encyclopedia-tome-drops.html.

Haaretz. "Report: Israeli Company Sold Surveillance Equipment to Iran." December 22, 2011. https://www.haaretz.com/1.5222231.

———. "Israel's Black Cube Campaigned against Liberal NGOs before Hungary's Election, Politico Says." July 7, 2018. https://www.haaretz.com/israel-news/report-israeli-firm-helped-discredit-ngos-ahead-of-hungarian-election-1.6246634.

Hafner-Burton, Emilie M., Susan D. Hyde, and Ryan S. Jablonski. "When Do Governments Resort to Election Violence?" *British Journal of Political Science* 44, no. 1 (2014): 149–79.

Hajizade, Ali. "ANALYSIS: Unveiling Iranian Pro-government Trolls and Cyber-Warriors." *Al-Arabiya*, January 17, 2018. https://english.alarabiya.net/en/perspective/features/2018/01/17/ANALYSIS-Unveiling-Iranian-pro-government-trolls-and-cyber-warriors.

Hakim, Danny. "Once Celebrated in Russia, Programmer Pavel Durov Chooses Exile." *New York Times*, December 2, 2014. https://www.nytimes.com/2014/12/03/technology/once-celebrated-in-russia-programmer-pavel-durov-chooses-exile.html.

Halper, Stefan. *The Beijing Consensus: Legitimizing Authoritarianism in Our Time*. New York: Basic Books, 2012.

Halperin, Morton H., and Kristen Lomasney. "Guaranteeing Democracy: A Review of the Record." *Journal of Democracy* 9, no. 2 (1998): 134–47.

Hamburger Fremdenblatt. No. 78, March 20, 1934 (evening edition). Quoted in Fritz Morstein Marx, "Propaganda and Dictatorship." *ANNALS of the American Academy of Political and Social Science* 179, no. 1 (1935): 211–18.

Hancock, Jan. *Human Rights and US Foreign Policy*. New York: Routledge, 2007.

Handley, Antoinette. "Ghana: Democratic Transition, Presidential Power, and the World Bank." In *Transitions to Democracy: A Comparative Perspective*, edited by Kathryn Stoner and Michael McFaul, 221–43. Baltimore: Johns Hopkins University Press, 2013.

Harding, Luke. "Vladimir Putin Hugs Polar Bear on Arctic Trip." *Guardian*, April 29, 2010. https://www.theguardian.com/world/2010/apr/29/vladimir-putin-polar-bear-arctic.

———. *Mafia State: How One Reporter Became an Enemy of the Brutal New Russia*. New York: Random House, 2011.

Harms, Philipp, and Heinrich W. Ursprung. "Do Civil and Political Repression Really Boost Foreign Direct Investments?" *Economic inquiry* 40, no. 4 (2002): 651–63.

Harnecker, Marta. "Hugo Chávez Frías: Un hombre, un pueblo." August 15, 2002. http://www.angelfire.com/nb/17m/Chavez/hombrepueblo.html#cap02.

Hauser, Christine. "From Putin's Hands: A Russian Passport for Steven Seagal." *New York Times*, November 25, 2016. https://www.nytimes.com/2016/11/25/world/europe/steven-seagal-russian-passport-putin.html.

Hegarty, Aoife, and Hans Fridlund. "Taking Stock—the Universal Periodic Review's Achievements and Opportunities." *Open Democracy*, August 11, 2016. https://www.opendemocracy.net/en/openglobalrights-openpage/taking-stock-universal-periodic-reviews-achievements-an/.

Heilbrunn, John R. "Equatorial Guinea and Togo: What Price Repression?" In *Worst of the Worst: Dealing with Repressive and Rogue Nations*, edited by Robert I. Rotberg, 223–49. Washington, DC: Brookings Institution Press, 2007.

Heller, Mikhail, and Aleksandr Nekrich. *Utopia in Power: The History of the Soviet Union from 1917 to the Present*. Manila: Summit Books, 1988.

Hellmeier, Sebastian, and Nils B. Weidmann. "Pulling the Strings? The Strategic Use of Pro-Government Mobilization in Authoritarian Regimes." *Comparative Political Studies* 53, no. 1 (2020): 71–108.

Henck, Nick. *Subcommander Marcos: The Man and the Mask*. Durham: Duke University Press, 2007.

Herczeg, Márk. "A köztévének egy német viccoldal álhírével sikerült bemutatnia, hogy Németország iszlamizálódik." *444*, May 20, 2018. https://444.hu/2018/05/20/a-koztevenek-egy-nemet-viccoldal-alhirevel-sikerult-bemutatnia-hogy-nemetorszag-iszlamizalodik.

Hermet, Guy. "State-Controlled Elections: A Framework." In *Elections without Choice*, edited by Guy Hermet, 1–18. London: Palgrave Macmillan, 1978.

Hess, Steve, and Richard Aidoo. "Democratic Backsliding in Sub-Saharan Africa and the Role of China's Development Assistance." *Commonwealth & Comparative Politics* 57, no. 4 (2019): 421–44.

Hille, Kathrin. "Russian Tax Law Aims to Coax Businesses Back Home." *Financial Times*, November 18, 2014. https://www.ft.com/content/1906b1d2-6f43-11e4-b50f-00144feabdc0.

Hirschman, Albert O. *Exit, Voice, and Loyalty: Responses to Decline in Firms, Organizations, and States.* Cambridge, MA: Harvard University Press, 1970.

Hobsbawm, Eric. *The Age of Extremes: A History of the World, 1914–1991.* New York: Vintage, 1994.

Hodges, Gabrielle Ashford. *Franco: A Concise Biography.* New York: Macmillan, 2002.

Hodos, George H. *Show Trials: Stalinist Purges in Eastern Europe, 1948–1954.* New York: Praeger, 1987.

Hollander, Paul. *From Benito Mussolini to Hugo Chávez.* Cambridge: Cambridge University Press, 2016.

Hollyer, James R., B. Peter Rosendorff, and James Raymond Vreeland. *Transparency, Democracy, and Autocracy: Economic Transparency and Political (In)Stability.* New York: Cambridge University Press, 2018.

Holpuch, Amanda. "Stolen Daughters: What Happened after #BringBackOurGirls?" *Guardian*, October 22, 2018. https://www.theguardian.com/tv-and-radio/2018/oct/22/bring-back-our-girls-documentary-stolen-daughters-kidnapped-boko-haram.

Holquist, Peter. "State Violence as Technique: The Logic of Violence in Soviet Totalitarianism." In *Stalinism: The Essential Readings*, edited by David L. Hoffman, 129–56. Malden, MA: Blackwell, 2003.

Hong Kong Watch. *Political Prisoners Database.* September 10, 2020. https://www.hongkongwatch.org/political-prisoners-database.

Hopkins, Valerie. "Orban Seeks Sweeping Changes to Hungary's Electoral Law." *Financial Times*, November 11, 2020. https://www.ft.com/content/7d8aa8d8-d07e-42f7-8fcc-e723b8c979e9.

———. "Hungary's Fidesz Finalizes EPP Divorce." *Financial Times*, March 18, 2021. https://www.ft.com/content/a10a928c-c9e8-4429-adfe-fd216d85dfoe.

Horn, Sebastian, Carmen M. Reinhart, and Christoph Trebesch. "How Much Money Does the World Owe China." *Harvard Business Review* 26 (2020). https://hbr.org/2020/02/how-much-money-does-the-world-owe-china.

Hornsby, Robert. "The Enemy Within? The Komsomol and Foreign Youth inside the Post-Stalin Soviet Union, 1957–1985." *Past & Present* 232, no. 1 (2016): 237–78.

Huang, Haifeng. "Propaganda as Signaling." *Comparative Politics* 47, no. 4 (July 2015): 419–44.

———. "The Pathology of Hard Propaganda." *Journal of Politics* 80, no. 3 (2018): 1034–38.

Huang, Zheping. "Your Five-Minute Summary of Xi Jinping's Three-Hour Communist Party Congress Speech." *Quartz*, October 18, 2017. https://qz.com/1105337/chinas-19th-party-congress-your-five-minute-summary-of-xi-jinpings-three-hour-speech/.

Hubbard, Ben. "MBS: The Rise of a Saudi Prince." *New York Times*, March 21, 2020. https://www.nytimes.com/2020/03/21/world/middleeast/mohammed-bin-salman-saudi-arabia.html.

———. *MBS: The Rise to Power of Mohammed bin Salman.* New York: Tim Duggan Books, 2020.

Human Rights Watch. "Singapore: End Efforts to Silence Opposition." October 17, 2008. https://www.hrw.org/news/2008/10/17/singapore-end-efforts-silence-opposition.

———. "Venezuela: End Harassment of TV Station." October 19, 2011. https://www.hrw.org/news/2011/10/19/venezuela-end-harassment-tv-station.

———. *Tightening the Grip: Concentration and Abuse of Power in Chávez's Venezuela*. July 17, 2012. https://www.hrw.org/report/2012/07/17/tightening-grip/concentration-and-abuse-power -chavezs-venezuela.

———. "World Report 2014: Iran." January 2014. https://www.hrw.org/world-report/2014 /country-chapters/iran#.

———. "Egypt: Rab'a Killings Likely Crimes against Humanity." August 12, 2014. https://www .hrw.org/news/2014/08/12/egypt-raba-killings-likely-crimes-against-humanity.

———. *"Kill the Chicken to Scare the Monkeys": Suppression of Free Expression and Assembly in Singapore*. December 12, 2017. https://www.hrw.org/report/2017/12/12/kill-chicken-scare -monkeys/suppression-free-expression-and-assembly-singapore.

———. "Egypt: Al-Sisi Should End Rights Abuses." April 10, 2018. https://www.hrw.org/news /2018/04/10/egypt-al-sisi-should-end-rights-abuses.

———. "Saudi Arabia: Mass Execution of 37 Men." April 24, 2019. https://www.hrw.org/news /2019/04/24/saudi-arabia-mass-execution-37-men.

———. *Tanzania: Climate of Fear*. October 28, 2019. https://www.hrw.org/news/2019/10/28 /tanzania-climate-fear-censorship-repression-mounts#.

Hungarian Spectrum. "András Dezső's Encounter with Natalie Contessa af Sandeberg." *Hungarian Spectrum*, September 8, 2019. https://hungarianspectrum.org/2019/09/08/andras -dezsos-encounter-with-natalie-contessa-af-sandeberg/.

Hungary Today. "Hungary Prepared to Host 'Just About Any' Sporting Event, Says Govt." August 7, 2019. https://hungarytoday.hu/hungary-prepared-host-any-sporting-event-govt/.

Hunt, Katie, and Cy Xu. "China 'Employs 2 Million to Police Internet.'" *CNN.com*, October 7, 2013. https://www.cnn.com/2013/10/07/world/asia/china-internet-monitors/index.html.

Huntington, Samuel P. *The Third Wave: Democratization in the Late Twentieth Century*. Norman: University of Oklahoma Press, 1993.

Hutchcroft, Paul. "Reflections on a Reverse Image: South Korea under Park Chung Hee and the Philippines under Ferdinand Marcos." In *The Park Chung Hee Era*, edited by Byung-Kook Kim and Ezra F. Vogel, 543–72. Cambridge, MA: Harvard University Press, 2011.

Hvg.hu. "Német vicclap álhíréről „tudósítva" számolt be a köztévé, micsoda állapotok uralkodnak nyugaton." May 21, 2018. https://hvg.hu/kultura/20180521_Nemet_vicclap_alhirerol _tudositva_szamolt_be_a_kozteve_micsoda_allapotok_uralkodnak_nyugaton.

Hyde, Susan D. *The Pseudo-Democrat's Dilemma: Why Election Observation Became an International Norm*. Ithaca, NY: Cornell University Press, 2011.

Hyde, Susan D., and Nikolay Marinov. "Which Elections Can Be Lost?" *Political Analysis* 20, no. 2 (2012): 191–210. http://www.jstor.org/stable/23260172.

Hyden, Goran, and Colin Leys. "Elections and Politics in Single-Party Systems: The Case of Kenya and Tanzania." *British Journal of Political Science* 2, no. 4 (October 1972): 389–420.

Ibrahim, Zuraidah, and Lydia Lim. "Lee Kuan Yew: This Is Who I Am." *Straits Times*, September 14, 2003. https://www.straitstimes.com/singapore/lee-kuan-yew-this-is-who-i-am.

Ibrahim, Zuraidah, and Andrea Ong. "Remembering Lee Kuan Yew: A Life Devoted Entirely to Singapore." *Straits Times*, March 24, 2015. https://www.straitstimes.com/singapore /remembering-lee-kuan-yew-a-life-devoted-entirely-to-singapore.

Ikenberry, John, and Anne-Marie Slaughter. "Democracies Must Work in Concert." *Financial Times*, July 10, 2008.

Ikenberry, G. John. "The Next Liberal Order." *Foreign Affairs* 99, no. 4 (July/August 2020): 133–42.

Ilko, Sergey. "Na vybori v Ukraine opredelen smotryashchy ot Kremlya?" *Unian.net*, February 23, 2012. https://www.unian.net/politics/612744-na-vyiboryi-v-ukraine-opredelen-smotryaschiy-ot-kremlya.html.

IMDB. "Running Wild with Bear Grylls: President Barack Obama." December 17, 2015. https://www.imdb.com/title/tt5006362/.

Inglehart, Ronald, and Christian Welzel. *Modernization, Cultural Change, and Democracy: The Human Development Sequence.* New York: Cambridge University Press, 2005.

Inter-American Commission on Human Rights. *Annual Report 2019.* 2019. http://www.oas.org/en/iachr/docs/annual/2019/docs/IA2019cap4BVE-en.pdf.

International Commission of Jurists. *Pakistan: Human Rights after Martial Law, Report of a Mission.* Geneva: International Commission of Jurists, April 1, 1987. https://www.icj.org/pakistan-human-rights-after-martial-law-report-of-a-mission/.

Interpol. *About Notices.* https://www.interpol.int/en/How-we-work/Notices/About-Notices.

Inter Press Service. "Peru: U.S./Canadian Press Group Protests Killings." *IPS-Inter Press Service*, December 5, 1991.

Ipsos. *Human Rights in 2018: A Global Advisor Survey.* https://www.ipsos.com/sites/default/files/ct/news/documents/2018-07/human-rights-in-2018-ipsos-global-advisor.pdf.

Iqbal, Sajid, Zoheb Hossain, and Shubh Mathur. "Reconciliation and Truth in Kashmir: A Case Study." *Race & Class* 56, no. 2 (October 2014): 51–65.

Iriye, Akira, and Petra Goedde. "Introduction: Human Rights as History." In *The Human Rights Revolution: An International History*, edited by Akira Iriye, Petra Goedde, and William I. Hitchcock, 3–24. Oxford: Oxford University Press, 2012.

Isakhan, Benjamin. "Read All about It: The Free Press, the Public Sphere and Democracy in Iraq." *Bulletin of the Royal Institute for Inter-Faith Studies* 8, no. 1–2 (2006): 119–53.

Islamic Human Rights Commission. "IHRC's UPR Report on Saudi Arabia." May 25, 2018. https://www.ihrc.org.uk/activities/ihrc-at-un/18145-ihrcs-upr-report-on-saudi-arabia/.

Jakhar, Pratik. "Confucius Institutes: The Growth of China's Controversial Cultural Branch." BBC.com, September 7, 2019. https://www.bbc.com/news/world-asia-china-49511231.

James, Ian. "Absent but Omnipresent, Chávez a Powerful Symbol." *Seattle Times*, January 25, 2013. https://www.seattletimes.com/nation-world/absent-but-omnipresent-chavez-a-powerful-symbol/.

Jensen, Nathan. "Political Risk, Democratic Institutions, and Foreign Direct Investment." *Journal of Politics* 70, no. 4 (2008): 1040–52.

Jessen, Ralph, and Hedwig Richter. "Non-Competitive Elections in Twentieth Century Dictatorships: Some Questions and General Considerations." In *Voting for Hitler and Stalin: Elections under 20th Century Dictatorships*, edited by Ralph Jessen and Hedwig Richter, 9–36. Frankfurt: Campus Verlag, 2011.

Ji, Fengyuan. *Linguistic Engineering: Language and Politics in Mao's China.* Honolulu: University of Hawaii Press, 2004.

Jiang, Steven. "Trial by Media? Confessions Go Prime Time in China." CNN, January 26, 2016. https://www.cnn.com/2016/01/26/asia/china-television-confessions/index.html.

Jiménez, Raúl, and Manuel Hidalgo. "Forensic Analysis of Venezuelan Elections during the Chávez Presidency." *PloS one* 9, no. 6 (2014). doi.org/10.1371/journal.pone.0100884.

Johns, Amelia, and Nikki Cheong. "Feeling the Chill: Bersih 2.0, State Censorship, and 'Networked Affect' on Malaysian Social Media 2012–2018." *Social Media + Society*. April 2019. doi:10.1177/2056305118821801.

Johnson, David T., and Franklin E. Zimring. *The Next Frontier: National Development, Political Change, and the Death Penalty in Asia.* New York: Oxford University Press, 2009.

Johnson, Ian. "Who Killed More: Hitler, Stalin, or Mao?" *NYR Daily*, February 5, 2018. https://www.nybooks.com/daily/2018/02/05/who-killed-more-hitler-stalin-or-mao/.

Jones, Derek. *Censorship: A World Encyclopedia.* New York: Routledge, 2001.

Jones, Graham. "Live Aid 1985: A Day of Magic." CNN, July 6, 2005. http://edition.cnn.com/2005/SHOWBIZ/Music/07/01/liveaid.memories/index.html.

Jones, Matthew. "Creating Malaysia: Singapore Security, the Borneo Territories, and the Contours of British Policy, 1961–63." *Journal of Imperial and Commonwealth History* 28, no. 2 (2000): 85–109.

Judt, Tony. *Postwar: A History of Europe since 1945.* London: Penguin Group, 2005.

Kalathil, Shanthi, and Taylor C. Boas. *The Internet and State Control in Authoritarian Regimes: China, Cuba, and the Counterrevolution.* Washington, DC: Carnegie Endowment for International Peace, 2001.

Kalinin, Kirill. "A Study of Social Desirability Bias in the Russian Presidential Elections, 2012." Working paper, presented at the 2014 APSA Annual Meeting, 2014.

———. "Exploring Putin's Post-Crimean Supermajority." SSRN 2658829 (2015).

Kampfner, John. *Freedom for Sale: Why the World Is Trading Democracy for Security.* New York: Basic Books, 2010.

Kato, Yoshikazu. "A Conversation with Francis Fukuyama." Asia Global Institute, Hong Kong, March 25, 2019. https://www.asiaglobalinstitute.hku.hk/news-post/a-conversation-with-francis-fukuyama.

Katsakioris, Constantin. "Creating a Socialist Intelligentsia." *Cahiers d'études africaines* 226 (2017): 259–88. doi.org/10.4000/etudesafricaines.20664.

Kay, Vee. "Kazakhstan President Lauds Lee Kuan Yew's Contribution in New Book." *Inside Recent*, February 5, 2018. https://www.insiderecent.com/kazakhstan-president-lauds-lee-kuan-yews-contribution-new-book-241.html.

Kazinform. "V ramkakh III Astaninskogo ekonomicheskogo foruma Glava gosudarstva Nursultan Nazarbayev provel ryad dvustoronnikh vstrech." July 1, 2010. https://www.inform.kz/ru/v-ramkah-iii-astaninskogo-ekonomicheskogo-foruma-glava-gosudarstva-nursultan-nazarbaev-provel-ryad-dvustoronnih-vstrech_a2283043.

Kazinform. "Kazakh Capital to Host 12th Astana Economic Forum on May 16–17, 2019." April 19, 2019. https://www.inform.kz/en/kazakh-capital-to-host-12th-astana-economic-forum-on-may-16-17-2019_a3518948.

Keck, Margaret E., and Kathryn Sikkink. *Activists beyond Borders: Advocacy Networks in International Politics.* Ithaca: Cornell University Press, 2014.

Kellam, Marisa, and Elizabeth Stein. "Trump's War on the News Media Is Serious; Just Look at Latin America." *Washington Post*, February 16, 2017. https://www.washingtonpost.com/news /monkey-cage/wp/2017/02/16/trumps-war-on-the-news-media-is-serious-just-look-at -latin-america/.

Kendall-Taylor, Andrea, and Erica Frantz. "Mimicking Democracy to Prolong Autocracies." *Washington Quarterly* 37, no. 4 (2015): 71–84.

Kendall-Taylor, Andrea, Erica Frantz, and Joseph Wright. "The Digital Dictators: How Technology Strengthens Autocracy." *Foreign Affairs* 99, no. 2 (March/April 2020): 103–15.

Kenyon, Paul. *Dictatorland: The Men Who Stole Africa*. London: Head of Zeus Ltd., 2018.

Kerr, Sarah. "Fujimori's Plot: An Interview with Gustavo Gorriti." *New York Review of Books*, June 25, 1992. https://www.nybooks.com/articles/1992/06/25/fujimoris-plot-an-interview -with-gustavo-gorriti/.

Kershaw, Ian. "War and Political Violence in Twentieth-Century Europe." *Contemporary European History* (2005): 107–23.

———. *To Hell and Back: Europe 1914–1949*. New York: Penguin, 2015.

Khashoggi, Jamal. "Saudi Arabia's Crown Prince Already Controlled the Nation's Media. Now He's Squeezing It Even Further." *Washington Post*, February 7, 2018. https://www .washingtonpost.com/news/global-opinions/wp/2018/02/07/saudi-arabias-crown-prince -already-controlled-the-nations-media-now-hes-squeezing-it-even-further/.

Khrushchev, Nikita. *Memoirs of Nikita Khrushchev*. Vol. 3, *Statesman, 1953–1964*. University Park: Pennsylvania State University Press, 2004.

Kim, Dong Choon. "Forgotten War, Forgotten Massacres—the Korean War (1950–1953) as Licensed Mass Killings." *Journal of Genocide Research* 6, no. 4 (2004): 523–44.

Kim, Hun Joon. "Why Do States Adopt Truth Commissions after Transition?" *Social Science Quarterly* 100, no. 5 (2019): 1485–1502.

Kim, Jinyoung. "Economic Analysis of Foreign Education and Students Abroad." *Journal of Development Economics* 56, no. 2 (1998): 337–65.

King, Gary, Jennifer Pan, and Margaret E. Roberts. "How Censorship in China Allows Government Criticism but Silences Collective Expression." *American Political Science Review* 107, no. 2 (2013): 326–43.

———. "How the Chinese Government Fabricates Social Media Posts for Strategic Distraction, Not Engaged Argument." *American Political Science Review* 111, no. 3 (2017): 484–501. doi:10.1017/S0003055417000144.

Kington, Tom. "Silvio Berlusconi Faces Inquiry over Bid to Block 'Hostile' TV Show." *Guardian*, March 15, 2010. https://www.theguardian.com/world/2010/mar/16/silvio-berlusconi -magistrates-phone-tap.

Kirilenko, Anastasia, and Daisy Sindelar. "Sleeping Tiger, Hidden Agenda?" Radio Free Europe Radio Liberty, March 15, 2012. https://www.rferl.org/a/putin_tiger_scam/24516781.html.

Klasa, Adrienne, Valerie Hopkins, Guy Chazan, Henry Foy, and Miles Johnson. "Russia's Long Arm Reaches to the Right in Europe." *Financial Times*, May 22, 2019. https://www.ft.com /content/48c4bfa6-7ca2-11e9-81d2-f785092ab560.

Klemperer, Victor. *I Shall Bear Witness: The Diaries of Victor Klemperer, 1933–41*. London: Weidenfeld & Nicolson, 1998.

———. *Language of the Third Reich: LTI: Lingua Tertii Imperii.* London: A&C Black, 2006.

Klishin, Ilya. "How Putin Is Bankrupting the Russian Opposition." *Moscow Times*, October 30, 2019. https://www.themoscowtimes.com/2019/10/30/how-putin-is-bankrupting-the-russian-opposition-a67971.

Knight, Brian, and Ana Tribin. *Opposition Media, State Censorship, and Political Accountability: Evidence from Chávez's Venezuela.* NBER Working Paper No. w25916. National Bureau of Economic Research, 2019.

Koestler, Arthur. *Darkness at Noon.* New York: Macmillan, 1940.

———. *The Invisible Writing.* New York: Random House, 2011.

Kommersant. "Vladimir Putin zayavil o neobkhodimosti zashchity ot 'destruktivnykh sil' v internete." January 30, 2018. https://www.kommersant.ru/doc/3534406.

Konan, Venance. "In Ivory Coast, Democrat to Dictator." *New York Times*, April 7, 2011. https://www.nytimes.com/2011/04/08/opinion/08konan.html.

Koon, Tracy. *Believe, Obey, Fight: Political Socialization of Youth in Fascist Italy, 1922–1943.* Chapel Hill: University of North Carolina Press, 1985.

Kopel, David. "Argentina's Free Press Is in Grave Danger: Book Review of 'Tiempos turbulentos.'" *Washington Post*, February 9, 2015. https://www.washingtonpost.com/news/volokh-conspiracy/wp/2015/02/09/argentinas-free-press-is-in-grave-danger-book-review-of-tiempos-turbulentos/.

Kott, Jan. "Controlling the Writing on the Wall." *New York Review of Books*, August 17, 1978.

Kozlov, Petr. "V Kremle izuchayut amerikanskie tekhnologii v kontekste vyborov v Dumu v 2016 godu." *Vedomosti*, March 10, 2015. https://www.vedomosti.ru/newspaper/articles/2015/03/10/elektoralnoe-importozameschenie.

Kozlov, Vladimir. "Belarus Emerges as Europe's Leading High Tech Hub." BNE Intellinews, February 18, 2020. https://intellinews.com/belarus-emerges-as-europe-s-leading-high-tech-hub-175911/.

Kramer, Andrew E. "Italians Win Yukos Units, but Gazprom Is to Benefit." *New York Times*, April 5, 2007. https://www.nytimes.com/2007/04/05/business/worldbusiness/05yukos.html.

Krastev, Ivan. "New Threats to Freedom: Democracy's 'Doubles.'" *Journal of Democracy* 17, no. 2 (2006): 52–62.

———. *Eksperimentalnaya rodina: Razgovor s Glebom Pavlovskym.* Moscow: Evropa, 2018.

Krastev, Nikola. "In the Heart of New York, Russia's 'Soft Power' Arm Gaining Momentum." Radio Free Europe Radio Liberty, February 15, 2009. https://www.rferl.org/a/In_The_Heart_Of_New_York_Russias_Soft_Power_Arm_Gaining_Momentum/1493429.html.

Krauss, Clifford. "U.S. Cuts Aid to Zaire, Setting Off a Policy Debate." November 4, 1990. https://www.nytimes.com/1990/11/04/world/us-cuts-aid-to-zaire-setting-off-a-policy-debate.html.

Krauze, Enrique. "The Shah of Venezuela." *New Republic* 240, no. 5 (March 31, 2009): 29–38. https://newrepublic.com/article/61787/the-shah-venezuela.

Kravtsova, Yekaterina. "Former 'Provocateur' Blames Police for Bolotnaya Clashes." *Moscow Times*, March 21, 2013. https://www.themoscowtimes.com/2013/03/21/former-provocateur-blames-police-for-bolotnaya-clashes-a22584.

Kricheli, Ruth, Yair Livne, and Beatriz Magaloni. "Taking to the Streets: Theory and Evidence on Protests under Authoritarianism." Unpublished paper, Stanford University, 2011.

Kucera, Joshua. "No One Rigs an Election Quite like Kazakhstan." *Atlantic*, April 5, 2011. https://www.theatlantic.com/international/archive/2011/04/no-one-rigs-an-election-quite-like-kazakhstan/236817/.

Kudaibergenova, Diana T. "Compartmentalized Ideology: Presidential Addresses and Legitimation in Kazakhstan." In *Theorizing Central Asian Politics: The State, Ideology and Power*, edited by Rico Isaacs and Alessandro Frigerio, 145–66. London: Palgrave Macmillan, 2019.

Kung, James Kai-Sing, and Shuo Chen. "The Tragedy of the Nomenklatura: Career Incentives and Political Radicalism during China's Great Leap Famine." *American Political Science Review* 105, no. 1 (2011): 27–45.

Kuran, Timur. "Now out of Never: The Element of Surprise in the East European Revolution of 1989." *World Politics* (1991): 7–48.

Kurlantzick, Joshua. "Why the 'China Model' Isn't Going Away." *Atlantic*, March 21, 2013. https://www.theatlantic.com/china/archive/2013/03/why-the-china-model-isnt-going-away/274237/.

L. L. "Stalinism in the Post-Stalin Regime: 'The Ministry of Truth' without 'Big Brother.'" *World Today* 10, no. 7 (July 1954): 300–309.

Lamb, David. *The Africans.* New York: Random House, 1987.

———. "Burmese Leader Ne Win." *Washington Post*, December 6, 2002. https://www.washingtonpost.com/archive/local/2002/12/06/burmese-leader-ne-win/e7be1659-d203-44cc-bf54-d05a18048ccc/.

Landau, David. "Abusive Constitutionalism." *UC Davis Law Review* 47 (2013): 189–260.

Landau, Mark J., Sheldon Solomon, Jeff Greenberg, Florette Cohen, Tom Pyszczynski, Jamie Arndt, Claude H. Miller, Daniel M. Ogilvie, and Alison Cook. "Deliver Us from Evil: The Effects of Mortality Salience and Reminders of 9/11 on Support for President George W. Bush." *Personality and Social Psychology Bulletin* 30, no. 9 (September 2004): 1136–50.

Lane, Charles. "The 'Self-Coup' That Rocked Peru." *Newsweek*, April 19, 1992. https://www.newsweek.com/self-coup-rocked-peru-197280.

Langer, Máximo, and Mackenzie Eason. "The Quiet Expansion of Universal Jurisdiction." *European Journal of International Law* 30, no. 3 (August 2019): 779–817. https://doi.org/10.1093/ejil/chz050.

Latinobarómetro. *Informe Latinobarómetro 2011.* http://www.infoamerica.org/primera/lb_2011.pdf.

Lauría, Carlos. "Confrontation, Repression in Correa's Ecuador." *CPJ.org*, September 1, 2011. https://cpj.org/reports/2011/09/confrontation-repression-correa-ecuador.php.

Law, David S., and Mila Versteeg. "The Declining Influence of the United States Constitution." *NYU Law Review* 87 (2012): 762–858.

———. "Constitutional Variation among Strains of Authoritarianism." In *Constitutions in Authoritarian Regimes*, edited by Tom Ginsburg and Alberto Simpser, 165–95. Cambridge: Cambridge University Press, 2013.

Lebovic, James, and Erik Voeten. "The Cost of Shame: International Organizations and Foreign Aid in the Punishing of Human Rights Violators." *Journal of Peace Research* 46, no. 1 (2009): 79–97.

Lee, Kuan Yew. "Address by Mr. Lee Kuan Yew, Senior Minister of Singapore, to the Kazakhstan Supreme Soviet on 20 September 1991." September 20, 1991. https://www.nas.gov.sg/archivesonline/data/pdfdoc/lky19910920.pdf.

———. *The Singapore Story*. Singapore: Marshall Cavendish Editions, 1998.

———. *From Third World to First: The Singapore Story: 1965–2000*. Singapore: Marshall Cavendish Editions, 2000.

Lees, Lorraine M. *Keeping Tito Afloat: The United States, Yugoslavia, and the Cold War, 1945–1960*. Pittsburgh: Pennsylvania State University Press, 1997.

Leese, Daniel. *Mao Cult: Rhetoric and Ritual in China's Cultural Revolution*. Cambridge: Cambridge University Press, 2011.

Legler, Thomas, and Thomas Kwasi Tieku. "What Difference Can a Path Make? Regional Democracy Promotion Regimes in the Americas and Africa." *Democratization* 17, no. 3 (2010): 465–91.

Lehoucq, Fabrice. "Electoral Fraud: Causes, Types, and Consequences." *Annual Review of Political Science* 6 (2003): 233–56.

Lemon, Edward. "Weaponizing Interpol." *Journal of Democracy* 30, no. 2 (2019): 15–29.

Lendvai, Paul. *Orbán: Hungary's Strongman*. New York: Oxford University Press, 2018.

Lenta.ru. "Moldavia gotova osvobodit vtorogo rossiiskogo nablyudatelya." July 19, 2005. https://lenta.ru/news/2005/07/19/deportation/.

Lerner, Samuel. *Informe Final de la Comisión de la Verdad y Reconciliación, Anexo 3: Compendio Estadístico*. Lima, Peru: Gobierno del Perú, 2013. http://www.cverdad.org.pe/ifinal/pdf/AESTADISTICO/ANEXO%20ESTAD%CDSTICO(PARA%20CD).pdf.

Levada Center. "Indikatory." https://www.levada.ru/indikatory/.

———. *Obshchestvennoe mnenie 2019*. Moscow: Levada Center, 2019.

———. "Aleksei Navalny: Otnoshenie i otravlenie." October 2, 2020. https://www.levada.ru/2020/10/02/aleksej-navalnyj-otnoshenie-i-otravlenie/.

———. "Kharakter i struktura massovoy trevozhnosti v Rossii." April 21, 2021. https://www.levada.ru/2021/04/21/harakter-i-struktura-massovoj-trevozhnosti-v-rossii/.

Levitsky, Steven, and Lucan A. Way. "International Linkage and Democratization." *Journal of Democracy* 16, no. 3 (2005): 20–34.

———.*Competitive Authoritarianism: Hybrid Regimes after the Cold War*. New York: Cambridge University Press, 2010.

Lewin, Tamar. "Gifts to Charity in US Topped $203 Billion in 2000, Study Says." *New York Times*, May 24, 2001. https://www.nytimes.com/2001/05/24/us/gifts-to-charity-in-us-topped-203-billion-in-2000-study-says.html.

Lewis, David. "Blogging Zhanaozen: Hegemonic Discourse and Authoritarian Resilience in Kazakhstan." *Central Asian Survey* 35, no. 3 (April 2016): 421–38.

Li, Quan, and Adam Resnick. "Reversal of Fortunes: Democratic Institutions and Foreign Direct Investment Inflows to Developing Countries." *International Organization* 57, no. 1 (2003): 175–211.

Liak, Teng Kiat. "Concern, Warmth . . . a Touch of Eloquence." *Straits Times*, October 10, 1985. https://eresources.nlb.gov.sg/newspapers/Digitised/Article/straitstimes19851010-1.2.22.8?ST=1&AT=filter&K=Lee%20Kuan%20Yew%20Reagan&KA=Lee%20Kuan%20Yew%20

Reagan&DF=&DT=&Display=0&AO=false&NPT=&L=&CTA=&NID=straitstimes&CT
=&WC=&YR=1985&QT=lee,kuan,yew,reagan&oref=article.

Liang, Chi Shad. *Burma's Foreign Relations: Neutralism in Theory and Practice*. Westport, CT:
Praeger, 1990.

Light, Matthew A. "What Does It Mean to Control Migration? Soviet Mobility Policies in Comparative Perspective." *Law & Social Inquiry* 37, no. 2 (2012): 395–429.

Lillis, Joanna. *Dark Shadows: Inside the Secret World of Kazakhstan*. London: I. B. Tauris, 2019.

Lipman, Maria, Anna Kachkaeva, and Michael Poyker. "Media in Russia: Between Modernization and Monopoly." In *The New Autocracy: Information, Politics, and Policy in Putin's Russia*,
edited by Daniel Treisman, 159–90. Washington, DC: Brookings Institution Press, 2018.

Lipton, Eric. "Feud in Kazakh President's Family Spills into U.S." *New York Times*, May 30, 2011.
https://www.nytimes.com/2011/05/30/world/asia/30kazakhstan.html?pagewanted=all.

Little, Andrew T. "Fraud and Monitoring in Non-competitive Elections." *Political Science
Research and Methods* 3, no. 1 (2015): 1–21.

———. "Propaganda and Credulity." *Games and Economic Behavior* 102 (2017): 224–32.

Lockwood, Nick. "How the Soviet Union Transformed Terrorism." *Atlantic*, December 23, 2011.
https://www.theatlantic.com/international/archive/2011/12/how-the-soviet-union
-transformed-terrorism/250433/.

Long, Gideon. "Living in Fear: Censorship under Pinochet." Journalism Is Not a Crime, June 18,
2015. https://journalismisnotacrime.com/en/news/90/.

Long, William. "Journalism: Ruling against Editor in Peru Shows Obstacles to Free Press." *LA Times*,
April 10, 1993. https://www.latimes.com/archives/la-xpm-1993-04-10-mn-21336-story.html.

Loong, Lee Hsien. "PM Lee Hsien Loong at the Debate on the Motion of Thanks to the Presi-
dent." September 2, 2020, Singapore Prime Minister's Office. https://www.pmo.gov.sg
/Newsroom/PM-Lee-Speech-at-the-debate-on-the-motion-of-thanks-to-the-president
-Sep-2020.

López Hurtado, Pablo. "Rafael Céspedes: 'Nosotros pactamos con Irene Sáez.'" *La Razón*, 2015.
https://www.larazon.net/2015/12/rafael-cespedes-nosotros-pactamos-con-irene-saez/.

Lorentzen, Peter. "China's Strategic Censorship." *American Journal of Political Science* 58, no. 2
(2014): 402–14.

Loudis, Jessica. "The Art of Escaping Censorship." *New Republic*, December 13, 2017. https://
newrepublic.com/article/146241/art-escaping-censorship.

Loushnikova, Ekaterina. "Comrade Stalin's Secret Prison." *Open Democracy*, January 13, 2015.
https://www.opendemocracy.net/en/odr/comrade-stalins-secret-prison/.

Lucas, Christopher, Richard A. Nielsen, Margaret E. Roberts, Brandon M. Stewart, Alex Storer,
and Dustin Tingley. "Computer-Assisted Text Analysis for Comparative Politics." *Political
Analysis* 23, no. 2 (2015): 254–77.

Ludwig, Arnold M. *King of the Mountain: The Nature of Political Leadership*. Lexington: University Press of Kentucky, 2002.

Luhn, Alec. "Vladimir Putin Declares All Russian Military Deaths State Secrets." *Guardian*,
May 28, 2015. https://www.theguardian.com/world/2015/may/28/vladimir-putin-declares
-all-russian-military-deaths-state-secrets.

Luxmoore, Matthew. "Putin Mania: Russian Personality Cult Obsessed with Powerful President." *Al Jazeera America*, January 24, 2016. http://america.aljazeera.com/articles/2016/1/24/putin-personality-cult-russians-obsessed.html.

———. "Google Censors Search Results after Russian Government Threat, Reports Say." Radio Free Europe Radio Liberty, February 7, 2019. https://www.rferl.org/a/google-censors-search-results-after-russian-government-threat-reports-say/29757686.html.

Lyons, Eugene. *Stalin, Czar of All the Russias*. Philadelphia: J. B. Lippincott, 1940.

Ma, Damien, and Neil Thomas. "In Xi We Trust: How Propaganda Might Be Working in the New Era." *Macro Polo*, September 12, 2018. https://macropolo.org/analysis/in-xi-we-trust/.

MacFarquhar, Neil, and Ivan Nechepurenko. "Aleksei Navalny, Viable Putin Rival, Is Barred from a Presidential Run." *New York Times*, February 8, 2017. https://www.nytimes.com/2017/02/08/world/europe/russia-aleksei-navalny-putin.html.

Machiavelli, Niccolò. "The Prince." In *The Prince and Other Political Writings*, edited by Bruce Penman. New York: Everyman.

Mackey, Danielle. "All the President's Trolls." *Rest of World*, June 16, 2020. https://restofworld.org/2020/ecuador-president-twitter-trolls/.

Magaloni, Beatriz. *Voting for Autocracy: Hegemonic Party Survival and Its Demise in Mexico*. New York: Cambridge University Press, 2006.

Maksymiuk, Jan. "Belarus: Lukashenka Eyes Union with Ukraine." Radio Free Europe Radio Liberty, November 24, 2006. http://www.rferl.org/content/article/1072956.html.

Malaysiakini. "Najib, Umno Sue Mkini over Readers' Comments." June 2, 2014. https://www.malaysiakini.com/news/264611.

Malesky, Edmund, and Paul Schuler. "Nodding or Needling: Analyzing Delegate Responsiveness in an Authoritarian Parliament." *American Political Science Review* 104, no. 3 (2010): 482–502.

Malkin, Elisabeth. "50 Years after a Student Massacre, Mexico Reflects on Democracy." *New York Times*, October 1, 2018. https://www.nytimes.com/2018/10/01/world/americas/mexico-tlatelolco-massacre.html.

Man, Chung. "Who Wants to Watch CCTV's Xinwen Lianbo Program?" *Ejinsight*, August 28, 2018. https://www.ejinsight.com/eji/article/id/1929046/20180828-who-wants-to-watch-cctvs-xinwen-lianbo-program.

Mander, Benedict. "Advertisers Feel Squeeze from Chávez." *Financial Times*, March 23, 2008. https://www.ft.com/content/21562624-f916-11dc-bcf3-000077b07658.

———. "Venezuelan Private Media Fear Fresh Assault." *Financial Times*, June 19, 2009. https://www.ft.com/content/4915a606-5cea-11de-9d42-00144feabdc0.

Manning, Molly Guptill. *When Books Went to War: The Stories That Helped Us Win World War I*. Boston: Houghton Mifflin Harcourt, 2014.

Manyika, James, Susan Lund, Jacques Bughin, Jonathan Woetzel, Kalin Stamenov, and Dhruv Dhingra. "Digital Globalization: The New Era of Global Flows." San Francisco, CA: McKinsey Global Institute, 2016. https://www.mckinsey.com/business-functions/mckinsey-digital/our-insights/digital-globalization-the-new-era-of-global-flows#.

Mao, Zedong. "Remarks at the Small Group Meeting of the Central Party Work Conference." In *Database for the History of Contemporary Chinese Political Movements*, edited by
Song Yongyi. Cambridge, MA: Fairbank Center for Chinese Studies, Harvard University,
1964.

Marcano, Cristina, and Alberto Barrera Tyszka. *Hugo Chávez*. New York: Random House,
2007.

Máriás, Leonárd, et al. *Centralised Media System: Soft Censorship 2018*. Mérték Media Monitor,
December 2009.

Markham, James M. "Germany's Trafficking in People." *New York Times*, July 29, 1984. https://
www.nytimes.com/1984/07/29/world/germanys-trafficking-in-people.html.

Markoff, John. *Waves of Democracy: Social Movements and Political Change*. New York: Routledge, 1996.

Markowicz, Karol. "Hollywood's Chávez-Cheering Stars and Venezuela's Victims." *New York
Post*, June 5, 2016. https://nypost.com/2016/06/05/hollywoods-chavez-cheering-stars
-venezuelas-victms/.

Márquez, Xavier. "A Model of Cults of Personality." Paper presented at American Political Science Association Annual Meeting, 2013. https://ssrn.com/abstract=2301392.

———. "Two Models of Political Leader Cults: Propaganda and Ritual." *Politics, Religion &
Ideology* 19, no. 3 (2018): 265–84.

Marshall, P. David. *Celebrity and Power: Fame in Contemporary Culture*. Minneapolis: University
of Minnesota Press, 2014.

Marthoz, Jean-Paul. "Venezuela's Foreign Policy: A Mirage Based on a Curse." Norwegian
Peacebuilding Resource Center, November 2014. https://www.files.ethz.ch/isn/186054/5a
c5220191adf69475fb57f9e303479c.pdf.

Martin, Paul. "Chávez, the Organization of American States, and Democracy in International
Law." *Alberta Law Review* 46, no. 4 (2008): 933–55.

Martínez-Torres, María Elena. "Civil Society, the Internet, and the Zapatistas." *Peace Review* 13,
no. 3 (2001): 347–55.

Mauzy, Diane K., and Robert Stephen Milne. *Singapore Politics under the People's Action Party*.
London: Psychology Press, 2002.

Mayr, Walter. "European Politicians Shill for Kazakh Autocrat." *Spiegel Online International*,
March 13, 2013. https://www.spiegel.de/international/europe/european-social-democrats
-lobby-for-kazakhstan-autocrat-a-888428.html.

Maza, Cristina. "Here's Where Paul Manafort Did Business with Corrupt Dictators." *Newsweek*,
August 7, 2018. https://www.newsweek.com/heres-where-paul-manafort-did-business
-corrupt-dictators-1061470.

Mazower, Mark. "Violence and the State in the Twentieth Century." *American Historical Review*
107, no. 4 (2002): 1158–78.

McClintock, Cynthia. "Peru's Fujimori: A Caudillo Derails Democracy." *Current History* 92,
no. 572 (1993): 112–19.

McCormick, Ty. "Is the US Military Propping Up Uganda's 'Elected' Autocrat?" *Foreign Policy*,
February 18, 2016. https://foreignpolicy.com/2016/02/18/is-the-us-military-propping-up
-ugandas-elected-autocrat-museveni-elections/.

McFaul, Michael. *Advancing Democracy Abroad: Why We Should and How We Can.* Lanham, MD: Rowman and Littlefield, 2009.

McMillan, John, and Pablo Zoido. "How to Subvert Democracy: Montesinos in Peru." *Journal of Economic Perspectives* 18, no. 4 (Fall 2004): 69–92.

M'Cormack-Hale, Fredline, and Mavis Zupork Dome. "Support for Elections Weakens among Africans; Many See Them as Ineffective in Holding Leaders Accountable." Afrobarometer Dispatch No. 425, February 9, 2021. https://afrobarometer.org/sites/default/files/publications/Dispatches/ad425-support_for_elections_weakens_in_africa-afrobarometer_dispatch-7feb21.pdf.

McPhail, Thomas L. *Global Communication: Theories, Stakeholders, and Trends.* Hoboken, NJ: Wiley-Blackwell, 2014.

Meduza. "What Putin Reads." July 16, 2020. https://meduza.io/en/feature/2020/07/17/what-putin-reads.

Melnikov, Nikita, "Censorship, Propaganda, and Political Popularity: Evidence from Russia." February 8, 2019. Mimeo, Princeton. https://ssrn.com/abstract=3276926 or http://dx.doi.org/10.2139/ssrn.3276926.

Memorial Human Rights Center. *Annual Report, 2013–14.* Moscow: Memorial Human Rights Center. https://memohrc.org/sites/all/themes/memo/templates/pdf.php?pdf=/sites/default/files/2013-2014-eng-b.pdf.

———. *Spisok lits, preznannykh politicheskimi zaklyuchennymi.* Moscow: Memorial Human Rights Center, August 16, 2021. https://memohrc.org/ru/bulletins/spisok-lic-priznannyh-politicheskimi-zaklyuchyonnymi-pravozashchitnym-centrom-memorial-5.

Mendick, Robert. "Tony Blair Gives Kazakhstan's Autocratic President Tips on How to Defend a Massacre." *Telegraph*, August 24, 2014. https://www.telegraph.co.uk/news/politics/tony-blair/11052965/Tony-Blair-gives-Kazakhstans-autocratic-president-tips-on-how-to-defend-a-massacre.html.

Meng, Anne. *Constraining Dictatorship: From Personalized Rule to Institutionalized Regimes.* New York: Cambridge University Press, 2020.

Meng, Xin, Nancy Qian, and Pierre Yared. "The Institutional Causes of Famine in China, 1959–61." *Review of Economic Studies* 82, no. 4 (2015): 1568–1611.

Menzel, Jiří. *Moja Hrvatska.* HTV. August 18, 2011.

Merl, Stephan. "Elections in the Soviet Union, 1937–1989: A View into a Paternalistic World from Below." In *Voting for Hitler and Stalin. Elections under 20th Century Dictatorships,* edited by Ralph Jessen and Hedwig Richter, 276–308. Frankfurt: Campus Verlag, 2011.

Metz, Helen Chapin. *Egypt: A Country Study.* Washington, DC: Federal Research Division of the Library of Congress, 1990.

Meusburger, Peter, and Heike Jöns. *Transformations in Hungary: Essays in Economy and Society.* Berlin: Springer Science & Business Media, 2012.

Mieczkowski, Z. "Foreign Tourism in the USSR: A Preliminary Investigation." *Geographical Survey* 3 (1974): 99–122.

Miller, Aaron D., and Richard Sokolsky. "An 'Alliance of Democracies' Sounds Good. It Won't Solve the World's Problems." *Washington Post*, August 13, 2020. https://www.washingtonpost.com/outlook/2020/08/13/biden-pompeo-trump-democracy/.

Miller, Judith. "Sudan Publicly Hangs an Old Opposition Leader." *New York Times*, January 19, 1985. https://www.nytimes.com/1985/01/19/world/sudan-publicly-hangs-an-old-opposition-leader.html.

Miller, Michael K., and Margaret E. Peters. "Restraining the Huddled Masses: Migration Policy and Autocratic Survival." *British Journal of Political Science* 50, no. 2 (2018): 1–31.

Milner, Helen V., and Bumba Mukherjee. "Democratization and Economic Globalization." *Annual Review of Political Science* 12 (2009): 163–81.

Mineev, Aleksandr. "'Krasnaya metka' dlya Interpola." *Novaya Gazeta,* December 13, 2013. https://novayagazeta.ru/articles/2013/12/13/57636-171-krasnaya-metka-187-dlya-interpola.

Miner, Luke. "The Unintended Consequences of Internet Diffusion: Evidence from Malaysia." *Journal of Public Economics* 132 (2015): 66–78.

Ministry of Foreign Affairs of the People's Republic of China, "Wang Yi: The Times of Arbitrary Interference in China's Internal Affairs by Fabricating Stories and Lies Are Long Gone." March 23, 2021. https://www.fmprc.gov.cn/mfa_eng/zxxx_662805/t1863431.shtml.

Mlechin, Leonid. *Yuri Andropov: Poslednaya nadezhda rezhima*. Moscow: Centrpoligraph, 2008.

Mokyr, Joel. "The Rise and Fall of the Factory System: Technology, Firms, and Households since the Industrial Revolution." *Carnegie-Rochester Conference Series on Public Policy* 55, no. 1 (2001): 1–45.

Montesquieu, Charles de. *The Spirit of the Laws*. Translated and edited by Anne M. Cohler, Basia Carolyn Miller, and Harold Samuel Stone. New York: Cambridge University Press, (1748) 1989.

Morgenbesser, Lee. *Behind the Façade: Elections under Authoritarianism in Southeast Asia*. Albany: State University of New York Press, 2016.

———. "The Autocratic Mandate: Elections, Legitimacy and Regime Stability in Singapore." *Pacific Review* 30, no. 2 (2017): 205–31.

———. "The Menu of Autocratic Innovation." *Democratization* 27, no. 6 (2020): 1053–72.

———. *The Rise of Sophisticated Authoritarianism in Southeast Asia*. New York: Cambridge University Press, 2020.

Morozov, Evgeny. *The Net Delusion: The Dark Side of Internet Freedom*. New York: Public Affairs, 2011.

Moscow Times. "Russia Passes Dual Citizenship Law, Hoping to Add 10M Citizens." April 17, 2010. https://www.themoscowtimes.com/2020/04/17/russia-passes-dual-citizenship-law-hoping-to-add-10m-citizens-a70036.

———. "Yakunin in Estonia Deal." December 22, 2010. https://www.themoscowtimes.com/2010/12/22/yakunin-in-estonia-deal-a3961.

———. "Opposition Meeting Point Likened to Concentration Camp (Photo)." April 14, 2013. https://www.themoscowtimes.com/2013/04/14/opposition-meeting-point-likened-to-concentration-camp-photo-a23269.

———. "Kremlin 'Aiming for 70% Victory' in 2018 Presidential Election." December 26, 2016. https://www.themoscowtimes.com/2016/12/26/the-kremlin-wants-70-turnout-on-presidential-elections-in-2018-a56641.

———. "Russian Protest Fines Surge Fivefold Since 2012—Study." July 2, 2019. https://www.themoscowtimes.com/2019/07/02/russian-protest-fines-surge-fivefold-study-a66239.

———. "Russia Freezes Bank Accounts Linked to Opposition Politician Navalny Following Raids." August 8, 2019. https://www.themoscowtimes.com/2019/08/08/russia-freezes-bank-accounts-linked-to-opposition-politician-navalny-following-raids-a66765.

Mozur, Paul. "Live from America's Capital, a TV Station Run by China's Communist Party." *New York Times*, February 28, 2019. https://www.nytimes.com/2019/02/28/business/cctv-china-usa-propaganda.html.

Mudde, Cas. "The 2014 Hungarian Parliamentary Elections, or, How to Craft a Constitutional Majority." *Washington Post*, April 14, 2014. https://www.washingtonpost.com/news/monkey-cage/wp/2014/04/14/the-2014-hungarian-parliamentary-elections-or-how-to-craft-a-constitutional-majority/.

Mukand, Sharun W., and Dani Rodrik. "The Political Economy of Liberal Democracy." *Economic Journal* 130, no. 627 (2020): 765–92.

Müller, Dominique, and Janine Häsler. "Liking or Sharing Defamatory Facebook Posts Can Be Unlawful." Lexology.com, April 7, 2020. https://www.lexology.com/library/detail.aspx?g=6e4845ad-af67-47aa-8b27-edbc721e0c0a.

Murphy, Kevin M., and Andrei Shleifer. "Persuasion in Politics." *American Economic Review* 94, no. 2 (2004): 435–39.

Mussolini, Benito. "The Political and Social Doctrine of Fascism." *International Conciliation* 306 (1935). Quoted in Fritz Morstein Marx, "Propaganda and Dictatorship." *ANNALS of the American Academy of Political and Social Science* 179, no. 1 (1935): 211–18.

Mutler, Alison. "Pro-Orbán Media Moguls Who Destroyed Hungary's Media Now Targeting European Outlets." *Coda*, June 28, 2019. https://www.codastory.com/disinformation/Orbán-media-moguls-targeting-european-outlets/.

MVD Rossii. "Sostav Obshchestvennogo soveta pri MVD Rossii sozyva 2011–2013 g." https://xn--n1ag.xn--b1aew.xn--p1ai/Sostav_Obshhestvennogo_soveta/Sostav_2011_2013.

Mydans, Seth. "Death of Pol Pot; Pol Pot, Brutal Dictator Who Forced Cambodians to Killing Fields, Dies at 73." *New York Times*, April 17, 1998. https://www.nytimes.com/1998/04/17/world/death-pol-pot-pol-pot-brutal-dictator-who-forced-cambodians-killing-fields-dies.html.

———. "Lee Kuan Yew, Founding Father and First Premier of Singapore, Dies at 91." *New York Times*, March 23, 2015. https://www.nytimes.com/2015/03/23/world/asia/lee-kuan-yew-founding-father-and-first-premier-of-singapore-dies-at-91.html.

Myers, Steven Lee. "How China Uses Forced Confessions as Propaganda Tool." *New York Times*, April 11, 2018. https://www.nytimes.com/2018/04/11/world/asia/china-forced-confessions-propaganda.html.

Myerson, Roger B. "The Autocrat's Credibility Problem and Foundations of the Constitutional State." *American Political Science Review* 102, no. 1 (2008): 125–39.

Nardelli, Alberto. "Revealed: The Explosive Secret Recording That Shows How Russia Tried to Funnel Millions to the 'European Trump.'" *BuzzFeed News*, July 10, 2019. https://www.buzzfeednews.com/article/albertonardelli/salvini-russia-oil-deal-secret-recording.

Natanson, George. "Duvalier, Terror Rule Haiti, Island of Fear: 'President-for-Life' and His Private Army Bogeymen Exact Hard Vengeance on Foes." *Los Angeles Times*, January 12, 1966, 17.

Nathan, Laurie. *A Survey of Mediation in African Coups*. African Peacebuilding Network Working Paper No. 15. Brooklyn, NY: Social Science Research Council. https://s3.amazonaws.com/ssrc-cdn1/crmuploads/new_publication_3/a-survey-of-mediation-in-african-coups.pdf.

National Archives of Singapore. "Speech by DPM Lee Hsien Loong at the Asian Launch of Channel News Asia at the Raffles Ballroom." Singapore: Media Division, Ministry of Information and the Arts, September 28, 2000. https://www.nas.gov.sg/archivesonline/data/pdfdoc/2000092803.htm.

National Commission on the Disappearance of Persons. *Nunca Más* (Never Again). Buenos Aires: Editorial Universitaria de Buenos Aires, 1984. http://www.desaparecidos.org/nuncamas/web/english/library/nevagain/nevagain_001.htm.

National Security Archive. "Inside Argentina's Killing Machine: U.S. Intelligence Documents Record Gruesome Human Rights Crimes of 1976–1983." May 30, 2019. https://nsarchive.gwu.edu/briefing-book/southern-cone/2019-05-30/inside-argentinas-killing-machine-us-intelligence-documents-record-gruesome-human-rights-crimes-1976.

Nazarbayev, Nursultan. *The Kazakhstan Way*. Translated by Jan Butler. London: Stacey International, 2008.

NBC News. "Belafonte: Bush 'Greatest Terrorist in the World.'" January 8, 2006. https://www.nbcnews.com/id/wbna10767465#.Xz_21MhKg2w.

Nechepurenko, Ivan. "Five Who Killed Boris Nemtsov, Putin Foe, Sentenced in Russia." *New York Times*, July 13, 2017. https://www.nytimes.com/2017/07/13/world/europe/boris-nemtsov-putin-russia.html.

New York Times. "Full Text of Clinton's Speech on China Trade Bill." March 9, 2000. https://movies2.nytimes.com/library/world/asia/030900clinton-china-text.html.

———. "Excerpts from an Interview with Lee Kuan Yew." August 29, 2007. https://www.nytimes.com/2007/08/29/world/asia/29iht-lee-excerpts.html.

———. "Foreign Government Contributions to Nine Think Tanks." September 7, 2014. https://www.nytimes.com/interactive/2014/09/07/us/politics/foreign-government-contributions-to-nine-think-tanks.html.

Ng, Irene. "Lee Kuan Yew: Behind the No-Nonsense Demeanour, a Heart That Beat for Singapore." *Straits Times*, April 7, 2015. https://www.straitstimes.com/opinion/lee-kuan-yew-behind-the-no-nonsense-demeanour-a-heart-that-beat-for-singapore.

Nguyen-Okwo, Leslie. "Hitler Had a Salute, Mao Had a Dance." *OZY*, December 11, 2016. https://www.ozy.com/true-and-stories/hitler-had-a-salute-mao-had-a-dance/74076/.

Nicolaevsky, Boris. *Power and the Soviet Elite*. New York: Praeger, 1965.

Nikolakakis, Michalis. "The Colonels on the Beach: Tourism Policy during the Greek Military Dictatorship (1967–1974)." *Journal of Modern Greek Studies* 35, no. 2 (2017): 425–50.

Noktara.de. "Essen benennt sich wegen Ramadan in Fasten um." May 19, 2018. https://noktara.de/essen-wird-zu-fasten/.

Nolan, Rachel. "The Realest Reality Show in the World." *New York Times*, May 4, 2012. https://www.nytimes.com/2012/05/06/magazine/hugo-chavezs-totally-bizarre-talk-show.html.

Noman, Omar. "Pakistan and General Zia: Era and Legacy." *Third World Quarterly* 11, no. 1 (1989): 28–54. http://www.jstor.org/stable/3992219.

Norris, Pippa, and Ronald Inglehart. "Silencing Dissent: The Impact of Restrictive Media Environments on Regime Support." Paper presented at the Midwest Political Science Association 66th Annual Meeting, Chicago, April 3–6, 2008. https://www.cpsa-acsp.ca/papers-2008/Norris.pdf.

. *Cultural Backlash: Trump, Brexit, and Authoritarian Populism.* New York: Cambridge University Press, 2019.

North, Douglass C., and Barry R. Weingast. "Constitutions and Commitment: The Evolution of Institutions Governing Public Choice in Seventeenth-Century England." *Journal of Economic History* 49, no. 4 (1989): 803–32.

NTV. "Odin den iz zhizni Putina." https://www.youtube.com/watch?v=DLmglD560-k.

Nugent, Paul. "Nkrumah and Rawlings: Political Lives in Parallel?" *Transactions of the Historical Society of Ghana* 12 (2009): 35–56.

Nyst, Carly, and Nick Monaco. *State-Sponsored Trolling: How Governments Are Deploying Disinformation as Part of Broader Digital Harassment Campaigns.* Institute for the Future, 2018. http://www.iftf.org/statesponsoredtrolling.

O'Grady, Mary Anastasia. "Winning Hearts and Minds inside the Beltway." *Wall Street Journal,* April 9, 2004. https://www.wsj.com/articles/SB108147181581878647.

O'Rourke, Tim. "Chronicle Covers: When a Shirtless JFK Caused a Stir at the Beach." *San Francisco Chronicle,* August 20, 2016. https://www.sfchronicle.com/chronicle_vault/article/Chronicle-Covers-When-a-shirtless-JFK-caused-a-9170798.php.

OECD. *OECD Convention on Combating Bribery of Foreign Public Officials in International Business Transactions.* 1997. http://www.oecd.org/corruption/oecdantibriberyconvention.htm.

OECD Stat. "Outbound Tourism." https://stats.oecd.org/Index.aspx?DataSetCode=TOURISM_OUTBOUND.

OECD Working Group on Bribery. *2018 Enforcement of the Antibribery Convention.* December 2019. http://www.oecd.org/corruption/anti-bribery/OECD-Anti-Bribery-Convention-Enforcement-Data-2019.pdf.

Office of the Federal Commissioner for the Stasi Records (BStU). *Stasi Note on Meeting with KGB Officials.* November 13, 1969, History and Public Policy Program Digital Archive, 88–110. https://digitalarchive.wilsoncenter.org/document/115714.

Ognjenović, Gorana. Introduction to *Titoism, Self-Determination, Nationalism, Cultural Memory: Volume Two, Tito's Yugoslavia, Stories Untold.* Edited by Gorana Ognjenović and Jasna Jozelić, 1–7. New York: Springer, 2016.

Ognjenović, Gorana, Nataša Mataušić, and Jasna Jozelić. "Yugoslavia's Authentic Socialism as a Pursuit of 'Absolute Modernity.'" In *Titoism, Self-Determination, Nationalism, Cultural Memory: Volume Two, Tito's Yugoslavia, Stories Untold,* edited by Gorana Ognjenović and Jasna Jozelić, 9–36. New York: Springer, 2016.

Ola Salem, Abdullah Alaoudh. "Mohammed bin Salman's Fake Anti-Extremist Campaign." *Foreign Policy,* June 13, 2019. https://foreignpolicy.com/2019/06/13/mohammed-bin-salmans-fake-anti-extremist-campaign/.

Olmsted, Kathryn. "Watergate Led to Sweeping Reforms. Here's What We'll Need after Trump." *Washington Post,* November 15, 2019. https://www.washingtonpost.com/outlook/2019/11/15/watergate-led-sweeping-reforms-heres-what-well-need-after-trump/?arc404=true.

Omelicheva, Mariya Y. "Authoritarian Legitimation: Assessing Discourses of Legitimacy in Kazakhstan and Uzbekistan." *Central Asian Survey* 35, no. 4 (October 2016): 481–500.

Ortiz-Ospina, Esteban, and Diana Beltekian. "Trade and Globalization." Our World in Data, October 2018. https://ourworldindata.org/trade-and-globalization. Using data from Michel

Fouquin and Jules Hugot. "Two Centuries of Bilateral Trade and Gravity Data: 1827–2014." CEPII Research Center, May 2016. http://www.cepii.fr/pdf_pub/wp/2016/wp2016-14.pdf.

Orwell, George. *1984*. London: Secker and Warburg, 1949.

Osiel, Mark. *Mass Atrocity, Ordinary Evil, and Hannah Arendt: Criminal Consciousness in Argentina's Dirty War*. New Haven: Yale University Press, 2001.

Ottaway, Marina. "Reluctant Missionaries." *Foreign Policy*, November 17, 2009. https://foreignpolicy.com/2009/11/17/reluctant-missionaries/.

Overy, Richard. *The Dictators: Hitler's Germany and Stalin's Russia*. New York: W. W. Norton, 2004.

Pacepa, Ion Mihai. *Red Horizons: Chronicles of a Communist Spy Chief*. Washington, DC: Gateway Books, 1987.

Pack, Sasha. *Tourism and Dictatorship: Europe's Peaceful Invasion of Franco's Spain*. New York: Springer, 2006.

Paddock, Richard C. "Democracy Fades in Malaysia as Old Order Returns to Power." *New York Times*, May 22, 2020. https://www.nytimes.com/2020/05/22/world/asia/malaysia-politics-najib.html.

Padgett, Tim. "Red Alert: Venezuelans Fleeing Their Regime Say Interpol Notices Derail Asylum." *WLRN*, April 29, 2019. https://www.wlrn.org/show/latin-america-report/2019-04-29/red-alert-venezuelans-fleeing-their-regime-say-interpol-notices-derail-asylum.

Painter, James. "The Boom in Counter-hegemonic News Channels: A Case Study of Telesur." Research paper presented to the Reuters Institute for the Study of Journalism, Oxford University, February 2007.

El País. "Chávez conquista a Robbins." June 9, 2008. https://elpais.com/cultura/2008/06/09/actualidad/1212962409_850215.html.

———. "Maradona rompe una lanza por la reelección indefinida de Chávez." January 29, 2009. https://elpais.com/internacional/2009/01/29/actualidad/1233183606_850215.html.

Panja, Tariq, and Kevin Draper. "US Says FIFA Officials Were Bribed to Award World Cups to Russia and Qatar." *New York Times*, April 6, 2020. https://www.nytimes.com/2020/04/06/sports/soccer/qatar-and-russia-bribery-world-cup-fifa.html.

Pantoja, Ary. "CEELA fue creado por Chávez." *El Nuevo Diario*, June 19, 2008. https://www.elnuevodiario.com.ni/politica/19160-ceela-fue-creado-chavez/.

Papaioannou, Elias, and Gregorios Siourounis. "Democratisation and Growth." *Economic Journal* 118, no. 532 (2008): 1520–51.

Parodi, Emilio. "Italian Prosecutors Probe Allegations of League Oil Deal: Sources." Reuters, July 11, 2019. https://www.reuters.com/article/us-italy-salvini-russia/italian-prosecutors-probe-allegations-of-league-oil-deal-sources-idUSKCN1U61JI.

Pearson, Tamara. "Venezuela: 'Only Ecuadorans Can Neutralise Coup Attempt.'" *Venezuelanalysis*, September 30, 2010. https://venezuelanalysis.com/news/5680.

Peh, Shing Huei. *Tall Order: The Goh Chok Tong Story (Volume 1)*. Singapore: World Scientific Publishing Company, 2018.

Pereira, Anthony W. *Political (In)justice: Authoritarianism and the Rule of Law in Brazil, Chile, and Argentina*. Pittsburgh: University of Pittsburgh Press, 2005.

Perović, Jeronim. "The Tito-Stalin Split: A Reassessment in Light of New Evidence." *Journal of Cold War Studies* 9, no. 2 (Spring 2007): 32–63.

Perraton, Hilary. "Foreign Students in the Twentieth Century: A Comparative Study of Patterns and Policies in Britain, France, Russia and the United States." *Policy Reviews in Higher Education* 1 no. 2 (2017): 161–86.

Pettersson, Therése, Stina Högbladh, and Magnus Öberg. "Organized Violence, 1989–2018 and Peace Agreements." *Journal of Peace Research* 56, no. 4 (2019): 589–603.

Pew Research Center. *What the World Thinks in 2002: Chapter 4: Global Publics View the United States.* Washington, DC: Pew Research Center, December 4, 2002. https://www.pewresearch.org/global/2002/12/04/chapter-4-global-publics-view-the-united-states/.

———. *Global Unease with Major World Powers.* Washington, DC: Pew Research Center, June 27, 2007. https://www.pewresearch.org/global/2007/06/27/global-unease-with-major-world-powers/.

———. *Global Economic Gloom—China and India Notable Exceptions.* Washington, DC: Pew Research Center, June 12, 2008. https://www.pewresearch.org/global/2008/06/12/chapter-7-which-governments-respect-the-rights-of-their-people/.

———. *Attitudes towards Democratic Rights and Institutions.* February 27, 2020. https://www.pewresearch.org/global/2020/02/27/attitudes-toward-democratic-rights-and-institutions/.

———. *US Image Plummets Internationally as Most Say Country Has Handled Coronavirus Badly.* September 15, 2020. https://www.pewresearch.org/global/2020/09/15/us-image-plummets-internationally-as-most-say-country-has-handled-coronavirus-badly/.

Pfaff, William. *The Bullet's Song: Romantic Violence and Utopia.* New York: Simon and Schuster, 2004.

Pi-Sunyer, Oriol. "Tourism in Catalonia." In *Tourism in Spain: Critical Issues,* edited by Michael Barke, John Towner, and Michael T. Newton, 231–64. Wallingford: CAB International, 1996.

Pike, Francis. *Empires at War: A Short History of Modern Asia since World War II.* London: Bloomsbury Publishing, 2011.

Pinchot, Gifford, and Elizabeth Pinchot. *The End of Bureaucracy and the Rise of the Intelligent Organization.* San Francisco: Berrett-Koehler, 1993.

Pingel-Schliemann, Sandra. *Zersetzen: Strategie einer Diktatur.* Berlin: Robert Havemann Gesellschaft, 2002.

Pinker, Steven. *The Better Angels of Our Nature.* New York: Penguin, 2011.

———. *Enlightenment Now: The Case for Reason, Science, Humanism, and Progress.* New York: Viking, 2018.

Pinto, António Costa. "Fascism, Corporatism and the Crafting of Authoritarian Institutions in Inter-war European Dictatorships." In *Rethinking Fascism and Dictatorship in Europe,* edited by António Costa Pinto and Aristotle Kallis, 87–117. London: Palgrave Macmillan, 2014.

Pivarnyik, Balázs. "László Kövér Is Heard Justifying Gerrymandering on Leaked Recording." *Budapest Beacon,* February 6, 2018. https://budapestbeacon.com/laszlo-kover-heard-attempting-justify-gerrymandering-leaked-recording/.

Plamper, Jan. "Abolishing Ambiguity: Soviet Censorship Practices in the 1930s." *Russian Review* 60, no. 4 (October 2001): 526–44.

Podeh, Elie. *The Politics of National Celebrations in the Arab Middle East.* New York: Cambridge University Press, 2011.

Podrez, Maksim, and Maria Prikhodina. "Znak pochtenia, znak otchayania." *rbc.ru*, April 17, 2014. https://www.rbc.ru/magazine/2014/05/56bc7e719a794701b81d2b8a.

Polgreen, Lydia. "Ghana's Unlikely Democrat Finds Vindication in Vote." *New York Times*, January 10, 2019. http://www.nytimes.com/2009/01/10/world/africa/10rawlings.html?pagewanted=all&_r=0.

Pomerantsev, Peter. *This Is Not Propaganda: Adventures in the War Against Reality.* New York: Public Affairs, 2019.

Pompeo, Michael R. "On Transparency and Foreign Funding of US Think Tanks." Washington, DC: U.S. State Department, October 13, 2020. https://2017-2021.state.gov/on-transparency-and-foreign-funding-of-u-s-think-tanks/index.html.

Pop-Eleches, Grigore, and Joshua A. Tucker. *Communism's Shadow: Historical Legacies and Contemporary Political Attitudes.* Princeton: Princeton University Press, 2017.

Popov, Genarii. "What Kind of Minister Was Shchelokov?" *Militsiya*, December 2000.

Popovic, Srdja, and Matthew Miller. *Blueprint for Revolution: How to Use Rice Pudding, Lego Men, and Other Nonviolent Techniques to Galvanize Communities, Overthrow Dictators, or Simply Change the World.* New York: Spiegel & Grau, 2015.

Potapova, Elizaveta, and Stefan Trines. "Education in the Russian Federation." *World Education News +Reviews*, June 6, 2017. https://wenr.wes.org/2017/06/education-in-the-russian-federation.

Potter, Mark. "Cuba Cracks Down on Illegal Emigration." CNN, July 26, 1999, http://www.cnn.com/WORLD/americas/9907/26/cuba.smugglers/.

Power, Jonathan. *Amnesty International: The Human Rights Story.* New York: McGraw-Hill, 1981.

———. *Like Water on Stone: The Story of Amnesty International.* Boston: Northeastern University Press, 2001.

Powers, William. "Hello World." *National Journal* 33, no. 26 (2001): 2082.

Pregelj, Vladimir. "The Jackson-Vanik Amendment: A Survey." Congressional Research Service Report for Congress. Washington, DC: Library of Congress, 2005.

President of Russia. "Interview with the German Newspaper *Suddeutsche Zeitung*." October 10, 2006. http://en.kremlin.ru/events/president/transcripts/23834.

———. "Seliger 2012 National Youth Education Forum." July 31, 2012. http://en.kremlin.ru/events/president/news/16104.

———. "Meeting of the Valdai International Discussion Club." September 19, 2013. http://en.kremlin.ru/events/president/news/19243.

———. "Russia Today TV Channel Starts Broadcasting in Argentina." October 9, 2014. http://en.kremlin.ru/events/president/news/46762.

Preston, Paul. *Franco: A Biography.* New York: Basic Books, 2003.

———. *The Spanish Holocaust: Inquisition and Extermination in Twentieth-Century Spain.* New York: W. W. Norton, 2012.

Prior, Markus. "The Immensely Inflated News Audience: Assessing Bias in Self-Reported News Exposure." *Public Opinion Quarterly* 73, no. 1 (Spring 2009): 130–43.

Pruce, Joel R. *The Mass Appeal of Human Rights.* New York: Springer, 2018.

Rachman, Gideon. "Lunch with the FT: Lee Hsien Loong Singapore's PM Talks about Japanese Aggression, Ukraine's Revolution and Why Nanny States Are Not All Bad." *Financial Times*, April 11, 2014. https://www.ft.com/content/4511f092-bf2c-11e3-8683-00144feabdc0.

———. "Chinese Censorship Is Spreading Beyond Its Borders." *Financial Times*, October 14, 2019. https://www.ft.com/content/cda1efbc-ee5a-11e9-ad1e-4367d8281195.

Rahimi, Babak. "Cyberdissent: The Internet in Revolutionary Iran." *Middle East Review of International Affairs* 7, no. 3 (2003): 101–15.

Rajah, Jothie. *Authoritarian Rule of Law: Legislation, Discourse and Legitimacy in Singapore*. New York: Cambridge University Press, 2012.

Rajak, Svetozar. "The Cold War in the Balkans, 1945–1956." In *The Cambridge History of the Cold War*, edited by Melvyn P. Leffler and Odd Arne Westad, 198–220. Cambridge: Cambridge University Press, 2010.

Ramírez, Erika. "Barack Obama: 10 Best Songs about the President." *Billboard*, November 7, 2012. https://www.billboard.com/articles/list/1516380/barack-obama-10-best-songs-about-the-president.

Rappeport, Alan. "Saudi Crown Prince Calls Khashoggi's Death 'Heinous.'" *New York Times*, October 25, 2018. https://www.nytimes.com/2018/10/25/world/middleeast/saudi-arabia-jamal-khashoggi-turkey.html.

Rauschning, Hermann. *Hitler Speaks: A Series of Political Conversations with Adolf Hitler on His Real Aims*. London: Kessinger Publishing, 1939.

———. *The Voice of Destruction*. Gretna: Pelican Publishing, 1940.

Rawnsley, Adam. "How Manafort's Work for the 'Torturer's Lobby' Came Back to Haunt Him." *Daily Beast*, February 25, 2019. https://www.thedailybeast.com/how-manaforts-work-for-the-torturers-lobby-came-back-to-haunt-him.

RBC. "Lidery oppozitsii B. Nemtsov i E. Limonov vyshli na svobodu." *rbc.ru*, January 15, 2011. https://www.rbc.ru/politics/15/01/2011/5703e24f9a79473c0df191b8.

———. "Kreml otsenil novuyu metodiku oprosa VTsIOMa o doverii Putinu." *rbc.ru*, May 31, 2019. https://www.rbc.ru/politics/31/05/2019/5cf0edf29a79479a20bbc0ea.

Reardon, Juan. "Latin America's TeleSUR Now Available to U.S. Viewers." *Venezuelanalysis.com*, August 4, 2011. https://venezuelanalysis.com/news/6405.

Reider, Bruce J. "External Support to Insurgencies." *Small Wars Journal* 10, no. 10 (2014): 1–18.

Rein, Lisa. "Federal Offices Are Still Waiting to Hang Trump's Picture." *Washington Post*, September 11, 2017. https://www.washingtonpost.com/politics/after-nine-months-federal-offices-are-still-waiting-to-hang-trumps-picture/2017/09/11/b36025c0-94b5-11e7-aace-04b862b2b3f3_story.html.

Rejali, Darius. *Torture and Democracy*. Princeton: Princeton University Press, 2007.

Reporters Without Borders. "Hungary: Orbán Allies Acquire Regional Press Monopoly." https://rsf.org/en/news/hungary-Orbán-allies-acquire-regional-press-monopoly.

Republic of Singapore. *Political Donations Act 2000*. June 23, 2000. https://sso.agc.gov.sg/Acts-Supp/20-2000/Published/20011231?DocDate=20000620.

Reuter, Ora John, and Graeme B. Robertson. "Subnational Appointments in Authoritarian Regimes: Evidence from Russian Gubernatorial Appointments." *Journal of Politics* 74, no. 4 (2012): 1023–37.

Reuters. "I'm the World's Only True Democrat, Says Putin." June 4, 2007. https://www.reuters .com/article/us-russia-putin-democracy/im-the-worlds-only-true-democrat-says-putin -idUSL0454405820070604.

———. "Sean Penn Joins Chávez on Campaign in Venezuela." August 25, 2012. https://www .reuters.com/article/entertainment-us-venezuela-election-penn/sean-penn-joins-chavez -on-campaign-in-venezuela-idUSBRE87503H20120806.

———. "Factbox: Hugo Chávez's Record in Venezuelan Elections." October 7, 2012. https:// www.reuters.com/article/us-venezuela-election-ballots/factbox-hugo-chavezs-record-in -venezuelan-elections-idUSBRE89702320121008.

———. "Illegal Immigration Clearly Linked with Terror Threat: Hungary PM." July 25, 2015. https://www.reuters.com/article/us-europe-migrants-hungary/illegal-migration-clearly -linked-with-terror-threat-hungary-pm-idUSKCN0PZ08F2015072.

———. "No Cult of Personality around Xi, Says Top China Party Academic." November 6, 2017. https://www.reuters.com/article/us-china-politics-xi/no-cult-of-personality-around-xi -says-top-china-party-academic-idUSKBN1D61DD.

———. "Singapore PM Files Defamation Suit against Blogger Who Shared Article on Facebook." December 5, 2018. https://www.reuters.com/article/us-singapore-politics-malaysia -scandal/singapore-pm-files-defamation-suit-against-blogger-who-shared-article-on -facebook-idUSKBN1O414L.

———. "How Sisi's Egypt Hands Out Justice." July 31, 2019. https://www.reuters.com /investigates/special-report/egypt-executions/.

RIA Novosti. "Aleksei Kochetkov nameren podat isk protiv MVD Moldavii." July 18, 2005. https://ria.ru/20050718/40925555.html.

Richardson, Christopher. "North Korea's Kim Dynasty: The Making of a Personality Cult." *Guardian*, February 16, 2015. https://www.theguardian.com/world/2015/feb/16/north -korea-kim-jong-il-birthday.

Richter, Monika L. "RT: A Low-Grade Platform for Useful Idiots," Atlantic Council, October 18, 2017. https://www.atlanticcouncil.org/blogs/ukrainealert/rt-a-low-grade-platform -for-useful-idiots/.

Roberts, Margaret E. *Censored: Distraction and Diversion inside China's Great Firewall.* Princeton: Princeton University Press, 2018.

———. "Resilience to Online Censorship." *Annual Review of Political Science* 23, no. 3 (2020): 401–19.

Roberts, Walter R. "Tito—Personal Reflections." *American Diplomacy*, February 2014. http:// americandiplomacy.web.unc.edu/2014/02/tito-personal-reflections/.

Rodan, Garry. "The Internet and Political Control in Singapore." *Political Science Quarterly* 113, no. 1 (Spring 1998): 63–89.

———. "Singapore in 1997: Living with the Neighbors." *Asian Survey* 38, no. 2 (1998): 177–82.

———. *Singapore "Exceptionalism"? Authoritarian Rule and State Transformation.* Working Paper No. 131. Perth: Murdoch University, 2006. https://researchrepository.murdoch.edu

.au/id/eprint/16148/1/Singapore_Exceptionalism_Authoritarian_Rule_and_State
_Transformation.pdf.

———. "Goh's Consensus Politics of Authoritarian Rule." In *Impressions of the Goh Chok Tong Years in Singapore*, edited by Bridget Welsh, James Chin, Arun Mahizhan and Tan Tarn How, 61–70. Singapore: Singapore University Press, 2009.

———. *Participation without Democracy: Containing Conflict in Southeast Asia.* Ithaca: Cornell University Press, 2018.

Rodrigo, Javier. "'Our Fatherland Was Full of Weeds': Violence during the Spanish Civil War and the Franco Dictatorship." In *If You Tolerate This . . . The Spanish Civil War in the Age of Total Wars*, edited by Martin Baumeister and Stefanie Schüller-Springorum, 135–53. New York: Campus, 2008.

Roessler, Philip G. "Donor-Induced Democratization and the Privatization of State Violence in Kenya and Rwanda." *Comparative Politics* (2005): 207–27.

Rogin, Josh. "In Malaysia, a Victory for Democracy—and an Opportunity for the US." *Washington Post*, June 7, 2018. https://www.washingtonpost.com/opinions/global-opinions/in -malaysia-a-victory-for-democracy--and-an-opportunity-for-the-us/2018/06/07/b365a928 -6a8e-11e8-bea7-c8eb28bc52b1_story.html.

Rogoff, Kenneth, and Anne Sibert. "Elections and Macroeconomic Policy Cycles." *Review of Economic Studies* 55, no. 1 (1988): 1–16.

Rogov, Kirill, and Maxim Ananyev. "Public Opinion and Russian Politics." In *The New Autocracy: Information, Politics, and Policy in Putin's Russia*, edited by Daniel Treisman, 191–216. Washington, DC: Brookings Institution Press, 2018.

Rohac, Dalibor. "A European Compromise Not Worth Making." *AEIdeas*, December 11, 2020. https://www.aei.org/foreign-and-defense-policy/a-european-compromise-not-worth -making/.

Roman, David. "How Hugo Chávez Helped Inspire Spain's Far-Left Podemos Movement." *Wall Street Journal*, February 6, 2015. https://www.wsj.com/articles/how-venezuelas-chavez-lives -on-in-spain-1425000737.

Romero, Simon. "Ecuador Leader Confounds Supporters and Detractors." *New York Times*, October 10, 2010. https://www.nytimes.com/2010/10/10/world/americas/10ecuador.html.

Romero, Simon, and Emily Schmall. "Battle between Argentine Media Empire and President Heats Up over Law." *New York Times*, November 30, 2012. https://www.nytimes.com/2012 /12/01/world/americas/media-law-ratchets-up-battle-between-kirchner-and-clarin-in -argentina.html.

Ron, James. "Varying Methods of State Violence." *International Organization* 51, no. 2 (1997): 275–300.

Roniger, Luis, Leonardo Senkman, Saúl Sosnowski, and Mario Sznajder. *Exile, Diaspora, and Return: Changing Cultural Landscapes in Argentina, Chile, Paraguay, and Uruguay.* New York: Oxford University Press, 2018.

Rosenbaum, Lorrin P., and Judith Kossy. "Indonesia's Political Prisoners." *Worldview* 19, no. 10 (1976): 36–40.

Rosenblum, Peter. "Prison Conditions in Zaire." Washington, DC: Human Rights Watch, 1994.

Roser, Max. "War and Peace." *OurWorldInData.org*, 2016. https://ourworldindata.org/war-and -peace.

Ross, Jenna. "Which Countries Are the Biggest Boost or Drag on the EU Budget?" *Visualcapital-ist.com*, September 20, 2019. https://www.visualcapitalist.com/which-countries-are-the -biggest-boost-or-drag-on-the-eu-budget/.

Ross, Michael L. *The Oil Curse: How Petroleum Wealth Shapes the Development of Nations*. Princeton: Princeton University Press, 2013.

Rosstat. *Rossia v tsifrakh 2013*. Moscow: Rosstat, 2013.

———. *Rossia v tsifrakh 2020*. Moscow: Rosstat, 2020.

Roth, Andrew. "Independent News Station, Feeling Kremlin's Wrath, Asks 'Why?'" *New York Times*, February 10, 2014.

———. "Russian State Watchdog Adds Navalny Network to Terrorism Database." *Guardian*, April 30, 2021. https://www.theguardian.com/world/2021/apr/30/russian-state-watchdog -adds-navalny-network-to-terrorism-database.

Rothenberg, Daniel, and Baltasar Garzón. "'Let Justice Judge': An Interview with Judge Baltasar Garzón and Analysis of His Ideas." *Human Rights Quarterly* 24, no. 4 (2002): 924–73.

Roucek, Joseph. "Yemen in Geopolitics." *Contemporary Review* 202 (December 1, 1962): 310–17.

Rozenas, Arturas, and Denis Stukal. "How Autocrats Manipulate Economic News: Evidence from Russia's State-Controlled Television." *Journal of Politics* 81, no. 3 (2019): 982–96.

Rozhdestvensky, Ilya, Mikhail Rubin, and Roman Badanin. "Chef i povar: Rassledovanie o tom, kak Rossia vmeshivaetsya v vybory v dvadsati stranakh." *proekt.media*, April 11, 2019. https:// www.proekt.media/investigation/prigozhin-polittekhnologi/.

RT. "Putin Talks NSA, Syria, Iran, Drones in RT Interview (FULL VIDEO)." June 12, 2013. https://www.rt.com/news/putin-rt-interview-full-577/.

Rubenstein, Joshua. "Introduction: Andrei Sakharov, the KGB, and the Legacy of a Soviet Dissident." In *The KGB File of Andrei Sakharov*, edited by Joshua Rubenstein and Alexander Gribanov, 1–85. New Haven: Yale University Press, 2008.

Rudnitsky, Jake, and Ilya Arkhipov. "Russia Turns Trampled Grass into Weapon against Opponents." Bloomberg News, September 12, 2019. https://www.bloomberg.com/news /articles/2019-09-12/russia-turns-trampled-grass-into-weapon-against-opponents.

Ruiz, Claudio. "Ecuador: Copyright as a Weapon for Censorship." *Derechosdigitales.org*, October 21, 2014. https://www.derechosdigitales.org/8125/ecuador-copyright-weapon -censorship/.

Rundlett, Ashlea, and Milan W. Svolik. "Deliver the Vote! Micromotives and Macrobehavior in Electoral Fraud." *American Political Science Review* 110, no. 1 (2016): 180–97.

Russmus.net. "Takogo kak Putin." http://russmus.net/song/1396.

Rusyaeva, Polina, and Elizaveta Surganova. "Mediakompaniu Kovalchuka i Mordashova otsenili v 150 mlrd. rub." *RBC.ru*, March 31, 2016. https://www.rbc.ru/technology_and_media/31 /03/2016/56fcf20c9a7947dd35dbd00f.

Rutenberg, Jim. "Larry King, the Russian Media and a Partisan Landscape." *New York Times*, September 19, 2016. https://www.nytimes.com/2016/09/19/business/media/moscow-joins -the-partisan-media-landscape-with-familiar-american-faces.html.

Sadr, Shadi. "Documenting the Perpetrators amongst the People." *Open Democracy*, May 19, 2015. https://www.opendemocracy.net/en/opensecurity/documenting-perpetrators -amongst-people/.

Safire, William. "Essay: The Dictator Speaks." *New York Times*, February 15, 1999. https://www .nytimes.com/1999/02/15/opinion/essay-the-dictator-speaks.html.

Sakr, Naomi. "Frontiers of Freedom: Diverse Responses to Satellite Television in the Middle East and North Africa." *The Public* 6, no. 11 (1999): 93–106.

Salem, Harriet, and Graham Stack. "Streetfighting Men: Is Ukraine's Government Bankrolling a Secret Army of Adidas-Clad Thugs?" *Foreign Policy*, February 6, 2014. https://foreignpolicy .com/2014/02/06/streetfighting-men/.

Sambrook, Richard. *Are Foreign Correspondents Redundant?* Oxford: Reuters Institute for the Study of Journalism, 2010.

Samuels, Brett. "Trump Ramps Up Rhetoric on Media, Calls Press 'Enemy of the People.'" *The Hill*, April 5, 2019. https://thehill.com/homenews/administration/437610-trump-calls -press-the-enemy-of-the-people.

Sánchez, Leonel. "San Diego Rally Backs Mexican Indian Revolt." *San Diego Union-Tribune*, January 7, 1994. https://advance.lexis.com/api/document?collection=news&id=urn:content Item:4P7G-PXY0-TWDC-M4RX-00000-00&context=1516831.

Sanger, David, and Katie Benner. "U.S. Accuses North Korea of Plot to Hurt Economy as Spy Is Charged in Sony Hack." *New York Times*, September 6, 2018. https://www.nytimes.com /2018/09/06/us/politics/north-korea-sony-hack-wannacry-indictment.html.

Sanovich, Sergey, Denis Stukal, and Joshua A. Tucker. "Turning the Virtual Tables: Government Strategies for Addressing Online Opposition with an Application to Russia." *Comparative Politics* 50, no. 3 (2018): 435–54.

Sassoon, Joseph. *Saddam Hussein's Ba'th Party: Inside an Authoritarian Regime*. Cambridge: Cambridge University Press, 2012.

Sauer, Pjotr. "'End of an Era': Russia Adds Navalny Political Network to 'Terrorist and Extremist' List." *Moscow Times*, April 30, 2021. https://www.themoscowtimes.com/2021/04/30/end -of-an-era-russia-adds-navalny-political-network-to-terrorist-and-extremist-list-a73796.

Saunders, David. "Xi Jinping's Threats of 'Crushed Bodies and Shattered Bones' Are an Echo of Another Violent Past." *Hong Kong Free Press*, October 20, 2019. https://hongkongfp.com/2019 /10/20/xi-jinpings-threats-crushed-bodies-shattered-bones-echo-another-violent-past/.

Scammell, Michael. "Pride and Poetry." *New Republic*, 2012. https://newrepublic.com/article /103341/joseph-brodsky-russian-literature-lev-loseff.

Schatz, Edward. "Transnational Image Making and Soft Authoritarian Kazakhstan." *Slavic Review* 67, no. 1 (Spring 2008): 50–62.

———. "The Soft Authoritarian Tool Kit: Agenda-Setting Power in Kazakhstan and Kyrgyzstan." *Comparative Politics* 41, no. 2 (January 2009): 203–22.

Schedler, Andreas. "The Menu of Manipulation." *Journal of Democracy* 13, no. 2 (2002): 36–50.

———. *The Politics of Uncertainty: Sustaining and Subverting Electoral Authoritarianism*. Oxford: Oxford University Press, 2013.

Schmidt, Gregory D. "Peru." In *Public Opinion and Polling around the World: A Historical Encyclopedia*. Vol. 1., edited by John Gray Geer, 683–88. Santa Barbara: ABC-Clio, 2004.

Schmitt, Carl. *Crisis of Parliamentary Democracy*. Berlin: Duncker and Humblot, 1923.

Schmitter, Philippe C. "The Impact and Meaning of 'Non-Competitive, Non-Free and Insignificant' Elections in Authoritarian Portugal, 1933–74." In *Elections without Choice*, edited by Guy Hermet, 145–68. London: Palgrave Macmillan, 1978.

Schudel, Matt. "Arthur Finkelstein, Quietly Influential GOP Campaign Mastermind, Dies at 72." *Washington Post*, August 19, 2017. https://www.washingtonpost.com/local/obituaries /arthur-finkelstein-shadowy-campaign-mastermind-and-gop-operative-dies-at-72/2017/08 /19/0bd638c6-84e8-11e7-902a-2a9f2d808496_story.html.

Searcey, Dionne, and Palko Karasz. "Laurent Gbagbo, Former Ivory Coast Leader, Acquitted of Crimes against Humanity." *New York Times*, January 15, 2019. https://www.nytimes.com /2019/01/15/world/africa/laurent-gbagbo-ivory-coast-icc.html.

Seddon, Max. "'Why Don't They Come and Sit in Jail with Me?'; Lunch with the FT Alexei Navalny." *Financial Times*, November 23, 2019. https://www.ft.com/content/c3adf28c-07d0 -11ea-a984-fbbacad9e7dd.

Selb, Peter, and Simon Munzert. "Examining a Most Likely Case for Strong Campaign Effects: Hitler's Speeches and the Rise of the Nazi Party, 1927–1933." *American Political Science Review* 112, no. 4 (November 2018): 1050–66.

Semmens, Kristin. *Seeing Hitler's Germany: Tourism in the Third Reich*. New York: Springer, 2005.

Service, Robert. *Stalin: A Biography*. Cambridge, MA: Harvard University Press, 2005.

Shabad, Theodore. "Soviet Waives Its Exit Tax for Five Leaving for Israel." *New York Times*, March 20, 1973. https://www.nytimes.com/1973/03/20/archives/soviet-waives-its-exit-tax -for-five-leaving-for-israel-visit-by.html.

Shadmehr, Mehdi. "Ideology and the Iranian Revolution." January 27, 2012. https://ssrn.com /abstract=1999826 or http://dx.doi.org/10.2139/ssrn.1999826.

Shafer, Jack. "Hail to the Return of Motherland-Protecting Propaganda!" *Slate*, August 30, 2007. https://slate.com/news-and-politics/2007/08/the-russians-drop-a-propaganda-bomb -with-their-washington-post-ad-supplement.html.

Shanor, Donald R. *Behind the Lines: The Private War against Soviet Censorship*. New York: St. Martin's Press, 1985.

Shapiro, Samuel. *Invisible Latin America*. North Stratford: Ayer Publishing, 1963.

Sharlet, Robert. "Dissent and Repression in the Soviet Union and Eastern Europe: Changing Patterns since Khrushchev." *International Journal* 33, no. 4 (1978): 763–95.

Shezaf, Hagar, and Jonathan Jacobson. "Revealed: Israel's Cyber-Spy Industry Helps World Dictators Hunt Dissidents and Gays." *Haaretz*, October 20, 2018. https://www.haaretz.com /israel-news/.premium.MAGAZINE-israel-s-cyber-spy-industry-aids-dictators-hunt -dissidents-and-gays-1.6573027.

Shih, Victor. "'Nauseating' Displays of Loyalty: Monitoring the Factional Bargain through Ideological Campaigns in China." *Journal of Politics* 70, no. 4 (October 2008): 1177–92.

Shuster, Simon. "Inside Putin's On-Air Machine." *Time*, March 5, 2015. https://time.com/rt -putin/.

Sikkink, Kathryn. *The Justice Cascade: How Human Rights Prosecutions Are Changing World Politics*. New York: W. W. Norton, 2011.

Silver, Laura, Kat Devlin, and Christine Huang. *Unfavorable Views of China Reach Historic Highs in Many Countries: Majorities Say China Has Handled COVID-19 Outbreak Poorly*. Pew Research Center, 2020.

Simon, Joel. *The New Censorship: Inside the Global Battle for Media Freedom*. New York: Columbia University Press, 2014.

Simpser, Alberto. *Why Governments and Parties Manipulate Elections: Theory, Practice, and Implications*. New York: Cambridge University Press, 2013.

Singapore Rebel. "1994–2015: A Chronology of Authoritarian Rule in Singapore." March 21, 2011. http://singaporerebel.blogspot.com/2011/03/1994-2011-chronology-of-authoritarian.html.

Singer, P. W., and Emerson T. Brooking. *LikeWar: The Weaponization of Social Media*. Boston: Mariner Books, 2018.

Skaaning, Svend-Erik, John Gerring, and Henrikas Bartusevicius. "A Lexical Index of Electoral Democracy." *Comparative Political Studies* 48, no. 12 (2015): 1491–1525.

Skarpelos, George M. "Communication Breakdown: The Chilean State and the Media, 1973–1980." *Berkeley Journal of Sociology* 36 (1991): 137–63.

Skidmore, Monique, and Trevor Wilson. *Dictatorship, Disorder and Decline in Myanmar*. Canberra: ANU Press, 2008.

Slackman, Michael. "Syrian Troops Open Fire on Protesters in Several Cities." *New York Times*, March 25, 2011. https://www.nytimes.com/2011/03/26/world/middleeast/26syria.html.

Slater, Dan. "Malaysia's Modernization Tsunami." *EastAsiaForum*, May 20, 2018. https://www.eastasiaforum.org/2018/05/20/malaysias-modernisation-tsunami/.

Slezkine, Yuri. *The House of Government: A Saga of the Russian Revolution*. Princeton: Princeton University Press, 2017.

Smith, Myles G. "Kazakhstan: CNN Blurs Line between News and Advertising." *Eurasianet*, July 20, 2012. https://eurasianet.org/kazakhstan-cnn-blurs-line-between-news-and-advertising.

Smith, Stephen W. "The Story of Laurent Gbagbo." *London Review of Books* 33, no. 10 (May 2011). https://www.lrb.co.uk/the-paper/v33/n10/stephen-w.-smith/the-story-of-laurent-gbagbo.

Sobolev, Anton. "Dictators in the Spotlight: What They Do When They Cannot Do Business as Usual." PhD diss., University of California, Los Angeles, 2019.

Socor, Vladimir. "Russia-Led Bloc Emerges in OSCE." *Eurasia Daily Monitor* 4, no. 214 (November 16, 2007). https://jamestown.org/program/russia-led-bloc-emerges-in-osce/.

———. "Russia Blocks Consensus at OSCE's Year-End Conference." *Eurasia Daily Monitor* 8, no. 225 (December 12, 2011). https://jamestown.org/program/russia-blocks-consensus-at-osces-year-end-conference/.

Soldatov, Andrei, and Irina Borogan. *The Red Web: The Struggle between Russia's Digital Dictators and the New Online Revolutionaries*. New York: Public Affairs, 2015.

———. *The Compatriots*. New York: Public Affairs, 2019.

Sosin, Gene. "Censorship and Dissent." *Studies in Comparative Communism* 19, no. 2 (Summer 1986): 149–57.

Southwick, Natalie, and John Otis. "Ecuador's U-turn away from Media Repression." *Columbia Journalism Review*, July 12, 2018. https://www.cjr.org/analysis/ecuador-moreno-correa-supercom-press-freedom.php.

Spar, Debora. "Foreign Investment and Human Rights." *Challenge* 42, no. 1 (1999): 55–80.

Specia, Megan. "Saudi Anti-Extremist Force Names Feminists as a Target. Briefly." *New York Times,* November 13, 2019. https://www.nytimes.com/2019/11/13/world/middleeast/saudi -feminism-extremism-video.html.

Spilimbergo, Antonio. "Democracy and Foreign Education." *American Economic Review* 99, no. 1 (2009): 528–43.

Spooner, Mary Helen. *Soldiers in a Narrow Land: The Pinochet Regime in Chile.* Berkeley: University of California Press, 1999.

Standaert, Michael. "Nike and H&M Face Backlash in China over Xinjiang Statements." *Guardian,* March 25, 2021. https://www.theguardian.com/world/2021/mar/25/nike-and-hm-face -backlash-in-china-over-xinjiang-statements.

Standish, Reid. "Where the War on Terror Lives Forever." *Foreign Policy,* September 2, 2016. https://foreignpolicy.com/2016/09/02/war-on-terror-forever-islam-karimov-uzbekistan -legacy-imu-isis-central-asia/.

Stanley, Alessandra. "Julian Assange Starts Talk Show on Russian TV." *New York Times,* April 18, 2012. https://www.nytimes.com/2012/04/18/arts/television/julian-assange-starts-talk -show-on-russian-tv.html.

Stein, Elizabeth A. "The Unraveling of Support for Authoritarianism: The Dynamic Relationship of Media, Elites, and Public Opinion in Brazil, 1972–82." *International Journal of Press/ Politics* 18, no. 1 (2013): 85–107.

Stein, Jana von. "Exploring the Universe of UN Human Rights Agreements." *Journal of Conflict Resolution* 62, no. 4 (April 2018): 871–99. https://doi.org/10.1177/0022002717721395.

Stevens, Colin. "Kazakhstan: A Model of Inter-Ethnic Tolerance and Social Harmony." *EU Reporter,* November 11, 2016. https://www.eureporter.co/featured/2016/11/11/kazakhstan-a -model-of-inter-ethnic-tolerance-and-social-harmony/.

Stone, Martin. *The Agony of Algeria.* New York: Columbia University Press, 1997.

Stoner, Kathryn, and Michael McFaul. "The Soviet Union and Russia." In *Transitions to Democracy: A Comparative Perspective,* edited by Kathryn Stoner and Michael McFaul, 27–61. Baltimore: Johns Hopkins University Press, 2013.

Straits Times. "Midnight Bomb Attack on Gimson." April 29, 1950, p. 1. https://eresources.nlb .gov.sg/newspapers/Digitised/Article/straitstimes19500429-1.2.2.

———. "The Clean-Up: Act Two." September 25, 1956. https://eresources.nlb.gov.sg /newspapers/Digitised/Article/straitstimes19560925-1.2.2.

———. "LBJ Gives Lee Red Carpet Welcome." October 18, 1967, p. 1. https://eresources.nlb.gov .sg/newspapers/Digitised/Article/straitstimes19671018-1.2.2?ST=1&AT=filter&K=Lee%20 Kuan%20Yew%20Johnson&KA=Lee%20Kuan%20Yew%20Johnson&DF=&DT=&Display =0&AO=false&NPT=&L=&CTA=&NID=straitstimes&CT=&WC=&YR=1967&QT =lee,kuan,yew,johnson&oref=article.

———. "Singapore 'A Dazzling Success.'" October 10, 1985, p. 13. https://eresources.nlb.gov.sg /newspapers/Digitised/Article/straitstimes19851010-1.2.22.11?ST=1&AT=filter&K=Lee%20 Kuan%20Yew%20Reagan&KA=Lee%20Kuan%20Yew%20Reagan&DF=&DT=&Display =0&AO=false&NPT=&L=&CTA=&NID=straitstimes&CT=&WC=&YR=1985&QT =lee,kuan,yew,reagan&oref=article.

Stukal, Denis, Sergey Sanovich, Richard Bonneau, and Joshua A. Tucker. "Detecting Bots on Russian Political Twitter." *Big Data* 5, no. 4 (2017): 310–24.

Sükösd, Miklós. "Democratic Transformation and the Mass Media in Hungary: From Stalinism to Democratic Consolidation." In *Democracy and the Media*, edited by R. Gunther and A. Mughan, 122–64. Cambridge: Cambridge University Press, 2000.

Sullivan, Andy. "U.S. Public-Relations Firm Helps Putin Make His Case to America." Reuters, September 12, 2013. https://www.reuters.com/article/us-syria-crisis-usa-ketchum -idusbre98c00s20130913.

Svolik, Milan. *The Politics of Authoritarian Rule*. New York: Cambridge University Press, 2012.

Szakonyi, David, and Ora John Reuter. "Electoral Manipulation and Regime Support: Survey Evidence from Russia." *World Politics*, 73, no. 2 (2021): 275–314.

Szeidl, Adam, and Ferenc Szucs. "Media Capture through Favor Exchange." *Econometrica*. New Haven: Econometric Society, 2020. https://www.econometricsociety.org/publications /econometrica/2020/08/01/media-capture-through-favor-exchange.

Tai, Qiuqing. "China's Media Censorship: A Dynamic and Diversified Regime." *Journal of East Asian Studies* 14, no. 2 (2014): 185–210.

Talbot, Ian. *Pakistan: A Modern History*. London: Hurst & Company, 2009.

Talley, Ian, and Drew Hinshaw. "U.S. Keeps Sanctions at the Ready Even as Trump Courts Hungarian Leader." *Wall Street Journal*, May 14, 2019. https://www.wsj.com/articles/u-s -keeps-sanctions-at-the-ready-even-as-trump-courts-hungarian-leader-11557867566.

Tan, Kenneth Paul. "The Ideology of Pragmatism: Neo-liberal Globalisation and Political Authoritarianism in Singapore." *Journal of Contemporary Asia* 42, no. 1 (2012): 67–92.

Tan, Netina. "Manipulating Electoral Laws in Singapore." *Electoral Studies* 32, no. 4 (2013): 632–43.

TASS. "'Mertvie dushi' po-amerikanski: Byli li falsifikatsii na vyborakh v SShA." February 13, 2017. https://tass.ru/mezhdunarodnaya-panorama/4018022.

Taussig, Michael T. *Defacement: Public Secrecy and the Labor of the Negative*. Stanford: Stanford University Press, 1999.

Taylor, Adam. "Was #Kony2012 a Failure?" *Washington Post*, December 16, 2014. https://www .washingtonpost.com/news/worldviews/wp/2014/12/16/was-kony2012-a-failure/.

Taylor, Brian D. *The Code of Putinism*. New York: Oxford University Press, 2018.

Taylor, Kathleen. *Brain Washing: The Science of Thought Control*. New York: Oxford University Press, 2004.

Tchoukarine, Igor. "The Yugoslav Road to International Tourism." In *Yugoslavia's Sunny Side: A History of Tourism in Socialism (1950s–1980s)*, edited by Hannes Grandits and Karin Taylor, 107–38. Budapest: Central European University Press, 2010.

Teele, Dawn Langan. *Forging the Franchise: The Political Origins of the Women's Vote*. Princeton: Princeton University Press, 2018.

Tengri TV. "Nazarbayev vystupil s poslaniem narodu Kazakhstana." October 5, 2018. https:// www.youtube.com/watch?v=OqagBfR3LIg.

Than, Krisztina. "Hungary's Government Plans to Tighten Control over Theaters." Reuters, December 6, 2019. https://www.reuters.com/article/us-hungary-orban-culture/hungarys -government-plans-to-tighten-control-over-theaters-idUSKBN1YA1UC.

Tharoor, Ishaan. "Hungary's Leader Says He's Defending Christian Europe; The Pope Disagrees," *Washington Post*, April 9, 2018. https://www.washingtonpost.com/news/worldviews /wp/2018/04/10/the-popes-challenge-to-orban-and-europes-far-right/.

Thomas, Kurt, Chris Grier, and Vern Paxson. "Adapting Social Spam Infrastructure for Political Censorship." Usenix Association, 2012. https://www.usenix.org/system/files/conference /leet12/leet12-final13_0.pdf.

Thompson, Wayne C. *Nordic, Central, and Southeastern Europe, 2018–2019*. Lanham, MD: Rowman and Littlefield, 2018.

Today Online. "The Evolution of Singapore's Speaker's Corner." October 21, 2016. https://www .todayonline.com/singapore/evolution-spores-speakers-corner.

Tolz, Vera, and Yuri Teper. "Broadcasting Agitainment: A New Media Strategy of Putin's Third Presidency." *Post-Soviet Affairs* 34, no. 4 (2018): 213–27.

Tong, James W. *Revenge of the Forbidden City: The Suppression of the Falun Gong in China, 1999– 2005*. Oxford: Oxford University Press, 2009.

Tong, Jingrong. "The Taming of Critical Journalism in China: A Combination of Political, Economic and Technological Forces." *Journalism Studies* 20, no. 1 (2019): 79–96.

Toobin, James. "The Dirty Trickster: Campaign Tips from the Man Who Has Done It All." *New Yorker*, May 23, 2008. https://www.newyorker.com/magazine/2008/06/02/the-dirty-trickster.

Toor, Amar. "How Putin's Cronies Seized Control of Russia's Facebook." *Verge*, January 31, 2014. https://www.theverge.com/2014/1/31/5363990/how-putins-cronies-seized-control-over -russias-facebook-pavel-durov-vk.

Toothaker, Christopher. "Last Anti-Chávez TV Station Faces Probe, Shutdown." *San Diego Union Tribune*, May 16, 2009. https://www.sandiegouniontribune.com/sdut-lt-venezuela -anti-chavez-tv-051609-2009may16-story.html.

Toro, Francisco. "Chávez Wasn't Just a Zany Buffoon, He Was an Oppressive Autocrat." *Atlantic*, March 5, 2013. http://www.theatlantic.com/international/archive/2013/03/chavez-wasnt -just-a-zany-buffoon-he-was-an-oppressive-autocrat/273745/.

———. "What Fidel Taught Hugo." *New Republic*, March 5, 2013. https://newrepublic.com /article/112596/hugo-chavez-dead-cuba-defined-him-much-venezuela-did.

Torpey, John. "Leaving: A Comparative View." In *Citizenship and Those Who Leave: The Politics of Emigration and Expatriation*, edited by Nancy L. Green and François Weil, 13–32. Champaign: University of Illinois Press, 2010.

Torres, M. Gabriela. "Bloody Deeds/Hechos Sangrientos: Reading Guatemala's Record of Political Violence in Cadaver Reports." In *When States Kill: Latin America, the US, and Technologies of Terror*, edited by Cecilia Menjívar and Néstor Rodríguez, 143–69. Austin: University of Texas Press, 2005.

Total. "Nazarbayev poruchil pravitelstvu izmenit podkhody v rabote." October 5, 2018. https:// total.kz/ru/news/gossektor/nazarbaev_poruchil_pravitelstvu_izmenit_podhodi_v _rabote_date_2018_10_05_11_30_52.

Tran, Mark. "Zimbabwe Election: Mugabe Threatens to Arrest Opposition Leaders." *Guardian*, June 17, 2008. https://www.theguardian.com/world/2008/jun/17/zimbabwe.

Treisman, Daniel. "Income, Democracy, and Leader Turnover." *American Journal of Political Science* 59, no. 4 (2015): 927–42.

———. "Authoritarian Elections as Inoculation." Paper presented at Annual Meeting of the American Political Science Association. Boston, 2018.

———. "Introduction: Rethinking Putin's Political Order." In *The New Autocracy: Information, Politics, and Policy in Putin's Russia*, edited by Daniel Treisman, 1–28. Washington, DC: Brookings Institution Press, 2018.

———. "Is Democracy in Danger? A Quick Look at the Data." Los Angeles: UCLA, 2018. https://www.danieltreisman.org/s/draft-june-7-58s2.pdf.

———. "Economic Development and Democracy: Predispositions and Triggers." *Annual Review of Political Science* 23 (2020): 241–57.

Trevizo, Dolores. *Rural Protest and the Making of Democracy in Mexico, 1968–2000*. University Park: Pennsylvania State University Press, 2011.

TRT World. "Saudi Journalist Saleh al Shehi Dies Shortly after Release from Prison." July 21, 2020. https://www.trtworld.com/magazine/saudi-journalist-saleh-al-shehi-dies-shortly-after-release-from-prison-38291.

Tucker, Joshua A. "Enough! Electoral Fraud, Collective Action Problems, and Post-Communist Colored Revolutions." *Perspectives on Politics* 5, no. 3 (2007): 535–51.

Tucker, Joshua A., Yannis Theocharis, Margaret E. Roberts, and Pablo Barberá. "From Liberation to Turmoil: Social Media and Democracy." *Journal of Democracy* 28, no. 4 (2017): 46–59.

Tyler, Patrick. "New Tapes Appear with Threats by Ukraine's President." *New York Times*, February 19, 2001. https://www.nytimes.com/2001/02/19/world/new-tapes-appear-with-threats-by-ukraine-s-president.html.

Tynan, Deirdre. "Kazakhstan: Top-Notch PR Firms Help Brighten Astana's Image." *Eurasianet*, January 18, 2012. https://eurasianet.org/kazakhstan-top-notch-pr-firms-help-brighten-astanas-image.

Ulfelder, Jay, and Benjamin Valentino. *Assessing Risks of State-Sponsored Mass Killing*. February 1, 2008. http://ssrn.com/abstract=1703426 or http://dx.doi.org/10.2139/ssrn.1703426.

UN Panel of Experts on Accountability in Sri Lanka. *Report of the Secretary-General's Panel of Experts on Accountability in Sri Lanka*. New York: United Nations, 2011. https://www.securitycouncilreport.org/atf/cf/%7B65BFCF9B-6D27-4E9C-8CD3-CF6E4FF96FF9%7D/POC%20Rep%20on%20Account%20in%20Sri%20Lanka.pdf.

UN World Tourist Organization. *Tourism Highlights, 2017 Edition*. New York: United Nations, https://www.e-unwto.org/doi/pdf/10.18111/9789284419029.

UNCTAD. "Digital Service Delivery Shows Potential for Developing World." March 29, 2019. https://unctad.org/en/pages/newsdetails.aspx?OriginalVersionID=2035.

———. *World Investment Report 2020*. New York: United Nations Publications, 2020. https://unctad.org/system/files/official-document/wir2020_en.pdf.

UNESCO Institute for Statistics, UIS.Stat Database. http://data.uis.unesco.org.

UNESCO. *Statistics of Students Abroad, 1962–1968*. Paris: UNESCO, 1971.

Urazova, Diana. "Nazarbayev about Lee Kuan Yew: I Considered Him a Good Friend." *Tengrinews*, March 26, 2015. https://en.tengrinews.kz/politics_sub/nazarbayev-about-lee-kuan-yew-i-considered-him-a-good-friend-259541/.

USAID. "Foreign Aid Explorer." https://explorer.usaid.gov/cd/EGY.

U.S. Bureau of Labor Statistics. "Employment by Major Industry Sector." https://www.bls.gov /emp/tables/employment-by-major-industry-sector.htm.

U.S. House of Representatives Permanent Selection Committee on Intelligence. "Exposing Russia's Effort to Sow Discord Online: The Internet Research Agency and Advertisements." https://intelligence.house.gov/social-media-content/.

Vandenbussche, Jerome, Philippe Aghion, and Costas Meghir. "Growth, Distance to Frontier and Composition of Human Capital." *Journal of Economic Growth* 11 (2006): 97–127.

Varol, Ozan O. "Stealth Authoritarianism." *Iowa Law Review* 100 (2014): 1673–1742.

Vázquez-Ger, Ezequiel. "What Can Tens of Millions of Dollars Buy Ecuador in the Empire?" *The Hill*, August 7, 2014. https://thehill.com/blogs/congress-blog/foreign-policy/214541 -what-can-tens-of-millions-of-dollars-buy-ecuador-in-the.

Venezuela Analysis. "Venezuelan President Chávez: The OAS Is Like a Corpse That Must Be Buried." March 26, 2010. https://venezuelanalysis.com/news/5220.

Vinokurova, Ekaterina. "To chto na ulitsu vydut desyatki tysyach lyudey, ne ozhidal nikto." *Gazeta.ru*, December 5, 2012. https://www.gazeta.ru/politics/2012/12/04_a_4878785 .shtml.

Vladimirov, Leonid. "Glavlit: How the Soviet Censor Works." *Index on Censorship* 1, no. 3–4 (1972): 31–43.

VOA. "VOA, BBC Protest China Broadcast Jamming." February 26, 2013. https://www.voanews .com/a/voa-bbc-jamming-china/1611431.html.

Voigtländer, Nico, and Hans-Joachim Voth. "Nazi Indoctrination and Anti-Semitic Beliefs in Germany." *Proceedings of the National Academy of Sciences* 112, no. 26 (June 2015): 7931–36.

Volchek, Dmitry, and Daisy Sindelar. "One Professional Russian Troll Tells All." Radio Free Europe Radio Liberty, March 25, 2015. https://www.rferl.org/a/how-to-guide-russian -trolling-trolls/26919999.html.

Von Salzen, Claudia. "Wie Gerhard Schröder als Türöffner für Gazprom agiert." *Der Tagesspiegel*, December 20, 2017. https://www.tagesspiegel.de/themen/agenda/pipeline-nord-stream -2-wie-gerhard-schroeder-als-tueroeffner-fuer-gazprom-agiert/20739366.html.

Vreeland, James Raymond. "Corrupting International Organizations." *Annual Review of Political Science* 22 (2019): 205–22.

Waisbord, Silvio. "All-Out Media War: It's Clarín vs. the Kirchners, and Journalism Will Be the Loser." *Columbia Journalism Review* (September/October 2010). https://archives.cjr.org /reports/allout_media_war.php.

Waldman, Simon A. "Turkey, Not Trump, Is the Biggest Threat to NATO Right Now." *Haaretz*, December 1, 2019. https://www.haaretz.com/middle-east-news/.premium-turkey-not -trump-is-the-biggest-threat-to-nato-right-now-1.8201531.

Walker, Sean. "'This Gentleman': Alexei Navalny, the Name Putin Dare Not Speak." *Guardian*, September 3, 2020. https://www.theguardian.com/world/2020/sep/03/this-gentleman -alexei-navalny-the-name-putin-dares-not-speak.

———. "Belarus Axed as Host of Ice Hockey Tournament over 'Security Concerns.'" *Guardian*, January 18, 2021. https://www.theguardian.com/world/2021/jan/18/belarus-axed-as-host -of-ice-hockey-tournament-over-security-concerns.

Wallis, Daniel. "Chávez Turns Up Heat on Globovisión in Venezuela." Reuters, June 15, 2010. https://www.reuters.com/article/us-venezuela-globovision/chavez-turns-up-heat-on -globovision-in-venezuela-idUSTRE65E5M220100615.

Warner, Judith. "A Hot Time in Washington." New York Times (Opinionator Blog), May 14, 2009. https:// opinionator.blogs.nytimes.com/2009/05/14/president/?login=email&auth=login-email.

Wedeen, Lisa. Ambiguities of Domination: Politics, Rhetoric, and Symbols in Contemporary Syria. Chicago: University of Chicago Press, 1999.

Weeks, Jessica. "Strongmen and Straw Men: Authoritarian Regimes and the Initiation of International Conflict." American Political Science Review 106, no. 2 (2012): 326–47. doi:10.1017 /S0003055412000111.

Weisbrot, Mark. "Changes in Latin America: Consequences for Health Development." International Journal of Health Services 37, no. 3 (July 2007): 477–500.

Welch, David. The Third Reich: Politics and Propaganda. New York: Routledge, 2008.

———. "'Opening Pandora's Box': Propaganda, Power and Persuasion." In Propaganda, Power and Persuasion: From World War I to Wikileaks, edited by David Welch, 3–18. London: I. B. Tauris, 2013.

Wells, H. G. "H. G. Wells: 'It Seems to Me That I Am More to the Left than You, Mr. Stalin.'" New Statesman, April 18, 2014. https://www.newstatesman.com/politics/2014/04/h-g-wells -it-seems-me-i-am-more-left-you-mr-stalin.

West, Richard. Tito and the Rise and Fall of Yugoslavia. London: Faber and Faber, 2012.

Wheelock, David C. "Comparing the COVID-19 Recession with the Great Depression." Economic Synopses, no. 39 (2020). https://doi.org/10.20955/es.2020.39.

White, Stephen, Richard Rose, and Ian McAllister. How Russia Votes. Chatham, NJ: Chatham House Publishers, 1997.

White House Gift Shop. "Barack Obama Collectibles & Gifts from the White House Gift Shop." https://www.whitehousegiftshop.com/category-s/2382.htm.

Whitman, Alden. "Antonio Salazar: A Quiet Autocrat Who Held Power in Portugal for 40 Years." New York Times, July 28, 1970. https://www.nytimes.com/1970/07/28/archives/antonio -salazar-a-quiet-autocrat-who-held-power-in-portugal-for-40.html.

Wiarda, Howard J. Corporatism and Comparative Politics: The Other Great Ism. Armonk, NY: M. E. Sharpe, 1996.

Wike, Richard, and Shannon Schumacher. Democratic Rights Popular Globally but Commitment to Them Not Always Strong. Washington, DC: Pew Research Center, February 27, 2020. https://www.pewresearch.org/global/2020/02/27/democratic-rights-popular-globally-but -commitment-to-them-not-always-strong/.

Wike, Richard, Laura Silver, and Alexandra Castillo. Many across the Globe Are Dissatisfied with How Democracy Is Working. Washington, DC: Pew Research Center, April 29, 2019. https:// www.pewresearch.org/global/2019/04/29/many-across-the-globe-are-dissatisfied-with -how-democracy-is-working/.

Wike, Richard, Bruce Stokes, Jacob Poushter, and Janell Fetterolf. US Image Suffers as Publics around World Question Trump's Leadership. Washington, DC: Pew Research Center, June 26, 2017. https://www.pewresearch.org/global/2017/06/26/u-s-image-suffers-as-publics -around-world-question-trumps-leadership/.

Wike, Richard, Bruce Stokes, Jacob Poushter, Laura Silver, Janell Fetterold, and Kat Devlin. *Trump's International Ratings Remain Low, Especially among Key Allies.* Washington, DC: Pew Research Center, October 1, 2018. https://www.pewresearch.org/global/2018/10/01/trumps -international-ratings-remain-low-especially-among-key-allies/.

Williams, Kevin. *International Journalism.* Thousand Oaks, CA: Sage, 2011.

Williams, Martyn. "South Korea Adjusts Some Radio Frequencies to Escape Jamming." *North Korea Tech,* October 2, 2019. https://www.northkoreatech.org/2019/10/02/south-korea -adjusts-some-radio-frequencies-to-escape-jamming/.

Willson, Perry. "The Nation in Uniform? Fascist Italy, 1919–43." *Past & Present,* no. 221 (November 2013): 239–72.

Wilson, Andrew. *Virtual Politics: Faking Democracy in the Post-Soviet World.* New Haven: Yale University Press, 2005.

Winter, Caroline. "Mansudae Art Studio, North Korea's Colossal Monument Factory." Bloomberg, June 6, 2013. https://www.bloomberg.com/news/articles/2013-06-06/mansudae-art -studio-north-koreas-colossal-monument-factory.

Witte, Joan. "Violence in Lenin's Thought and Practice: The Spark and the Conflagration." *Terrorism and Political Violence* 5, no. 3 (1993): 135–203.

Wolf, John Baptiste. *France, 1814–1919: The Rise of a Liberal-Democratic Society.* New York: Harper & Row, 1963.

Wong, Sin-Kiong. "Subversion or Protest? Singapore Chinese Student Movements in the 1950s." *American Journal of Chinese Studies* 11, no. 2 (2004): 181–204.

Wong, Stan Hok-Wui. "Gerrymandering in Electoral Autocracies: Evidence from Hong Kong." *British Journal of Political Science* 49, no. 2 (2019): 579–610.

Wood, David. "The Peruvian Press under Recent Authoritarian Regimes, with Special Reference to the Autogolpe of President Fujimori." *Bulletin of Latin American Research* 19, no. 1 (January 2000): 17–32.

Wootliff, Raoul. "Israelis Arrested for Spying on Romanian Anti-Corruption Czar." *Times of Israel,* April 6, 2016. https://www.timesofisrael.com/israelis-arrested-for-spying-on -romanian-anti-corruption-czar/.

World Bank. "Industry (Including Construction), Value Added (% of GDP)." World Bank Data. https://data.worldbank.org/indicator/NV.IND.TOTL.ZS.

———. "International Tourism, Number of Arrivals." World Bank Data. https://data.worldbank .org/indicator/ST.INT.ARVL.

———. "International Tourism, Number of Departures." World Bank Data. https://data .worldbank.org/indicator/ST.INT.DPRT.

———. "Personal Remittances, Received (Current US$)." World Bank Data. https://data .worldbank.org/indicator/BX.TRF.PWKR.CD.DT.

———. "Labor Force, Total." World Bank Data. June 21, 2020. https://data.worldbank.org /indicator/SL.TLF.TOTL.IN.

World Bank. "Net ODA Received (% of Central Government Expense) - Tanzania." World Bank Data. October 15, 2021. https://data.worldbank.org/indicator/DT.ODA.ODAT.XP .ZS?locations=TZ.

World Trade Organization. "Trade Shows Signs of Rebound from COVID-19, Recovery Still Uncertain." October 6, 2020. https://www.wto.org/english/news_e/pres20_e/pr862_e.htm.

World Values Survey. "Online Data Analysis." http://www.worldvaluessurvey.org/WVSOnline.jsp.

Wright, Joseph, and Abel Escribà-Folch. "Are Dictators Immune to Human Rights Shaming?" IBEI Working Papers 2009/25. October 2009. https://ssrn.com/abstract=1483607 or http://dx.doi.org/10.2139/ssrn.1483607.

Wrong, Michela. *Do Not Disturb: The Story of a Political Murder and an African Regime Gone Bad.* New York: Public Affairs, 2021.

Wuerth, Ingrid. "International Law in the Post-Human Rights Era." *Texas Law Review* 96, no. 2 (December 2017): 279–350.

Wuttke, Alexander, Konstantin Gavras, and Harald Schoen. "Have Europeans Grown Tired of Democracy? New Evidence from Eighteen Consolidated Democracies, 1981–2018." *British Journal of Political Science* (2020): 1–13.

Xu, Xu. "To Repress or to Co-opt? Authoritarian Control in the Age of Digital Surveillance." *American Journal of Political Science* (2020). doi: 10.1111/ajps.12514.

Yee, Chen May. "Malaysia's Ex-Police Chief Admits to Beating Anwar." *Wall Street Journal*, March 1, 1999. https://www.wsj.com/articles/SB920179149246563500.

Yoong, Sean. "Singapore's Lee Has Anwar Opinion." AP, August 17, 2000. https://apnews.com/article/e3ca7e03a64ab4ff41664d3efd4100cb.

Young, Lauren E. "The Psychology of State Repression: Fear and Dissent Decisions in Zimbabwe." *American Political Science Review* 113, no. 1 (February 2019): 140–55.

Yudin, Greg. "In Russia, Opinion Polls Are Being Used to Cover Up a Divided Society." *Open Democracy.org*, July 2, 2020. https://www.opendemocracy.net/en/odr/russia-opinion-polls-referendum/.

Yurchak, Alexei. *Everything Was Forever, until It Was No More: The Last Soviet Generation.* Princeton: Princeton University Press, 2013.

Zakaria, Fareed. *The Future of Freedom: Illiberal Democracy at Home and Abroad.* New York: Norton, 2003.

———. "The New China Scare: Why America Shouldn't Panic about Its Latest Challenger." *Foreign Affairs* 99 (2020): 52–69.

Zambrano, Diego. "The Constitutional Path to Dictatorship in Venezuela." *Lawfare.com*, March 18, 2019. https://www.lawfareblog.com/constitutional-path-dictatorship-venezuela#.

Zamyatina, Tamara. "Speakers' Corners in Moscow Have Not Gained Expected Popularity Yet." *TASS*, October 15, 2013. https://tass.com/opinions/762700.

Zaslavsky, Victor, and Robert J. Brym. "The Functions of Elections in the USSR." *Soviet Studies* 30, no. 3 (July 1978): 362–71.

Zelikow, Philip, Eric Edelman, Kristofer Harrison, and Celeste Ward Gventer. "The Rise of Strategic Corruption." *Foreign Affairs* 99 (2020): 107–20.

Zen_Pickle. "The Craziest Lies of the Hungarian State-Controlled Media—The Top 100 List." *Medium*, January 18, 2019. https://medium.com/@smalltownhigh/the-craziest-lies-of-hungarian-state-controlled-media-the-top-100-list-9d2a82ea6c44.

Zhao, Suisheng. "Xi Jinping's Maoist Revival." *Journal of Democracy* 27, no. 3 (2016): 83–97.

Zhussupova, Dilshat. "Kazakhstan to Present Its First Report to UN on SDG Progress." *Astana Times*, February 2, 2019. https://astanatimes.com/2019/02/kazakhstan-to-present-its-first -report-to-un-on-sdg-progress/.

Zlobin, Nikolai. "Humor as Political Protest." *Demokratizatsiya* 4 (1996): 223–31.

Zloch-Christy, Iliana. *Debt Problems of Eastern Europe.* Cambridge: Cambridge University Press, 1987.

Zygar, Mikhail. *All the Kremlin's Men: Inside the Court of Vladimir Putin.* New York: Public Affairs, 2016.

INDEX

Page numbers in *italics* indicate figures or tables.

A NOTE ON THE TYPE

This book has been composed in Arno, an Old-style serif typeface in the
classic Venetian tradition, designed by Robert Slimbach at Adobe.